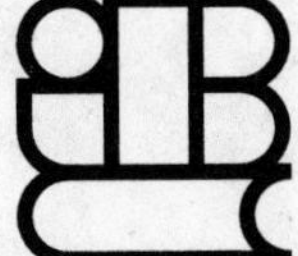

COMING INTO HER OWN

COMING INTO HER OWN

Educational Success in Girls and Women

Sara N. Davis

Mary Crawford

Jadwiga Sebrechts

Editors

Jossey-Bass Publishers
San Francisco

The material in Chapter Ten is based upon work supported by the National Science Foundation under Grant No. HRD-9553486. Any opinions, findings, and conclusions or recommendations expressed in this publication are those of the author(s) and do not necessarily reflect the views of the National Science Foundation.

Jossey-Bass books and products are available through most bookstores. To contact Jossey-Bass directly, call (888) 378-2537, fax to (800) 605-2665, or visit our website at www.josseybass.com.

Substantial discounts on bulk quantities of Jossey-Bass books are available to corporations, professional associations, and other organizations. For details and discount information, contact the special sales department at Jossey-Bass.

Manufactured in the United States of America on Lyons Falls Turin Book. This paper is acid-free and 100 percent totally chlorine-free.

Library of Congress Cataloging-in-Publication Data

Coming into her own : educational success in girls and women / Sara N. Davis, Mary Crawford, and Jadwiga Sebrechts, Editors.
p. cm.
Includes bibliographical references and index.
ISBN 0-7879-4490-4 (acid-free paper)
1. Women—Education—United States. 2. Women—Education (Higher)—United States. 3. Feminism and education—United States. 4. Women's studies—United States. I. Davis, Sara N., date. II. Crawford, Mary (Mary E.) III. Sebrechts, Jadwiga, date.
LC1503 .C65 1999
371.822'0973—dc21

99-6037

FIRST EDITION

HB Printing 10 9 8 7 6 5 4 3 2 1

CONTENTS

PART THREE
Transforming Math and Science

PART FOUR
Changing Individual Expectations

PART FIVE
Creating Healthy Environments

PREFACE

ON A BEAUTIFUL DAY in May several years ago, a group of women scholars gathered in Amherst, Massachusetts, to share thoughts and strategies for fostering academic success and achievement for girls and women. The occasion was the fourth annual Nag's Heart conference—a conference devoted to exploring various issues that affect the professional and academic lives of women. Our particular sessions addressed the topic of resilience in girls and women and explored programming and pedagogies designed to bring change to academic institutions and to extend opportunities to women students.

Despite the diversity of perspectives offered on the subject—everything from leadership development to teaching statistics, from multicultural advising to use and abuse of alcohol on campuses—the unity of purpose behind the strategies outlined suggested that there was a much-needed book to be written on the array of positive programs and approaches. We proceeded to create a comprehensive volume that is both practical and theoretical, that addresses pedagogical concerns as well as campus-environment issues.

Theoretical research undergirds and frames each chapter; we then proceed to provide practical lessons for those who wish to create environments where girls and women can flourish. Although many chapters deal with teaching and learning on college campuses, the examples offered are applicable to broader academic experience on all levels. These models can be applied in any environment in which teaching is a priority—most especially responsive and responsible teaching. We provide examples of collaborative and interactive classrooms in which communities of learners are engaged in constructing knowledge and understanding. We hope that this book suggests some models for transforming the classroom and the campus climate, and that it will serve as a stimulus for those who would like to create their own innovative approaches.

Acknowledgments

Like the teaching and learning outlined in our book, our work has resulted from a process of collaboration. Some of our collaborators are obvious;

others worked behind the scenes, offering comments, insights, and encouragement. We wish to send our heartfelt thanks to the many who made our work possible.

We start with the mastermind of our weekend at Nag's Heart, Faye Crosby, whose vision and organizational acumen brought the original scholars together. Faye created the spirit that allowed us to engage in dialogues, which showed us the richness of issues that could be explored.

From the beginning our editor, Leslie Berriman, was a partner in our endeavor. Her perceptive insights helped to fashion the book's contours. Her deep engagement with the book and belief in its value inspired the enterprise throughout. More than giving our book structure, she gave it soul.

The three coeditors of this volume began work as colleagues and ended as friends. We would like to thank each other for making the collaboration an enjoyable, satisfying, and personally rich undertaking.

All of the authors who contributed to the book have been ideal team members, whether they were part of the project from its inception at Nag's Heart or joined at a later time. Their expertise, eloquence, and enthusiasm have made the book a satisfying whole.

The pioneering work of Elizabeth Tidball made possible a project focusing on women-centered education. Her concern for and research on the characteristics that provide an empowering educational environment for women opened the door for the contemporary interest in these issues. The Jessie Ball duPond Fund generously supported the research agenda of the nation's women's colleges that brought together a critical mass of scholars to explore women's education.

Each of us would like to thank the following institutions and people for their support and effort in bringing this project to fruition: Margaret M. Healy, president of Rosemont College; Pat Gross; Debra Klinman; Anne Marie Lopes; the Women's College Coalition; and Marci Meadows.

Finally, each of us would like to thank our primary and loving collaborators, our husbands: Bill Davis, Roger Chaffin, and Marc Sebrechts.

We write this in hopes that the experiences of the next generation (our children) will be enriched: Eli and Rebecca; Mary, Mark, and Ben; and Alixandra, Peter, and Luc.

Rosemont, Pennsylvania
Storrs, Connecticut
Washington, D.C.
June 1999

Sara N. Davis
Mary Crawford
Jadwiga Sebrechts

ABOUT THE EDITORS

SARA N. DAVIS is associate professor of psychology and women's studies at Rosemont College. She is active in the Women's Studies Consortium of Philadelphia. In addition to the experiences of women in the classroom, her interests include study of comprehension of narrative texts. She is a member of several international organizations, where she has presented her research on these topics. She recently coedited (with Mary Gergen) *Toward a New Psychology of Gender.* Recent publications include "Blurring the Boundaries: Stories in Literature and the Social Sciences," "Narrative Structure and Emotional Response," and "Reading Together: Discourse in the Literature Classroom."

MARY CRAWFORD is professor of psychology and director of women's studies at the University of Connecticut. She is the author of *Talking Difference: On Gender and Language,* coauthor of the forthcoming third edition of *Women and Gender: A Feminist Psychology,* and coeditor of other volumes, including *Gender Differences in Human Cognition, Gender and Thought: Psychological Perspectives* and *In Our Own Words.* She is currently the North American editor of the international journal *Feminism and Psychology* and coeditor of a special double issue of *Psychology of Women* quarterly on innovative research methods. She is a Fellow of the American Psychological Association and the American Psychological Society.

JADWIGA SEBRECHTS is president of the Women's College Coalition, an association of the nation's seventy-nine women's colleges that makes the case for these institutions, sponsors research on optimal learning environments for women and girls, and acts as an advocate for the higher education of women before policy makers, the press, and the public. Initiator of a gender-equity public service ad campaign, Sebrechts has worked with educators, youth-serving organizations, and parents on strategies that promote academic achievement by girls in middle school through college. She has written on women and science, effective learning and teaching strategies, and women-centered pedagogy, as well as served on advisory boards to the Department of Education, National Science Foundation, and National Institutes of Health and on numerous higher education commissions. Her Ph.D. is in French literature from Yale University, where she was also an instructor.

ABOUT THE CONTRIBUTORS

NEAL B. ABRAHAM is vice president for academic affairs and dean of the faculty at DePauw University. He taught physics from 1980 to 1998 at Bryn Mawr College, from which he earned his Ph.D. in 1977 after receiving his B.S. in physics in 1972 from Dickinson College. A Fellow of the American Association for the Advancement of Science, the American Physical Society, and the Optical Society of America, his research in nonlinear dynamics, chaos, and spatiotemporal dynamics has involved more than fifty undergraduate students and colleagues in Spain, France, Germany, Italy, China, Russia, and Belarus. He has served in leadership roles in Project Kaleidoscope and in the science education activities of the National Research Council, coauthoring *Science Teaching Reconsidered*. He also provided leadership to the National Conferences on Undergraduate Research and the Council on Undergraduate Research.

JANIS S. BOHAN is a professor of psychology at Metropolitan State College of Denver. She is the author of *Psychology and Sexual Orientation: Coming to Terms* and editor of *Re-Placing Women in Psychology: Readings Toward a More Inclusive History* and *Seldom Seen, Rarely Heard: Women's Place in Psychology*. In addition, she has numerous presentations and publications dealing with feminist psychology and the psychology of sexual orientation.

CAROLE BAROODY CORCORAN codirected a State Council of Higher Education Funds for Excellence Grant that launched Mary Washington's interdisciplinary Race and Gender Curriculum Transformation project. The Race and Gender project was featured in *Black Issues in Higher Education* and cited as a model program by the Commission on the University of the 21st Century. She is cochair of the American Psychological Association's Division 35 (Psychology of Women) Task Force on Teaching Undergraduate Feminist Psychology. She received the 1994 Outstanding Faculty Member Award from Mortar Board and was nominated for the State Council of Higher Education Outstanding Faculty Award in 1996.

DEBBIE COTTRELL is assistant dean of the faculty at Smith College. Prior to her work at Smith, she served as assistant professor of history and assistant dean of the faculty at Cottey College in Missouri. Her research and teaching have focused on U.S. women's history, political history, and the history of education. Cottrell authored *Pioneer Women Educator: The Progressive Spirit of Annie Webb Blanton* (1993), which received the Liz Carpenter Award for the best scholarly book on the history of women and Texas. She has also published articles in the *Missouri Historical Review, Southwestern Historical Quarterly, Journal of Physical Education*, and *Recreation and Dance* and contributed to the *American National Biography* and *Historical Dictionary of Women's Education.* Her scholarship on women's education has been shared at numerous conferences.

ESTELLE DISCH is an associate professor of sociology at the University of Massachusetts, Boston, where she works on general education reform, diversity initiatives, and faculty development. She edited *Reconstructing Gender: A Multicultural Anthology*; her research focuses on sexual exploitation by health and mental health professionals and clergy. She is on a lifelong quest to overcome the limitations of a privileged white Protestant upbringing in a white suburb in the fifties.

GEORGE DOWDALL is professor of sociology at St. Joseph's University, Philadelphia. A graduate of Holy Cross College, he has a Ph.D. from Brown University and was a postdoctoral fellow at the UCLA School of Public Health. While a visiting lecturer at the Harvard School of Public Health, he served as a consultant to the College Alcohol Study. He is the author of two recent books: *The Eclipse of the State Mental Hospital* and *Adventures in Criminal Justice Research: Data Analysis Using SPSS for Windows*. His publications include several books about mental health and research methods and papers about college binge drinking and other public health issues.

HELENE ELTING recently joined the faculty of the Wharton School of Business of the University of Pennsylvania. She teaches in the Leadership and Communication Program, specializing in issues of gender, power, and leadership. She is a frequent lecturer on issues of interdisciplinary and feminist pedagogy in both academic and psychoanalytic institutions. Some recent talk titles are "Whose Class/Text Is It Anyway?" "American Women's Fiction and Feminist Psychoanalytic Narrative," and "Only Connect: Cross-Disciplinary Pedagogy Within the Liberal Studies Curriculum." For the past eleven years, as a lecturer at Bryn Mawr College, she has actively worked to facilitate the inclusive curriculum and to speak across disciplinary boundaries.

ELLEN A. ENSHER is assistant professor of management at Loyola Marymount College in Los Angeles. She received her Ph.D. in organization psychology from Claremont Graduate University. She is particularly interested in mentoring relationships and has published and presented papers on this topic.

KARI L. FRASER is a clinical psychologist currently employed as a school-based adolescent and family psychotherapist in a new program focused on providing integrated therapeutic and educational services to students in Boulder's public schools. A major research interest is exploring the processes by which experiential education and therapy promote learning and psychological change. She has most recently examined women's participation in a full-force self-defense course that facilitates changes in their sense of themselves and their abilities and has presented this research at a national conference. Other publications and presentations include "The Relation of Connection, Regulation, and Support for Autonomy to Adolescents' Functioning"; "The Possible Selves During Early Adolescence: Impressions of Now Shaping Visions of When"; and "Hopes, Fears, and Making It Through Middle School: A Longitudinal Analysis of Adolescents' Academic Possible Selves."

SHARON G. GOTO received her B.A. from the University of California, Los Angeles. She received her A.M. and Ph.D. in social/organizational psychology from the University of Illinois, Urbana-Champaign. She is an assistant professor at Pomona College, where her research focuses on cultural diversity issues. Specifically, her published work includes topics such as cross-cultural interpersonal interactions both within and beyond the workplace and strategies that foster success for ethnic minorities. Her research has concentrated largely on Asian American populations. She is currently working on a collaborative project that looks at Asian American perceptions of discrimination and its effects on mental health. She derives enormous pleasure from teaching both in and out of the classroom and recently received a Wig award for teaching excellence.

MARY B. HARRIS is Regents Professor at the University of New Mexico in the educational psychology program and associate dean for research and administration of the College of Education. She has published more than 170 articles on a broad range of topics, including aggression, gender role stereotypes, attitudes toward obesity and weight control, and behavior modification. She is the author of *Basic Statistics for Behavioral Science Research* (second edition) and editor of *School Experiences of Gay and Lesbian Youth: The Invisible Minority*. Her recent articles include "Experiences of Gay and Lesbian Teachers and Parents with Coming Out in a School Setting"; "Knowledge, Attitudes, and Concerns about Portfolio Assessment"; "Challenges for Older Students in Higher Education"; "Parents' Behaviors, Knowledge, and Beliefs Related to Unintentional Firearm Injuries Among Children and Youth in the Southwest"; and "Introductory Nutrition Students' Attitudes Toward Obesity: Ethnic and Gender Differences."

JUDITH GIBLIN JAMES is associate professor of English at the University of South Carolina, where she has been a leader in women's studies, serving as interim director in 1993–94 and 1995–96 and founding director of the graduate program in 1992–93. She teaches graduate and undergraduate courses in literature by women and American women writers. A textual scholar concerned with material evidence of the creation, transmission, and reception of literary works, James has published three books and numerous articles on nineteenth- and twentieth-century American literature. Her most recent book is *Wunderkind: The Reputation of Carson McCullers*. She is currently at work on two books: *Dramatizing Difference: The American Social Novel on Stage* and *Intimate Fictions: The Life in the Work of Sylvia Ashton Warner*. In addition to her research, she is an award-winning teacher and a nationally recognized consultant on evaluation of writing.

ERIKA KATES is a senior research associate at both the Heller School of Social Policy at Brandeis University, and the Project on Women and Social Change at Smith College. She has focused on access to postsecondary education as a way out of poverty for low-income mothers since 1986, publishing numerous articles and policy papers on the subject. She has worked with national and state networks of educators, researchers, and low-income women in attempts to improve overall access to substantive education and training. She also has extensive experience as an evaluation researcher, most recently at the Harvard Family Research Center and at Tufts University, where her focus was on reviewing the state of the art of evaluation in family support and in writing evaluation guidelines for family preservation programs. Currently, she is a cochair of WETAC (Welfare, Education, Training Access Coalition), an organization in Massachusetts that is engaged in education and outreach, policy development, and documentation.

ELLEN KIMMEL is Distinguished Professor, Education and Psychology at the University of South Florida. Based in the College of Education, she has long had an interest in teaching and has written and conducted workshops extensively on feminist pedagogy. She is a former president of Division 35 of the APA and the Southeastern Psychological Association, and a Fellow of the American Psychological Association, the American Psychological Society, and the American Association of Applied and Preventive Psychology. She served on the governing boards of all four of these organizations and has been active in these groups as well as on campus and in state politics to advance the status of women. Together with Mary Crawford, she has edited two forthcoming special double issues of the *Psychology of Women Quarterly* on innovative methods in feminist research.

MARY E. KITE is professor of psychological science at Ball State University, teaching undergraduate courses in statistics, research methods, and social psychology. She is also coordinator of graduate training for her department. She received her Ph.D. in social psychology from Purdue University in 1987. Her research interests include gender-associated stereotyping and prejudice; relevant publications include "Do Heterosexual Women and Men Differ in Their Attitudes Toward Homosexuality?" "Warming Trends: Improving the Chilly Campus Climate"; and "Sex Differences in Attitudes Toward Homosexual Persons, Behaviors, and Civil Rights: A Meta-Analysis." She has made numerous presentations at national conferences and has received grants for two research projects, on gender roles through the life span and on broadening undergraduate education (business school–liberal arts collaboration). She is one of five science, engineering, and mathematics mentors for the NSF grant "Awareness, Skills, and Mentoring Add Up to Success for Girls in Science, Engineering, and Mathematics Careers."

DEBORAH MAHLSTEDT is associate professor of psychology and women's studies at West Chester University in Pennsylvania. Her research on sexual violence prevention with young men has received recognition at national and international conferences. She is the author of articles on sexual assault in *Feminism and Psychology* and the *Journal of Human Justice*. In 1995, she cofacilitated an invitational seminar, "Feminism, Activism, and Scholarship: Studying Violence Against Women," for the Nag's Heart Feminist Psychology Seminar Series at Smith College. She completed a professional video in March 1998, "College Men Confront Violence Against Women." She serves as a reviewer of sexual-assault manuscripts for *Psychology of Women Quarterly* and *Feminism and Psychology*.

ROXANA MOAYEDI is an associate professor at Trinity College in Washington, D.C. She received her Ph.D. in sociology from American University and a management diploma from the International Management Center in Fujinomia, Japan. She is interested in teaching sociological perspectives on race, class, and gender by involving students in community service projects, such as mentoring minority students or volunteering in community centers. She believes this approach brings life and clarity to the concepts studied and allows students to see personal troubles such as poverty and divorce as public issues and socially structured. She has given a number of presentations on this topic.

SUSAN E. MURPHY is assistant professor of psychology at Claremont McKenna College, where she also teaches in the graduate school. She is also associate director of the Kravis Leadership Institutes. Her research interests include leadership, mentoring, small-group decision making, and motivational processes.

REBECCA L. PIERCE is an associate professor of mathematical sciences at Ball State University, teaching undergraduate and graduate statistics courses that incorporate the use of statistical software. She has made more than twenty-five presentations on statistics, statistical methods, and career opportunities for mathematics and statistics majors at national and regional conferences, state colleges, and local public schools. Most recently she has been codirecting a National Science Foundation–sponsored model project for women and girls, "Awareness, Skills, and Mentoring Add Up to Success for Girls in Science, Engineering, and Mathematics Careers."

VIRGINIA KAIB RATIGAN holds a Ph.D. in religious studies from Marquette University. She has taught in the theology departments at Wheeling Jesuit College, Villanova University (both graduate and undergraduate), and St. Joseph's University. She is currently associate professor of religious studies at Rosemont College, where she serves as coordinator of religious studies and on the core committee for the women's studies program. She has written about women and ministry in *A New Phoebe: Perspectives on Roman Catholic Women and the Permanent Diaconate*. In 1996 she wrote a major review article on the biographies of Cornelia Connelly, founder of the Society of the Holy Child Jesus, for the Records of the Catholic Historical Society of Philadelphia.

GLENDA M. RUSSELL is a research associate in women's studies and a clinical instructor in psychology at the University of Colorado, Boulder. She has conducted numerous research projects dealing with the psychological impact of antigay activities, as well as the costs, rewards, and motives of heterosexuals who take a stand for gay rights. This work has been presented at several conferences and also served as the basis for a documentary video and an oratorio. In addition, she has numerous publications dealing with these and related topics. She is currently working on *Voices of Trauma, Voices of Hope: Qualitative Analyses of the Effects of Amendment 2* and *Sexual Orientation: The Meanings We Make—Conversations About Psychology and Sexual Orientation* (with Janis Bohan).

CANDACE SCHAU is a professor at the University of New Mexico (UNM) in the educational psychology program. She received a B.S. in physics and a Ph.D. in psychology with a graduate minor in statistics. She was awarded UNM's Outstanding Teacher of the Year award, has been a Faculty Scholar, and received the UNM chapter of Phi Delta Kappa's Research Award. She loves to teach (especially statistics) and also loves doing research, especially as a collaborative activity with students and colleagues. Her research and evaluation activities explore the psychology of teaching and learning statistics and science, with an emphasis on cognition and assessment; gender equity; sex-role attitudes and behaviors; and educational programs and their students and instructors. She is an author or coauthor of more than thirty-five research-based articles and book chapters and coauthor of an undergraduate educational psychology textbook.

JESSICA A. SUCKLE is a doctoral student in experimental psychology at the University of Rhode Island. Her research interests include violence against women and teaching psychology. She has presented her work in both of these areas at the annual conferences of the Association for Women in Psychology as well as the 1998 conference of the American Psychological Association.

HENRY WECHSLER is a social psychologist with a strong interest in high-risk behaviors of adolescents and young adults. A primary focus of his studies has been binge, or heavy episodic, alcohol use. His research has pointed to the problems college binge drinkers cause for themselves and for others on campus, through secondhand effects. He is principal investigator of the College Alcohol Study and lecturer in the Department of Health and Social Behavior at the Harvard School of Public Health. He has published widely on the epidemiology of alcohol abuse and the role of public policies and institutions in fostering or preventing alcohol problems.

Coming Into Her Own *is dedicated to our parents whose love and belief in our attaining an education provided the foundation for this book.*

Francine L. Needle
William B. Needle

Mary Drummer Crawford
Wallace Barckley Crawford

Anna Seliwoniuk
Nicholai Seliwoniuk

COMING INTO HER OWN

INTRODUCTION

THE RESURGENCE OF CONTEMPORARY FEMINISM in the late 1960s and early 1970s included important critical commentary on the experience of women within traditional educational environments. The earliest work addressed evidence of sex bias in textual materials as well as gender inequity in the classroom (Frazier and Sadker, 1973; Hall and Sandler, 1982). The aim of this early research was to highlight the problems that mitigated against full and equal development of girls' and women's potential.

Acknowledgment of these inquiries led some feminist scholars to explore the particular nature and implications of women's experience. Gilligan (1982) proposed a special path for women's development. Belenky, Clinchy, Goldberger, and Tarule (1986) considered what women-centered education should or could be. These works, together with a series of other efforts, were the catalyst for many attempts to create equitable learning environments for women and to integrate scholarship by and about women. Soon, studies followed that examined classroom experiences, social climate, academic relationships, and differing experiences at coed and single-sex institutions.

Positive attempts to enhance the learning experiences of women students in higher education are flourishing. To date, the full range of this contemporary work, integrating theoretical perspectives with exemplary classroom strategies, has not been collected in a single volume. *Coming Into Her Own* seeks to begin the process.

A discussion of feminist pedagogy is not without political risk, and this political dimension can undermine the very objectives that are sought. Rather than expand and enrich the number and quality of approaches and educational contexts available, a "pedagogy for women" could contribute to the relegation of women's education to the sidelines, stigmatizing women as needing something different in order to perform. Moreover, a pedagogy focusing on females and on alternative educational environments embroils us in the claim that separate *can* be equal—if not better. In proposing classroom environments where knowledge is seen as growing from engagement, one runs the risk of promoting a "nurturing" environment where deficits in development, rather than transmission of "true knowledge," are addressed. There are always lingering suspicions that difference from the norm implies inferiority.

We seek to explore alternative pedagogies and teaching strategies because they expand educational opportunities, which we posit as an indisputable good. Alterity does not need to throw us onto the horns of a values dilemma or compel us to dismiss one method as inferior to another. We explore many alternative approaches, some of which are particularly effective for some constituencies and less effective for others. By offering strategies that respond to differences in background, motivation, and objectives, we expand the array of possibilities and pedagogical options and embrace the *both-and* dynamic in education, not the reductionist *either-or* model of pedagogy that is in place. Inclusion rather than exclusion is the abiding theme and operating principle, for college campuses are complex places with many constituencies that have differing relationships both to learning and to the process of education. We are talking about profoundly altering a campus environment—one that generally assumes a single optimal pedagogy or perhaps divides into two pedagogies (one for men and one for women; or one for the majority and one for a "special" population).

The complexity of the student population requires reexamination of strategies and an enrichment of approaches. In this book, we seek to frame approaches to teaching and learning that are sufficiently flexible to address the diverse needs of students of different genders, race, ethnicity, class, ages, and sexual orientation. Such a multiplicity of approaches is enriching to the learning environment for all.

The research focus throughout this volume is on solutions: strategies that optimize women's educational experience. Our interest is in laying out the contours of an education that is women-centered and the attendant strategies that make a positive difference to the efficacy of that educational experience.

Coming Into Her Own combines theoretical positions and practical strategies for implementing new pedagogies and attitudes. It explores feminist issues in the classroom, on campuses, and in individual relationships (that is, teacher-student, advisor-student, student-student). The chapters address a full range of components necessary to create optimal educational environments for women. This volume had its beginnings when Jadwiga Sebrechts and Mary Crawford organized a conference, in Amherst, Massachusetts, in 1995, on resilient women and education, bringing together scholars from around the country. While participating in the conference, Sara Davis recognized the importance of collecting this work into a new volume on beneficial, educational environments for women. Since theoreticians of feminist pedagogy are also its practitioners, this book integrates the two—a kind of simultaneous manifesto and blueprint for pedagogical reform.

Women and Education: Why Now?

Awareness and interest in the issue of gender in the classroom has grown appreciably over the last decade. The Anita Hill–Clarence Thomas hearings in the fall of 1991 brought both the vocabulary and the images of gender discrimination to a broad American public. Previously, these issues had been reserved for discussions among feminists and academics. Americans who had no particular professional or political interest in gender discrimination or other feminist topics were riveted by the U.S. Senate hearings that made household terms of such concepts as sexual harassment and sex bias. Moreover, the image of the Senate seeking unsuccessfully to identify a woman member to sit on the panel—from among its two women and ninety-eight men—could never be erased from the American consciousness. Gender inequality as practiced at the highest levels of the federal government was undeniable. This stark image of women's underrepresentation in the Senate and the hearings themselves inaugurated 1992 as the year of the woman.

Women had run for political office before that time, but never in such numbers and never as self-consciously and overtly as women candidates. The unprecedented entry of women into the political process was matched by the new focus put on education for girls and women beginning in February 1992 with publication of the AAUW report "How Schools Shortchange Girls." The data were not new—in fact, the report offered an analysis of some eleven hundred studies, surveys, and reports that had been released over the previous decade or further back. What this research showed was a systematic pattern of bias against girls in the K–12 classroom in the United States, a bias that was inadvertent, not maliciously intended. The sins were those of omission, rather than commission: girls had been excluded from the educational benefits and opportunities that males received by virtue of their sex. Virtually every news organization in the country gave front-page coverage to the dramatic, unequivocal findings of the report, altering how educational equity could be discussed. This report, like the many others that followed (Orenstein, *Schoolgirls,* 1994; Mann, *The Difference: Growing Up Female in America,* 1994; Sadker and Sadker, *Failing at Fairness: How Schools Cheat Girls,* 1994; and

Pipher, *Reviving Ophelia: Saving the Selves of Adolescent Girls,* 1994), compellingly showed that an educational system that was less than optimal for all students was failing female students even more.

Interest in the education of girls became widespread and motivated a series of diverse efforts to reform the system and find better ways of educating the female majority. Eager to address the demonstrated educational inequity, researchers set out to identify questions of equity. Teaching styles and dynamics became issues of concern, and the conversation moved to finding solutions to the inhospitable climate that pervaded all levels of educational experience.

Why Focus on Women?

Women seem to be doing rather well in U.S. education. Their grades at every academic level are equal to or better than the grades of their male peers. The gender gap in math and science enrollments is narrowing, as is the gap in math performance on standardized tests. The majority of students currently enrolled in higher education are female. Indeed, some critics have suggested that a focus on women in educational settings is unwarranted, since they are at an advantage relative to men. Liberal arts colleges report concern about a new gender gap—the absence of male students—and some are implementing "affirmative action" plans to recruit and retain them (Gose, 1997).

Although women certainly should not be viewed as a homogeneous group of "victims" of higher education, and full access for men must continue, there are compelling reasons to justify a continued focus on optimizing educational environments for diverse women. Although they represent a numerical majority, the *experience* of education for women is often that of being in a minority partly because the institutional climate remains organized around men and masculinity. Kathryn Pauly Morgan argues that women have been forced to adapt through

> a kind of colonized assimilation of our educational sensibilities . . . we become increasingly comfortable seeing primarily images of white boys and men active in the world and in positions of authority and dominance. We come to find it normal to read primarily the writings of white male authors and we inordinately appreciate those teachers, professors, and colleagues who make even modest attempts to be more inclusive of women in their defining of the canon. Through the process of colonization we internalize a misogynistic censor. This process is complete when we believe and feel that, yes, our concerns, our ideas,

> our feelings, and our life experiences are educationally irrelevant, secondary, limited, and inappropriately particularistic [Morgan, 1996, pp. 112–113].

The myth of coeducation pretends that equal numerical access to higher education gives women and men the *same* education. But for girls and women, participating in coeducation as it is currently structured often leads to "devastating experiences of mutilation, gender neutering, schism, and internalized misogyny" (Morgan, 1996, p. 117).

Morgan's charge is borne out by a great deal of empirical research. Kim Thomas (1988), for example, conducted ethnographic interviews with undergraduates studying physics and English in universities in the United Kingdom. As in the United States, physics and the liberal arts are gendered as masculine and feminine respectively, in the United Kingdom Thomas found that the physics students were introduced to a masculinist culture of laboratory science, while English students fared little better, reading mostly male authors. The female physics students were treated as a class of interlopers by the male majority; however, the male liberal arts students were treated as individuals even though they were in a numerical minority.

In the United States, classroom climate studies (such as that of Crawford and MacLeod, 1990) have repeatedly shown that women are less likely to speak in class and more likely to report inequitable treatment from professors. Also well documented is a lowering of self-confidence, expectations for success, and career goals as talented women "progress" through the educational system. Karen Arnold's longitudinal study of eighty Illinois high school valedictorians presents this defeatist trajectory only too vividly in *Lives of Promise: What Becomes of High School Valedictorians* (1995). Half of the valedictorians who were followed through their college careers and beyond were women. In surveys throughout their four years of college, these exceptional achievers were asked to evaluate themselves relative to their peers. Whereas one quarter of the male valedictorians persisted in their belief that they were intellectually "far above average" throughout their college career, no female valedictorians rated themselves as such beyond their sophomore year. This was true despite the women receiving objectively better grades than their male valedictorian counterparts.

Moreover, using gender as the only lens for comparison obscures the differential effects of educational inequities on particular groups of women. As Erika Kates documents in the final chapter of this volume, low-income women have educational needs that differ from those of upper-income women as well as from their male peers. Differential attention from teachers is directed not only to male students but to white students of both sexes, with African American girls becoming progressively more shut out of classroom interaction (Sadker and Sadker, 1994). To understand educational issues for women, we must specify *which* women, as well as which settings.

Focusing on women also compels us to examine *structural* issues in higher education. Issues and problems such as violence against women and against lesbian, gay, and bisexual people; alcohol abuse and associated health risks on campus; and access to higher education for low-income women: none of these can be adequately addressed without attention to structural causes and correlates. The current climate of backlash against feminism and women's studies can cloud the vision needed to address these issues, yet it accentuates the importance of doing so.

The Impetus: A Model of Women's Education

This book originated in a setting that is a unique model of women's education. The brainchild of psychologist Faye Crosby, the whimsically named Nag's Heart Conferences are small residential conferences. They usually occur in the summer; in recent years there have been five conferences annually, lasting four days. Each includes eight to fourteen participants, of whom two act as group facilitators. Usually, half or so of the participants are college professors.

Each conference has its own individual theme—such as dilemmas of teaching, dilemmas of spirituality, dilemmas of balancing work and family—and its own structure; but every conference must conform to the general mission of Nag's Heart, which is to replenish the feminist spirit.

Crosby writes: "What is the feminist spirit and why does it need replenishment? When we refer to the feminist spirit, we have in mind the communal effort to enhance true gender equity. The spirit resides within individuals, but individuals in isolation cannot bring about real change. Collective efforts are necessary. Replenishment is needed because any effort at true change drains people of energy, even as it satisfies and invigorates them. When one is in the trenches, the war can seem mighty long, even for the winning side" (unpublished correspondence).

The effectiveness of Nag's Heart conferences derives from their unusual format and attention to process. Participants live together in informal settings, often sharing bedrooms and bathrooms. Day One starts in the afternoon with cocktails, dinner, and brief introductions. Days Two and Three involve intensive small-group interactions in the morning, free time for relaxation in the afternoon, and communal meals and activities in the evening. The final day is devoted to achieving closure, both substantively and emotionally. Ceremonies matter at all points in the process.

During the intensive work sessions, each participant is allocated one-half hour in which to present a "dilemma" of personal import relevant to the issues at hand. Dilemmas can be broad or narrow. Participants may use their half-hour slot in any way they wish; they may speak for twenty-nine minutes and get one minute of comments from the group, or speak for one minute and get twenty-nine minutes of discussion. Extra sessions are devoted to issues that appear in more than one individual's presentation.

Throughout the four days, staffers pamper participants as much as limited budgets allow. More important than the material comfort is the intellectual, emotional, and spiritual comfort of knowing that one can speak and listen without fear and without pretense. Enormous benefit comes from the release of pent-up worries and frustrations. Constructive feedback greatly helps participants find ways to put their dilemmas in perspective and develop practical and workable new strategies for achieving personal goals. Many participants speak of the solace of companionship. As Crosby points out, "It is always helpful to change-agents to find out that they are not alone" (unpublished correspondence).

Our holistic experience at Nag's Heart occurred over the course of four days in which discontinuities fell away. Discussions merged with social interactions and flowed naturally into shared cultural and recreational activities. It was an experience that engaged the total person—so that both body and mind could be nourished and restored. As Crosby would say, "Sometimes the cook, too, needs to eat a meal that is served to her in the grand ballroom."

The theme of the workshop from which this book emerged was "Educating for Resilience: Girls and Women in the Classroom." Many educational pathologies had been explored by others at countless conferences, but this conference set for itself the task of analyzing the characteristics of females who survived and thrived in the classroom. Suspecting that the female students themselves were not the only ones responsible for reaching this desirable goal, the assembled community of educators, scholars, college presidents, and educational policy advocates considered teaching strategies that had been particularly successful both in and out of the classroom. Each participant presented a lesson that she had learned in teaching. These ranged from descriptions of leadership development programs in women's colleges to the teaching of statistics, business theory, psychology, and history, and to academic advising strategies that seemed effective with Asian students.

The work of this book has been to make the transition from workshop to a practical yet theoretically grounded compendium of strategies. Authors were added to the original cluster to make *Coming Into Her Own* as comprehensive, or at least as representative, as possible of the many areas in which the educational experience for women can be reformed. Our goal was to present ideas that faculty could adapt to their own campuses to effect the types of change that engage all students.

Organization of the Book

Our goal in organizing this book was to highlight successful innovations taking place in and around academic institutions.

We begin in Part One, "Women-Centered Education," by examining an overview of the enterprise of women's studies and look as well at the benefits that accrue in attending a women's college.

Part Two, "Restructuring the Classroom," then moves to a presentation of classroom dynamics and how they have been transformed by the principles and strategies of feminist pedagogy. Although embedded in a theoretical framework, our examples describe actual classroom situations in abundant detail to suggest techniques that a reader might readily adopt or adapt.

Part Three, "Transforming Math and Science," looks at a particular area of classroom experience that has provided some of the greatest challenges and has yielded some of the greatest results. Having described examples from the academic sphere, we look beyond the classroom at ways to enhance the student's whole-life experience.

In Part Four, "Changing Individual Expectations," we describe situations and programs in which the student develops her own resources—whether in an advising relationship or in a more formal program such as lessons in self-defense.

None of this would be successful without complementary changes at the institutional level, and so our fifth and final part, "Creating Healthy Environments," looks at changes in the institution that can create an environment open to the needs of all students.

We emphasize creating an atmosphere on campus that enables each student to feel stimulated and valued and therefore to be maximally productive. This has often meant attention to what happens in the classroom; yet no student performs optimally in an environment where she does not feel comfortable. Thus we have chosen to emphasize overall campus-environment issues as well as interactive and responsive teaching milieus. The complementary themes of *mentoring* and *changing the culture* resonate throughout this volume.

Mentoring

The concept of mentoring appears repeatedly throughout the chapters of the book, both the ones that focus on classroom interaction and those that deal with other facets of campus life. Mentoring has been variously defined, from very broad conceptions to much more sharply delineated relationships. For example, a recent issue of the *APA Monitor* offered several all-encompassing definitions, saying "mentoring occurs anytime someone transfers knowledge to another" (Murray, 1998, p. 34, citing Reich). In looking at how this theme develops in the various chapters, we emphasize aspects concerned with guidance along new pathways. We look at relationships between more experienced people who can become models for and guide novice individuals in a variety of behaviors. The former do not simply teach or represent information but rather impart a way of being in the world, whether professionally, academically, or socially. In particular, we look at advising relationships, role modeling, students who choose to take a leadership role in social groups, and using the life experiences of others as a way of learning and growing.

Mentoring has played a very important role for women expanding their horizons. Many successful women recognize the importance of sharing their experiences and thus opening the field to younger women. The sciences have led other disciplines in identifying the mentoring relationship between teacher and student as the crucial one for educating all students, most notably women. In disciplines as male dominated as the scientific and technical ones, informal mentoring arrangements were often too infrequent, inconsistent, and selective to be useful to the underrepresented group. Hence, each scientific society has established a women's division where mentoring is identified as a priority for all women students in the pipeline. For example, Division 35 of the American Psychological Association (Psychology of Women) has set up mentoring programs for young psychologists. The guiding principle is that psychologists with experience can instruct as well as provide models for less-experienced psychologists, facilitating the process of integration into the profession. Mentors illustrate productive attitudes and behaviors. By offering their personal examples of productive attitudes and behaviors, mentors extend direct, as well as more subtle, help to newcomers entering the field.

Education is a process of acculturation through which, for example, one learns not only, say, the principles of physics but what it means to be a physicist. In Chapter Twelve, Neal Abraham explains how both components play a necessary part in the model program at Bryn Mawr College, attracting as well as retaining students in the study of physics. He describes how students are successfully introduced to the world of physics at Bryn Mawr. Faculty members interact with students on both programmatic and individual levels. From the outset, they seek to represent physics broadly, engaging students in their own hands-on experiences in the lab, in departmental presentations of research, and as research assistants (at Bryn Mawr and at other institutions). By working as assistants, students are intimately exposed to the joys and discouraging moments that are part of being a physicist. At the same time, faculty work with student preconceptions of physics on the individual level. Because each student enters college with unique ideas and experience of physics, it is important to deal with each individual perspective directly.

Rebecca Pierce and Mary Kite also use mentoring as an important part of their work with high school students being introduced to the idea of math and science as career choices. As they relate in Chapter Ten, high school students visit Ball State University to gain insight into the worlds of science and math and to be encouraged to pursue these fields in college. As part of their introduction to psychology, students communicate with established women psychologists by way of the Internet. This activity serves two purposes: the students learn to use the Internet as an important academic tool, and at the same time they have the opportunity to learn about important professional and lifestyle issues from women scientists. Each student is put in touch with a successful female psychologist who is willing to discuss her career and her life. The students ask questions that open a window on life as a psychologist. This exercise also symbolically includes students as colleagues of the psychologists by affording an intimate form of access to the women's life stories.

Role modeling, as documented by Jadwiga Sebrechts, has long been considered a critical factor in the success of graduates from women's colleges (Chapter Two; see also Tidball, 1980). In women's colleges, where a high proportion of faculty members and administrators have traditionally been women, students have had the opportunity to see how women can achieve. These women role models expand the realm of the possible for all women. Even so, their role as models of achievement is often augmented by mentoring relationships in which the faculty guide students in their movement toward careers.

In the classes she taught at Trinity College, Roxana Moayedi (the author of Chapter Thirteen) maximized the relationship between role modeling and mentoring. She provided an interactive relationship creating links between professors and their college student mentees, who were, in turn, mentoring at-risk high school girls. The college students were thus in the dual roles of mentors and mentees. Moayedi's goal was to help the college students develop in their mentoring role by enabling them to benefit from the role modeling provided by their professor. Sara Davis, too, was interested in the advantages of role modeling when she developed collaborative methods for interacting in the classroom (Chapter Seven)—a style of teaching in which her greater expertise and experience served as a model for students rather than a source of information to be imposed. She modeled processes of doing research and engaged her students as colleagues in the process.

Helene Elting explores the interplay between the life stories presented in literary texts and those of the reader. Her concern is with the emotional and intellectual space within the classroom and how it is developed and shared by teacher and students alike. Intercutting her own experiences of visits with her dying mother and discussions in her literature class in Chapter Six, she reveals how she models an understanding of life that may transcend the experiences of her students. She reflects on how her understanding of characters and situations differs from what her students see. Her engagement with difficult issues and her willingness to describe how these issues affect her thinking constitute an important model for students. Her concern is with the levels of feeling and of meaning that are created through different levels of experience. Her students cannot experience what she sees—they have not lived enough; nor can she allow her own needs to dominate in the classroom. She can, however, introduce her students to new ways of experiencing and understanding.

Benefits of mentoring extend beyond the classroom setting to the wider social climate of the campus, as Deborah Mahlstedt and Carole Corcoran show in Chapter Eighteen's exposition of their work with fraternities. In an attempt to alter perceptions and behavior, especially in regard to attitudes toward women and sexuality, Mahlstedt developed a peer education program, associated with a class, to educate fraternity leaders in new conceptions of behavior. The goal was to diminish sexually aggressive behavior toward women by training profeminist male leaders. Men were attracted to the program because of the leadership opportunities and compensation, as well as by their own sensitivities and desire to promote change. The class also exploited the benefits of layers of mentoring: Mahlstedt was, visibly, a mentor for the peer facilitators who conducted the bulk of the class, and they in turn trained fraternity peer educators who became facilitators of change within fraternity settings.

Even though mentoring is clearly important, as a highly sensitive activity it must build from the needs of the mentees rather than be imposed on them. There are many possible goals for any student; an advisor must be sensitive to these possibilities and not attempt to favor a single pathway. In Chapter Fourteen, Susan Murphy, Sharon Goto, and Ellen Ensher describe how advisors need to be sensitive to the cultural and experiential heritage that students bring with them, and help them make the most appropriate choices. So, while others have emphasized the role-modeling component of mentoring in which an advisor or professor actively moves the student into professional life, these authors caution that this may not always be the most appropriate goal. The advisor should be aware that variation in cultural (both ethnic and class) background leads to differing expectations that may not be clearly delineated. For example, a student's cultural background might support her higher education but only if it does not interfere with the marriage plans that her family has made for her. Or a family may encourage educational goals yet be reluctant to permit travel beyond a narrow geographical area, creating conflict with professors who offer opportunities for study abroad or at graduate schools far afield. One must be sensitive to the particular goals of each student; they represent the many threads of her life and coalesce in different and often surprising ways.

Changing the Culture

Much has been written in the last fifteen years about the "chilly climate" that is the norm for girls and women at educational institutions (Hall and Sandler, 1984)—with the understanding that campus culture in its unexamined form is what is seen as regular or normal. Early on, numerous researchers, prominently the Sadkers (1994), emphasized how classrooms are historically structured to meet the needs of some male students and thus reinforce aggressive, monopolizing behaviors. It has been documented that women are often ignored in these classrooms because they do not make demands for teacher attention. Differential treatment may be the source of some of the paradoxes of women and education discussed earlier. Albeit inadvertently, many talented and smart women (and men) have been casualties of insensitive pedagogical practices.

However, research emerging from many arenas, including the sciences, demonstrates that when collaborative and engaged teaching is available, most students are responsive. In fact, establishing "communities of learners," partnerships among students and with faculty, produces positive results—even for those who were managing well in the hierarchical classroom (cf. Project Kaleidoscope, 1992). In addition, all aspects of campus life must converge to create a climate in which all students can thrive. Two strains of effort complement each other: those attempting to alter the culture and those empowering women students and giving them the tools for change.

On the broadest level, Judith James opens our book by charting the change in institutions as women's studies courses, and later women's studies programs, emerged. In many instances, these developments were the result of student demands. Although many initially believed that women's studies courses would never be viewed as substantial and would thus remain marginalized, in fact they came to have major consequences across the curriculum. "Women's studies scholarship diversifies and strengthens our knowledge of the world, adding the experiences and insights of women in all times and places to the historical record and exposing the errors that allowed their exclusion," James says in the opening chapter of this volume. Women's studies courses addressed the place of all women in our society and questioned the types of research that had underscored our understanding of women. As the content changed, so too did the method; new forms of classroom interaction became the norm for women's studies classes. The emphasis shifted from transmission of knowledge to its co-construction.

Several of the chapters in this book describe specific, concrete practices that can change the classroom culture. Some involve the feminist impetus to learn from the voices and experiences of women. For example, Deborah Cottrell (Chapter Four) built a course on the history of women in the United States around autobiographies and biographies of women. Rather than focusing on external events, she used an in-depth study of the texture of women's lives in different eras as a way of exploring historical change and life in different eras. Sara Davis and Virginia Ratigan transcended disciplinary boundaries to develop a course about studying women's lives that gave students access to a diverse group of women, with the focus on how they became agents of change (Chapter Five).

Other innovative practices are attempts to disrupt the socialized passivity and individualism of students in traditional classrooms. The authors of these chapters take very seriously Ellen Kimmel's claim in Chapter Three that feminist pedagogy is characterized by concerns about the distribution of power in the classroom. They explore the benefits—and limits—of creating a different classroom culture. Mary Harris and Candace Schau (Chapter Eleven) tackle statistics, a subject that is a gateway to social science careers and that is often badly taught. They describe specific factors that increase student involvement and success. As was pointed out earlier in this Introduction, Sara Davis develops collaborative teaching techniques that require cooperation, not competition (Chapter Seven). Estelle Disch reports in Chapter Eight on the contexts and strategies that enable women to speak and be heard. Sharing this concern with voice, in Chapter Nine Mary Crawford and Jessica Suckle look at how to deal with students' resistance to feminist content without silencing them. As a group, these chapters show concern with pragmatic outcomes, willingness to take risks, and readiness to learn from ongoing interaction with students.

However skilled and caring the classroom teacher may be, women cannot fully "come into their own" in symbolically masculine institutions. Higher education in the United States reflects the larger society in incorporating a masculinist culture of male entitlement, heterosexism, and biases of class and ethnicity. Aspects of this reality are addressed in several chapters, each of which documents structural inequities and then suggests practical ways of redressing them. For example, Janis Bohan and Glenda Russell examine how heterosexism was enacted in a conservative community when students attempted to form a gay and lesbian student group. Their ethnographic research project (Chapter Sixteen) goes beyond documenting inequities of sexual orientation; it shows how allies for change can emerge in unlikely and unexpected places.

Mary Crawford, George Dowdall, and Henry Wechsler (Chapter Seventeen) examined data from a large national study of alcohol use and abuse on college campuses. Their research indicates that there are significantly different patterns at women's colleges than at coed institutions. Attitudes at women's colleges are more strongly affirming of students who choose not to drink; consequently there are fewer alcohol-related problems, of both a direct and a secondary nature, at women's colleges. Students are less likely to have alcohol-related problems such as unplanned sexual activity and academic difficulties, to binge frequently, or to experience the consequences that drinking entails for others in their environment. In part, a different culture exists on women's college campuses. Socializing occurs frequently in contexts where there is less drinking, and the lack of fraternity and sorority systems seems to minimize the drinking. Crawford and associates call for innovative and systemic attempts to alter the culture at coed campuses so that there is less drinking.

Glenda Russell and Kari Fraser analyze the strategies of a program that seeks to empower individual women, Model Mugging, in Chapter Fifteen. Throughout the course of this program in self-defense training, women are taught not only techniques for physically protecting themselves but complementary psychological attitudes such as personal boundary setting. Russell and Fraser analyze how effective pedagogical strategies can be translated to this setting in which much of the work is physical and psychological. The course is viewed as empowering to women, who feel a sense of control and are moved to believe in their ability to use their physical skills to defend themselves rather than rely on others.

Erika Kates has investigated the needs of low-income mothers in the college setting. Assumptions about age of students, developmental stage, personal priorities, and so forth are different with this older, independent population who are juggling multiple roles (Chapter Nineteen).

Clearly, there is much more to be done in interrogating institutional norms not just of masculinity but of whiteness (Maher and Tetreault, 1997; Fine, Weis, Powell, and Wong, 1997), heterosexism (Wilkinson and Kitzinger, 1993), and class privilege (Lather, 1988). Ellen Kimmel, in Chapter Three's central contribution to this volume, describes four themes underlying feminist pedagogies: concern with distribution of power in the classroom, the idea that reflection on one's emotional reactions is central to learning, the importance of social responsibility and action, and recognition and inclusion of diversity (diverse people and diverse ideas). As ideals, they are inspiring; as templates for everyday practices, they are daunting. Yet the editors of this volume believe that these pedagogical themes are advanced, imperfectly but importantly, in the work of our contributors.

Using This Book

Many dimensions of diversity are represented in the pages of this book. Its contributors work in a wide variety of educational settings—single sex and coed, public and private, large and small. Some work outside formal settings altogether. Their methods vary from the traditional surveys, experiments, and quasi-experimental methods of the social sciences to discourse analysis, case studies, ethnographic interviews, and social action research. As individuals, they offer perspectives grounded in differing genders, sexual orientations, and ethnicities. As professionals, they represent a wide range of disciplines, and their experience in higher education runs from relatively recent to long-standing. What they share is the firm belief that "women's issues" are fundamental issues for higher education.

Above all, we consider this book to be a compendium of practical strategies and methods that "work"—that foster optimal learning environments for diverse women in diverse settings. We invite our readers to consider it, reflect upon it, and adapt it to their own situations, rather than treat it as a set of prescriptions. We hope that it guides teachers, administrators, and others who interact with women in higher education and who care about helping each woman student come into her own.

REFERENCES

American Association of University Women. "The AAUW Report: How Schools Shortchange Girls." Researched by Wellesley Center for Research on Women. Washington, D.C.: AAUW Foundation, 1992.

Arnold, K. *Lives of Promise: What Becomes of High School Valedictorians.* San Francisco: Jossey-Bass, 1995.

Belenky, M. F., Clinchy, B. M., Goldberger, N. R., and Tarule, J. M. *Women's Ways of Knowing: The Development of Self, Voice, and Mind.* New York: Basic Books, 1986.

Crawford, M., and MacLeod, M. "Gender in the College Classroom: An Assessment of the 'Chilly Climate' for Women." *Sex Roles,* 1990, *23,* 101–122.

Fine, M., Weis, L., Powell, L. C., and Wong, L. M. (eds.). *Off White: Readings on Race, Power, and Society.* New York: Routledge, 1997.

Frazier, N., and Sadker, M. *Sexism in School and Society.* New York: Harper-Collins, 1973.

Gilligan, C. *In a Different Voice.* Cambridge, Mass.: Harvard University Press, 1982.

Gose, B. "Liberal-Arts Colleges Ask: Where Have the Men Gone?" *Chronicle of Higher Education,* June 6, 1997, p. A35.

Hall, R. M., and Sandler, B. R. "The Classroom Climate: A Chilly One for Women?" *Project on the Status and Education of Women.* Washington, D.C.: Association of American Colleges, 1982.

Hall, R. M., and Sandler, B. R. "Out of the Classroom: A Chilly Campus Climate for Women?" *Project on the Status and Education of Women.* Washington, D.C.: Association of American Colleges, 1984.

Lather, P. "Feminist Perspectives on Empowering Research Methodologies." *Women's Studies International Forum,* 1988, *11*(6), 569–581.

Maher, F. A., and Tetreault, M.K.T. "Learning in the Dark: How Assumptions of Whiteness Shape Classroom Knowledge." *Harvard Educational Review,* 1997, *67*(2), 321–349.

Mann, J. *The Difference: Growing Up Female in America.* New York: Warner, 1994.

Morgan, K. P. "Describing the Emperor's New Clothes: Three Myths of Educational (In-)Equity." In A. Diller, B. Houston, K. P. Morgan, and M. Ayim (eds.), *The Gender Question in Education.* Boulder, Colo.: Westview Press, 1996.

Murray, B. "Mentoring: No Longer Just for Students." *APA Monitor,* 1998, *29*(9), 34–35.

Orenstein, P. *Schoolgirls: Young Women, Self-Esteem, and the Confidence Gap.* New York: Doubleday, 1994.

Pipher, M. *Reviving Ophelia: Saving the Selves of Adolescent Girls.* New York: Warner, 1994.

Project Kaleidoscope. *What Works: Building Natural Science Communities.* Vol. 2. Washington, D.C.: Project Kaleidoscope, 1992.

Sadker, M., and Sadker, D. *Failing at Fairness: How America's Schools Cheat Girls.* New York: Scribner, 1994.

Thomas, K. "Gender and the Arts/Science Divide in Higher Education." *Studies in Higher Education,* 1988, *13*(2), 123–137.

Tidball, E. "Women's Colleges and Women Achievers Revisited." *Signs,* 1980, *5*(3), 504–517.

Wilkinson, S., and Kitzinger, C. *Heterosexuality: A Feminism and Psychology Reader.* London: Sage, 1993.

PART ONE

WOMEN-CENTERED EDUCATION

AMERICAN HIGHER EDUCATION has a long and venerable tradition, although it is a largely masculine one. Even the most respected women-centered institutions—the women's colleges that emerged in the middle of the nineteenth century—took as their model, the educational structure, teaching strategy, and curriculum of existing male institutions. In many instances, the women's institutions were founded as pale reflections of their male counterparts and recognized the destinies of their students to be quite different from those of the students coming out of the male academy. Women's colleges mirrored the values of society and sought to cultivate the intellectual capacities of women, which had long been neglected, rather than restructure society or women's roles in it. Although arousing some suspicion, women's colleges were tolerated precisely because they did not overtly threaten the social order; nor were they completely understood by the male establishment. The students populating the women's colleges came primarily from the middle class and did not seek higher education because of feminist proclivities. Once in college, however, they often did experience intellectual awakenings and gain a new identity as "educated women"; and increasingly they drew fire from detractors. Women's colleges evolved and became distinct institutions. In the last few decades, this divergence from their male models has become a difference in kind. Women's colleges now offer a truly alternative educational model.

The historical role that women's colleges have played in American higher education is not the principal reason for which they are considered in Part One. Ours is not merely an obliging nod to a venerable and necessary foremother. Women's colleges today continue to be the only higher educational environments that unabashedly and unapologetically make the education, advancement, and achievement of women their first and only priority. As a function of this clear priority, they are also the institutions whose curricula and pedagogy have undergone dramatic and innovative change. They have conspicuously sought to be leadership training grounds for women, as women have—appropriately and in greater numbers than ever—raised their professional and personal aspirations.

Increasingly reflecting the changes in society and the growing diversity of women who are attending college, women's colleges have responded vigorously to this evolution and to the needs of their diverse populations. These are places in higher education where high expectations for student achievement and rigorous standards are the norm, yet where flexible programming has evolved in response to the needs of working women. These are institutions where service learning was pioneered decades ago because of the perceived need to establish a curricular connection between the classroom and the lived experience of the extracampus community. These are also the institutions where first-generation college goers and underprepared but motivated urban women alike have been given an opportunity to succeed.

Arguably, women's colleges provide the best contemporary answers to the question, What would an educational environment designed to be optimal for educating women and girls look like? All educational institutions should seek to answer this question, not only because it is right to do so but also because women constitute the majority in higher education nationwide. Their numeric superiority does not ensure priority status within traditional, historically male-centered institutions. Effective women-centered educational models should be developed and implemented in all of higher education. Today's women's colleges provide an important laboratory for growing, examining, and testing these models.

Women's studies, too, was born, not in the educational mainstream but on the margins of the disciplines. Its evolution as a field of study and scholarly research has been important in establishing a history of accomplishment for women, by enlarging the content areas of all disciplines and by incorporating women's contributions into the canon. As a multidisciplinary approach to study that interweaves a variety of fields, women's studies has enriched our intellectual history. More than a content area, women's studies offers a methodology and a pedagogical strategy that are women-centered and challenging to the established academic discourse. The women's studies approach can fundamentally transform a curriculum, by revolutionizing the relationships among students, between teachers and students, and between knowledge and interpretation. As a method of inquiry, the women's studies approach is a powerful tool, able to probe and question assumptions about the nature of learning and authority. When infused globally into the curriculum, it has the power to revitalize any discipline fundamentally, because the pedagogical stance that it assumes transcends the experience of women and provides a means of accessing the experience of the other, of the excluded. Far from being a limited perspective or a peripheral consideration of a single aspect of the disciplines, women's studies opens up a broad vista on every discipline that can then be reexamined and discussed—even rediscovered.

The paradox of women-centered pedagogy, whether the one modeled by women's colleges or the one animating women's studies, is that it results in an inclusive and dynamic reinvigoration of the educational experience for all students.

I

THE CONTRIBUTION OF WOMEN'S STUDIES PROGRAMS

Judith Giblin James

THE ACADEMIC MISSION of women's studies programs is to increase teaching and research about women in colleges and universities the world over. The first such program was established at San Diego State University in 1969, although the first women's studies courses at that university were offered in 1966 (Boxer, 1981/82). In the ensuing thirty years, women's studies programs have flourished nationally and internationally to such a degree and with such widespread impact that the *Chronicle of Higher Education* in 1987 called the growth in scholarship and teaching about women the most significant development in twentieth-century higher education (McMillen, 1987). By the mid-1990s, more than six hundred active programs existed in the United States, and women's studies courses were taught in two-thirds of universities, one-half of four-year colleges, and one-fourth of two-year colleges (Spaid, 1993). Internationally, the current decade began with vital programs in Great Britain, Western Europe, Australia, New Zealand, Mexico and portions of South America, India, Bangladesh, the Philippines, Korea, Japan, and China (Klein, 1991). Most U.S. programs offer both undergraduate majors and minors, and more than one hundred offer graduate programs at the master's or doctoral levels.

Philosophically, women's studies grows out of the recognition of a staggering conceptual error: that the history, psychology, biology, and artistry of men adequately represent "human" experience (Minnich, 1990). In the popular imagination and in the canons of most academic disciplines until the mid-1970s, this misperception held sway. For this reason, and for the exclusions it implies, higher education's central role in forming and transmitting cultural values became increasingly suspect under the challenges of women students and faculty. The women's studies program at the University of South Carolina, where I teach, for instance, was born out of student agitation for courses on women's experience in the wake of the U.S. Supreme Court decision on *Rowe* v. *Wade* in 1973. As a consequence of such events and the impetus of second-wave feminism generally, women and men throughout the United States and in other countries began to challenge the power of higher education to define what constitutes knowledge, especially if that knowledge has been limited to the experiences and insights of a single gender, race, or class.

Student challenges resulted in courses, and courses gave rise to programs. The first attempt to profile the emerging phenomenon in U.S. higher education came in 1976 when Florence Howe reported on fifteen representative programs and their common characteristics. In addition to establishing or retaining close alliances with activist women within their local communities—a sign of their overtly political agendas—the profiled programs had significant intellectual influence in the lives of their institutions, fostering new scholarship on women and engaging in informed and socially committed pedagogy.

Howe concluded that women's studies is "the perfect liberal art":

- It is interdisciplinary and unifying.
- It teaches skills in critical analysis.
- It assumes a problem-solving stance.
- It clarifies the issue of value judgment in education.
- It promotes socially useful ends [quoted in O'Barr, 1994, p. 90].

Other signs of professionalization followed quickly: founding of the National Women's Studies Association in 1977; inception of the journals *Signs* and *Feminist Studies* in the mid-1970s and *Sage: A Scholarly Journal on Black Women* in 1983; development of feminist journals encouraging scholarship on women in almost every discipline and women's studies lists in mainstream university presses by the end of the 1980s.

These developments were not extensively or fully supported by the institutions they served. Instead, the growth of women's studies in its first two decades was fostered principally by grants from private foundations and governmental agencies such as the Ford Foundation, the Rockefeller Foundation, the National Endowment for the Humanities (NEH), and the

Fund for the Improvement of Postsecondary Education (Stimpson and Cobb, 1986; Guy-Sheftall, 1995). The leadership of these granting agencies was especially instrumental in developing the large-scale curriculum transformation projects that emerged in the early 1980s with the goal of integrating women's studies scholarship and teaching across the disciplines in selected U.S. colleges and universities. However, as Reagan-era domestic policies foreclosed public funding for these projects, the role of private foundations became critical. The budgetary priorities of the NEH in this period are particularly revealing of the first stages of backlash against a strongly and rapidly developing women's studies presence in the academy and the feminist scholarship it fostered. Lynne Cheney, who followed William Bennett as chair of the NEH in 1986, spoke publicly on numerous occasions of her fear that "feminist criticism, Marxism, various forms of poststructuralism, and other approaches" would displace "the traditional concept of Western civilization." In the early 1990s, under Cheney's leadership, "projects related to women, gender, or feminism accounted for only 164 of 1,776 projects funded by all NEH divisions, and amounted to only 2 percent of the funds awarded by the NEH Division of Research" (Ginsberg and Lennox, 1996, p. 183).

Curtailment of government funding led women's studies scholars and administrators to private foundations (particularly the Ford Foundation) to support their efforts to bring insights from black studies and ethnic studies to the design of more inclusive women's studies programs. Throughout their growth in the last half of this century, feminism and women's studies, in the United States and internationally, have undergone an extremely self-conscious process of recognizing inequalities that the movements themselves initially and unwittingly perpetuated: the privileging of white women over black women and other women of color; of bourgeois women over working-class women; of Eurocentric experience over that of Third World women; of heterosexual women over lesbian or bisexual women; of educated over uneducated women; and of academic women over nonacademic women. We have learned, as a result, to speak of feminisms, of pluralistic dimensions of women's experience.

Out of the struggles and rung-by-rung progress of the last thirty years, women's studies has largely corrected its own early tendency to assert that women could and should speak with one voice. As a consequence, women's studies grew stronger, more inclusive, and more acutely perceptive in its analysis of and teaching about "difference." It has now become one of the most important forces in fostering sophisticated scholarship designed to understand and undo the tyranny of difference in modern societies. Such scholarship cuts across disciplinary lines and reshapes curricula.

Campuswide Benefits of Women's Studies

Perhaps because of the vital and revolutionary nature of their mission, women's studies programs have generated a centrifugal energy that propels feminist challenges to academic hierarchies, rigid disciplinarity, and male-biased teaching and course content into the university at large. Fears that women's studies would be ghettoized and easily containable within the institutional hierarchy have proved unfounded. The inevitable direction of student enlightenment and the explosion of new knowledge about women is outward, and pointedly aimed at transformation of the knowledge base.

The impact of such centrifugal movement is, on practical and philosophical levels, revolutionary—no matter at what pace it occurs. It shatters long-established paradigms of hierarchical and dualistic thinking. As Susan Griffin has observed, "Everywhere the old either-or begins to break down. . . . Thus, we may have to relearn thinking" (1981/82, p. 291). The emphasis in women's studies on inclusionary and cooperative approaches to teaching and research reflects the postmodern shift from either/or to both/and. Griffin recognizes such a shift in Darwin's finding that the health of an environment depends as much on the existence of diverse life forms as on struggle for the fittest to survive. Similarly, in twentieth-century science's discovery that light is both a particle and a wave, "the seeming existence of contradiction can be a gift of knowledge in a disguised form. So often in the history of thought a paradox has led to the discovery of a larger and more fundamental truth. . . . And we may fail to see this more fundamental truth precisely because we have been blinded by our belief in an old paradigm, an ideology" (pp. 289–290). In challenging the paradigm that has equated male experience and achievement with a definition of what it means to be "human," women's studies scholarship diversifies and strengthens our knowledge of the world, adding the experiences and insights of women in all times and places to the historical record and exposing the errors that allowed their exclusion.

A leader in the growth of women's studies and the effort to expand its influence throughout the curriculum, Paula Rothenberg makes Griffin's point about old paradigms forcefully. For better or worse, she says, "the curriculum defines what is real or unreal, what counts or is unimportant, what is normal or abnormal. It determines where the margins are and who occupies them. It has the power to render people, places, things, entire cultures, and continents invisible." Rothenberg's work to integrate scholarship on gender into the curricula of New Jersey colleges and universities is part of a larger effort to introduce race, class, gender, ethnicity, and sexuality as categories of analysis. "If you haven't been taught to use those categories, you won't see them. And if you don't know to look for them, everyone loses," she says. Emphasizing the social construction of "the knower and the known," Rothenberg proposes two questions with which to approach the transformation of learning: "Whose view of the world am I teaching or studying in this course?" and "In whose interest is it that I learn to see myself and others in this way?" (Rothenberg, 1993). The personal and institutional consequences of asking such questions can be transformative. The answers reveal the layers of prejudice and ignorance that we have been taught to see as "normal" and provide new and clearer lenses with which to view every dimension of experience, inside or outside the classroom.

The relationship among knowledge, power, and pedagogy is seamless within institutions of higher education. One of the most important effects of the influence that women's studies scholarship and individual programs bring to bear on higher education generally is increased awareness of biased teaching, wherever it appears. This awareness and the actions and interactions that result from it have had, in many cases, the salutary effect of warming what Roberta Hall and Bernice Sandler (1982) describe as a "chilly climate" for women in U.S. colleges and universities. "Sooner or later," say Jean O'Barr and Mary Wyer, "women's studies students realize that they are seeking an education within an environment that is predicated on the exclusion of women" (1992, p. 73). In male-centered classrooms, faculty create a climate in which women speak less than men and their contributions are taken less seriously. Faculty often have not learned new knowledge about women or do not incorporate it in their teaching. Some teachers persist in assuming that masculine pronouns (the so-called generic *he*, for example) include women and choose out-of-date textbooks that employ sexist language. Women are sometimes made to feel unwelcome in disciplines historically dominated by men, and in any area of study teacher attitudes can show lack of respect for women and their ideas. The cumulative effect of such disregard for women can be daunting, O'Barr and Wyer say, especially when students first realize the extent of institutional sexism and have found the words to label it. Women's studies has assumed a leadership role in educating faculty about how their assumptions about women may detract from the effectiveness of their teaching.

A women's studies model has been shown to "provide substantial benefits for all students, but especially for those who need them most: women of color, white women, and men of color" (Rosser and Kelly, 1994, p. 50). The difference of this model from the teaching-as-usual model, still too prevalent in colleges and universities, dramatically exposes feminism's challenge to the construction of teacher as knower and student as the recipient of knowledge (see, for example, Ellen Kimmel's Chapter Three in this volume). However, the introduction of so-called feminist pedagogy has met with vitriolic resistance—even though the techniques associated with feminist and other liberation pedagogies are those that schools of education have heretofore hallowed as simply "good teaching." In seeking to displace the model of Teacher as Prime Knower and bearer of the light, whose rays may fall unevenly or diffusely over more or less passively receptive students, feminist methods substitute the model of Student as Knower, actively cooperating in her or his own enlightenment, with the teacher serving as a conductor of electric intellectual currents. When introduced into the world of large lecture halls, which encourage the strut-and-pose model of teaching, feminist pedagogy is often perceived as threatening and therefore stigmatized as alien, inferior, disreputable. That is why defenders of teaching-as-usual have a stake in portraying the women's studies classroom as anti-intellectual, whiny, and (when not whiny) warm and fuzzy.

We have Elizabeth Kamarck Minnich to thank for exposing the self-interest and special pleading of critics of feminist and other liberation pedagogies. Minnich describes a key feature of such overreactions as the "excellence argument": the putative need to maintain standards that this more patient, more nurturing—read "coddling"—teaching would water down. She exposes the logical flaw of "applying definitions of what is real and/or central to any field . . . to categories for which they were never designed." This circular reasoning "leads to sloppy—and cruel—thinking, not to preservation of excellence." This is to be seen in the process whereby "definitions and standards derived from the study of men . . . , applied to the study of women, show women to be less 'real' and less worthy than men." These are unfair standards, illogically applied in the confusion of equality with sameness. "Excellence and prejudiced elitism are not the same" (Minnich, 1989, p. 281).

Excellence, all systems in our society and thirty years of women's studies research and teaching combine to tell us, is never absolutely clear, precise, and coherent. Excellence is complex, contingent, messy, and therefore richly perceptive. The insistence on recognizing and valuing complexity—the both/and as more reliable than the either/or—is one of the foremost contributions of women's studies scholarship to a transformation of research and teaching across the disciplines and within professional schools.

Direct Benefits of Women's Studies

From the beginning, women's studies curricula were identified with innovations in pedagogy, based on a belief in the inseparability of content from form, of message from method. Teaching the social construction of gender and the intersecting categories of race, class, ethnicity, age, nationality, and sexuality (to name just a handful of the modes of difference now considered indispensable to feminist critique) has, from the first, required a restructuring of students' and faculty's experience of the classroom: "Circular arrangement of chairs, periodic small-group sessions, . . . assignments that required journal keeping, 'reflection papers,' cooperative projects, and collective modes of teaching with student participation all sought to transfer to women's studies the contemporary feminist criticism of authority and the validation of every woman's experience. These techniques borrowed from the women's movement also were designed to combat the institutional hierarchy and professional exclusiveness that had been used to shut out women" (Boxer, 1981/82, pp. 243–244).

The collaborative, nonhierarchical methodology of consciousness raising gave rise to many innovations in pedagogy, particularly in the first decade of women's studies courses. By 1979, classroom practice had grown, of necessity, more complex, moving through stages, as identified by Cheri Register, "from compensating, to criticizing, to collecting and constructing, and finally to conceptualizing anew" (quoted in Boxer, 1981/82, p. 249). I would add that a signal feature of feminist pedagogy has been respect for women and the ideas of women, as well as valuing the knowledge and intellectual strengths of all students.

Attempts to document the effects of women's studies courses on those who enroll in them have rarely been as systematic as might be desirable, and many have been hampered by small sample size, particularly in gauging the responses of male students (Thomsen, Basu, and Reinitz, 1995). Several early studies demonstrated positive outcomes on measures of students' attitudes toward themselves, their women's studies classes, and their preparation for life outside the university (Bose, Steiger, and Victorine, 1977; Brush, Gold, and White, 1978; Howe, 1985). The most prominent recent studies are reported in *Engaging Feminism: Students Speak Up and Speak Out,* edited by Jean O'Barr and Mary Wyer (1992); *The Courage to Question: Women's Studies and Student Learning,* edited by Caryn Musil (1992); and *Women's Studies Graduates: The First Generation,* by Barbara F. Luebke and Mary Ellen Reilly (1995). Musil's collection analyzes seven women's studies programs, focusing on the voices of students in evaluating the effect of curricula and pedagogy on their development as thinkers. Luebke and Reilly draw from a national sample of eighty-nine women's studies graduates who recount the effects of their programs of study and the efficacy of their degrees. O'Barr and Wyer analyze more than one hundred excerpts from student writing in graduate and undergraduate classes at Duke University for evidence of common learning experiences.

In a smaller study, O'Barr, director of women's studies at Duke and former editor of *Signs,* undertook to verify the claims of students that women's studies provides an analysis of women's experience that intellectually validates frustrations they had felt but lacked ways of explaining (O'Barr, 1994). With colleagues Silvia Tandeciarz and Kathryn West, O'Barr attempted to discover "how different students develop a cognitive framework affected by an awareness of gender roles" (p. 154). After assembling full dossiers on sixty-five students in an introductory women's studies course (three course evaluations, four class assignments, and the final exam), they then conducted follow-up interviews a year later with the twenty-two students for whom they had the fullest documentation. Four students, whose experiences seemed representative, were profiled in depth. O'Barr and her colleagues concluded that although students readily adapt course content and methods to their individual needs, they had a number of motives in common: "a desire to gain a general knowledge of women's studies and feminist issues; a desire for a better understanding of themselves as women; a search for how gender relates to other defining characteristics in their lives (race, class, religion, region, and sexuality, among others); ideas on how to become more involved in working to change inequality; and a desire for frameworks that tie together previous courses, life experiences, and feelings about women's issues" (O'Barr, 1994, p. 155).

The researchers found Carol Gilligan's model (1991) of achieving "voice" appropriate for describing the learning students identified and affirmed one year after their participation in the introductory course. Instead of being content with silently seething at the gender inequities they now recognized, these students displayed the confidence to act on their beliefs, particularly insofar as was necessary to resolve interpersonal conflicts with stereotyping. O'Barr and colleagues concluded that these students' new knowledge was both intellectual and practical. They recognized at a personal as well as a societal level "that social conditioning is formative of . . . identity, . . . feelings, . . . actions, and [often, for women] guilt." Moreover, they "gained a political awareness that has allowed them to use their knowledge and to turn their resistance outward" (O'Barr, 1994, p. 177).

O'Barr's earlier and larger study, with Mary Wyer (1992), found that the current generation of college-age women receive mixed messages about their future. They have internalized the expectation fostered by thirty years of feminist activism: that women are powerful and capable of defining and achieving what constitutes success in their lives. However, women of this generation also know that they "live at risk of sexual abuse, rape, and domestic violence in a culture, both public and private, that . . . persists in conflating womanhood and motherhood. Women's studies offers a safe place to explore mixed reactions to these mixed messages" (O'Barr and Wyer, 1992, pp. 2–3).

Students of women's studies also confront and resolve another form of cognitive dissonance. The promise of feminist pedagogy is "a tension-filled promise because, of necessity, feminists must incorporate the unlearning of the old dyads—living and learning, emotion and reason, community and individual, teacher and student, creator of knowledge and consumer of knowledge, powerful and powerless—into the search for more productive paradigms" (O'Barr and Wyer, 1992, p. 9). An analysis of more than one hundred excerpts from student writing confirmed that reflection on the learning process is one of the chief characteristics, and benefits, of a feminist education. The Duke University undergraduates reported increased class participation and gains in self-confidence and analytical skills (O'Barr and Wyer, 1992).

Of the three large studies of student learning published in the 1990s, only Barbara F. Luebke and Mary Ellen Reilly (1995) focus on women's studies majors and attempt a nationwide survey. Their conclusions, added to those of Caryn Musil (1992) and O'Barr and Wyer (1992), buttress Florence Howe's earlier claim that, in fostering critical acuity, social responsibility, and interdisciplinary awareness, women's studies courses provide the best in liberal arts education.

One of the women's studies graduates surveyed by Luebke and Reilly was, as a result of work experiences accumulated before returning to college, no stranger to society's double standards. She credits majors in both women's studies and sociology at the University of Rhode Island with significantly sharpening her analysis of institutionalized sexism and other forms of discrimination in American culture and with inspiring her "to become a change agent" (quoted in Luebke and Reilly, 1995, p. 135). She makes her contribution as a teacher in the state of Washington.

A Yale University graduate and a practicing attorney said that the interdisciplinary range of women's studies allowed her to bring "a completely untraditional perspective" to coursework in traditional disciplines, "something which has only enhanced my ability to be a critical thinker" (quoted in Luebke and Reilly, 1995, p. 163). A young man who now manages a large cooperative grocery was inspired by Bettina Aptheker's celebrated "Intro to Feminism" course at the University of California at Santa Cruz (see, for example, Kamen, 1991). As a result, he changed his major from environmental studies to women's studies to acquire "a 'big picture' view of our culture" rather than isolated fragments of understanding that obscure "underlying causes" of the dilemmas human beings face. Women's studies proved "an incredible resource for gaining a clearer perspective," he said (quoted in Luebke and Reilly, 1995, p. 46).

One of Luebke and Reilly's most compelling narratives comes from a woman, now a writer, who left school in the eighth grade because she was legally blind and her family too impoverished to afford glasses. At the age of fifty-eight at the University of Minnesota, she found a women's studies program she calls "my lifeline." Her coursework gave sharp focus to the racism, sexism, and class prejudice that had afflicted her own life in patriarchy and the lives of her mother, sisters, and friends. Far from being discouraged by her new knowledge, she said, "I felt I was really coming alive at last. . . . I began to breathe and *think* more clearly" (quoted in Luebke and Reilly, 1995, p. 64).

Luebke and Reilly emphasize that the most common outcomes perceived by the women's studies majors they surveyed are consistent with outcomes identified in Musil's earlier study (1992) of women's studies and student learning on seven U.S. campuses. Graduates reported acquiring a repertoire of critical perspectives. They learned "to examine every premise, to become critics of the media, to question assumptions before and during research, and to challenge the status quo" (Luebke and Reilly, 1995, p. 199). Their women's studies courses, they said, gave them crucial insights into the social construction of difference and the forces that lead to oppression. Luebke and Reilly conclude that such insights made women's studies students "better at whatever they have done since graduation. The accusation that feminism is mainly concerned with white, middle-class women's lives is not substantiated in our study" (p. 199). The researchers also believe their findings exonerate women's studies of irresponsible charges that its courses are intellectually undemanding and impractical.

It is probably no exaggeration to say that women's studies programs offer women in large coeducational universities the closest approximation of the academic challenge and confidence building shown to be characteristic of women's experiences in single-sex institutions (see Jadwiga Sebrechts's discussion in Chapter Two of this volume). To think and write, Virginia Woolf famously asserted, a woman needs a room of her own.

Something similar appears to be required for women, in the aggregate, in higher education: the availability of what Jane Aaron and Sylvia Walby call "intellectual space": "Building a world in which women are not subordinated requires the development of a world view in which this is possible. To do this, intellectual space is needed. Ideas are not simply produced from an individual's everyday experience but from discussion with others and the sharing and debating of personal histories, acts which give conceptual form to experience and reveal the personal as the political" (Aaron and Walby, 1991, p. 1).

Women's studies currently constitutes that space. No matter how effectively the study of gender (and its intersection with other categories of difference) may be dispersed throughout the disciplines, there will always be a need for women's studies programs within the academy and for the introductory and core courses that provide first exposure to feminist methodologies; the critique of patriarchy; and the ideal of cooperative, rather than competitive, learning. Such programs offer a "feminist intellectual space" that optimally serves the needs of women students and faculty for a "room" of their own in historically and persistently patriarchal institutions.

The Future of Women's Studies Programs

Australian scholar Renate Klein offers a stirring assessment of the promise of women's studies: "Passion and politics, in interaction with a politics of curiosity *and* a politics of responsibility, are magic ingredients in the creation and distribution of the sort of feminist knowledge/vision which has the potential to move women's studies—and its participants with it—'out of the margins' in the 1990s and beyond" (1991, p. 75). Moving out of the margins, for Klein and others, is synonymous with resurrecting particular goals that have been pushed to the edges as women's studies concentrated on establishing strong programs, inclusive of race, class, and other differences. These include honoring women's studies' ties to feminist activism and improvement of the material conditions that affect women's lives. When thirty prominent women's studies scholars and program leaders from the United States met in 1992 to consider priorities for the next millennium, Bonnie Thornton Dill urged a revaluation of "the interconnections between the production of knowledge and the creation of public policy"; Beverly Guy-Sheftall suggested that "building women's studies infrastructure in regions outside the United States and fostering global understandings and perspectives within the United States" will claim an increasingly large share of feminist attention in subsequent decades; and Gail Hornstein called for increased focus on women and science (Hatton, 1994, pp. 256–263). (See Part Three, on bringing girls and women to math and science, in this volume.) These priorities, it should be noted, will be pursued, to a considerable extent, by a generation of scholars, teachers, and other citizens trained in women's studies programs over the last three decades.

It is a hopeful and, perhaps, inevitable development that the many current discussions of the future should emphasize, on the near edge of the millennium, the need to keep faith with the original vision of women's studies, particularly its commitment to activism, inclusivity, and interdisciplinarity. Other perennial themes are the need to promote wide access to the enormous amount of new knowledge about women generated in the last thirty years; to extend women's studies scholarship and teaching to new audiences, as in secondary schools and adult education programs; and, at all costs, to resist the entropic tendencies that would substitute the narrow and compartmentalized intellectual frameworks we have sought to abandon for the rich, complex, and difficult analysis of experience we have struggled to achieve.

Women's studies has a distinguished, though relatively brief, past and important work to do in the future. Begun in an era of campus activism to obtain greater representation and freedoms for historically oppressed groups, women's studies has never abandoned its commitment to research and teaching to understand and improve the lives of all women. Most often with scarce resources and against waves of conservative backlash that have threatened progressive scholarship and teaching throughout the academy, women's studies has struggled to forge a finely reciprocal relationship between establishing core courses dedicated to feminist theory and methodology and transforming existing courses, disciplines, and pedagogies throughout the university to reflect new knowledge about women and concepts of difference. The documented experiences of students demonstrate that the effects of women's studies curricula and pedagogy—collectively touted, and sometimes mocked, as the "empowerment" of women—are complex, widespread, and intellectually transformative. As such programs have grown in strength and inclusivity, they have become the safe intellectual space where women (and men) can confront the challenges of contemporary life with optimal chances for success.

REFERENCES

Aaron, J., and Walby, S. "Towards a Feminist Intellectual Space." In J. Aaron and S. Walby (eds.), *Out of the Margins: Women's Studies in the Nineties.* London: Falmer, 1991.

Bose, C., Steiger, J., and Victorine, P. "Evaluation: Perspectives of Students and Graduates." *Women's Studies Newsletter,* 1977, *5*(4), 6–7.

Boxer, M. J. "For and About Women: The Theory and Practice of Women's Studies in the United States." In N. O. Keohane, M. Z. Rosaldo, and B. C. Gelpi (eds.), *Feminist Theory: A Critique of Ideology.* Chicago: University of Chicago Press, 1981/82.

Brush, L. R., Gold, A. R., and White, M. G. "The Paradox of Intention and Effect: A Women's Studies Course." *Signs,* 1978, *3*(4), 870–883.

Gilligan, C. "Joining the Resistance: Psychology, Politics, Girls, and Women." *Michigan Quarterly Review,* 1991, *29*(4), 501–536.

Ginsberg, E., and Lennox, S. "Antifeminism in Scholarship and Publishing." In V. Clark, S. N. Garner, M. Higonnet, and K. H. Katrak (eds.), *Antifeminism in the Academy.* New York: Routledge, 1996.

Griffin, S. "The Way of All Ideology." In N. O. Keohane, M. Z. Rosaldo, and B. C. Gelpi (eds.), *Feminist Theory: A Critique of Ideology.* Chicago: University of Chicago Press, 1981/82.

Guy-Sheftall, B., with Heath, S. *Women's Studies, a Retrospective: A Report to the Ford Foundation.* New York: Ford Foundation, 1995.

Hall, R., and Sandler, B. *The Classroom Climate: A Chilly One for Women.* Washington, D.C.: Association of American Colleges, 1982.

Hatton, E. "The Future of Women's Studies: A Ford Foundation Workshop Report." *Women's Studies Quarterly,* 1994, *3/4,* 256–264.

Howe, K. G. "The Psychological Impact of a Women's Studies Course." *Women's Studies Quarterly,* 1985, *25*(1,2), 125–131.

Kamen, P. *Feminist Fatale: Voices from the "Twentysomething" Generation Explore the Future of the "Women's Movement."* New York: Fine, 1991.

Klein, R. D. "Passion and Politics in Women's Studies in the 1990s." In J. Aaron and S. Walby (eds.), *Out of the Margins: Women's Studies in the Nineties.* London: Falmer, 1991.

Luebke, B. F., and Reilly, M. E. *Women's Studies Graduates: The First Generation.* Athene series. New York: Teachers College Press, 1995.

McMillen, L. "More Colleges and More Disciplines Incorporating Scholarship on Women into the Classroom." *Chronicle of Higher Education,* Sept. 9, 1987, pp. A15–A17.

Minnich, E. K. "From the Circle of the Elite to the World of the Whole: Education, Equality, and Excellence." In C. S. Pearson, J. G. Touchton, and D. L. Shavlick (eds.), *Educating the Majority: Women Challenge Tradition in Higher Education.* New York: American Council on Education; Macmillan, 1989.

Minnich, E. K. *Transforming Knowledge.* Philadelphia: Temple University Press, 1990.

Musil, C. M. (ed.). *The Courage to Question: Women's Studies and Student Learning.* Washington, D.C.: Association of American Colleges; National Women's Studies Association, 1992.

O'Barr, J. F. *Feminism in Action: Building Institutions and Community Through Women's Studies.* Chapel Hill: University of North Carolina Press, 1994.

O'Barr, J., and Wyer, M. (eds.). *Engaging Feminism: Students Speak Up and Speak Out.* Charlottesville: University Press of Virginia, 1992.

Rosser, S. V., and Kelly, B. *Educating Women for Success in Science and Mathematics.* National Science Foundation Model Project Report. Division of Women's Studies, University of South Carolina, 1994.

Rothenberg, P. "Engendering Knowledge: Women's Studies and Multicultural Perspectives." Keynote address, University of South Carolina Systemwide Women's Studies Conference, Columbia, Mar. 19, 1993.

Spaid, E. L. "Women's Studies Matures as an Academic Discipline." *Christian Science Monitor,* Mar. 22, 1993, p. 12.

Stimpson, C. R., and Cobb, N. K. *Women's Studies in the United States.* New York: Ford Foundation, 1986.

Thompsen, C. J., Basu, A. M., and Reinitz, M. T. "Effects of Women's Studies Courses on Gender-Related Attitudes of Women and Men." *Psychology of Women Quarterly,* 1995, *19*(31), 419–426.

2

THE WOMEN'S COLLEGE DIFFERENCE

Jadwiga Sebrechts

NUMEROUS REPORTS over the last decade have chronicled the inequities of the educational experience for girls and women—from gender bias in standardized achievement tests to sexist language in books, stereotypical depiction of females in the curriculum, and a general failure to address proactively the underperformance by females in such male domains as math and science. This pervasive "chilly climate" on college campuses, profiled in Hall and Sandler's eponymous report (1984), has discouraged women's achievement and has exposed them to harassment and eroded their self-esteem. Not invigorated, as are their male counterparts, by the triple-strength tonic of faculty attention, opportunities to speak, and high expectations, female students have gradually lowered their sights with respect to their own performance and have opted out of challenges and opportunities. Few outside the feminist academic community noticed, until *How Schools Shortchange Girls* was released in 1992 and galvanized media attention.

The study, commissioned by the American Association of University Women and produced by the Wellesley Center for Research on Women, focused on precollege girls. The forty concrete recommendations in which the document culminated transformed it from a mere report into a manifesto. It called upon educators and policy makers to inscribe girls indelibly into the national agenda for educational reform. Moreover, the report underscored an important feature of the remaining inequities for females at any level in their education: gender inequity in education was now largely a sin of omission rather than of commission and as such could be even more difficult to extirpate. Most educators and institutions did not do anything actively to disadvantage their female students; most wanted to be equitable and fair. Yet the entire educational system was inherently gender-biased, with powerfully ingrained practices and expectations that resulted in inadvertent discrimination.

Alexander Astin's important analysis of the college experience, *What Matters in College? Four Critical Years Revisited* (1993), pointed out that failure to actively and specifically address the educational needs of women was highly effective in creating an inhospitable climate for them. In college, such "shortchanging" risked deforming a woman's development just as she was preparing for a career and positioning herself in her societal role. Colleges effectively reinforced societal gender bias by failing to counter it proactively:

> Women enter college already differing considerably from men in self-rated emotional and psychological health, standardized test scores, GPAs, political attitudes, personality characteristics, and career plans, and most of these differences widen during the undergraduate years. . . . Even though men and women are presumably exposed to a common liberal arts curriculum and to other common environmental experiences during the undergraduate years, it would seem that their educational programs preserve and strengthen, rather than reduce or weaken, stereotypical differences between men and women in behavior, personality, aspirations, and achievement. A similar conclusion was reached nearly twenty years ago in *Four Critical Years* [pp. 405–406; reference to Astin, 1977].

Astin's study also debunks the myth that was promulgated during the coeducational euphoria of the early 1970s, that as long as they participate in the same educational settings as men, women inevitably receive a comparable education. It becomes clear that achieving an equal educational experience for women requires conscious, deliberate effort. Women must figure in an institution's explicit priorities. Women must be valued and become a value that the institution promotes.

What would a postsecondary institution look like if it were designed to fully meet the educational needs of women and to be a place where women were valued? It would probably not look like the typical and prolific contemporary, coeducational institutions.

Coed institutions are a reflection of social norms, where dualism is enlisted to deal with questions of gender, where opposition is established in which the two sides of the equation are not equal. One—namely, the male element—is taken to be the norm against which the other—the female element—is compared and found, by definition, to be inadequate. The difference in prestige of the two genders evidences itself prototypically in education, where the characteristics attributed to the male—such as rationality, objectivity, abstraction—are those valued in the academy, while traditional attributes of the female—intuition, subjectivity, connectedness—are undervalued. For women, the degree of success in the male academy often depends on their ability to conform with the characteristics that are posited as superior. This is especially true in the supposedly masculine disciplines such as math and science. These "dueling" gender archetypes are locked in an either-or dynamic rather than the inclusive one of both-and. In this design, there *must* be winners and losers.

The peer culture on a coed campus can also militate against women's academic performance and achievement. Unlike their male counterparts, who are valued and rewarded for academic, athletic, and leadership prowess by their male and female peers, women derive their prestige from their attractiveness to men. In their eye-opening study of a southern coed campus, Holland and Eisenhart (1990) found that approximately 80 percent of women succumbed to the social pressure of subsuming their own accomplishments into the quest for, and retention of, a prestigious male. From him, their worth derived; from his accomplishments, their stock rose and fell. Only 20 percent of females resisted this social imperative and derived their self-worth from their own achievements and victories. Significantly, the latter, *resister* group was found by the researchers to be engaged in "real world" applications of their knowledge and expertise, whether as lab assistants, student interns, or trainees. Preliminarily at least, these extracurricular *mastery* activities seemed to contribute to a sense of purpose and enhanced self-esteem.[1]

The Women's College Culture

A women's college posits an alternative culture and tradition from that found at a typical coed institution. It is a place where the history, the values, the *statues* as well as the *statutes* affirm the value of women and give them a legacy of achievement with which to identify. In their 1988 study of twelve colleges and universities, Kuh and Whitt defined the climate of an institution as a cultural fabric, "a persistent pattern of norms, values, practices, beliefs, and assumptions that shape the behavior of individuals and groups in the community and provide a frame of reference within which to interpret the meaning of events and actions on and off campus" (p. 3). At the heart of the cultural assumptions at a women's college lies the notion that the education and empowerment of women is crucially important. Women are not "the other," introduced after the structure most conducive to male learning patterns has been firmly entrenched. They are the chief participants for whom the system has been designed.

We already have rich data from women's colleges and from independent research that show the single-sex setting to be especially conducive to the intellectual, developmental, and professional needs of women. Starting with the pioneering analyses of Astin and continuing through the studies of Daryl Smith (1990), Myra and David Sadker (1994), Catherine Krupnick (1985), and Elizabeth Whitt (1992, 1994), the evidence suggests that women optimize their intellectual development, enhance their sense of self-efficacy, keep their aspirations and self-esteem high, and build leadership skills in women's colleges. The statistics about women's college graduates provide eloquent testimony for these claims.

Women's colleges have been remarkably prolific in producing math and science graduates. At some of them, 25–40 percent of the students major in math, natural science, and economics. In fact, the percentage of majors in economics, math, and the life sciences was higher in women's colleges than it was even for men in coed institutions, and substantially higher than for women at those institutions. Women's college graduates were two to three times more likely to continue toward advanced degrees in math and science, including medical school and engineering, than their coed counterparts (Tidball and Kistiakowsky, 1976). Approximately one-half of all graduates of women's colleges entered traditionally male, and therefore higher-paying, fields (Women's College Coalition Study, 1985). They were also represented in senior positions and on boards of Fortune 1000 companies at six times the rate that one would have expected given their proportion in the population of graduate women; and almost one quarter of the women in Congress[2] had attended women's colleges (although only about 3 percent of all women who had attended college in the last forty years attended women's colleges).

Traditionally, when researchers make systematic comparisons between women's colleges and coed colleges they define "better" in terms of the heights of academic and postgraduate achievement among the respective institutions' students (Tidball and Kistiakowsky, 1976; Miller-Bernal, 1993). Women's college graduates outperform their coed counterparts in comparably selective institutions. Though impressive, such comparisons only tell half of the story, since these measures rely on masculine standards of achievement and success, especially the attainment of important positions at higher levels of compensation. Other criteria can and should be used to judge whether the women's college environment is indeed a "better" one for women students. Using current methodology and the High School and Beyond database (compiled by UCLA for more than twenty years now), researchers have found that women at women's colleges are more likely to stay in school to graduation, more predictably exhibit a concern for social change, grow in their acquisition of leadership skills, and continue with their education after graduation. Moreover, women's college graduates express stronger views favoring gender equality, have higher self-esteem, and are more likely to achieved occupational satisfaction and success (Smith, 1990; Astin, 1977). The benefits of such an environment extend well beyond the classroom and postgraduate occupational success, into the social, personal, and societal arenas.

The inevitable question entailed by such results: What is it about the women's college experience on the campus, in the classroom, and in the curriculum that can account for such desirable pedagogical and civic outcomes? The short answer might be: everything.

Contemporary women's colleges are diverse institutions—distinct from each other in their history, profile, student body, and strengths, and internally diverse with respect to the race, ethnicity, socioeconomic status, age, and life experience of their students. Women's colleges are found in twenty-four states, with Massachusetts and Pennsylvania claiming about a dozen each. They are located in large urban centers as well as in suburban and rural settings. Small, private, liberal arts institutions with an average undergraduate student population of one thousand students, women's colleges range twentyfold in size from three hundred to six thousand students; in terms of selectivity and prestige they vary from the Seven Sisters,[3] with their national reputations, substantial endowments, and illustrious alumnae network, to the one-third of women's colleges with historic affiliations to the Catholic church and their traditions of service and provision of educational access to the underserved in their local and regional communities. Some women's colleges have a primarily residential, full-time, traditional-age student population; others have innovated flexible and even off-site programming for a growing population of highly motivated adult women seeking the credentials that will allow them greater job opportunities and will enable them to better provide for their families.

Despite their diversity as institutions, women's colleges share a common mission of educating women and expanding women's opportunities. Women's colleges exist *because* women's education is important. Whatever their particular characteristics, women's colleges offer environments in which high expectations for student achievement and success characterize all faculty-student interactions, where the mentoring relationship between faculty member and student underlies the process of education, and where positive role modeling is provided by female faculty and administrators. High expectations, mentoring, and the presence of abundant female role models—although important to accomplishment in any field—are critical to achievement for women in the sciences and traditionally male arenas of accomplishment (as Abraham outlines in Chapter Twelve of this volume). Moreover, the women's college environment is permeated by respect for the contributions of women. It is a place where the substantial history of women's achievement is celebrated and where a critical mass of students of the same sex come together to support each other's efforts. A women's college allows the female pronoun to become the norm. As one researcher recounted, it was only when she stepped onto a women's college campus that she encountered her own prejudice about what is normal. She had always assumed that only the male pronoun could follow a reference to a person of accomplishment, prestige, and power. The prevalence of *she* in that privileged position startled her at first but then became a source of pride and tremendous self-affirmation.

In a recently published, comparative study of two radically different women's colleges—Bennett, an historically black, regional, less-selective institution in Greensboro, North Carolina, and nationally known Bryn Mawr, one of the Seven Sisters, outside of Philadelphia—Lisa Wolf-Wendel (Tidball, Smith, Tidball, and Wolf-Wendel, 1998)[4] identified the characteristics that were most important to student satisfaction and academic performance. She found the characteristics to be common to both institutions, despite the differences in tradition, selectivity, and prestige. The two institutions were identical in their explicitly demonstrated commitment to mission, values, and caring about their students' achievement. The students' perception of these institutional priorities resulted not only in high levels of satisfaction but also in enhanced self-concept, which in turn led to heightened levels of engagement and achievement. If the quality of an institution's mission makes a difference to women's achievement, then there is no better example of a women's college mission dedicated to an explicitly articulated set of core values and expectations about student growth than that formulated by St. Mary of the Woods College in Indiana. In its "Statement of Student Outcomes," the college declares that "our students must master new ideas, new technologies, and new ways of creating community. As we envision success, it cannot exist without this human dimension. If we hope to contribute to a world in need of healing and understanding, we must come to the same conclusion. . . . We see success in terms of fulfillment brought about by active lives."

Johnnetta Cole, former president of Spelman College (also an historically black women's college) explained, when asked to suggest a reason for the effectiveness of these special environments, "As a young woman at a women's college, I see others like me, who are valued, and learn that I, too, am valuable." In her book *Conversations: Straight Talk with America's Sister President* (1993), Cole offers a series of lessons that Spelman can teach other institutions that are neither historically black nor women's. Among the six lessons that she outlines is this one: "At Spelman, students see individuals who look like them serving as the president of the college, a professor of biology or economics, the president of the student body, editor of the newspaper, and captain of the basketball team. Lesson: Positive role models encourage high self-esteem, which is a necessary ingredient for learning. Positive role models boost a student's pride and sense of self-worth" (p. 180).

For those in a minority position, whether by virtue of their race or their gender, likeness is empowering. Seeing oneself as part of the whole, not as different and marginalized, leads to a sense of possibility, opportunity, and efficacy. A symmetrical argument is difficult to make for likeness of a majority group, of a dominant and empowered cohort. The reaffirmation of one's majority status may lead to an unhealthy catharsis, and this may be the reason that no research has yet shown corresponding benefits to white men in all-male institutions.

Two concepts of identity are at work in the development of an empowered woman, and a women's college feeds both. First, each student sees herself to be the same as the valued students of the institution; second, she recognizes her uniqueness, as an individual with a particular set of talents and competencies, which her institution respects.

Both senses of identity are promoted by the existence of a critical mass of women, most especially in the disciplines where women are underrepresented. Eccles (1989) emphasizes the importance of creating a critical mass of women students and scientists to create an environment that does not promote the sense of isolation that afflicts young women, who find themselves part of a small minority in a traditionally male discipline, in a traditionally male institution. An informal proposal by Carnegie Mellon University to establish an engineering institute for women was predicated on the belief that a critical mass of women is important for encouraging them to achieve in a field as male-dominated as engineering. At the large, coed University of Seattle, a pilot study was conducted in the early 1990s, comparing a women's-only program for chemistry majors and two coed counterparts. Not only did the women's-only classes have higher retention rates of students than did the others but also the classes were especially beneficial to minority women (primarily Asian at the University of Seattle), whose attrition rate was traditionally even more severe than that of the majority women. The results suggested clear benefits of single-sex settings even in the context of a large coed institution for retaining and encouraging persistence among "underrepresented" groups.

Role Modeling and Mentoring Success

The process of developing a sense of identity as a competent, independent thinker and agent is importantly undergirded at a women's college by the abundance of role models and mentors. Students at women's colleges have a four-in-five chance of seeing a woman exercise presidential authority at their college; at a coed college, it is about one in eight. The boards of trustees, the administration, and the faculties have a much higher proportion of women than at coed colleges. And it is axiomatic that at a women's college, the student leaders are women.

The crucial role of mentoring in academic success and in leadership development has been explored in classic studies such as those of Tidball and Kistiakowsky (1976) and countless others; yet a systematic and all-inclusive effort to mentor and provide appropriate role models for women students has not been a priority at most institutions. It has been left to the individual initiative of faculty. Recent studies by Eccles (Eccles and Jacobs, 1986, Eccles, 1989), have put mentoring and role modeling into the positions of prominence they deserve.

In outlining the importance of role modeling and mentoring to cultivating women's achievement, success, and leadership potential, the example of the sciences is prominent in most studies. It is notable, therefore, that more than half of all faculty are female at women's colleges; among math and science faculty, 45.6 percent are women, compared to less than 14 percent at coed institutions and only 4 percent at technical institutes. Young women aspiring to careers in math and science need to see women who have achieved the careers to which they themselves are aspiring and who are eager to encourage their efforts. According to Tidball and Kistiakowsky, "the more adult women of accomplishment present in the environment, the more likely are women students to proceed to their own post-college accomplishments" (1976, p. 651). Hence, the concerted effort on the part of institutions to increase the numbers of female faculty at all academic ranks is fundamental, not only to achieving gender equity for the faculty but also to promoting gender equity for students.

The positive impact of role modeling is not reserved for the classroom. A young woman's developing ego is profoundly affected by affiliation with an institution that is led by a woman president (90 percent at women's colleges compared to 16 percent in coed institutions), where women constitute the majority of the faculty (55 percent at women's colleges), and whose senior administration is equally divided between men and women, as is the board of trustees. In the nation's eighty women's colleges, women not only constitute the vast majority of the student population but also teach and govern the institution in numbers equal to or better than the number of men.

American popular culture plays an important role in dissuading girls and young women from taking themselves seriously and aspiring to greatness. In addition to depicting achieving women as unappealing bluestockings or negligent mothers, the media and the popular press typically offer only masculine images of achievement. There is a paucity of female images and names in positions of authority to nurture the imaginations of young women.

Mentoring is a critical component of the process of plotting and embarking upon a career direction. Mentoring and support for a developing vision of the self are at the heart of pedagogical strategies that overdetermine success for women. Inherent in the mentoring relationship is the underlying expectation that students achieve and are worthy of the faculty's attention. As Etta Falconer, director of science programs at Spelman, replied when asked the secret to Spelman's success, "We expect them to succeed, and they do." High expectations and one-on-one mentoring leave little room for failure. They are central to the empowering process—nowhere more so than in the sciences.

Leadership and developing a sense of expertise are also dependent upon the opportunity to practice both. As Whitt (1994) elaborates, leadership is learned within a climate that supports such learning and offers encouragement to assimilate the lessons. The absence of male competition for student leadership positions is an important factor, in obvious as well as subtle ways. Since all student leadership positions are filled by women at a women's college, more women have the experience of leading, without facing even the option of deferring to males. If an organization on campus is to be organized and operate effectively, a woman has to do it or else it does not function. Moreover, any previously held gender expectations among faculty advisors that might perpetuate gender stereotypes must be put aside. Dependence on women students to provide leadership, if any student leadership is to be had, stimulates faculty to encourage women to take on these roles. In coed institutions, participation of women in the leadership arena depends solely on self-selection. Since women are likely to underestimate and undervalue their abilities and potential, the expectation that large numbers of women will place themselves in the position of competing for a leadership position just because it is available is unrealistic. Hence the "same" opportunity that a coed institution offers women and men is weighted against a woman's participation. If a student does not experience leadership in college, it is less likely that she or he will seek it out after college.

Classroom Dynamics

On the micro level, the women's college classroom offers lessons as important as those taught by the macro level of campus climate, institutional mission, and philosophy. Numerous studies cite the differing learning strategies that students use in the classroom and show that the very conditions most conducive to one student's learning can be the least amenable to another's. Men are more likely to assume the adversarial, debating stance and engage in negative criticism of posited claims with some zeal; female students often prefer a cooperative, positive approach to learning and withdraw from discussions that become confrontational. Moreover, men's response time to questions is habitually quicker; hence their tendency to monopolize discussions. Women are more likely to reflect before speaking and to withhold comment if it contradicts what has already been articulated. Krupnick of the Harvard School of Education and the Sadkers of American University's School of Education have also published compelling studies of the differences in approach to verbal intervention in classes on the part of teachers. Men command more class time responding to questions than women in the same classroom—about 2.5 times more—because they respond instantly and are called upon more frequently, but they also receive very different responses from the teacher when they make a mistake. Women students are more often asked to respond to factual questions, requiring little, if any, analytic reasoning and are corrected by the teacher if they make an error. Their male counterparts are targeted for responses to more complex questions requiring critical judgement, and if they make a mistake they are encouraged to try to figure out the correct response. An easy correction is not offered to them, and they learn that the correct reply lies within their capacities (Krupnick, 1985; Sadker and Sadker, 1994). Since women are less likely to participate in class, it is important to target women for participation in discussions. Students need to experience participation in classroom discussion even if their own proclivities would cause them to defer to others. Research has shown that female faculty work to create a better environment in the classroom for all their students (Crawford and MacLeod, 1990). Hence an increase in the number of female faculty in college would be beneficial to all students, both in the increase in role models and in enhancement of the classroom experience.

Because classroom performance and the teacher's expectations about classroom performance contribute to the development of the student's ego and self-esteem, it is crucial to encourage active participation of women in classroom life. In areas of traditional male dominance such as the sciences, active participation includes hands-on exposure to instrumentation and equipment so that competence is developed. Women students should not have the option of deferring to a male lab partner whenever equipment is manipulated. Access to instrumentation is crucial to all students expecting to become adequately trained in the technical disciplines. Women are particularly challenged in this area. Not only do they compete with men for time with equipment but women typically have less *informal* experience with equipment than their male counterparts and are less likely to grab the opportunities to experiment in an area that is still relatively novel.

Project Kaleidoscope (begun in 1990 and sponsored by the National Science Foundation), a comprehensive investigation of the best practices in teaching math and science at the undergraduate level, has paid special attention to what the most successful programs do and how these successful strategies can be translated into other contexts. After examining a variety of institutions, including women's colleges and historically black colleges—where some of the most dramatic and positive results were found—the investigators recommended that undergraduate science and math training be done in the context of "communities of learners and scientists," who work in close proximity to each other and where collaboration gives dynamic force to the educational experience. Establishing these communities depends upon transforming the educational context from one that favors competitiveness and an exclusive model to one that fosters cooperation and inclusiveness. The garden, rather than the playing field, is the helpful metaphor in understanding the qualitative difference in perspective. Women's colleges do not seek to "weed out" the underprepared or intimidated from the academic garden. Instead, there is a concerted effort to recruit, and then to retain through such reinforcing practices as counseling and extensive extracurricular opportunities and internships. In *Achieving Educational Excellence,* Astin calls this the "talent development approach to undergraduate education." Every teacher is considered "capable of producing significant improvements in the performance of students, whatever their performance level at college entry." Abraham's model for teaching physics (Chapter Twelve) relies on this new understanding of science education.

A Women-Centered Curriculum

The curriculum at women's colleges is an extension of the campus culture and the classroom's pedagogical goals and has been developed to serve the diverse needs of the student population. The Bryn Mawr physics course is only one of many innovative courses that can serve as models for teaching women and other populations more effectively. Ursuline College in Cleveland redesigned its entire four-year program of study to incorporate contemporary research on optimal curricular construction and student development. The result is an academically rigorous, progressive, and developmentally sensitive program that puts women at the very center of the enterprise.

Most curricular innovations have not been as radical but instead have taken the form of additional courses and foci for study that reflect a changing society and new areas of interests. These include courses such as "Dispute Resolution"; "Women, Leadership, and Social Change"; and "Strategies for Transitions." Other curricular adaptations have been broader and more inclusive of the evolving sense of social responsibility that pervades the campus culture. The increasing diversity of the population has catalyzed the development of multidisciplinary and interdisciplinary programming, as well as new models of instruction. Mount St. Mary's College in Los Angeles has developed a national model for incorporating the multidisciplinary approach into college curricula through its Center for Cultural Fluency. It is a fundamental part of the college's unique institutional structure (a two-year campus for the underprepared, regional population and a four-year campus with a primarily residential, full-time student cohort that includes the graduates of the two-year campus); the center develops and pilots curricula and pedagogical approaches in the richly diverse college. The college community offers a demographic mirror image of the local population, being 40 percent Latina, 18 percent African American, and 16 percent Asian.

The College of New Rochelle in New York has evolved a flexible curriculum within its alternative institution, called the School of New Resources, in response to the growing population of nontraditional-age students in college (80 percent of which are female, nationwide). These highly motivated adult learners, who work full-time, are able to carry a full-time course load because the faculty come to the students' workplace and instruction is scheduled in the evenings. At other women's colleges similar alternative, flexibly scheduled programs are offered through the weekend-college format.

Although the entire educational experience at a women's college is oriented toward developing leadership in its students, separate and intensive leadership development curricula and leadership institutes—complete with faculty and journals—have arisen at women's colleges in the past decade. Explicitly focused on developing those qualities and competencies that the rest of the college experience seeks to reinforce, these programs are highly replicable in other settings.

The Benefits of a Women's College Model

Women's colleges have been part of the American educational scene since the 1830s. Their first hundred years were certainly a challenge, yet they thrived and played a widely recognized and valid societal role. During the second hundred years, women's colleges fell victim to their own success. The debates of the last twenty-five years about the optimal educational context for women are, arguably, the byproduct of the achievements of women's colleges in helping to change the societal norms for women.

The U.S. civil rights movement of the 1960s had a galvanizing effect on women's demands for greater participation in American society, similar to that of the nineteenth century. Women were among the leaders of the struggle for achieving civil rights for blacks, and they analogized their situation once more to that of oppressed minorities. The response in American education to women's activism was the implementation of virtually universal coeducation in 1972. In that year, discrimination on the basis of sex was outlawed in the nation's publicly funded educational institutions by Title IX; even prestigious, private men's institutions that were not required to comply with Title IX opened their doors to women. This second wave of emancipation by women almost brought about the demise of women's colleges. It decimated their numbers and forced the remaining ones into a defensive posture. Instead of standing at the vanguard of opportunity for women, women's colleges became symbols of the discredited notion that separate can ever be equal.

Despite a 150-year history of educating women in the United States, it is only since the early 1970s that American educational reformers have begun to even ask the appropriate questions about women's education. The very existence of women's colleges in the past obviated the questions. Educational inadequacy, if not actual failure in American schools, has forced important questions about learning environments, appropriate measures of achievement, and sensible criteria for determining outcomes that now occupy educators and policy makers. Ironically, we are learning some of the most important answers about the education of women from the institutions that were most threatened with extinction. Not only do women's colleges today provide continuing benefits to their students but they offer themselves as laboratories in which pedagogical theory can be tested, and from which curricular innovations can be adapted for broader use.

As leaders in curricular design, and in responsiveness to a changing population, women's colleges continue to play a vital role in advancing our societal agenda, whether through agitation for more leadership opportunities, or by producing women scientists, or by putting the spotlight on the gender equity agenda. Women's colleges offer the numeric majority a majority role in its education.

Moreover, there is a double benefit to be derived from overhauling programs in such a way as to encourage more women to succeed at education. As has been underscored by many studies, the effective educational practices that work best for women and minorities are those that are the most effective for all students: giving teaching a priority, being inclusive, seeking to develop the talent that is present, and exploring diverse methodologies.

NOTES

1. Eisenhart has continued her research of mastery by examining gender differences in developing a sense of expertise in scientific professions.
2. The most recent data from the 105th Congress were used. Twelve of the fifty women in Congress attended women's colleges.
3. Barnard, Bryn Mawr, Mount Holyoke, Smith, Radcliffe, Vassar (coed), and Wellesley.
4. Wolf-Wendel presented the paper as part of a symposium in Washington, D.C., cosponsored by the Department of Education, called "A Closer Look at Women's Colleges," in January 1998.

REFERENCES

American Association of University Women. "The AAUW Report: How Schools Shortchange Girls." Researched by Wellesley Center for Research on Women. Washington, D.C.: AAUW Foundation, 1992.

Astin, A. W. *Achieving Educational Excellence.* San Francisco, Jossey-Bass, 1985.

Astin, A. W. *Four Critical Years.* San Francisco: Jossey-Bass, 1977.

Astin, A. W. *What Matters in College? Four Critical Years Revisited.* San Francisco: Jossey-Bass, 1992.

Cole, J. *Conversations: Straight Talk with America's Sister President.* New York: Doubleday, 1993.

Crawford, M., and MacLeod, M. "Gender in the College Classroom: An Assessment of the 'Chilly Climate' for Women." *Sex Roles,* 1990, *25,* 101–122.

Eccles, J. S. "Bringing Young Women to Math and Science." In M. Crawford and M. Gentry (eds.), *Gender and Thought: Psychological Perspectives.* New York: Springer-Verlag, 1989.

Eccles, J. S., and Jacobs, J. E. "Social Forces Shape Math Attitudes and Performance." *Signs,* 1986, *11*(2), 367–380.

Hall, R., and Sandler, B. *Out of the Classroom: A Chilly Campus Climate for Women.* Project on the Status and Education of Women. Washington, D.C.: Association of American Colleges, 1984.

Holland, D. C., and Eisenhart, M. A. *Educated in Romance: Women, Achievement, and College Culture.* Chicago: University of Chicago Press, 1990.

Krupnick, C. G. "Women and Men in the Classroom: Inequity and Its Remedies." *On Teaching and Learning,* May 1985, pp. 18–25.

Kuh, G. D., and Whitt, E. J. *The Invisible Tapestry: Culture in American Colleges and Universities.* ASHE-ERIC, Higher Education Report Series No. 1. Washington, D.C.: Association for the Study of Higher Education, 1988.

Miller-Bernal, L. "Single-Sex Versus Coeducational Environments: A Comparison of Women Students' Experiences at Four Colleges." *American Journal of Education,* 1993, *102,* 22–54.

Pascarella, E. T., and Terenzini, P. T. *How College Affects Students.* San Francisco: Jossey-Bass, 1991.

Project Kaleidoscope. *What Works: Building Natural Science Communities. A Plan to Strengthen Undergraduate Science and Math.* Vols. 1, 2. Washington, D.C.: Project Kaleidoscope, 1990–92.

Riordan, C. "Single- and Mixed-Gender Colleges for Women: Educational, Attitudinal, and Occupational Outcomes." *Review of Higher Education,* 1992, *15*(3), 327–346.

Sadker, M., and Sadker, D. *Failing at Fairness: How America's Schools Cheat Girls.* New York: Scribner, 1994.

Smith, D. *The Challenge of Diversity: Involvement or Alienation in the Academy?* No. 5. Washington, D.C.: School of Education and Human Development, George Washington University, 1989.

Smith, D. "Women's Colleges and Coed Colleges: Is There a Difference for Women?" *Journal of Higher Education,* 1990, *61*(2), 181–197.

Stoecker, J. L., and Pascarella, E. T. "Women's Colleges and Women's Career Attainments Revisited." *Journal of Higher Education,* 1991, *62*(4), 394–411.

Tidball, M. E. "Baccalaureate Origins of Entrants into American Medical Schools." *Journal of Higher Education*, 1985, *56*, 385–402.

Tidball, M. E. "Women's Colleges: Exceptional Conditions, Not Exceptional Talent, Produce High Achievers." In C. S. Pearson, D. L. Shavlik, and J. G. Touchton (eds.), *Educating the Majority: Women Challenge Tradition in Higher Education.* New York: American Council on Education; Macmillan Series on Education, 1989.

Tidball, M. E., and Kistiakowsky, V. "Baccalaureate Origins of American Scientists and Scholars." *Science*, 1976, *193*, 646–652.

Tidball, M. E., Smith, D. G., Tidball, C. S., and Wolf-Wendell, L. E. *Taking Women Seriously: Lessons and Legacies for Educating the Majority.* Washington, D.C.: Oryx Press, 1998.

Whitt, E. J. "Taking Women Seriously: Lessons for Coeducational Institutions from Women's Colleges." Paper presented at annual meeting of American Educational Research Association, San Francisco, Mar. 1992.

Whitt, E. J. "'I Can Be Anything!': Student Leadership at Three Women's Colleges." *Journal of College Student Development*, 1994, *33*(3), 198–207.

Women's College Coalition Study. *Profile of Graduates of Women's Colleges.* Washington, D.C.: Women's College Coalition Study, 1985.

PART TWO

RESTRUCTURING THE CLASSROOM

IN HER CHAPTER elucidating the practices of feminist pedagogy, Ellen Kimmel says, "Perhaps the simplest yet most powerful metaphorical act—the pedagogical shot heard 'round the world—was to place the chairs in a circle." This act may be considered emblematic of the mood of collaboration that exists within the feminist classroom. The circle of chairs symbolizes and enables the change of relationship that occurs in the feminist classroom by making possible an environment of partnership among students and professor. In modifying hierarchies that give power and privilege to a professor, one makes room for reflexivity and an atmosphere where knowledge is constructed by students and professor together.

Another component is critical in defining the feminist classroom: the focus on the experiences of women. Women have so often been missing from the discussion, and the research, that a feminist pedagogical approach rectifies this gap with an explicit focus on women. Complementing this perspective is an emphasis on action. In the feminist class, the message is often presented that knowledge generated about the status of women needs translation into proactive behavior.

In Part Two, we offer a series of chapters in which professors describe and reflect upon how they bring change to their classes. These innovations incorporate new ways of understanding and selecting material to be presented, and simultaneously emphasize more collaborative classroom structures. It is our intention that these chapters offer models as well as concrete ideas that can be adapted by readers. Our goal has been to find examples where the theory of feminist pedagogy is translated into practice within the classroom. We feel that many wonderful ideas exist yet have not been collected so as to combine theory and practice.

We begin with a chapter in which Ellen Kimmel outlines comprehensive principles and accompanying strategies underlying feminist pedagogies. The chapter is not prescriptive, suggesting a single pedagogy; instead, it emphasizes the many variations that derive from a set of general principles.

With Kimmel's chapter providing the theoretical groundwork, we move to instantiations of these principles. The other chapters in Part Two move across disciplines and demonstrate a variety of strategies for implementing the principles of feminist pedagogy. Chapters Four, Five, and Six represent a cluster addressing the study of women's lives. Describing a literature class in Chapter Six, Helene Elting explores the limits of the personal. She questions how the life experiences of professors and students alike affect the dynamics of the class discussion and hence the interpretation of the literary works. Her concern is with locating the boundary between life experiences viewed as appropriate material for broadening and deepening interpretation and the same experiences appearing as intrusions into the interpretive process.

In a class on U.S. women's history, Debbie Cottrell chose to begin with women's own narratives about their lives (Chapter Four). Students moved from the particulars of women's lives as expressed in autobiographical writings to construct a broader picture of the society in which these women lived. Students made comparisons with life as they know it in the twentieth century and the characteristics of lives in other time periods. For a culminating project, students worked collaboratively to create a presentation for their college depicting an aspect of women in history.

Sara Davis and Virginia Ratigan, authors of Chapter Five, worked from an interface of their two disciplines, psychology and religious studies, in developing ways of studying women's lives. The emphasis was on techniques—using archival material, developing interview styles, interweaving multiple sources for learning about women—as well as on approaches to developing an understanding of the lives. They emphasized how multiple sources inevitably present different perspectives on a life and engaged students in a project to evaluate the different ways in which the story of a life can be told.

Sara Davis and Estelle Disch each illustrate how they structure the classroom interaction to maximize participation. Disch's Chapter Eight describes a situation in which female students felt silenced; she shows how participation in classroom activities enabled them to find and express their voices. Teaching in a large public university with much diversity, she has developed classroom techniques that encourage openness, welcoming student input in establishing goals for the class as well as critiquing it throughout the semester. As revealed in Chapter Seven, Davis also seeks to maximize participation within her class. Rather than lecture in her course on feminist research approaches, she works with students to collaboratively plan and engage in research projects. With this format, the strengths of each student have the opportunity to flourish.

The switch to different pedagogical methods is not without difficulties. Many students feel threatened if the traditional classroom methods are altered. Further, the knowledge of discrimination toward women may frighten rather than empower students. In Chapter Nine, Mary Crawford and Jessica Suckle provide a taxonomy of the types of resistance that emerge and describe approaches for dispelling this resistance.

In these chapters there is much evidence of success. There are also new issues to confront; the chapters suggest the importance of an ongoing evaluation process as the authors reflect on the impact of their endeavors. One important issue is the question of the limits of the personal. Although one of the key factors in these classroom transformations is integration of personal and theoretical knowledge, the question arises about when the personal becomes burdensome and fails to enrich the learning process. There is a delicate balance between enhancing and overwhelming the class process. How can one best achieve these important linkages while maintaining a focus of interest to all students? What expectations develop in students who have been encouraged to share life experiences with the class? What are the best ways to integrate individual feelings and responses in the class while still working with theories and ideas? Where is there a limit to the personal? It requires great skill to work with feelings and simultaneously keep the class focused.

Should the class be a place where the feelings of all are valued equally? What happens if some students who are not sympathetic to the material continually disagree and disrupt the class? Several of the chapters approach these forms of resistance and suggest ways of maintaining a productive environment.

Several other sequelae of the change in classroom milieu are raised. These interactive approaches stress a level of student participation that some may find difficult. How can all students best be encouraged to become part of the class? Within these chapters are examples of techniques for structuring the interaction so that a variety of individual skills may become part of the classroom interaction. A traditional hierarchical class requires the same attributes of all students. However, as the classroom activities become more diverse, there is more opportunity for students to display their unique skills.

Another issue to be confronted is how grading fits in with emphasis on the students' experiences and feelings. As a result of the level of discussion, many students develop a deep connection with both the classroom community and the work they produce. Can our traditional system of quantifying work with a letter grade adequately convey the diverse achievements of students?

The chapters in Part Two present a few of the innovative transformations that exist in the larger community. We hope they stimulate others to experiment in their classes.

3

FEMINIST TEACHING, AN EMERGENT PRACTICE

Ellen Kimmel

WHAT IS FEMINIST PEDAGOGY? Who practices it? Just as there are many feminisms, so are there many forms of feminist pedagogy. Since there are no licensing exams for the right to call oneself a feminist pedagogue, a wide range of feminists are rightly justified in taking on the label to describe how they conduct their classrooms. This is not to say that the term is meaningless, since the literature abounds with stories from those who claim membership in the category. In reading this chapter, you can decide if you subscribe to some of the principles and strategies of instruction that help define the emergent practice of feminist pedagogy.

Are You a Feminist Pedagogue?

To personalize the reading of this chapter, a self-scoring survey (Table 3.1) allows you to think about some of the specific principles and classroom behaviors that have been endorsed by feminist teachers in terms of your own commitment and actions related to teaching. Take a moment to complete the two-part questionnaire and score it.

No doubt you have many questions, qualifications, or other reactions to the survey. Remember, it is intended to stimulate your thoughts, not to evaluate you for entrance into a "club." That is, the instrument was created as a teaching device (there are no psychometric data about the validity of this test!) and is an example of the type of active learning activity you may use in your classrooms to get students to engage personally with

Table 3.1. Survey on Principles and Strategies of Feminist Pedagogy.

Listed below are the principles of feminist pedagogy as defined by a group of feminist psychologists. Assess yourself on your support of them.

Self-assessment: To what degree, if at all, do you subscribe to each principle? Mark your answers in the appropriate column, 1 being the lowest and 6 the highest.

Principles	1 actively oppose	2 moderately oppose	3 slightly oppose	4 slightly support	5 moderately support	6 actively support
1. Fundamental to feminist pedagogy is a consciousness of differential power, privilege, and oppression that is made explicit through the instructor's planning, articulation of values and goals, and classroom policies.						
2. Acknowledging the power inherent in the teaching role, feminists seek ways to empower students in the training process.						
3. All voices are encouraged, valued, and heard; that is, a climate of respect for difference is fostered.						
4. Feminist teachers are committed to recognizing and accommodating multiple learning styles and respecting the different contexts of students' lives.						
5. Learning should be holistic, integrating cognitions, feelings, and experiences.						
6. Feminist pedagogy makes the connection between personal experiences and social-political reality.						
7. Feminist pedagogy assumes both teachers and students are engaged in a mutual learning process.						

Principles	1 actively oppose	2 moderately oppose	3 slightly oppose	4 slightly support	5 moderately support	6 actively support
8. Feminist teachers continually strive to increase their knowledge of and sensitivity to diverse cultural realities.						
9. Feminist teachers model an acceptance of their own authority and expertise.						
10. Knowledge is contextual and emergent; therefore feminist teachers are committed to including multiple sources of knowledge.						
11. Learning is in the service of social change.						
12. Learning is in the service of increasing self-awareness and personal growth.						
13. Feminist teachers help to reclaim women's histories and cultures.						
14. Feminist pedagogy is aimed at transforming the curriculum by examining critically existing constructs and working to develop theory that reflects the breadth of human experience.						

Subtotal ________

Scoring on Principles

The total scores range from 14 to 84 points. If you score 75 or higher, chances are you identify yourself as a feminist pedagogue. This likelihood diminishes as your score gets lower.

Table 3.1. Survey on Principles and Strategies of Feminist Pedagogy, Cont'd.

Strategies

Now rate how frequently you use the strategies that support the principles.

Self-assessment: How often do you use each strategy?

Strategies	**1 have never used**	**2 rarely use**	**3 occasionally use**	**4 frequently use**
1. I sensitize students to the oppressive and transformative power of language.				
2. I require nonsexist, inclusionary language in all communications.				
3. I help students develop a sense that they can be social change-agents.				
4. I use assignments that engage students in social-change efforts.				
5. I make use of a developmental view of the consciousness-raising process.				
6. I encourage affirmative attitudes about and views of women.				
7. I enhance and make accessible resources relevant to the lives of women.				
8. I bring in a variety of women to serve as role models.				
9. I contextualize learning materials and activities.				
10. I highlight the experiences of marginalized people.				
11. I use narratives, journals, and other activities to explicate life stories.				
12. I facilitate creation of a safe learning environment.				
13. I model appropriate self-disclosure to encourage students to make the learning process personally relevant.				
14. I ask unasked questions and listen for silences.				
15. I develop activities to assist students who find it difficult to participate in class.				

Strategies	1 have never used	2 rarely use	3 occasionally use	4 frequently use
16. I share my learning process, incomplete thoughts, errors, ideas in progress, and personal reactions and invite students to do the same.				
17. I make use of group activities.				
18. I use cooperative learning activities.				
19. I use the class process to illustrate feminist principles.				
20. I illuminate the group process as a teaching tool.				
21. I employ experiential learning activities.				
22. I have students function as experts in the learning process.				
23. I provide opportunities for students to direct aspects of their learning experience.				
24. I make use of respectful debate.				
25. I include course assignments that teach students they can contribute to the knowledge base.				
26. I make evaluation a dialogic process.				
27. I invite student feedback and provide opportunities for anonymous evaluation.				
28. I provide opportunities for students to review and evaluate constructively the work of their peers.				

Subtotal ________

Scoring on Strategies

Here the total scores range from 28 to 112. The higher the score the more you act like a feminist pedagogue. A score of 80 or higher suggests you live out your feminist beliefs.

Now, mentally compare the strength of your commitment to the principles to the frequency with which you use the strategies in your teaching. Is there a match? Is there a discrepancy between your scores?

Source: These principles and strategies are published in Kimmel and Worell, 1997.

the material. It is one mark of a feminist classroom that the personal is not only political but often pedagogical.

Forms of Feminist Pedagogy

Feminist activism in the United States in the 1960s and 1970s found its way into the academy and led to the intensive critique of many disciplines and the structure of the university that housed them. As women faculty and their students deconstructed and reconstructed what was known and how we know it, there was an explosion of "new" scholarship. These new data and theories about women's lives and experience demanded a new approach to the entire educational enterprise. Not just the content (curriculum) but also the process (pedagogy) used to develop the next generation of scholars and citizens had to depart radically from the patriarchal models that had always dominated institutions of higher learning. Teaching was, or could be, a key way to disrupt the traditional, hierarchical male-female arrangements and avoid reproducing the very structures feminists intended to eliminate.

Perhaps the simplest yet most powerful metaphorical act—the pedagogical shot heard 'round the world—was to place the chairs in a circle. What is more incongruous than students lined neatly in rows like silent soldiers, taking notes on the evils of not speaking out or being active participants in their own destiny? The medium *is* the message. Many early feminist pedagogues sensed this truth and began quietly to shift classroom power relations—along with its content—to begin what has evolved into the many feminist pedagogies. The forms derive from the differences in how feminists theorize about the origins of women's subordination to men, the factors that sustain inequality, and thus the approach that should be taken to change it (Acker, 1994). Different feminisms imply diverse assumptions and methods of teaching and learning.

Originally, contemporary Western feminism was divided into three major theoretical camps: radical, socialist, and liberal. Postmodern and poststructural influences (see Crowley and Himmelweit, 1992; Benhabib, 1995), along with developments in feminist theory, have since blurred this typology. Thus, at least two other types must be added: cultural (essentialist) and multicultural.

Radical feminists hold that exploitation of women is one of the forms of human oppression—if not the oldest and most pervasive—and that teachers must attend to the sexual politics of everyday life in educational institutions. Every arrangement should be up for investigation, from the curriculum to decision-making processes, since all institutions are webbed in the domination of women as a group. Patriarchal power structures must be challenged in all their manifestations, in and out of the classroom, making radical feminist teachers among the most activist.

Arguing that economic oppression, based on a capitalistic economy, serves to perpetuate class and gender oppression, *socialist feminists* focus on how schooling (public and higher education) reproduces class- and gender-based power arrangements. As teachers, they encourage students to examine bourgeois practices of social interaction and class values critically.

Liberal feminists believe that equal opportunity regardless of sex leads to women's liberation. Their aim is to end discrimination on the basis of gender in the classroom and the workplace and ensure fair treatment and freedom from gender stereotypes. Women can and will do the rest. This form of feminism does not seek major alterations to present capitalist democratic structures or economies.

Cultural feminists (also known as *essentialist feminists*) hold that women's strengths and contributions have been devalued in Western society while men's have been privileged. Cultural feminists attempt to develop teaching practices that highlight connection, collaboration, and inclusion as the way to increase their value in the larger society (see Belenky, Clinchy, Goldberger, and Tarule, 1986).

Finally, recognizing that women possess multiple subjectivities, the very category of "woman" has been called into question as to its usefulness. *Multicultural feminists* recognize our multiple identities based on gender, race, sexual orientation, class, etc. Hence, they strive to avoid privileging one identity over another by not using teaching strategies that emphasize only one aspect of identity.

Although these political positions form and inform the various pedagogies, many feminist pedagogues do not self-identify their camp. Some may not see themselves as belonging to any particular group and, if asked, might call themselves "eclectic feminists." These positions and movements have nonetheless influenced the practice of feminist teaching and must be acknowledged, along with other important forces to be described below.

Just as teachers bring their various forms of feminism into the classroom, the classroom itself is inherently political (Goslin, 1990). Sociologists have promoted three major theories of the purpose and function of schools: Parsonianism, Marxism, and Weberianism. Briefly, the Parsonians or functionalists regard the primary purpose of schools to be transmission of culturally based knowledge and preparation of individuals for their adult roles in society. They argue that the schools function neutrally and are egalitarian. However, if the history of disenfranchised groups is examined, this assertion rings hollow. The fact is that ascribed characteristics of race, class, and gender determine school treatment and outcomes for students, and the school as the great equalizer has been an unfulfilled promise of American education. For example, teachers have placed less importance on the professional achievement of girls and women, who in turn continue to be underrepresented in careers involving math and science.

Parsonians deny the interest-group bias in how our schools function, but the other two theories do not. Marxists contend that schools exist to reproduce existing class structures through promoting capitalist ideology. Weberians extend this to other dominant groups (religious, political, and cultural). This is achieved by restricting subordinate groups' access to credentials for powerful roles in society and by indoctrinating members of these groups to accept their domination as "natural" and right. Teachers who simply follow the tradition may be blind to the political nature of their work, but they perpetuate existing group differences no less.

In short, there is no escape from the political realities of teaching. As a feminist, the fairest thing one can do is make this fact explicit. Heald (1991) asserted that, to be useful, "feminist pedagogy needs to be grounded in the understanding that education is an apparatus of social regulation" (p. 147). Understanding how it helps form our various subjectivities enables us also to learn how to resist a narrow definition of ourselves so that a place can be created for a wider range of human "subjects."

We influence our students and hope that it is for the better of society *as we see it*. When all is said and done, we are in the business of "conversion" (Kinsler and Zalk, 1996). Those of us trained in the sciences particularly are reluctant to admit this view. The image of ourselves as preachers feels morally wrong. Yet, it would be morally bankrupt to allow the prevailing data and theories of our disciplines to be left unchallenged by the feminist critique that we have labored so long to develop. It is also unlikely that we would present our theory and data in a neutral fashion, assuming that students are capable of sorting through the complexities on their own. Feminist teachers make their cases, too, often with passion. At the same time, they should recognize there is no whole and universal truth, and they must be open to debate and discussion as undefensively as possible. This is an emergent practice.

Principles and Strategies of Feminist Pedagogy

In the summer of 1994, a group of feminist psychologists gathered for a conference at Boston College to examine feminist practice in psychology in the broadest sense. For many attendees, this "practice" meant therapy, but for just as many others it meant teaching and research as well as supervision. In small working groups, the attendees deliberated and developed consensus about the nature of various areas of practice, sharing each day's work with the other groups. The final product was an edited book (Worell and Johnson, 1997). The feminist pedagogy group, consisting of nine faculty and one graduate student, created the set of principles and strategies presented in Table 3.1 (Kimmel and Worell, 1997). The group struggled with many questions about the nature of feminist pedagogy, emerging with a matrix that mapped each of the fourteen principles with one or more of the twenty-eight strategies that enacted them. Thus, our approach to the question of whether there was such a thing as feminist teaching that could be differentiated from "good" or student-centered teaching was empirical. It existed if the group could identify a unique set of assumptions, goals, behaviors, and beliefs by which to define it. Following the conference, an extensive review of the literature was tied to the principles and strategies articulated by the Boston group.

Four Themes of Feminist Pedagogy

The literature mirrors the Boston discussions and reveals four recurrent themes in feminists' versions of educational reform. Of these issues, power dominates the discourse.

Power

Many feminists have attempted to counter the prevailing imbalance of power in traditional classrooms by promoting a "liberatory" (à la Paulo Freire [1971] and Henry Giroux [1988]) or democratic classroom (Klein, 1987; Schniedewind, 1987; Shrewsbury, 1987). One vision is similar to how feminist organizations are run, with their emphasis on antielitism and collective decision making. A circle has no head and no tail! Although one cannot ignore the differential power accorded to faculty by the institution (they evaluate the students' performance as learners), authors such as Schniedewind and the Boston group urge creation of a democratic environment by inviting students to participate in decisions about the content and process of the class, asking for feedback about the class and teaching methods throughout the course, and coteaching the course.[1] Many feminists promote the concept of a community of learners, a cohesive group working together to enhance their own and the group's understanding. This includes flexibility of teacher-student and student-teacher roles and the feminist principles of egalitarian power relationships, sisterhood, and consciousness raising (see principles 7 and 12 in Table 3.1). The prevailing competitive nature of education is countered by a more cooperative process. There are many strategies to support the community concept, including cooperative learning groups, other groupings and pairings, and peer feedback and support as part of the evaluation process.

What is meant explicitly by equality also has been widely discussed and debated. If each person in the class should be given a voice that is valued, then are all voices equally welcome? This question divided the Boston working group. One position challenges or negatively evaluates the bigot, the sexist, or the homophobic and restricts its opportunity to be heard. Those in opposition argue that all voices should be encouraged, but the instructor should also refrain from honoring ideas that are demeaning to others. The Boston group concluded that feminist teachers must model the value of open discussion and inclusion of divergent views but shoulder the responsibility to confront slurs and attacks (see principle 3). To silence the dissenter communicates intolerance—and perhaps inability to facilitate free discourse, the foundation of liberatory education.

Issues of power as reflected and promoted by language were mentioned throughout the discussion in Boston and in the literature, and they led to the first two strategies in the survey (Table 3.1): namely, that feminist teachers *sensitize students to the oppressive and transformative power of language* and that they *require that nonsexist, inclusionary language be used in all communication.* Interestingly, there was dissention about the use of the term *oppression,* since some felt it was an inflammatory word that could close student minds before they heard how it in fact operates. Given its historical use, though, the term was left in.

Feminists have confronted the paradox of power and authority that are differentially accorded faculty as they attempt to create equality among themselves and their students (see especially Morgan, 1987; Matthews, 1994; Luke, 1992). Inside and outside the classroom, faculty have the power to write the syllabus; evaluate students; control the teaching methods; and offer resources, opportunities, and support for jobs, awards, and entrance to programs. If we give voice to students, then it is within our power to give it! (See principle 1.) The issue then becomes how to share power, empower students, and still claim our expertise and accomplishments. This leads to principle 2 (*Feminist teachers acknowledge the power in their teaching role and seek ways to empower students in the learning process*) and principle 9 (*Feminist teachers model acceptance of their own authority and expertise*).

Emotions in Learning

A second major tenet of feminist pedagogy found in the literature and reflected in the work of the Boston group is that emotions are central to learning.[2] Inclusion of the affective domain is part of a student-centered education movement that focuses on student development as part of the instructional mandate. Here, values are explicitly examined and challenged by encouraging students (and faculty) to seek connections between course content and their own lives, seeing their lives in a larger social perspective, journaling, employing experiential activities, and including the arts in nontraditional ways.[3] Despite evidence that supports these affective techniques (and short courses at local teaching enhancement centers for faculty and student teaching assistants on how to employ them), most professors ignore them (see for example Blackburn, Pellino, Boberg, and O'Connell, 1980), out of ignorance or an entrenched belief that the lecture defines teaching (Thielens, 1987). Being a feminist, however, *is* a predictor of the use of such affective strategies (Wakai, 1994). In fact, the feminists' fight to discredit dualistic thinking that divides human characteristics along gender lines (systematically devaluing those things deemed "feminine," such as emotions) has led to valuing the affective *and* intellectual in their classrooms. One has to chuckle (in vindication) upon reading recent psychological research suggesting that every thought is accompanied by a feeling. . . . So much for the dualism of thoughts and emotions, now seen as inseparable.

Social Responsibility and Action

Social responsibility and action are a third central concept in feminist thought and pedagogy. Certainly, feminists are not the only educators who have promulgated these concepts. They are central to the liberatory education of Freire (1971), for example, and the experiential learning model of Kolb (1984), both of which hold action as critical to learning and social change. Social action fosters a sense of agency and connects ideas to action, keeping feminism alive and evolving to meet the changing conditions of women's lives. Feminists at the Boston conference were emphatic in including social action as a cornerstone of a feminist classroom.[4]

Diversity

The fourth theme is diversity in all its complexity.[5] The classroom is the site for highlighting our multiple identities as humans and confronting how our society responds to myriad types of difference. This is done by dealing with how privilege works in the here-and-now with members of the class. Even all-women classes provide a laboratory for teasing out the operation of privilege, given that women embody all other differences except gender. To confront women's oppression of women means addressing all other forms of inequality; "anything less than this vision of total freedom is not feminism, but merely female self-aggrandizement" (Smith, 1982, p. 49). As bell hooks (1989) warned, we must guard against an empty rhetoric and be reflexive about our own identities that blind us to others'.

Calling attention to group process helps students understand how power operates and the dynamics of privilege based on group membership. A key skill implied here is that of managing classroom dynamics. One reason that many are loath to tread this terrain is that it is difficult and can lead to negative student reactions (and evaluations). However, transformation of any kind has inherent risks as well as rewards. It is part of the feminist pedagogy agenda (see principle 14) and should not be avoided. Rather, we are well served to do whatever is necessary to acquire these critical teaching competencies. Along with that, it is imperative that feminists educate themselves about histories and present realities of groups other than their own (principle 8) as well as take advantage of the new scholarship to learn more of their own history, so sadly absent from the curriculum when they were students. A feminist pedagogue must be a lifelong learner!

What Are the Perils and Joys of Feminist Teaching?

At this point, you may be asking, as did Penny Welch (1994), if the task of conducting a feminist classroom is possible, given all the demands suggested in the literature and by the long list of principles and strategies in Table 3.1. We must see our teaching as an emergent practice, one that continuously develops through experience, attendance at conferences and workshops, reading, and reflection on the feedback provided by our students. Welch described her own process of becoming a feminist teacher, and the writings and experiences she found particularly helpful in the process. She also pointed out that being a feminist does not necessarily mean one employs feminist pedagogy (see Forrest and Rosenberg, 1997). Even more, commitment to the ideals of feminist pedagogy does not predict the extent to which one practices them in the classroom.

Julie Kmiec, Faye Crosby, and Judith Worell (1996) attempted to document to what degree feminist professors actually put into practice their ideological commitments to feminist pedagogy. They randomly sampled seventy-seven women members of Division 35 (Psychology of Women) of the American Psychological Association. They found minimal association between the measures of commitment to feminist pedagogy and the actual behaviors the faculty reported in their sample. Although it may be, the authors suggest, that the participants were just boasting (full of hot air), a more likely interpretation is that being a feminist—regardless of level of commitment to feminist pedagogy—may predispose one to teach nontraditionally so that no differences emerged. Or, on a less positive note, it could be that feminists in their sample did not deviate from traditional instruction despite their values, perhaps from lack of exposure to newer teaching strategies. In fact, it might be interesting for you to review the scores you earned on the two surveys (Table 3.1) to assess the match between your values and your behavior.

A number of books and articles describe the experiences of feminist teachers who *have* adapted new strategies. For example, Bannerji and others (1991); Culley and Portuges (1985); Davies, Lubelska, and Quinn (1994); Holland and Blair (1995); Luke (1996); Luke and Gore (1992); Reinardy (1992); and Stone (1994) are recommended as a start. Terry Threadgold (1996) posed two additional, difficult questions: Once our pedagogy erases the "voice of the master," how do we "others" learn to speak in our own bodies and still hold credibility within the academy? Can we reconstruct, from within, the institutions that have made us outsiders, with less power to begin with, in order to conduct our version of emancipatory education? As Vicki Kirby (1994) forthrightly asserted, "feminism is a specific articulation of the complexity of phallocentrism . . . [and its] parasitic residence inside the body of power changes the nature of that power in the very act of taking sustenance from it. Consequently feminists can never offer the definitive 'how to' guide. . . ." (p. 20). Since our classrooms are not ahistorical spaces but particular, situated locales embedded in specific cultures and time, there are no universal answers to these questions.

All of this translates into the fact that feminist teachers face many paradoxes, dilemmas, and uncertainties when they enter their classrooms. If they refuse the binary roles of either benevolent and self-sacrificing mom (a virgin in struggles with power) or all-powerful leader, where can they tread? How can they own their passion for intellectual engagement *and* valuing of the personal and emotional? How can they sit in a circle *and* be chair of the faculty senate while criticizing the structure of education and the society it mirrors? Further, a pedagogy-politic that is simply oppositional does little to further our ability to create change in ourselves, our students, or our institutions.

The Boston group's report of their experience as feminist teachers reflects the diversity of angst and inspiration found in the literature (Kimmel and Worell, 1997; see especially Table 2 in that work). Here again, it is well to remember that not all students are alike, nor colleges, nor majors, nor faculty. Vastly different stories result from the confluence of all these variables and the mix of strategies the feminist teacher employs. For instance, a tenured, senior professor still finds negative student evaluations painful but is not so threatened as would be a beginning faculty member struggling to gain credibility and, ultimately, tenure. The threat is magnified if the woman is of color, disabled, openly lesbian or bisexual, or possessed of any characteristics not central to the dominant American image of "the professor." The title of Ava McCall's article (1994) "Rejoicing and Despairing: Dealing with Feminist Pedagogy in Teacher Education" may say it for feminist pedagogues in any discipline! Crawford and Suckle (Chapter Nine of this volume) offer interesting insights into the complex dynamics that make feminist teachers laugh and cry and how those dynamics have changed in the last two decades. What can be said for certain is that practicing feminist pedagogy is an adventure, sure to afford a roller-coaster ride of high rewards and breathtaking risks.

Student Responses to Feminist Pedagogy

It is not all a victory narrative! The literature of feminist pedagogy abounds with feminist teachers' accounts of student responses to their instruction. Usually the feminist pedagogue/researcher retells students' responses and restates, or quotes, key student comments, and then interprets them. These data are often only by-products of their classroom stories, not data resulting from direct queries of students about how they experience feminist teaching. More systematically gathered reactions from students are sorely needed to begin to appreciate their realities.

As the list below suggests, a major reaction to feminists and their pedagogy is resistance:

TYPES OF STUDENT RESISTANCE

Silence

Anger

Denial

Defensive behaviors

Conflict over teacher as nurturer

Acting out

Victim blaming

Lack of empathy

Embarrassment over an error

Chagrin at espousing an interpretation that is dismissed

Distress at confronting in more complexity problems conveniently ignored

Confusion about engaging private matters in public

Low evaluations of course, faculty

These forms of resistance were extracted from articles and chapters written most often by instructors about their students and (less often) by independent observers of instruction. Cheryl Johnson (1994) recounted students' reactions to her as the instructor of a course on African American literature. Her presence as a black woman disrupted traditional notions about who should occupy the position of authority in the classroom. The students' assumptions that black women belonged in subservient or demeaning roles clashed with Johnson's reality as professor. One manifestation of students' dis-ease was hesitancy—even fear—of engaging with her in speaking about African American literature and culture. Students were uncertain, worried that they might insult with their language the person who stood in front of them with the "right answer" and a grade book. If not with silence, they responded with discourse that was so neutral, so bland, that she claimed it "disinfects the very subjects under discussion" (p. 132).

Luke (1992) wrote about another aspect of the silent response. She described feminist scholars as the "archeologists of discourse, digging away at buried sites of women's knowledges" (p. 214). Their teaching project has been to give students their "voice," equated with a politically positive and empowering move. Luke interrogates this premise, asking, What if silence is a "politics of resistance"? Silence could be read as a refusal to "confess" and expose oneself. Such analysis might lead us to reconstruct our pedagogical strategies, reframe our experience, and respond to students' silence with less frustration and, hopefully, greater effectiveness.

Although silence is one of the worst student responses to a teacher invested in "giving voice," it is not a simple reaction to interpret. Student silence, resistance, and ignorance may not be a passive state—an absence of information—but may be an active form of negation that effective teachers must engage. Inevitably, feminist classrooms are "as conflicted as nurturing, as competitive as collaborative, and as contradictive as complementary" (Finke, 1993, p. 7). It's important not to reproduce an easy dichotomy that places oppression, anxiety, and resistance either in the student or outside in the culture. We cannot, as Finke put it, "be content with either an apolitical theory or an untheorized politics" (p. 10).

Student responses to feminist pedagogy can be problematic even under the most ideal circumstances, that is, classes with dedicated feminist students who have chosen to be there, a campus with strong women's studies programs and feminist presence, and friendly colleagues supportive of feminist projects. For example, how close can or does one get to students, who often are the same age and who depend on their professor's power while aspiring to her position? These students can be overly dependent, relying on the faculty person to provide tough criticism as well as a lot of support. If we faculty are negotiating the transformation from sixties radical to full professor, as are a number of feminists who began their careers in the late 1960s and early 1970s, we in turn may need our students to affirm our radicality, to assure ourselves that we have not "sold out" (Scheman, 1994). Boundary issues emerge on many levels.

Feminist teachers and authors not only provide lengthy descriptions of students' growth and "regression," transformation, and dependency; they also offer a number of strategies to deal with problematic student responses. The next list presents suggestions extracted from the literature (along with a few of my own):

FACULTY RESPONSES TO STUDENT RESISTANCES

Shift focus from social issues to classroom dynamics

Legitimize meanings women bring to their experiences (turn challenges back on the questioner)

Disrupt order-of-speaking hierarchy

Require men in the class to own their own privilege (rather than the limits on women and their own privilege)

Encourage self-reflexive critique of unequal power relations

Stay attentive to political content of women's lives

Attend to how women historically invested in contradictory practices to survive

Set ground rules for discussion

Recognize students' individual and cultural differences

Facilitate inclusion and group cohesion

Encourage broad participation

Facilitate a *classroom* atmosphere, not group therapy

Encourage objectivity

Recognize and manage diversity in academic preparedness

Infuse race and culture throughout

Apply collaborative teaching strategies

Establish connection between students and ourselves

Facilitate relationships among students

Enable students to articulate their experiences and knowledges

Foster meaningful engagement with course context (tell their stories)

(This list and the preceding one were developed in collaboration with Patricia Martini-Clark, a doctoral student at the University of South Florida.)

It should be noted that several of these recommendations mirror some of the Boston group's strategies listed in Table 3.1 (the second part of the survey). Crawford and Suckle (Chapter Nine) elaborate both the sources of resistance and ways to handle counterproductive student behavior and undesired (even dreaded) teaching incidents and outcomes. There are always students who challenge teachers who question the status quo. We are compelled to learn to be effective champions of change to the fullest extent possible. This includes reflecting on *our own resistance* and adopting a nondefensive response when we meet students' defenses. Appreciating that change involves loss, risk, and/or anxiety can help us join students, reduce the "restraining forces," and develop their willingness to entertain new ideas and practice new behaviors (Greenman, Kimmel, Bannon, and Radford-Curry, 1992).

This chapter has asked you to think about your values and behavior as a feminist who teaches. Many scholars and practitioners have written and spoken about feminist pedagogy over the last three decades. They have urged us to stretch our knowledge and skills to enlarge our performance in the roles of student developer and institutional change-agent. They have set high standards. We must remember to use these ideas and ideals as a guide and source of inspiration, not as a bludgeon. Scheman (1994) retells the story of a girl who, at age ten, with no anxiety about it, asked her parents what parents are for. When she looked back and reflected, it became clear to her that her parents had instilled in her such a sense of security and agency as to leave their role invisible. This is a model many of us might aspire to emulate with our students, but it is not a standard. Ours is an emergent practice.

NOTES

1. See also strategies 12, 14, 15, 16, 19, 20, 22, 23, 25, 26, 27, and 28 in Table 3.1.
2. See principles 5, 6, 10, and 12.
3. See strategies 5, 8, 9, 11, 13, 17, 18, 21, and 24.
4. See principles 11, 13, and 14 and strategies 3 and 4 (and others to a lesser degree).
5. Principles 3, 4, 8, 10, 13, and 14 all speak to the theme of diversity.

REFERENCES

Acker, S. "Feminist Theory and the Study of Gender and Education." In S. Acker (ed.), *Gendered Education: Sociological Reflections on Women, Teaching, and Feminism.* Buckingham, England: Open University Press, 1994.

Bannerji, H., and others (eds.). *Unsettling Relations: The University as a Site for Feminist Struggles.* Boston: South End Press, 1991.

Belenky, M. F., Clinchy, B. M., Goldberger, N. R., and Tarule, J. M. *Women's Ways of Knowing.* New York: Basic Books, 1986.

Benhabib, S. "Feminism and Postmodernism: An Uneasy Alliance." In S. Benhabib, J. Butler, D. Cornell, and N. Fraser (eds.), *Feminist Contentions.* New York: Routledge, 1995.

Blackburn, R., Pellino, G., Boberg, A., and O'Connell, C. "Are Instructional Programs off Target?" *Current Issues in Higher Education,* 1980, 2(1), 32–48.

Crowley, H., and Himmelweit, S. (eds.). *Knowing Women: Feminism and Knowledge.* Oxford: Polity Press, 1992.

Culley, M., and Portuges, C. (eds.). *Gendered Subjects: The Dynamics of Feminist Teaching.* New York: Routledge, 1985.

Davies, S., Lubelska, C., and Quinn, J. C. (eds.). *Changing the Subject.* Bristol, Pa.: Taylor and Francis, 1994.

Finke, L. (1993). "Knowledge as Bait: Feminism, Voice, and the Pedagogical Unconscious." *College English,* 1993, *55*(1), 7–26.

Forrest, L., and Rosenberg, F. "A Review of the Feminist Pedagogy Literature: The Neglected Child of Feminist Psychology." *Applied and Preventive Psychology,* 1997, 6, 179–192.

Freire, P. *Pedagogy of the Oppressed.* New York: Herder and Herder, 1971.

Giroux, H. A. "Literacy and the Pedagogy of Voice and Political Empowerment." *Educational Theory,* 1988, *38*(1), 61–75.

Goslin, D. "The Functions of the School in Modern Society." Reprinted in K. Dougherty and F. Hammack (eds.), *Education and Society.* Orlando: Harcourt Brace, 1990.

Greenman, N. P., Kimmel, E., Bannon, H. M., and Radford-Curry, B. "Institutional Inertia to Achieving Diversity." *Educational Foundations,* 1992, *6,* 89–111.

Heald, S. "Pianos to Pedagogy: Pursuing the Educational Subject." In H. Bannerji and others (eds.), *Unsettling Relations: The University as a Site of Feminist Struggles.* Boston: South End Press, 1991.

Holland, J., and Blair, M. (eds.). *Debates and Issues in Feminist Research and Pedagogy.* Clevedon, Okla.: Multilingual Matters, 1995.

hooks, b. *Talking Back: Thinking Feminist, Thinking Black.* London: Pluto Press, 1989.

Johnson, C. "Disinfecting Dialogues." In J. J. Matthews (ed.), *Jane Gallop Seminar Papers.* Canberra: Australian National University, 1994.

Kimmel, E., and Worell, J. "Preaching What We Practice: Principles and Strategies of Feminist Pedagogy." In J. Worell and N. Johnson (eds.), *Shaping the Future of Feminist Psychology.* Washington, D.C.: American Psychological Association, 1997.

Kinsler, K., and Zalk, S. R. "Teaching Is a Political Act: Contextualizing Gender and Ethnic Voices." In K. F. Wyche and F. J. Crosby (eds.), *Women's Ethnicities.* Boulder, Colo.: Westview Press, 1996.

Kirby, V. "Response to Jane Gallop's 'The Teacher's Breasts': Bad Form." In J. J. Matthews (ed.), *Jane Gallop Seminar Papers.* Canberra: Australian National University, 1994.

Klein, R. D. "The Dynamics of the Women's Studies Classroom: A Review Essay of the Teaching Practices of Women's Studies in Higher Education." *Women's Studies International Forum,* 1987, *10*(2), 187–206.

Kmiec, J., Crosby, F. J., and Worell, J. "Walking the Talk: On Stage and Behind the Scenes." In K. F. Wyche and F. J. Crosby (eds.), *Women's Ethnicities.* Boulder, Colo.: Westview Press, 1996.

Kolb, D. *Experiential Learning: Experience as the Source of Learning and Development.* Upper Saddle River, N.J.: Prentice-Hall, 1984.

Luke, C. "Women in the Academy: The Policies of Speech and Silence." *British Journal of Sociology of Education,* 1992, *15*(2), 211–230.

Luke, C. (ed.). *Feminism and Pedagogies of Everyday Life.* Albany: State University of New York Press, 1996.

Luke, C., and Gore, J. (eds.). *Feminisms and Critical Pedagogy.* New York: Routledge, 1992.

Matthews, J. J. (ed.). *Jane Gallop Seminar Papers.* Canberra: Australian National University, 1994.

McCall, A. L. "Rejoicing and Despairing: Dealing with Feminist Pedagogy in Teacher Education." *Teaching Education,* 1994, *6*(2), 59–69.

Morgan, K. P. "The Perils and Paradoxes of Feminist Pedagogy." *Resources of Feminist Research,* 1987, *16,* 49–52.

Reinardy, M. "Feminist Teaching: An Outline and Resource Guide." Paper presented at the American Association of University Women, Mills College Conference, Oakland, Calif., 1992.

Scheman, N. "On Waking Up One Morning and Discovering We Are Them." In J. J. Matthews (ed.), *Jane Gallop Seminar Papers.* Canberra: Australian National University, 1994.

Schniedewind, N. "Teaching Feminist Process." *Women's Studies Quarterly,* 1987, *15*(13/14), 15–31.

Shrewsbury, C. "What Is Feminist Pedagogy?" *Women's Studies Quarterly,* 1987, *15*(3/4), 6–14.

Smith, B. "Racism and Women's Studies." In G. T. Hull, P. B. Scott, and B. Smith (eds.), *All the Women Are White, All the Blacks Are Men, But Some of Us Are Brave.* Old Westbury, N.Y.: Feminist Press, 1982.

Stone, L. (ed.). *The Education Feminism Reader.* New York: Routledge, 1994.

Thielens, W., Jr. *The Disciplines and Undergraduate Lecturing.* Paper presented at the annual meeting of the American Educational Research Association, Washington, D.C., Apr. 1987. (ED 286436.57, pp. MF01/PC-03)

Threadgold, T. "Everyday Life in the Academy: Postmodernist Feminisms, Generic Seductions, Rewriting, and Being Heard." In C. Luke (ed.), *Feminisms and Pedagogies of Everyday Life.* Albany: State University of New York Press, 1996.

Wakai, S. T. *Barriers to and Facilitators of Feminist Pedagogy in College and University Teaching.* Paper presented at the annual meeting of the Association for the Study of Higher Education, Tucson, Ariz., Nov. 1994. (ED 375 729, pp. MF01/PC-02)

Welch, P. "Is a Feminist Pedagogy Possible?" In S. Davies, C. Lubelska, and J. Quinn (eds.), *Changing the Subject: Women in Higher Education.* London: Taylor and Frances, 1994.

Worell, J., and Johnson, N. *Shaping the Future of Feminist Psychology.* Washington, D.C.: American Psychological Association, 1997.

4

TEACHING THROUGH NARRATIVES OF WOMEN'S LIVES

Debbie Cottrell

A HISTORY CLASSROOM can be a crowded place, regardless of how many students are enrolled in it. Voices from the past are, of course, an integral part of the study of history. But, sometimes those voices are too loud, authoritative, and Godlike—making history seem a predetermined science chronicling events and individuals far removed from the mere humans trying to make sense of it.

The ominous voices of this type of history are often made louder by third-person textbooks or detached scholarly works that tie history into neat conclusions, false sequences, resolved issues, and forced endings. Such works can have, even if unintended, the effect of distancing students from the past. Especially for novice students of history, they can also obscure the role of interpretation, evidence, and bias in studying the past.

As Ellen Kimmel notes in the preceding chapter, the practice of feminist pedagogy incorporates principles that allow a different avenue of studying the past. Power and politics, deeply embedded in many traditional studies of history, can be confronted, challenged, and changed by recognizing multiple sources of knowledge, a purpose of recentering women in history, and a goal of holistic learning.

One feminist teaching technique that challenges the authoritative approach to history and moves toward history as a form of empowerment involves, quite simply, using autobiographical narratives to introduce more complex, real, and relatable voices to students. As Trev Lynn Broughton and Linda Anderson have noted, women's autobiographical writings provide a "complex interrelation between the personal, the theoretical, and the political" (Broughton and Anderson, 1997, p. xi). In a history class, replacing "objective" scholarly voices with the voices of those directly involved in an event or issue reframes history and changes the dynamics of power.

The Course and Its Context

A course in the history of women in the United States, taught in spring semesters at Cottey College (a small women's college located in Nevada, Missouri), has given me an opportunity to use narrative autobiographical works to create a more seamless pipeline between the past and my students. The setting in which this course is taught deserves some explanation, before the course itself is described.

Cottey College is unique. In addition to its single-sex status, it is a selective two-year institution with an enrollment of 300–350 students. Located in the rural Midwest, it is owned and operated by the P.E.O. Sisterhood, a women's philanthropic educational organization. In addition to owning the college, this organization provides a wealth of scholarships to our students; this tie, then, makes Cottey quite affordable for a private institution and further gives the college the distinction of being a women's institution that is also owned and operated by women. Students—almost all of whom are traditional-age, residential, and in need of financial aid—come from all over the country and from many other nations. The student enrolled at Cottey is usually a woman who is looking for a strong academic environment and preparation, who is lively and eager to learn, who is comfortable with her gender and her abilities (although not necessarily a self-described feminist), and who sees college as an exciting beginning to her future. Many of our students are from rural areas, many are uncertain about their undergraduate major and career plans, and many have connections to the P.E.O. Sisterhood.

Clearly, this is a very fruitful environment for teaching a course on women's history. In fact, most courses in Cottey's curriculum are viewed first and foremost in terms of their transferability, since we are a two-year college. However, some courses, such as this one, are seen as so integral to the college's mission and purpose that they are included in the curriculum even if they might not transfer easily or be readily identified as lower-division courses. The college has no official women's studies program but does offer, in addition to this women's history course, several courses that address women in different disciplines. Among these are women in literature, women in psychology, women and society, and women in music.

My course consists of both first- and second-year students, most of whom have taken a survey course in U.S. history as a prerequisite to this class (if that is lacking, a strong high school history background is required). Enrollment in the class usually ranges from ten to twenty students. Often, these students will have taken (or be enrolled in) one of the other women's courses; most students do not attempt to create a women's studies program by taking all of these classes.

Course Structure

The first week is spent introducing students to the study of women's history. I emphasize that this is not a traditional history class with a few women thrown in, but rather a study of history with women at its center. I try to convey to them the concept, in Joan Scott's words, of making "women a focus in enquiry, a subject of the story, an agent of the narrative" (Scott, 1992, p. 237). This leads me to talk about issues of periodization, "great men" theories, social and cultural history, and the study of individuals to examine larger themes—all of which helps demonstrate how this course is different from other history courses these students have had. I pose questions about the need for this type of course, especially if other history courses are becoming more integrated and diverse. I present my view that regardless of how other history courses are structured, I believe studying history from the perspective of women is uniquely instructive and capable of yielding a better and more complete understanding of the past. I also talk about my delight in teaching this type of course at a women's college where women's history is being made. Finally, I encourage the students to talk about what sort of criticisms of a course such as this exist, and how valid they might be. My goal in this opening discussion is not only to raise students' awareness of the academic issues surrounding this course they enroll in but also to provide a direct, fearless consideration of what this course is about.

A more theoretical approach follows the introduction, exposing students to different approaches to the study of women, such as compensatory history, contributory history, and gender studies. Sources for the study of women are discussed, and I bring in various samples, ranging from journals to the National Women's History Project catalog and to indices from various women's history archives.

In the first week, I attempt to integrate students into the past by having them consider their own histories and how those differ from their mother's histories. The complex issue of feminism as a part of women's history is also introduced, with a promise to return to that topic and to consider its historical context later in the semester.

In the early part of the course, I ask students to give me some brief information on index cards relating to their academic and personal backgrounds, as well as to the issues just described. After receiving the cards, I talk about them in class (and continue to do so throughout the semester). I quote from them to get across the various (and diverse) ideas the students have about women's history. I talk about what they identify as their expectations in this course and what they see as major concerns as the semester begins.

Using this specific background allows me to then introduce the content of the course in a way that is relevant to the individual students in this specific semester. Still within the first two weeks of the course, I explain to them what major topics we study and how they relate to the students' expectations and goals for the course. I talk about the narratives that will be read to help everyone understand those issues better and why I believe the women's voices in these narratives are so essential to our semester's study. I tell them how students have reacted to these works in the past, why I might change a book from one year to the next, how I expect them to read these works, and what kind of help (in the form of study guides, clear assignments, firm deadlines, class discussions) they can expect in order to get the most out of these books. I tell the students that the readings in this class are in some ways representative but more important are illustrative of the complexity and differences in women's lives, and that, of course, in selecting these readings I am being forced to leave out many other important works.

Although this course is quite different from the one that Sara Davis and Virginia Ratigan describe in the next chapter in this book, it has a very similar goal of helping students not just learn about what women have done but reach an understanding of the richness, complexity, and diversity of women's lives and make connections to those elements. Part of the goal, of course, includes some recognition of my own life. Early in the course, I tell the students a lot about my academic work, about my commitment to and belief in women's colleges, about my interest in generational issues in women's history (noting my place in the generation between them and most of their mothers). I make it clear that I am more interested in *their* voices than my own, but I also tell them that my views, experiences, and reactions will be included when the students indicate that they are helpful. They never fail to exercise this option.

After the first week or so, the course is divided into four major topics:

1. Early American women, prehistoric times to 1820
2. Women's life and work in early industrial times, 1820–1880
3. Redefining womanhood, 1880–1920
4. Women in the modern United States, 1920–1990

Each topic is covered through class discussion, discussions of readings, and some lecture material. Students are graded in the course on class participation, written responses to readings, project work, and midsemester and final examinations.

The division of discussion and lecture varies and is tailored to the size of the class. For example, when enrollment is in the range of ten students, I shift to teach it in more of a seminar fashion. In this situation, I rely less on group assignments and more on individual discussion. Discussions also vary in format. Book discussions are scheduled in advance, usually to coincide with written-material deadlines. These discussions then flow from the ideas students have generated and dealt with in their papers. Because written assignments usually require students to tackle a broad question ("What does this work teach us about women's experiences?" or "How does this narrative demonstrate the feminist nature of the subject?"), students respond in varying and often opposing ways, which makes for lively and rich discussions. Discussion is also used to help students think about other assigned readings or to express their opinions on strategies, reactions, and approaches of different women (for example, when we study the issue of suffrage in our topic of redefining womanhood, I ask students to evaluate the role of radical efforts and to project whether or not they would have supported the more radical element of the suffrage wing at the time).

In addition to this organization, and in an effort to enhance interaction with women's voices, students are asked to become involved directly with history through a course project. I have structured this part of the course in different ways, but one option that I always offer students is the opportunity to create an exhibit on some aspect of our college's history for display in the campus gallery. This project requires students to do research in the college archives, collaborate in creating a thematic exhibit, do presentations on the exhibit to the college community, and design and hang the exhibit. This element of the course is a very important reinforcement to the idea—which the use of narratives for course readings also uses—that history is accessible to students and that vantage points for learning history are not limited to the classroom. It also allows them to experience firsthand the challenges and power that rest with the person who interprets and writes history.

I find this part of the course extremely important and rewarding, yet also quite challenging. I am trained as a historian, not a curator or artist, so I must rely on the (extensive) help of other professionals on our campus to make this project work. Initially, I attempted to give the students (nearly) complete autonomy to select a research project and conceptualize its design. A few semesters of that effort made it clear that the students needed more direction and more certainty that our archives could support the topic they chose. In recent semesters, I have worked with our college archivist in advance to identify workable topics and have provided shorter (and firmer) deadlines for the students to complete their research. "Beyond Our Borders: Cottey's International History" and "Notes from Our Past: The History of Cottey's Music Program" were the most recent topics, both of which yielded a wealth of information about women's history all around us. For both of these topics, the students learned how much was available on women as well as how hard it was to fill some simple gaps in the college's past. They learned that a good archivist is essential to directing a researcher through primary sources. They struggled with different historical and artistic interpretations, as well as the inconsistencies they found in college materials.

Probably the most instructive aspect of this assignment comes when the students open their exhibit to the public. At this point, they are required to organize a brief presentation and be available that evening to discuss the work they have done. Criticisms, questions, and accolades greet them quickly, reinforcing both what they have learned and what they do not know. After this evening, we spend some time in class talking about how their experiences relate to those of professional historians. A few weeks after the exhibit comes down, students are asked to evaluate the project and provide some specific information on what they learned about women's history, how their ideas about studying the past have changed because of this work, how they can connect this work to the issue of narrative studies and interpretations, and whether they would have future classes participate in a similar exercise. (So far, despite many helpful suggestions and many complaints about the excessive work, the overwhelming majority of students insist that it must remain a part of the course.)

The Use of Narratives

The heart of this course, and the aspect that ties together all of the elements I have described, is the use of narrative autobiographical works as the focus of outside readings. In some semesters, these narratives are supplemented with a textbook, such as *Women's America: Refocusing the Past* (Kerber and De Hart, 1995). In other semesters, I have used a supplementary documentary reader, such as *Early American Women: A Documentary History, 1600–1900* (Woloch, 1997) and *Modern American Women: A Documentary History* (Ware, 1997). In some semesters, I supplement the autobiographical monographs with an assortment of shorter autobiographical works, such as those found in Jill Ker Conway's *Written by Herself* (1992). It is, however, the narrative autobiographical works of individual women assigned for reading, discussion, and written responses that form the central part of this course and bring women's voices straight to the students.

In the past five years, I have used six narrative autobiographical studies to frame this course. My choice of books has derived from my desire to find readable narratives that preserve the voice of the woman's life they are telling, even if historical editing is introduced in some way. I look for works that rely on diaries or letters and that reveal stories that would probably otherwise be lost to history. I am interested in works that reveal something about the process of a woman's education (whether it be formal or informal), since I believe that college students relate well to these types of chronicles and I also believe that these stories reinforce the idea of knowledge as a form of empowerment. I search for accounts that portray "rounded human beings" whose lives are detailed by both events and the female subjects themselves (Helgesen, 1990, p. 68). I also look for creative approaches to women examining their lives, and I rely on student feedback on these works to see if changes need to be made from one year to the next.

Of course, the pedagogical impact of the books I select is guided by not only the authors and their works but by the vantage points of those of us studying them. Abigail Stewart (1994) notes that it is helpful to analyze one's own role as it affects one's understanding as well as to avoid searching for a unified or coherent self or voice (thereby seeking to impose a false order or unity on our subjects). I find that in teaching narrative works the issue of "relatability" is always important, sometimes helping and sometimes hindering. All of us in this course are drawn to those with whom we feel a common bond, which only concerns me when it keeps us from learning from those who are very different. In my most recent experience in teaching this course, one student in the class was adjusting to the relatively new role of mother—as was I. Thus, every narrative that dealt with motherhood, children, and life choices about career and marriage resonated rather loudly for us. Our vantage point was different from that of others in the class, but it was also quite different between the two of us (she a twenty-year-old college student and I a forty-year-old professor). This fact allowed our views to be more inclusive than exclusive for others in the class, forced us to look at history from a more personal angle, and, I believe, made the class better in the process.

But the opposite can also occur. When some students in that same class read Betty Friedan's *The Feminine Mystique* (third edition, 1996), many found her vantage point unapproachable. Her arguments seemed important but not necessarily relevant to them, making the distance from the 1960s to the 1990s seem quite large (in fact, larger in some ways than the distance from the 1920s to the 1990s). Helping these students get past their initial reaction of irrelevancy to grapple with the complex ideas of this significant woman was a challenge, one that was overcome only as they came to understand Friedan's larger impact on the women's movement and how this work was part of it.

One work that I have used each time I have taught this course, and have always found to be well received and instructive, is *A Midwife's Tale: The Life of Martha Ballard Based on Her Diary 1785–1812* (Ulrich, 1990). This highly acclaimed, Pulitzer Prize–winning work immediately introduces students to several critical elements. Being able to read Ballard's diary entries directly, even when they are brief and not immediately revealing, connects students to the thinking and writing skills and processes of an eighteenth-century woman. Students usually indicate some trouble wading through her spelling and phrasing initially and then take pride in their ability to make sense of it easily as they continue to read. This book also allows students to see directly how historians do their work and how it is possible for a historian to enlighten the subject with which she is working without detracting from its original integrity. My students are usually unanimous in crediting Ulrich with making Ballard's diary come to life, even if a few of them indicate a desire for more diary and less editorial comment!

Discussions and a written assignment allow students to delve into the significance of the book. In many ways, the students in my class have little in common with Ballard other than their gender. She is an eighteenth-century woman of little education, a mother of many children, an older woman at the time she writes her diary, and a woman who spends most of her time delivering children and assisting those who are ill. Yet her autobiographical story seems to bridge those gaps and to connect young twentieth-century students to her. Students comment on her determination—both for what she does all day and for the time she takes to write about her days. They recognize her abilities and commitment, while at the same time they learn more about daily life in colonial America from the perspective of a woman. Students are usually surprised to find that standards for sexual conduct were not particularly rigid and that Ballard is quite direct in dealing with a host of moral problems in colonial New England.

Written responses to this book are usually geared to asking students to indicate what larger themes about women's history they find in this work. Themes of social medicine, female support groups, the limits of separate-sphere ideology, and the potential significance of one individual life are among those that have been identified.

This semester, the reading of *A Midwife's Tale* was supplemented with the viewing of the 1996 feature film based on this book. Like the book, the movie tells both Martha Ballard's story as well as Laurel Ulrich's story of researching and telling Ballard's story. It thus creates another level of interpretation to add to Ballard's and Ulrich's. Seeing the movie after the book was read and discussed and the papers on it were turned in allowed students to contemplate visually what they had already encountered in writing; it added to their understanding of the multilayered study of history and the richness inherent in such an approach.

A Midwife's Tale helps me achieve my goals of reframing history, shifting the dynamics of power, and teaching history in a more integrated and scholarly style because it uses one powerful female voice, long overlooked, to tell a broader colonial story. Ballard's words provide the promise of new life, the despair of exhaustion, the unfairness of the male medical profession's progressive encroachment on the practice of midwifery, the generational trials of a woman passing through middle age, and the ongoing challenge of finding meaning and making sense of the myriad events that are an individual life. With Ulrich's diligent and careful work wedded to Ballard's words, the use of this narrative has the added benefit of highlighting feminist scholarship at its best.

A very different, and less-known, autobiographical work that I have used for several semesters is *The Making of a Feminist: Early Journals and Letters of M. Carey Thomas* (Dobkin, 1978). This work is used to illustrate further the issue of women's education in the nineteenth century. Thomas, of course, becomes one of the leading women in higher education in this country in the early twentieth century, but that is not the story that is examined (or desired) here. Rather, this book is used to introduce the issues involved when a young girl desires a quality, advanced education in a time before it is readily accessible to her.

The young M. Carey Thomas compiled a diary that is feisty, smart, revealing, entertaining, and surprising. For all of these reasons, students respond and relate easily to it. Although her story, too, is somewhat foreign to a generation of young women who have never questioned their right to attend college, Thomas's articulation of frustration with her elders, alienation from others, and an inner drive to succeed is much less foreign to them.

In using this work, I usually have students briefly read other contemporary accounts of Thomas and introduce them to the critical views of her that have resulted from some of her policies at Bryn Mawr—especially her more racist tendencies. I also encourage students to consider how the editor of this work approached Thomas's writings and to contrast her treatment with Ulrich's. Students make distinctions here and sense that Dobkin uses a traditional (and perhaps less revealing) method of editorializing and is more concerned with (what they see as) insignificant elements of Thomas's life and how history deals with those. Like Ballard's story, Thomas's diary gives students a direct link to history while at the same time making them think critically about the work of historians in this process.

Thomas's young, rebellious voice provides an excellent opportunity to begin to explore the meanings of feminism and how they can be acted upon. The fact that Thomas wrote her diary before the word *feminism* was used in this country yet the editor chose to use that word in her title for Thomas's writings provides an opening for grappling with the meaning of Thomas's life with this word in mind. Within the broader framework of women's education, Thomas's voice gives us generational issues, woman-centered lifestyles, rebellion against sexism, impatience with incompetence, and a sense of hope that seemingly insurmountable barriers can be overcome. I remind students of the foundation that Thomas benefited from, as she was able to take advantage of some of the earlier ideas about education put forth by Catharine Beecher, Emma Willard, and Mary Lyon. I also encourage them to see how she did things her own way and became, in her own right, a pioneer for women's education. The seemingly simple words in her diary and letters reveal an increasingly complex life, which again helps us reframe history and look at her use of power and the significance of that usage.

Selection of M. Carey Thomas's writings resulted from the need for a replacement for another narrative autobiographical work that I used and then found I had to change. That eventuality is equally revealing pedagogically and so is explained here. Upon arriving at Cottey College in 1993, I quickly learned that the founder of our college, Virginia Alice Cottey, had been greatly influenced by the legendary woman educator Mary Lyon. Cottey, in fact, aspired to create a school much like Mount

Holyoke for females in the Midwest. Cottey never met Mary Lyon but instead drew her inspiration from reading Lyon's life story several times and believing there were undeniable links between what Lyon achieved and what Cottey wanted.

This situation led me to believe that introducing an autobiographical work about Mary Lyon would be most appropriate at Cottey. I was pleased to learn that one such work that used Lyon's writings was still in print: *Mary Lyon and Mount Holyoke: Opening the Gates* (Green, 1979). I assigned it the first semester I taught this course. Although this work did not have as much contextual richness as Martha Ballard's story, I saw it as having other benefits and thus being equally capable of demonstrating larger themes through an individual voice.

My students saw it differently. Mary Lyon may have influenced the founder of the college they were attending, but she was not particularly influential to them. In part, her writings were too direct, too pat and resolved, too noncontroversial for them to find much meaning in them. Devoutly religious and pious, Lyon seemed somewhat unreal to them as well as frequently monotonous. Students found it difficult to get past her tendency to approach every problem with a great deal of prayer (and not much else). Her voice provided a unique Cottey connection, but it did little else. I found it difficult to inspire students to find the larger themes her life encompassed or to see in her struggles anything that made much sense to them.

Feedback on this book made it clear that another work would be better. Looking for a work that focused on issues related to women's education, but in a more relevant manner, I found the spunky writings of M. Carey Thomas to be an apt replacement. Although neither work is as widely acclaimed as Martha Ballard's story, I am convinced that Thomas's voice is more helpful than Lyon's in my efforts to reframe history and provide an avenue for integrated scholarly study in this course.

A fourth work that I have used most semesters is *The Long Day: The Story of a New York Working Girl* (Richardson, 1990). This work introduces students to dual voices: the heroine of this fictional account of a young woman who moves through a series of working-class jobs *and* the middle-class author who herself held a series of jobs in order to research the working-class environment for women early in the twentieth century. Obviously, this is a more complex approach than the first narratives I assign, yet even in its fictional approach it allows students to encounter the female experience directly.

Using *The Long Day* as a narrative autobiographical story lets the voice of the fictional heroine survive intact, even while it introduces the issue of class perspective to historical studies. The version of the work I use includes an introduction (by Cindy Sondik Aron), which lays out very clearly the ideas of the author and how they influenced her creation of this fictional account. With that background and context, students follow the heroine through a series of jobs in such places as a box factory, an artificial flower warehouse, and a laundry, as well as her experiences in boarding rooms and with a range of frightening employers.

This is a world the Cottey students do not know. The personal voice taking them through this world makes it more real; the fact that the heroine is a young woman close to their age reinforces this reality. Even so, slang phrases and obscure references to the work culture frequently confuse them and leave them feeling that they are encountering an environment so foreign that it is difficult to believe it is based on a situation in this country and in this century.

Reading this work forces students to remember that it is a constructed account, but also that it is one based on firsthand observations. Students usually identify an inherent sense of unfairness in the working world of the lower east side, and they question the accuracy of the details Richardson provides. Some want to believe that Richardson must have gotten some it wrong, in the hope that inaccurate history might erase unpleasant elements. This reaction opens ways to separate the heroine's voice from Richardson's, while at the same time seeing where those voices overlap. *The Long Day* is an emotional, personal story and because of that, I believe, my students see the working-class culture more humanely than they might otherwise. The heroine at the center of this study is both empowered and empowering, and her voice demonstrates a particular set of challenges that my students are better off for recognizing.

In the latter part of this course, I often use the well-known *Coming of Age in Mississippi* by Anne Moody (1968) to show the anger and impact of a young woman directly involved in the civil rights movement in the United States. Reading this work is much like having someone take you with her through a very personal and difficult journey that does not have a particularly happy ending. It demonstrates the cost of commitment and the price of pain in very vivid terms, even as it draws readers to its volatile and intriguing protagonist.

I enjoy using this book because it turns history on its head. It throws objectivity aside and replaces it with unabashed emotion. It always causes students to ask, "What happened to her?" The fact that what happened to her is not easily answered (Moody has been institutionalized for many years and is not available for direct contact) only adds to the power and pain of this work.

Using this work also allows for fruitful explorations of the extent to which this book is truly "women's history" or whether it is more a story of "black history" or, as one student said, "just human history." Moody's anger is clearly more race-related than gender-related, but by the end of the semester in which this book is read many students in my course are not comfortable drawing overly rigid lines in these areas.

Students come to this book with a working knowledge of the civil rights movement and, often, with a romantic sense of what being involved meant. Moody's story scrapes the romance away and replaces it with deep scars, ambivalence, and unpleasant detail. With Moody's perspective, they are forced to rethink history and see the complexity—both personal and beyond—involved in large-scale social movements. One semester, when I asked students to prepare written responses to the book in the form of a letter to Anne Moody, I found over and over that students asked her how she found the strength to go on, to avoid being overwhelmed, and to believe that what she did would matter later. Of all the books I use in all the classes I teach, this one consistently elicits the most personal responses.

As noted above, I have also used Friedan's *The Feminine Mystique* to confront women's experiences in the United States in recent times. As one of the compelling reasons to introduce this book to students, in discussing the modern women's movement with my classes I found that usually only a few students had heard of this work and virtually none of them had read it. Since it is both a historic and historical work, I believe it is an important personal narrative, as well as primary source, for the study of women.

The Feminine Mystique also allows an important base for discussing generational issues in more depth. How Friedan has dealt with her label as the "mother of the modern women's movement," how her leadership style has incorporated those of different ages and ideas, and what she has done since writing *The Feminine Mystique* opens up those issues very clearly for students. As noted, at least some students have a hard time not reading Friedan too literally and thus finding her ideas removed from them. But others quickly make interdisciplinary connections with her work, using their studies in psychology and sociology as well business to help them understand the points she is making.

What each of these books provides is a connection to students that causes them to reframe their approach to and understanding of history. The pedagogical discovery in choosing works of this nature is clear: when students focus on direct life stories, they hear more clearly the voices of doubt, the searching, the imperfection, the triumph, and the human elements that are so essential to the study of history. For students, the discovery comes in seeing the timeless quality of women's lives and in understanding better how and why individuals did what they did (or did not do) in their context.

The use of narratives, in short, brings history alive. It helps students make connections that then allow them to analyze women's historical developments with a fuller view of history. In this women's history course, intellectual connection is built upon to allow students the opportunity to act on their personal connection to history. Students are asked to use their insights into history as they create their semester project. Carrying out their own firsthand research, using college archives, working side by side with professors and archivists, making their own judgments and interpretations, conducting oral history interviews, selecting material artifacts, and keeping notes on their experiences—all of this places these students (who made their first step with a personal connection to history through reading women's life stories) clearly in the stream of thoughtful searchers, recipients of the power of historical investment, and analyzers of the past from an informed and relevant perspective.

From a pedagogical view, building a course on women around narrative works has allowed me to delve deeply into feminist issues and to consider carefully the layers of women's lives. It has given me the opportunity to gauge student reaction and interaction closely and thus led me to quickly acknowledge when a new book should be tried, a project assignment refined, a discussion strategy modified, or a learning technique adjusted to fit more closely with the characteristics and needs of a specific (collective and individual) class. As Ellen Kimmel notes, feminist teaching must be viewed as an emergent practice that develops through experience; in this course, as much as any other I have taught if not more so, I have certainly experienced the sense that I must not be afraid to try new approaches, take some risks, and deal continuously with finding the right mix of guidance, leadership, and instruction to match a less-authoritative, less-power-driven arrangement of teaching and studying history. Teaching this course makes me feel very much a part of "the struggle for more egalitarian and inclusive knowledge that reflects far-reaching epistemological revolutions in the scholarly disciplines" (Maher and Tetreault, 1994, p. 2).

This course has reinforced for me the belief that the best history is truthful, holistic, and inclusive. It demonstrates each semester that students learn best when they are invested in what is being studied. The investment that I seek to establish comes through learning to relate to issues and individuals; experiencing firsthand the challenges of good scholarship; and approaching history as a subject to be studied through reading, writing, discussing, and interpreting. I often feel in this course that I am removing the dust from the past; pulling history in closer; and helping students find a more accessible, personal, and direct sense of what preceded them. Although this course, for the time being, remains more discipline-specific than interdisciplinary, I believe it does contribute to an informal arrangement of women's studies under way on our campus and could someday be part of a more formal arrangement here. Through either arrangement, I expect this course to continue to allow our students to become (as Judith James alludes in the first chapter of this book) more self-conscious learners, seeing more clearly the vagaries, prejudice, and injustices found both in history as well as in the approach one uses to study it.

REFERENCES

Broughton, T. L., and Anderson, L. (eds.). *Women's Lives/Women's Times: New Essays on Auto/biography.* Albany: State University of New York Press, 1997.

Conway, J. K. *Written by Herself*. New York: Vintage, 1992.

Dobkin, M. H. (ed). *The Making of a Feminist: Early Journals and Letters of M. Carey Thomas*. Kent, Ohio: Kent State University Press, 1978.

Friedan, B. *The Feminine Mystique*. (3rd ed.) New York: Norton, 1996.

Green, E. A. *Mary Lyon and Mt. Holyoke: Opening the Gates*. Hanover, N.H.: University Press of New England, 1979.

Helgesen, S. *The Female Advantage: Women's Ways of Leadership*. New York: Doubleday, 1990.

Kerber, L. K., and De Hart, J. S. *Women's America: Refocusing the Past*. New York: Oxford University Press, 1995.

Maher, F. A., and Tetreault, M.K.T. *The Feminist Classroom*. New York: Basic Books, 1994.

Moody, A. *Coming of Age in Mississippi*. New York: Laurel, 1968.

Richardson, D. *The Long Day: The Story of a New York Working Girl*. Charlottesville: University Press of Virginia, 1990.

Scott, J. "Women in History: The Modern Period." In J. A. Kourany, J. P. Sterba, and R. Tong (eds.), *Feminist Philosophies*. Upper Saddle River, N.J.: Prentice-Hall, 1992.

Stewart, A. J. "Toward a Feminist Strategy for Studying Women's Lives." In C. E. Franz and A. J. Stewart (eds.), *Women Creating Lives: Identities, Resilience, and Resistance*. Boulder, Colo.: Westview Press, 1994.

Ulrich, L. T. *A Midwife's Tale: The Life of Martha Ballard Based on Her Diary 1785–1812*. New York: Vintage, 1990.

Ware, S. *Modern American Women: A Documentary History.* New York: McGraw-Hill, 1997.

Woloch, N. *Early American Women: A Documentary History, 1600–1900.* New York: McGraw-Hill, 1997.

5

STUDYING WOMEN'S LIVES IN AN INTERDISCIPLINARY CONTEXT

Sara N. Davis, Virginia Kaib Ratigan

DURING THE PAST THIRTY YEARS cries for educational reform on the collegiate level have often included interdisciplinary courses. At the same time that some disciplines have shown increasingly narrow specialization, many educators favor interdisciplinary courses that incorporate critical literatures across several disciplines. The expectation is that foundational interdisciplinary courses raise awareness of major intellectual issues. Many feel that work across disciplines broadens the questions that can be asked and the methodologies that can be applied.

A benefit of the interdisciplinary foundational course that arises repeatedly in the literature[1] is that the course is frequently designed around a question that is then examined from multiple perspectives. Questions are on the order of "What is the meaning of art within cultures?" (Gesiakowska and LoSardo, 1991, p. 39). This particular question formed the basis for a course at DePaul University, incorporating the relationship of social and political history of Western cultures with contemporary artwork. Another introductory course that many colleges have presented is "Representations of Coming of Age," which exposes students to literature, art, psychology, and sociology. One appeal of such courses is the opportunity to look to classical as well as contemporary work to incorporate broad perspectives. Furthermore, students are encouraged to consider large questions as they address material and learn to integrate ideas from several sources, rather than simply pursuing a linear trajectory across time. As students move through the curriculum, interdisciplinary courses can serve a different purpose, that of joining perspective and methodology in ways that best address a question. For example, many fields—literature and religion, to name two—turn to psychology for an understanding of developing cognitive process as well as methodology. There are numerous instances where psychological methods have been used to empirically test literary and religious theories (Andringa and Davis, 1994; Fowler, 1981).

The growth of interdisciplinary research has spawned the development of many new fields that integrate research from two or more disciplines. Some noteworthy examples of these are women's studies, environmental studies, and African American studies. Interdisciplinary fields emerge from, as well as continue to influence, the original disciplines, thus generating the possibility of an ongoing feedback loop. Since many scholars see their work residing in their original discipline and the developing (inter)discipline, they continue to provide new ideas that stimulate growth in the two areas.

In this chapter, we describe an interdisciplinary course, "Studying Women's Lives," which we taught jointly. It was always our intention to draw on the women's studies literature to provide the main structure for the course. Within this structure were ideas and readings that came from our own disciplines (religious studies and psychology). We want to examine different concepts of disciplinarity and interdisciplinarity and explore where our course fit within these concepts. We also want to explore how the interdisciplinary nature of the course served to develop an understanding of the complexity of women's lives in our students.

Disciplinarity, Multidisciplinarity, and Interdisciplinarity

Disciplines have their own ways of viewing the world, their own vocabulary, their own techniques. People working within a discipline learn particular ways of assessing validity, which influence their perspectives not only in doing research but also in what they want to achieve in the classroom. Donald (1997) describes differences among the divisions of the natural sciences, social sciences, and humanities. For example, whereas social scientists look for empirical evidence and conceptual frameworks as explanations, "humanistic truth involves something other than logical or scientific validity" (Donald, 1997, p. 33). This distinction was described by Bruner (1986) as a difference between paradigmatic truth and narrative truth. The paradigmatic, often associated with the natural sciences, draws on objective procedures to test for empirical truth, while the narrative relies on intuitive and dramaturgical truth. Immersion in these particular ways of seeing the world forges identities that can be powerful. For some, the identity within a discipline is extremely important, whereas others find this orientation to be limiting and look for ways to import ideas and methods from other disciplines and fields.

Instances of interdisciplinary courses vary widely.[2] At issue is how much synthesis occurs across disciplines and how much is considered desirable. Bidisciplinary or multidisciplinary courses bring together input from two or more different fields but do not necessarily attempt to integrate them. For example, a course might bring together chemistry and political science to investigate evidence for a crime. The chemistry part of the course would use chemical procedures to construct the evidence; political science would then use this evidence to try the case in a mock trial. Although both fields are crucial to the course, the questions would be addressed sequentially. In fact, the chemistry professor may conduct the class in her lab for the first half of the semester, the political science instructor in her classroom during the second half.

An interdisciplinary course, on the other hand, strives to achieve integration between or among the disciplines in question. Rather than a sequential approach in which the insights of one discipline are employed followed by those of another, one employs broader concepts that transcend a single discipline; "in an interdisciplinary course faculty work together as much as alone, interacting instead of merely working jointly" (Newell, 1983, as cited by Richards, 1996, p. 116). This view emphasizes the generation of new interpretive frameworks, which are the result of the cross-fertilization of two or more disciplines. "Thus approaches, methodologies, and theories from different fields work together to shape a new model" (Fulcher, 1978, as quoted by Richards, 1996). This is seen as more than simply juxtaposing different ideas; it transforms and extends one's perspective. Davis and Gergen (forthcoming) have explored how literature and the social sciences interact to create narratives that "enrich the context from which we can understand the multiple communities that [constitute] an individual's life." These narratives are generated and understood by drawing on what we know from both disciplines. For example, in looking at how readers respond to literary works, we are concerned with the role of memory and previous experiences as well as examining how textual structures stimulate responses. Jamieson and Cappella (1996) have described how scholars in different disciplines may be doing similar work unbeknownst to one another. To eliminate this duplication of work and to coordinate research questions, there are clear benefits to working across disciplines. Specifically, these authors show that a union of political science and communications fosters emphasis on the content of political messages as well as their impact, instead of on one or the other.

The conception of an interdisciplinary field requires dialogue among the constituent participants. Each field is in and of itself complex. Any synthesis involves selecting ideas and approaches from the field and is influenced by the participants. This should not be seen as a static configuration; new perspectives are always asking to be part of the dialogue. Although integration across disciplines is often a desirable goal, fundamental differences across disciplines can complicate the process. Newell (1983, cited by Richards, 1996) states that for these reasons one often wants to stop short of the goal of total synthesis and be sensitive to the limitations imposed by different orientations. In our case, we believed that there have been bridges connecting our disciplines for a long time. In the setting of undergraduate college teaching, the study of women and religion has translated into development of new courses in feminist theologies, spiritualities, ethics, and literature, as well as attention to the impact of these interdisciplinary courses on traditional offerings. Many programs in religious studies incorporate the work of feminists from a variety of disciplines. The same can be said for the links between psychology and women's studies as courses develop in such areas as feminist research methods and feminist therapeutic strategies.

Individually, we were interested in using narratives, investigating styles of interpretation, and working from the perspective of multiple interpretations. Each of us had taught courses linking our disciplines with women's studies. We were also linked by common experiences in our respective fields, such as our awareness of the marginalization of women's voices and experiences.

As we designed our course, "Studying Women's Lives," we were motivated by deep questions of how to understand women's lives. As a framework, we selected a group of guidelines described by Abigail Stewart (1994, discussed later in this chapter), formulated from research in women's studies. We saw the course as being guided by women's studies and not by our specific disciplines. We specifically avoided labeling the material that we presented as belonging to either religious studies or psychology; instead, we continuously emphasized the questions we used to frame the course. We were comfortable that these guidelines resonated with trends in our individual disciplines. However, despite the mutuality between our disciplines and the use of the women's studies framework, there were times when we each reflected our own areas of expertise within our disciplines and, more generally, aspects of our disciplines.

From the point of view of religious biography, deeper questions about life and death and the role of faith, as well as the meaning of suffering, became an important part of the course. Sometimes these were related to the lives of religious women, but they extended to themes in the lives of women in a variety of contexts as well. Once these themes became part of how we could understand a woman's life, it was important to understand how they applied to all women. From the point of view of psychology, the tools that can be used to question the meaning of life were explored, employed, and critiqued. Feminist psychology furnished the perspectives of a critique of logical positivism, the mandate to look at women's agency and to consider women as knowable in relationship.

Our Own Stories

As we realized our common ground in designing and proposing this course, we were led to reflect on our own academic histories. We present these stories here to introduce and illustrate our individual and common concerns and how they were integral to the course.

Virginia Ratigan

My undergraduate major in English and theology provided grounding in narrative literature, and this interest has been sustained throughout my career. The 1960s found me in graduate school in the broader field of religious studies, where I developed a strong interest in biblical narrative and religious biography and autobiography.

This was a time when interreligious dialogue as well as dialogue within traditions (such as Vatican II for Catholics) were the order of the day. It was also a time when voices of women across traditions were still falling on deaf ears in the "malestream." Thus my career in teaching spans three decades of work and study during the critical years in which feminist voices have been heard a little more clearly in the academy.

My involvement with grassroots movements such as the Women's Ordination Conference, along with feminist scholarship in religion and my work in the classroom, have all served to highlight the centrality of narrative in the intersection of religion with other disciplines, especially in the humanities and social sciences. But even the idea of narrative in religious studies is itself problematic. Whose narrative is told? Whose left out? Whose story becomes normative? Though diverse in many ways, the sacred texts of each tradition—and perhaps more important the interpretations of the texts—carry the common themes of patriarchy with their histories of dominance and oppression (Christ, 1992). As feminists have developed critical hermeneutical tools and methodologies for analysis, the results have gone far beyond the inclusionary concerns of the 1960s to create major shifts in understanding basic questions of theological anthropology. Narratives of women's lives are at the heart of the task.

During my thirty years of teaching, the classroom setting has provided my greatest insights into the transformative aspects of feminist methods and models of teaching. My earlier efforts revolved around the classical model of lecture-and-discussion, which paid attention to student's questions and input. The interactive classroom today creates a context for collaboration, unlocking a much greater potential for students to take responsibility in the teaching and learning process.

Sara Davis

Throughout my career, I have been intrigued by questions that I feel cannot be answered by straightforward, disciplinary research. In graduate school, working on a project studying filmmaking, I read the theoretical work of the legendary Sergei Eisenstein, who said of his goal as a filmmaker, "In fact every spectator, in correspondence with his individuality, and in his own way and out of his own experience . . . creates an image in accordance with the representational guidance suggested by the author" (1942, p. 33).

As a student of psychology, I was interested in observing just how this process could come about. Where do the correspondences lie between the total of the spectator's lifetime experiences and the image that the filmmaker is trying to stimulate this individual to create? I felt I had to go beyond the laboratory to begin to understand how the interplay developed between the individual and the work of art. I began to combine film theory and literary theory with the empirical methodology offered by some psychologists. I wanted to observe the development, over time, of cognitive and emotional responses to a work of art and see how they were related to textual strategies. Fortunately, there was a growing movement in psychology at that time to promote study of individuals through narratives generated in context (Gergen, 1985; Gruber, 1981). Using the case-study method (Gruber, 1981) encouraged in-depth study of small numbers of subjects as they had contact with a literary text over time.

These same ideas continued to interest me as I have turned my attention to feminist pedagogy. My interest is in how one stimulates the growth of ideas in the classroom. The concept of the interactive, collaborative classroom again raises questions about how to provide the elements that enable diverse groups of students to grapple with concepts and give them meaning within their own intellectual contexts. Other critical questions include: What constitutes knowledge within the classroom? How is personal experience used to enhance learning? What different types of relationship are beneficial within the classroom?

Overview of "Studying Women's Lives"

In the course of working together for five years, we realized our mutual concern with women's journeys and began to plan for an interdisciplinary course. We were fortunate in receiving immediate support from our administration, which is interested in developing interdisciplinary courses. From the beginning, our focus was on the question of how to study women's lives; we developed the course from that point of view without specific concern for how to emphasize inputs from our disciplines.

There were certain major ideas that we wanted to emphasize throughout the course. Perhaps most pivotal was the idea of multiple perspectives: there is no single story of a life, but many. Each recounting varies according to the perspective of the person telling it and the audience reading it. This concept of multiple perspectives was reflected in another principle: that students be exposed to multiple techniques for generating information about lives because each technique yields certain information that may not be available from others. Finally, we accepted the validity of each student's experiences and encouraged them to use those experiences in their attempts to understand the lives of others. We were interested in a variety of women's lives, both living and dead, both famous and ordinary.

In organizing this class (and in responding to opportunities that arose once it was in progress), we expanded the class beyond the traditional walls of the classroom to include participation in a major conference, Feminism Across the Generations,[3] which we were involved in organizing; visits to local archives; presentation of a one-woman play chronicling the life of Jeannette Rankin;[4] a filmmaker showing and describing the genesis of her film; several speakers in and outside of class; and visits with women in a retirement community who were creating an archive of life stories.

We emphasized interaction in our class. Although at times we needed to provide an analysis or describe a way of doing things, we primarily organized our classes to be experiential. We encouraged students through a variety of activities to work with and think about the material so that they would become involved with it. We also shared our own professional and feminist development with the class. We modeled collaborative behaviors through our own interactions, working together in all classes and eschewing the model in which each of us would handle sections representing our own disciplines. We discussed our ideas with each other as well as the class. In so doing, we used our own experiences, both intellectual and personal, to make points. We hoped to model the way in which personal experiences provide a trigger for reflection, not a digression from the material at hand.

A chapter written by Stewart (1994) that gives seven guidelines for how to study women served as an interpretive framework throughout the class. These guidelines exhort the researcher to be sensitive to the missing pieces, reflect on how her own perspective and presence affect the research process, consider the role of gender, and be comfortable with the complexities of a life story. In addition, she emphasizes the need to "identify women's agency in the midst of social constraint" (p. 21).

The series of assignments and classroom activities in which we engaged were designed to enable students to process these principles in a variety of ways. For example, we encouraged each student to be aware of her own history and to look at how it led her to certain conclusions, while students with different life experiences tended to interpret things slightly differently. Every story has multiple threads that can be braided together in different ways; they need not form a single story. This point was emphasized in a biography project (which we describe later). We devised multiple ways of getting at our own biographies. In almost every activity, we asked students to think about how there might be threads in their own life histories that formed a connection with our class readings and presentations. In each class we had whole-group discussions, and a variety of small-group activities that varied from week to week, designed to encourage students to expand the ability to understand varieties of lives.

Implementation of Strategies

Our overarching goal for the class was to enable students to understand the complexity and richness of women's lives. We exposed students to diverse methods for collecting the stories of women's lives; we encouraged the ability to listen to and learn from women's stories and to look at possibilities for translating stories or testimony to action. We wanted our students to view women in their social, religious, and historical contexts. Finally, we wanted to enable our students to think critically and ask questions.

A good part of our course centered on teaching students techniques for collecting material about women's lives. Various approaches to collecting information were examined in preparation for two major projects: an interview with a woman about her major life concerns, and the biography project. In all cases, analysis was sensitive to the guidelines adopted from Stewart. Additionally, we drew on these guidelines to select speakers for the class. We wanted to emphasize how the idea of women as change-agents became an important organizing theme.

Techniques for Studying Women's Lives

Throughout the course of the semester, students were exposed to several techniques for gathering information about women's lives. We spent time with the college archivist, who introduced the types of material that exist in archives and how to access them. Students then went to local archives to gather material pertaining to women who have been significant in local history and beyond. Students worked through multiple sources of data in a particular time period—newspaper articles, yearbook entries, letters, programs from award dinners, and so forth—to piece together a picture of a particular woman's life. At the archives, many of them were presented with boxes of material they had to sort through to find what was significant. This was a different experience for students who deal primarily with computers and not artifacts. Many found this to be a rewarding experience. The assignment occurred in conjunction with a speaker who described her archival work as preparation for a major biographical study. She described starting with boxes of collected materials and finding systems of organizing and bringing meaning to the life.

In preparation for the project in which students conducted interviews, we examined theoretical positions on interviewing (Franklin, 1997; Reinharz, 1992). Our aim was to sensitize students to the range of potential relationships that can be developed during the interview and the outcomes that result. We were concerned that students be cognizant of how their input and structuring of the interview would influence the process. Students then went out and conducted their own interviews in which they were concerned with not only what they learned about the woman's life but also what happened during the interview. Did they feel their techniques were productive, and did they feel comfortable with these techniques? Were they able to make the woman comfortable so she could explore her life during the interview?

This is discussed more fully in the next section, on biographies.

Biographies

Several weeks of the semester were devoted to our biography project, culminating in a "biography day" in which we examined the multiplicity of stories that have been told about particular lives. In preparation, we spent a certain amount of class time exploring ways of collecting information for the study of individual biographies. We wanted to inculcate the idea that there is no single biography of a person but rather many possible compilations of a person's life, each filtered through the understanding and perspectives of a particular author. We therefore wanted to introduce the students to multiple sources of information as well as ways of gathering and organizing it.

We had two speakers address biographical projects. Mary Elizabeth Strub SHCJ described an innovative way of organizing copious boxes of unpublished materials from the life of Cornelia Connelly, the founder of her religious community (which in turn founded Rosemont College). Her project, a position paper on the life of Mother Connelly (Strub, 1987), demonstrated how many threads there are to a life and how no single organization of the material is capable of presenting all potential interpretations. Strub had a particular purpose to her own interpretive work: documentation of the life as part of the process of canonization. Virginia Ratigan had also published a paper on the life of Cornelia Connelly (1996). She described to the class her experience of positioning the many published biographies from the last hundred years in her review article. She examined the particular orientations embedded in biographies written in different eras and for different purposes. In both of these talks, the emphasis fell on the multiple possibilities for organizing any life and not seeing it as a single closed story.

In conjunction with a campus talk, students read an autobiographical essay by theologian Diana Hayes (1995) in which she discussed the evolution of her faith and the other choices that grew out of her religious commitments. In her book, she intertwined growing theological interests with experiences within the African American culture. She detailed her struggles with physical disabilities; experiences with discrimination; and her growing faith, which enabled her to give meaning to the difficulties and questions in her life.

Concomitant with these other activities, we included opportunities for students to explore their own biographies and how those stories might connect with the materials we were studying. For example, after reading Hayes, we used an activity designed to connect her life with that of the students. Each student wrote a personal reaction to the book on a piece of paper and then passed it to another student, who responded and then passed it along. There were several go-arounds in which interesting and thoughtful written discussions developed. Students were stimulated to think about how their lives (which surely were constituted differently) still might have some commonality with Hayes's life and with each other's. The activity also enabled them to use their own lives to forge connections to Hayes's life and use these connections to enrich their understanding of her issues. At another point, we drew on student biographies in a different way: we created a mural representing aspects of their lives. We posed several questions and requested that each member of the class write something on a piece of paper and add it to the mural. For example, we asked them to reflect on when they first became conscious of inequality, to think about aspects of their lives that did not easily cohere, and so forth. Students seemed to respond positively to the opportunity to address theory by personalizing it with their own experiences and to see the panorama created by the conjunction of their life histories.

The culminating project was our biographical study, in which students worked in small groups, each of which selected a person to study. Each student within a particular group consulted different biographical material on that person: written biographies, material in reference books, autobiographies, archival materials, material on the Internet. Every student analyzed her own sources for the points of view they espoused. The different points of view included when was it written, the perspective of the author, what new information was incorporated, what was missing, what the popular story of this person's life was, and how the particular information varied in any given biography. When these groups collaborated on what they had learned about their subject, students were able to address differences that were due to various time frames, as well as being the result of different types of relationship and purpose on the part of the biographers.

Women as Change-Agents

An important theme that was highlighted throughout the class was examination of how women made major changes in their lives. Speakers invited to the class provided examples of having radically altered their own lives. Several were political refugees from countries in tremendous turmoil; all of these women had in common the experience of harrowing escapes once they realized that their lives were in jeopardy. We focused discussion on an individual coming to the realization that change is necessary and then finding a way to do so in risky or dangerous situations. Several young women presented stories of escape from oppression—one from female genital mutilation in West Africa, two others from the war in Bosnia. One of these women brought along her immigration lawyer, who herself had an interesting story of change. The attorney had gone from a secure university position to devoting herself to assisting people who were seeking asylum and had to deal with tremendous pain and difficulty every day;

she felt compelled to respond to the needs of people who had already suffered greatly and needed advocates within the system.

We were fortunate in bringing to campus a one-woman play, *The Year of the Woman,* written by Kate Walbert (copyright 1996). This play, based on the life of Jeannette Rankin, the first woman to be elected to the U.S. Congress, posed one more example of a woman breaking out of the social, political, and educational constraints placed on women. Rankin was eager to be elected to Congress to fight for her belief in pacifism and suffrage. We had the opportunity to discuss ways of constructing a life with both the playwright and the actress. Walbert, who spoke with us, described how she came upon the Rankin story in a brief newspaper article and traversed the country, looking in records offices and interviewing distant relatives to piece together and reconstruct what she could about the life of this important woman who had been lost to history. The actress spoke with the audience after the presentation about how she was able to construct the essence of this life through her acting.

Reflections on Interdisciplinarity

The ultimate questions about human experience posed by religion and psychology were always present in this course. These two disciplines are particularly congenial and mesh well within the framework of women's studies. It was our goal throughout the course to focus on the questions rather than the disciplines.

We believe that students entered the class with fixed ideas about the nature of psychology and religion. They tended to consider the entire field of psychology as being represented by clinical psychology, with its goal being to help people better understand their dynamics, but this tended to ignore the large part of the field devoted to understanding such aspects as human emotions, personality, cognition, and behavior. Religion was seen more from the perspective of its institutional or creedal dimensions, not so much from the universal themes of the spiritual journey and human search for God. This led some students to expect clearly demarcated inputs from each discipline. In fact, we received feedback from a faculty member that a student had complained to her that it was difficult to tell when we were doing psychology and when we were doing religion. Although this was meant as a criticism of our class from someone not sympathetic to the interdisciplinary endeavor, we were pleased at hearing that we had achieved this degree of integration. However, when given the opportunity to evaluate the class, many students saw psychology and religion integrating well in the study of women's lives. In the words of one student evaluation, "The two disciplines both complement and stimulate discussion. Since most of us are religious and all have a psychological package to carry, it is a good format to blend the two."

Many saw the relationship of the two disciplines as much more closely linked than they had initially imagined. They were impressed with the flexibility within the fields that allowed them to expand and examine different sorts of life situations. We viewed it as part of our task to open students to the possibility of moving beyond the disciplinary to the interdisciplinary.

In our view, the course represented a serious effort toward integration. We saw ourselves as working under the aegis of women's studies and drew our organizing questions from within that (inter)discipline. Much of the specific material we used in class came from scholars in our fields who were bridging the disciplines (religious studies or psychology) with feminist scholarship. For example, we drew on the work of Margery Franklin, who has made contributions in the fields of psychology and women's studies. Her critique of traditional styles of interviewing within psychology opened the way to different and more flexible modes in her interviews of women artists. Similarly, Stewart urges a level of self-reflexivity in the study of women's lives that is rare for many psychologists.

We believe that our course provides another example of viewing a woman's life not as a fixed entity but instead drawing on scholarship in women's studies, religious studies, and psychology to unlock the dynamics of the life. A woman's story can be told in terms of the spiritual search, the circumstances in which she lives and the changes she makes, and how they are affected by gender, religion, ethnicity, sexual orientation. In other words, the life of any woman has many stories, depending on the narrator and the audience. It was our goal to encourage students to reveal the necessity to seek out multiple story lines and allow them to coexist.

NOTES

1. See Reithlingshoefer (1991) for a series of chapters addressing implementation of interdisciplinary teaching.
2. For a fuller explanation, see Richards (1996).
3. This conference was sponsored by the Women's Studies Consortium of the Greater Philadelphia area.
4. The play, *The Year of the Woman* (copyright 1996), was written by Kate Walbert. The playwright can be contacted in the English department of Yale University, New Haven, Connecticut.

REFERENCES

Andringa, E., and Davis, S. N. "Literary Narrative and Mental Representation or How Readers Deal with 'A Rose for Emily.'" In H. Van Oostendorp and R. Zwaan (eds.), *Naturalistic Text Comprehension.* Norwood, N.J.: Ablex, 1994.

Bruner, J. *Actual Minds, Possible Worlds.* Cambridge, Mass.: Harvard University Press, 1986.

Christ, C. "Feminist Sojourners in the Field of Religious Studies." In C. Kramerae and D. Spender (eds.), *The Knowledge Explosion.* New York: Teachers College Press, 1992.

Davis, S. N., and Gergen, M. "Blurring the Boundaries: Stories in Literature and the Social Sciences." *Spiel: Siegener Periodicum zur Internationalen Empirischen Literaturwissenschaft* (forthcoming).

Donald, J. *Improving the Environment for Learning.* San Francisco: Jossey-Bass, 1997.

Eisenstein, S. *The Film Sense.* Orlando: Harcourt, Brace, 1942.

Fowler, J. W. *Stages of Faith: The Psychology of Human Development and the Quest for Meaning.* New York: HarperCollins, 1981.

Franklin, M. "Making Sense: Interviewing and Narrative Representation." In M. Gergen and S. N. Davis (eds.), *Towards a New Psychology of Gender.* New York: Routledge, 1997.

Gergen, K. "The Social Constructionist Movement in Modern Society." *American Psychologist,* 1985, *40*(3), 265–275.

Gesiakowska, J., and LoSardo, B. "Team Teaching and Interdisciplinary Courses." In S. J. Reithlingshoefer (ed.), *Developing Effective Interdisciplinary Instruction. Selected Papers from the Ninth Annual Conference on Nontraditional and Interdisciplinary Programs.* Fairfax, Va.: George Mason University, 1991.

Gilligan, C. *In a Different Voice.* Cambridge, Mass.: Harvard University Press, 1982.

Gruber, H. E. *Darwin on Man: A Psychological Study of Scientific Creativity.* Chicago: Chicago University Press, 1981.

Hayes, D. L. *Trouble Don't Last Always.* Collegeville, Minn.: Liturgical Press, 1995.

Jamieson, K. H., and Cappella, J. N. "Bridging the Disciplinary Divide." *PS: Political Science and Politics,* 1996, *17*(1), 13–17.

Ratigan, V. K. "In Search of Cornelia Connelly: Biographical Sources." *Records of the American Catholic Historical Society of Philadelphia,* 1996, *107*(1/2), 25–45.

Reinharz, S. *Feminist Methods in Social Science.* New York: Oxford University Press, 1992.

Reithlingshoefer, S. J. *Developing Effective Interdisciplinary Instruction: Selected Papers from the Ninth Annual Conference on Nontraditional and Interdisciplinary Programs.* Fairfax, Va.: George Mason University, 1991.

Richards, D. G. "The Meaning and Relevance of 'Synthesis' in Interdisciplinary Studies." *JGE: The Journal of Education,* 1996, *45*(2), 114–128.

Stewart, A. J. "Toward a Feminist Strategy for Studying Women's Lives." In C. E. Franz and A. J. Stewart (eds.), *Women Creating Lives: Identities, Resilience, and Resistance.* Boulder, Colo.: Westview Press, 1994.

Strub, E. M. *Informatio. Documentary Study for the Canonization Process of the Servant of God: Cornelia Connelly.* Rome: Sacred Congregation for the Causes of Saints, 1987.

6

THE INFLUENCE OF THE PERSONAL ON CLASSROOM INTERACTION

Helene Elting

Teachers are not abstract; they are women or men of particular races, classes, ages, abilities, and so on. The teacher will be seen and heard by students not as an abstraction, but as a particular person with a defined history and relationship to the world.

—Weiler (1991)

I have come to distrust any pedagogy that does not begin in the personal . . . I have come to distrust any pedagogy that does not conclude in the communal: subject to the checks and balances of the others, the teacher, the tradition, and the texts.

—O'Reilly (1993)

I REMEMBER an antediluvian era in which the professor acknowledged neither the students' embodied lives nor his own—the academic experience premised to be one of pure intellection. A tweedy, pipe-or-cigarette-smoking graybeard entered the class and gave his gift to his students: a fund of knowledge and ideas. The hour was carefully scripted, yet offhandedly interrupted by well-rehearsed "personal" anecdotes that somehow enhanced the professor's stature while divorcing him even further from us. I suppose that we, the students, found comfort in his seamless narrative, much as we would in a story with a precise beginning, middle, and ending. At the same time, I recall my frustrations with the unspoken biases of his interpretations and the single-mindedness of his arguments. The texts were his, not mine.

Of course, the flood waters of feminism have washed away those patriarchal practices. As Ruth Spack puts it: "The focus on the person teaching in the classroom and on the personal in scholarly writing has evolved out of feminist challenges to the Western academy's traditional privileging of objectivity. . . . Educator Kathleen Weiler points out that the feminist pedagogy that emerged from this research has adopted liberatory pedagogy's notion of transforming the teacher from lecturer to participant in the learning process" (1997, p. 10).

In the last several years of teaching English, writing, and women's studies at a small women's liberal arts college, much of my work has been an effort to help students recognize that they have points of view of their own that are discoverable through articulation. Constituting one's reality in words "for consumption" is no mean feat. To ask them for that kind of authenticity, I believe that I must ask as much of myself. The risk taking must be shared. I must model willingness to put forth provisional, partial positions vis-à-vis text or idea.

Is that really what students have come here for? Or do students want answers? What if the students do not cooperate in our joint venture, or wrest control of the text, or have nothing to say? I struggle with conflictual desires to produce a participatory, open-ended narrative around a given text and the far-less-noble impulse to squelch any resistance to my modulated discourse on the text. Mary O'Reilly's analogy of the writing classroom to a "heart of darkness" seems particularly apt here. In *The Peaceable Classroom* (1993), she divulges how easily she, the professor, begins to signify the students as the uncivilized "other" who might savage her script:

> One year, I discovered that I had begun to hate students. It came upon me while I was trying to pull together a conference paper on student-centered teaching. . . . That year, I had a class of twenty-four freshmen who were stonewalling me day after day. . . . English 102 sat silent, resistant, glowering: an implacable force brooding over an inscrutable intention, as Joseph Conrad might have put it.

> Is it any wonder that while writing up my conference proposal, I should scrawl across the top of it, like Mr. Kurtz under similar pressure, "Exterminate all the brutes"? This was the phrase that I was mumbling under my breath as my younger and presumably more idealistic colleagues talked about what was going on in their classrooms. And I began to think more and more of Mr. Kurtz as a prototype of the writing teacher. Indeed, the Heart of Darkness strikes me as appropriate metaphor for the classroom in more ways than one. It's here we confront chaos and misrule, savage silence, chills, fever, and, at least in some places where I've taught, failure of the air conditioning [O'Reilly, 1993, p. 64].

O'Reilly's confession points to what has become a crucial negotiation for me as to how to share the classroom space and collaborate in producing meaning around texts. Whose class is it, anyway? What does the space of the classroom actually feel like? Is it a contact zone (Pratt, 1991) or an "Oprah" show? Is it horizontally configured, or vertically? If "the process [that] feminist pedagogy seeks to describe is not the student's discovering a voice that is already there, but her fashioning one from the discursive environment through and in which the feminist subject emerges" (Finke, 1993, p. 14), how does the professor's position matter to the kind of environmental provision?

My frame question, "Whose class is it, anyway?" derives from a film with Christine Lahti and Richard Dreyfuss in which a physician and a patient struggle over the patient's right to make the choice to die. In *Whose Life Is It Anyway?* the doctor (Lahti) is a woman of strong principles that she wishes to practice upon her patient (Dreyfuss), a man who is paralyzed from the neck down in a car crash. From his supine position in the hospital bed, reduced to a kind of infantilism by his injuries, the patient demands that he authorize what happens to him, that he participate in his own treatment—that is, the patient refuses to allow his narrative to be subsumed by the competing narrative of the physician. What is radical about the closure to film is the physician's recognition of the patient's competency. The film suggests that, with renegotiation of power relations between physician and patient, outcomes are liable to change.

The precise nature of the medical encounter does not speak to classroom experience. But what does resonate is the destabilization of the equation between subject (doctor/teacher) and object (patient/student). The feminist classroom also puts the relation between actor and acted-upon into question. The professor, like the physician, possesses script and prescription. She is the "knower" who claims the education, expertise, and discourse required to examine the issue (pathology). The patient or "learner" is asked to collaborate (claim responsibility for) the "text" (the body). The notion of ownership of the text-body, the treatment-illness, is thus central to both conversations. Whose life or whose class is it, anyway?

In "The (In)visibility of the Person(al)," Spack remarks, "I believe that academics can and should find a way to open up a conversation about 'unspeakable things' and to make our classrooms safe places to continue the conversation" (1997, p. 25). Spack's statement refers specifically to the (in)visible differences of sexual orientation and race. I would argue that her thesis is also relevant to making the classroom a site for contending with such unspeakable things as disease and dying, pain and grieving.

In this chapter, I remember the discursive environment of my class during the semester when I, the professor, was emotionally and psychologically shaken by my mother's dying. I want to figure out how my role playing, subject positions, and speech acts gave permission for certain kinds of conversations to take place. Without discounting the particular "content" of the course, it seems to me that the politics of the class, to paraphrase Oedipus in Muriel Rukeyser's "Myth," "was what made everything possible." How, then, did practice of feminist pedagogy enable the self-fashioning of both students and professor when the latter admitted that she was "a particular person" who was losing her mother to cancer?

The Syllabus: A Well-Wrought Map

In fall 1993, I designed and taught a liberal studies/women's studies seminar that I somewhat ceremoniously titled "Subject Positions: Euro-American and African American Women Writing Fiction." I was able to propose its thematic orientation and structure its readings somewhat freely within the context of the larger curricular needs of the college. Funded by the English department, "my" course satisfied the college writing requirement as well as that of the feminism and gender studies concentration.

The ostensible topic of the course was the feminist narrative of agency. The syllabus that I handed out on the first warm September day of class was a well-wrought map of the months to come. In my habitual fashion, I worked hard to name the theoretical matrix of the course and to articulate its framing questions: "Our interest is the feminist narrative of agency. What I mean by this phrase is the story that contends with the female figure's capacity to make meaning in relation to others. The course theorizes that this productivity depends upon recognition by that 'other.'"[1]

I wanted to test and textualize the notion of "intersubjectivity" (Benjamin, 1988). The syllabus premised that "fictions seem to imply that certain kinds of interaction facilitate self-signification while other relations are disabling to the self." Underlying that assumption was the hunch that, without recognition, without relation to an other, the female figure's capacity for self-signification was implausible. The syllabus then spoke more particularly to how we would look at *Tell Me a Riddle, Dessa Rose, The House of Mirth,* and *Their Eyes Were Watching God*: "For instance, we want to know what an Olsen or Williams or Wharton might argue are practices that cause silence, submission, objectification, 'spirit murder'" [Williams, 1991, p. 73], death to the female figure.

I am certain that, on an intellectual level, I shaped the course content as a way of narrativizing the arguments of Maureen Mahoney and Barbara Yngvesson (1992). Their essay "The Construction of Subjectivity and the Paradox of Resistance: Reintegrating Feminist Anthropology and Psychology" focused on the question of what impels women to "resist domination and make change." In particular, Mahoney and Yngvesson's definition of "subjectivity" (p. 45) seemed to provide the logic for yoking together Stowe, Alcott, Williams, Morrison, Walker, and Olsen. To quote my syllabus: "Each of these American women writers considers the possibility of a female figure who acts, who has wants, and who must sometimes act against the grain in the face of contradictory desires."

The rationale for the syllabus is a bit disingenuous, however. Another narrative was already insinuating itself—albeit unconsciously—into the course. Why were we to look at the causes of "spirit murder" and of the "death of the female figure"? Why were we to ask "how a sense of self is consolidated or disrupted" (Benjamin, 1988, p. 19)? My guess is that I was trying to contend with the implacable reality that metastatic breast cancer was going to kill my mother. Was the course therefore endlessly and always about a woman in her mid-sixties sedated by morphine and confined to her second-floor apartment? Actually, no. The question that the course really sought to answer was: how does the daughter survive? For that, the professor had neither script nor prescription. "*That August summer,*" I wrote in my journal,

> *my mother had begun to wither away. "A big-boned woman," she had always called herself, slowly she lost her appetite. She wanted little but ginger ale and applesauce. Her taupe Sable sedan sat parked uselessly on the street. My father gave away her cherished oversized-head tennis racquet.*

The syllabus, then, embraced paradoxical intentions. It set out an agenda that fit within departmental norms and met institutionalized standards. As the first text of the course, this document predicted the issues that would be integral to course content. I want to stress the conventionality of its academic discourse. The surface text was about nineteenth- and twentieth-century Euro- and African American women writers. At the same time, the syllabus was utterly self-reflexive; unconsciously, my psychic and emotional investment in comprehending the death of the mother informed the symbolic economy of the course. I wanted my students to enable me to "solve a problem . . . to fashion a subject-position from which to produce (rather than repeat) language, a relation to particular disciplinary discourses and practices" (Finke, 1993, p. 25).

At the time that I made up the syllabus, I was haunted by my visual and auditory image of the closure to *Beloved*. Towards the end of Morrison's 1987 novel, the female protagonist, Sethe, lies prone on her bed, depressed and indifferent to life outside 124 Bluestone. Paul D comes into the room and desperately tries to rouse her from her inertia. He pleads with her to get up rather than to die on him.

Here was a mother who had lost all desire to act, who was utterly depleted of hope. Yet, it seemed to me that the final lines of *Beloved* were intimation that Sethe might revive in the presence and through the recognition of Paul D. Perhaps the grip of his hand and the persuasiveness of his words would inspire Sethe to hold on to life. "Subject Positions" would provide the discursive environment to share that interpretive stance and to find out whether my students envisioned Sethe's rebirth in the same terms that I did. I wanted them to tell me whether Sethe would get out of bed.

Narrative (In)commensurability and the Classroom Space

I came face to face with the dilemmas that arise out of teachers' own embodied existences.

—Ruth Spack, "The (In)visibility of the Person(al)"

My class that fall was a group of twenty women students at Bryn Mawr College. We sat scrunched elbow-to-elbow around a shiny seminar table. In my mind, I imagined that we would produce the model of (female) community that seemed infinitely possible at a small liberal arts college.

Each Friday after class, I would gather my sheaf of papers and books and make the four-hour pilgrimage by trains and taxi to my parents' apartment in East Norwich, New York. I would return to my own home outside Philadelphia every Sunday, exhausted, anguished, even tormented by the ravaging that I had witnessed. At 11:00 A.M. on Monday, I would greet my students and begin to teach.

That lived experience and subjective knowledge of fear, loss, abandonment, and disintegration became part of the narrative of the course. The seminar room became a site of negotiation for reconciling the seemingly incommensurate and competing narratives of American woman writer, professor, and students. In fact, the stories of Tillie Olsen, Edith Wharton, and Toni Morrison structured the discursive environment of the classroom in ways that related very specifically, even intimately, to my unspeakable feelings of hurt and uncertainty.

On the first day of class, I handed out Patricia Williams's postscript to *Alchemy of Race and Rights*. Why was "A Word on Categories" the first reading that I gave my students? Williams's first-person voice, at once autobiographical, self-questioning, at-risk, but also somehow brilliant and hard-edged, became a persona through which I could enact my own "ideology of style." She introduces herself as neither unitary nor whole, but rather "constantly reconfiguring herself in the world by (means of) a number of governing narratives or presiding fictions" (1991, p. 256). Williams makes palpably real for her readers the somewhat abstruse postmodernist notion of how the self fashions herself in relation(s) and in language. We are dazzled by her discourse as she narrativizes her sense of self as conflicted, confused, and angry.

> *It is Rosh Hashanah, the Jewish New Year. My mother comes to our home in Philadelphia. It will be her final trip. We put her up in a room for the "physically challenged" at a nearby hotel. I navigate her wheelchair across the damp tile floor of the Marriott's indoor pool so that she can watch her nine-year-old granddaughter, Lindsey, swim. My mother remarks on the gracefulness of her stroke, the likeness to my own free style in the water thirty years earlier. The holiday is cut short when the grinding pain in her spine countermands her wish to "celebrate" the year to come* [my journal].

"The Brass Ring and the Deep Blue Sea" was the first formal assigned reading for "Subject Positions: American Women Writers." In this opening chapter of *Alchemy of Race and Rights,* Williams explores her own radical and feminist pedagogical practice at Columbia School of Law. She recuperates specific episodes from her course "Women and Notions of Property" that suggest that, for Williams, teaching is a performance art, and that crisis shapes her performance.

Williams begins with the assertion that "subject position is everything in her analysis of the law." Her discourse is self-reflexive and spliced with slang as well as legalese: "I am very depressed. It always takes a while to sort out what's wrong, but it usually starts with some kind of perfectly irrational thought such as: I *hate* being a lawyer" (p. 3).

Williams then segues from these remarks on her own mental state to an examination of a case involving a runaway slave named Kate. She describes "an 1835 decision from Louisiana, involving the redhibitory vice of craziness" to her reader. The question that the case poses is as to the state of mind of the aforementioned slave: is Kate "crazy" or "only stupid"? Williams challenges the reader/student to realize the "subject position" of the silent, oppressed black woman who is denied voice under the law. Curiously, Williams does not speak to the case precisely; in fact, she gives no opinion as to the merits of *Icar* v. *Suar.* Rather, she shares her sense of her own embodied existence with the reader:

> As I said, this is the sort of morning when I hate being a lawyer, a teacher, and just about everything else in my life. It's all I can do to feed the cats. I let my hair stream wildly and the eyes roll back in my head.
>
> So you should know that this is one of those mornings when I refuse to compose myself properly; you should know you are dealing with someone who is writing this in an old terry bathrobe with a little fringe of blue and white tassels dangling from the hem, trying to decide if she is stupid or crazy [p. 4].

These personal remarks seem utterly tangential to the "text" itself: are we to focus on a slave named Kate or the narrator in her terry bathrobe? My sense is that Williams wants her readers/students to see and feel both subjects. What strikes me as marvelously clever and complicated here is Williams's series of rhetorical maneuvers that negotiate among her own "discomposed" persona, the reader, and the ostensible textual subject: the stupid-or-not-stupid, crazy-or-not-crazy slave named Kate.

Williams appeals to us to empathize with her own feelings of alienation and anger toward the patriarchal establishment. She does so by asking that we decry the abuse directed at the historical figure, Kate. Neither we her readers nor, by extension, her students are quite sure who or what is the subject of her discourse. The boundaries between teacher and text, between teacher and students, are suddenly blurred.

Williams's law students react as disgruntled consumers. Her parables defy their explanation, her positions bewilder and alarm them. They feel betrayed by this professor who offers them fragments and asks them somehow to construct their own texts. They assume that the class should be a well-wrought argument modeling a logical development of idea.

> My students, most of whom signed up expecting to experience that crisp, refreshing, clear-headed sensation that "thinking like a lawyer" purportedly endows, are confused by this and all the stories that I tell them in my class on Women and Notions of Property. They are confused enough by the thought of dogs and women as academic subjects, and paralyzed by the idea that property might have a gender and that gender might be a matter of words.
>
> But I haven't been able to straighten things out for them because I'm confused too. I have arrived at a point where everything I have ever learned is running around and around in my head; and little bits of law and everyday life fly out of my head in weird combinations. Who can blame the students for being confused? On the other hand, everyday life is a confusing bit of business. And so my students plot my disintegration, in the shadowy shelter of ivy-covered archways and in the margins of their notebooks [pp. 13–14].

Williams's admission is the point for me. She confesses that her "depression" and "confusion" inscribe her pedagogy. She cannot separate out the legal discourse from the "little bits of everyday life." Moreover, she struggles to clarify and organize the text of her teaching so that it does not become an exercise in self-reflexiveness. She is teaching out of that confusion and depression. The politics of Williams's classroom, the conversational dynamics and the meanings produced there, are necessarily shaped by her pain and anger and power. Is this a discursive environment through which her students can fashion their own voices?

> *I must say good-bye to what never was. Wittingly and wistfully, I constructed a good mother whose warmth and devotion answered to my huge needs for affection. Her cool blue eyes had always insisted on the*

fiction of that figure. I never listened. I worked on her image. Cancer has deprived me of that fantasy [my journal].

We turn to Tillie Olsen's *Tell Me a Riddle* (1956) and Nancy Chodorow's essay "Gender, Relation, and Difference in Psychoanalytic Perspective" (1988).[2] The title piece, "Tell Me a Riddle," invites us to problematize "unspeakable ideas" about a mother's anger at her family's neediness, a daughter's feeling of abandonment and lack of mothering, and the wasting of the body by metastatic liver cancer. Much of "Tell Me a Riddle" takes place within the maternal consciousness; the narrative often centers on Eva's unspoken resistance to her family's will. I give my students Rukeyser's "Myth" and suggest that they envision Eva as sphinxlike, immobile, a marker/monster in the journeys of others.[3]

We explore the daughter's attempt to consecrate her mother's life by narrativizing it. I ask my students to sense Vivi's passionate need for her mother's recognition of a shared past:

> And Vivi's tears and memories, spilling so fast, half the words not understood.
>
> She had started remembering out loud deliberately, so that her mother would know the past was cherished, still lived in her. . . .
>
> Lowering a hem: How did you ever . . . when I think how you made everything we wore. . . . Tim, just think, seven kids and Mommy sewed everything we wore [Olsen, 1956, p. 87].

What does Vivi wish to produce through her recuperation of childhood memories of washday, of reading books, of nursing?

I ask my students what they make of the mother's resistance to remembering: "Stop it, daughter, stop it, leave that time." Why does Eva stifle Vivi's desire to sentimentalize the past? I challenge my students to explain the roots of the protagonist's repressed anger toward her children. Why can Eva not tolerate "day after day, the spilling memories?" As their professor, I cannot transmit that information to my students; I have not mastered the text. Rather, "Tell Me a Riddle" becomes a site for our collaborative production "of language, of relation to particular disciplinary discourses and practices" (Finke, 1993, p. 25).

I piece together fragments from trips taken to see her. She seems to wait for me—I hope—sphinxlike, humbled, finite in strength.

> *I tell her what I see and how I make those images mean for me. I hear her gravelly voice too cheerfully chime, "Rise and shine. . . ."*
>
> *I see the green wool carpet on stairs, living room and landing.*
>
> *I see the dark brown wood Queen Anne baby grand piano and feel the warmth of dry heat from the radiator at which I sit. I look out at snow and rain. I see her at the pink formica rectangular kitchen table eating Ebinger's coffee cake or Thomas's date nut bread with cream cheese, reading the Times Magazine Section. The word "cholesterol" had not been coined. I see her pulling me on a sled on South Oyster Bay Road.*
>
> *I think that, finally, my capacity to connect past present and future gives her something material. I can embody her. She can feel through me. I make of her life a text to share. She survives in me. She thanks me often* [my journal].

My students label Eva's cancer "psychosomatic." They sense the old woman's sphinxlike impenetrability . . . but for them, Eva is more monster than mother. They view her as pitiable but not heroic. We talk about the good-enough mother, separation-individuation, and the children's unwillingness "to accord the mother her own selfhood" (Chodorow, 1988, p. 7).

> Now one by one the children came, those that were able. Hannah, Paul, Sammy. Too late to ask: and what did you learn with your living, Mother, and what do we need to know? . . .
>
> Lennie, suffering not alone for her who was dying, but for that in her which never lived. . . . From him too, unspoken words: *good-bye, Mother, who taught me to mother myself* [Olsen, 1956, p. 108; emphasis mine].

Our exegesis takes us to the realization not only of maternal anger but also to the acknowledgment of the children's feeling of lack of environmental provision by the mother. Hannah, Paul, Lennie are selfish, perhaps, as they watch their mother die, but they are also needy. They want recognition from her. Is intersubjectivity possible?

Ultimately I structure our conversation around Eva's granddaughter, Jeannie. I make Jeannie into a protagonist and stress her capacity for ministering to the needs of Eva. Jeannie senses Eva's desire to let go and urges her grandfather: "Help her to die." Even as Jeannie seems to teach her grandfather about how to care for and relate to his dying wife, she inspires me. I identify quite literally with the fictional character, floating signifiers and semiotics be damned.

> *I sit by her bedside and cry silently in the half-darkness.*
>
> *I tell her that I will be back within the week. I tell her that she will be bathed, that her sheets will be changed, that the nurse will take care of her* [my journal].

Midsemester, the class reads Edith Wharton's *The House of Mirth* ([1905] 1994). Wharton's authorial voice endlessly compels me as it insinuates itself into her storytelling. I hear her ambivalence, her self-doubts, and her conflictual sense of self in both her fiction and her autobiographical memoir. In fact, my construction of Wharton's authorial identity as an American Victorian woman writer inscribes our discussion.

We begin with portions of Wharton's memoir, *A Backward Glance* (1934). I want my students to have a feel for the material culture as well as for the family dynamics that help to produce Wharton as writer. Several of the excerpts, taken from chapters entitled "Knee High" and "Little Girl," represent Wharton's adult memory of her mother's neglect of her emotional and intellectual needs. These anecdotes describe Lucretia Wharton as a "chilly woman who censored her daughter's reading, denied her writing paper, withheld physical affection, and met her literary efforts with 'icy disapproval'" (Showalter, 1991, p. 102).

> *She spoke of herself in the third person as "Mrs. Elting." I could not get close to her no matter how well I did in school or sports. She liked the medals and honors and trophies but did not seem to see me* [my journal].

From that site of memory, we turn to *House of Mirth* itself. I pose several framing questions that belie my point of view toward the text. "What prevents Lily Bart from developing a sense of agency and authenticity? What does she seek? What interactions are disabling to her? Why does Lily die?" Like Eva and Patricia Williams (and me), Lily Bart seems thwarted in her capacity to integrate pieces of herself and to articulate who she is for others. I want us to discover what produces this "lostness." I put forth the argument that Wharton produces a female figure who has internalized a sense of self as less than, as other (Chodorow, 1988). Not knowing how to "mother herself," Lily seeks "rescue" from the first moments of the novel.

I offer five collaborative presentation or paper topics on *The House of Mirth* to generate student interaction around primary text and their own writing. Included are issues of (1) Selden as spectator or voyeur, (2) the crisis of masculinity in the novel, (3) the significance of the *tableau vivant*, and (4) that of Simon Rosedale's position outside the dominant class structure. I want to stress that the assigned text mattered to the kinds of conversation I authorized as professor. We problematized the novel from a variety of angles while focusing our lens on "the feminist narrative of agency."

My students balk at my arguments about Lily. To Bryn Mawr College women, she is a shallow narcissist who has not got her values straight. They disdain both her obsessive concern with how she appears as well as her manipulation of men. They voice a postfeminist impatience, even incredulity, at her lack of capacity to empower herself. My investment in their reading of *House* becomes a defense of Lily Bart. I try to protect her against my students' callow impulse to belittle her efforts to achieve autonomy. I ground my counterargument in the text by proposing a fifth and last topic: "Explore Lily's homelessness and its connection to her lack of self-possession. If Lily often seems to be a child fearful of abandonment, does she have good cause? Consider Lily's lack of agency as she is disinherited, excluded, cast ashore. How do Mrs. Peniston, Mrs. Trenor, Mrs. Dorset figure in this struggle to achieve a stable sense of self? Is Lily a somewhat infantilized female figure whose quest is for the good mother?"

> *I bring Thanksgiving dinner to my parents' apartment, a rental unit into which they had moved some two years earlier. My mother sleeps fitfully on the hospital bed installed in the bedroom. I go through her dishes and pots in order to set the table. I find the grater which she used thirty years ago to make egg salad and the orange Creuset pot which held her brisket. I remember that the frozen vegetables never seemed to thaw. I don't think that she knows it is a holiday . . . or that I am in the next room* [my journal].

We spend the last several weeks of the semester on *Beloved*. I ask students to return to Patricia Williams so as to understand the admixture of pain, anger, confusion, and promise that suffuses Morrison's novel. Both Williams's essay "On Being the Object of Property" and *Beloved* thematize the relation of the living to the dead and suggest that one must let go but also hold on to the spirits of those one loves. Williams remembers her intersubjective relation with her godmother, Marjorie:

> Two years ago, my godmother Marjorie suffered a massive stroke. As she lay dying, I would come to the hospital to give her meals. My feeding the one who had so often fed me became a complex ritual of mirroring and self-assembly. The physical act of holding the spoon to her lips was not only a rite of nurture and sacrifice, it was the return of a gift. . . . The quiet woman who listened to my woes about work and school required now that I bend my head down close to her and listen for mouthed word fragments, sentence crumbs. I bent down to give meaning to her silence, to her wandering search for words [p. 229].

When we turn to *Beloved,* my students surprise me. They do not want to flesh out what might become of Sethe, the mother, so much as they want to speak to her daughter Denver's promise for the text. Denver has been neglected, they say, Denver has not been given environmental provision by her mother, yet she survives. In spite of Denver's belief that she's "lost her mother," she goes forth and discovers a female community that recognizes her need for nurturance. "She turning out fine. Fine" (Morrison, 1987, p. 266).

> *"It's Helene, mommy."*
> *"I know, darling. . . .*
> *"Good-bye, darling."*
> *"Good-bye, mommy"* [my journal].

My mom died the last day of the semester.

Closure: What Was Lost and What Was Won?

> *Teaching, then, I would argue, not only engages the unconscious, but is implicated in the very formation of the unconscious itself. The unconscious constitutes what Felman has called a kind of unmeant knowledge which escapes intentionality and meaning, a knowledge which is spoken by the language of the subject, but which the subject cannot recognize, assume as* hers *and thus appropriate.*
>
> —Finke, 1993, p. 15 (emphasis added)

What happened to the performance art of teaching in the presence of personal crisis? What did the students learn from me, from one another, from the assigned texts? What did I, the professor, take from collaborating in the production of meaning around fictional narratives within the context of a female community?

Texts became a way for me and for my students to apprehend and constitute the "unspeakable" realities of death and survival in words. The female community of the class—separate as they were from my homeplace—engaged ideas of agency and authenticity, fractured subjectivity, spirit murder, maternal anger, and environmental provision for the daughter from their own sites of feeling and knowledge. The class was not a heart of darkness; I was not Kurtz. No conversion took place. Their disparate convictions about how to live in the world became part of the narrative of the course and of my story as well.

NOTES

1. The vocabulary of my syllabus borrows from the rhetorical strategies of Mahoney and Yngvesson (1992). I lifted their definitions out of the original context; it seemed to me that this displacement was essential to making the theory manifest and real for my students.
2. Though not transparently evident in this essay, Chodorow's vocabulary was seminal to course development. Notions of "agency and authenticity," "environmental provision," etc. derived from her analysis of the child-parent bond (1988).
3. The notion of Eva as sphinx, suggested by Marianne Hirsch in *The Mother/Daughter Plot* (1989), connects "Tell Me a Riddle" to the Oedipus text. I argued that Sophocles' drama might provide an interpretive stance for making sense of the title and italicized choral elements of the Olsen story. The Oedipal plot also resonates in the third part of the story, where Eva inches along the sand: "Once she scooped up a handful, cradling it close to her better eye; peered and flung it back. And as they came almost to the brink and she could see the glistening wet, she sat down, pulled off her shoes and stockings, left him and began to run" (p. 93). I asked my students whether Eva's journey toward death initiates a heightened consciousness of the mystery of life.

REFERENCES

Benjamin, J. *The Bonds of Love: Psychoanalysis, Feminism, and the Problem of Domination.* New York: Pantheon, 1988.

Chodorow, N. "Gender, Relation, and Difference in Psychoanalytic Perspective." In H. Eisenstein and A. Jardine (eds.), *The Future of Difference.* New Jersey: Rutgers University Press, 1988.

Finke, L. "Feminism, Voice, and the Pedagogical Unconscious." *College English,* 1993, *55,* 7–27.

Hirsch, M. *The Mother/ Daughter Plot.* Bloomington: Indiana University Press, 1989.

Mahoney, M., and Yngvesson, B. "The Construction of Subjectivity and the Paradox of Resistance: Reintegrating Feminist Anthropology and Psychology." *Signs: Journal of Women in Culture and Society,* 1992, *18*(1), 44–73.

Morrison, T. *Beloved.* New York: Plume, 1987.

Olsen, T. *Tell Me a Riddle.* New York: Bantam, 1956.

O'Reilly, M. R. *The Peaceable Classroom.* Portsmouth, N.H.: Boynton/Cook, 1993.

Pratt, M. L. "Arts of the Contact Zone." *Profession, 91,* 1991.

Showalter, E. *Sister's Choice: Tradition and Change in American Women's Writing.* Oxford: Clarendon Press, 1991.

Spack, R. "The (In)visibility of the Person(al)." *College English,* 1997, *59*(1), 9–31.

Weiler, K. "Freire and a Feminist Pedagogy of Difference." *Harvard Educational Review,* 1991, *61,* 449–473.

Wharton, E. *The House of Mirth.* Boston: Bedford Books, 1994. (Originally published 1905.)

Wharton, E. *A Backward Glance.* New York: D. Appleton-Century Company, Inc., 1934.

Williams, P. *The Alchemy of Race and Rights: Diary of a Law Professor.* Boston: Harvard University Press, 1991.

7

CREATING A COLLABORATIVE CLASSROOM

Sara N. Davis

MUCH HAS BEEN WRITTEN about feminist values and theories as they have been translated into feminist pedagogy. Collaboration is one of the critical values that have been developed in the setting of the feminist classroom. Conceptually, collaboration describes several different relationships within the classroom, always connoting a sense of students in interaction—with the professor, with each other, and with the material. Viewing the classroom as collaborative moves one away from a static image of both knowledge and place to an environment in which ongoing discovery becomes a paramount goal. In this chapter I describe a course I designed and taught, "Feminist Styles of Inquiry," in which collaboration underlies the *process* that occurred within the classroom, the *content* that was covered, and the system of *relationships* that developed.

The course was planned to present students in the social sciences with a sense of alternative ideologies and priorities that can guide research, as conceptualized by a large body of feminist scholars.[1] Throughout the semester students read and discussed feminist critiques of traditional social science and then went on to read examples of research that was informed by feminist theory. Simultaneously, as a class, we planned, conducted research, and analyzed data for two different studies. We collaborated on all aspects of research design. In other words, together the students and I decided what it was we would study, collected and assessed sources for the literature review, determined analytic methods, trained to code the data, and, finally, discussed the results.

Feminist Teaching Practices

Several years ago, for an entirely different project (Davis, 1994), I observed several literature classes. My concern was with the ways in which personal experience became a legitimate tool for literary interpretation. I was struck by the vast differences in attitude among teachers with regard to a variety of input from students.

One professor, after a long monologue describing the meaning of a Hemingway story, asked the class if they understood what he had been saying. One student tried to rephrase a concept in line with an experiential interpretation. The professor responded by saying: "Well, this is a very philosophical story, as I've already made clear; Hemingway is not interested in a sociological analysis of his character." He then continued his exegesis of the story.

By contrast, a second professor began discussion of an Ibsen play by saying, "Tell me what you think of the characters." Her interaction with the class occurred largely through asking questions (often quite general) and then encouraging the students to develop their response to them. This approach frequently stimulated discussions in which divergent views emerged and were debated. Students were guided through the process of building an argument for their case.

These two approaches led to very different experiences on the part of the students. The first professor supplied students with a wealth of information about scholarly work on interpretation. This style of teaching has aptly been described with a financial metaphor (Maher, 1985, p. 31, taken from Freire) in which deposits of knowledge are made in the vaults of students' minds. In this view, as in a safe deposit box, information is inert capital that resides in the mind until it is withdrawn for future needs. The goal of the professor in this model is to make the deposit—to be sure the student has taken in the correct information. The second professor facilitated students in drawing on their life experiences to extrapolate from and give meaning to the dilemmas within the play. She used her expertise to guide them in constructing an argument and in showing them what to look for in reading a play (for example, what information can be gleaned from stage directions). If one were to also cast this process in terms of a financial metaphor, it would be couched in terms of investment. With investment there is also an initial deposit, but the accent is on growth. In this case, the emphasis is less on the professor's initial deposit than on the joint process of co-investing—student and professor working together to bring about development of the investment.

As a result of the different processes within the two classrooms, there were very different constructions of knowledge. In the first, the teacher-as-expert was the single person with a voice. He imparted his distilled version of the history of interpretation of the Hemingway story. The emphasis was ultimately on information, pieces that the student could carry with her upon leaving the class and that would fill notebooks to be consulted in the future. Students often find this approach tremendously reassuring. After all, they are in school to learn, and here is expert knowledge provided by an acknowledged scholar far more experienced than they. Moreover, this is the model that students have traditionally encountered.

The knowledge that arises from the second class is more fluid, constructed during the class. The students came to know Ibsen's play through their active engagement with it. In their discussion, this particular group of students came to see moral dilemmas as a result of their response to the play. They struggled to come to an understanding of the nature of honesty. Another group of students might have selected another element that was of greater concern to them. It was not inevitable that the discussion developed as it did. Rather than a logical sequence of facts, for students there will remain the memory of a developed argument. However, the teacher used her expertise to guide the development of the argument—for example, she posed questions based on her knowledge of past interpretations of the story or directed students to details that enhanced their arguments. In this class, many students were actively engaged in responding to other points of view, struggling with their own understanding of the characters and of the moral dilemmas they felt were posed in the play. This active processing enabled students to learn about the particular play—but also about how to approach a literary work, build a critical argument, think about opposing points of view, and talk to their peers or colleagues.

The alternate vision embraced by the second class put the emphasis on students constructing their own understanding. The assumption is that students must actively engage with the material for it to become meaningful. The emphasis shifts from a concern for knowledge as truth to a concern with the process of arriving at a version of knowledge. What did they learn? They learned multiple approaches to the interpretation of this play. They struggled with competing interpretations, which have the potential to enlarge any single person's perspective. They learned how to engage in an intellectual discussion with, and value the contributions of, their peers. In a recent book, Gross (1997) employed the metaphor of the theater to describe collaborative teaching. In her conception, teachers and students jointly create a curriculum in the same way that players and director work together to bring a vision of the world to the theater.

Clearly, there is no single model of the feminist classroom (Kimmel's Chapter Three in this volume), but there are certain ideas that seem to appear across perspectives, mainly, emphasis on both process and content, which are often viewed as inseparable. Many of the ideas exemplified in the practices of the second class I have described are similar to processes often seen in the feminist classroom: constructive, experiential learning. In describing the feminist and personalist teaching methodologies, Homan (1997) has said, "Students and teachers take learning and the construction of knowledge seriously. They are not only critical thinkers; they become interdependent, reflexive, constructive thinkers" (p. 254). However, many (see for example Kimmel and Worell, 1997) feel that in addition there is a requisite content component: the centrality of women. In my course, "Feminist Styles of Inquiry," my intent was to use processes that enabled experiential, interactive learning sensitive to feminist critiques of traditional education and research. At the same time, I wanted to create experiences for students that focused on women and their experiences within our culture. My goal was to guide students through a wealth of material that would give them access to critiques of the assumptions traditionally associated with psychological research and provide the opportunity to rethink research approaches. Constraints of the seminar necessarily led to research projects that were kept simple but selected with emphasis on how they could contextualize women, look at their sense of agency, and come to consider how their own presence influences the course of the research.

Maher sets out a number of critical ideas that appear in reviews of feminist teaching: "A pedagogy appropriate for voicing and exploring the hitherto unexpressed perspectives of women and others must be collaborative, cooperative and interactive. . . . It assumes that each student has rights and potential contributions to the subject matter. Its goal is to enable students to draw on their personal and intellectual experiences to build a satisfying version of the subject, one that can be used productively in their lives. . . . The teacher is a major contributor, a creator of structure and a delineator of issues, but not the sole authority" (1985, p. 30).

One can see emphasis in this quotation on the student: what she brings to the class, her experiences in the classroom, and what she takes away from her experience. Notably, Maher's description of feminist teaching practices veers away from a set concept of the knowledge to be gained and redirects the focus to constructions of a "version." In an early paper describing feminist teaching methods, Schniedewind (1983) provides five guidelines: atmosphere of mutual respect and trust, shared leadership, cooperative structures, integration of cognitive and affective learning, and a call to activism. Again, process and interaction, as well as social learning, become paramount; "learning comes to be seen as an evolving creation. Knowledge is no longer seen as a ready-made body of stuff that is received and repeated in tones of sacredness" (Homan, 1997, p. 255).

Description of the Class

"Feminist Styles of Inquiry" was an honors seminar open to students who had already completed the research methods course required of all psychology majors. The course was taught at Rosemont College, a small, Catholic women's college in suburban Philadelphia. All of the students in the class had previously studied statistics with me. The goal was to engage students in alternative conceptions by way of examining the practices of traditional psychology and to provide some hands-on experience in carrying out the research. This was an elective course designed to sensitize students to research that was concerned with women's experiences and expectations. The structure of the class combined discussion of readings with research experience. The collaborative format of the class became as important an educational goal as the content, and the two can be seen as intimately related.

Process

The procedures that I established were geared to creating an atmosphere of active learning through engagement in viable short-term research. It was my goal that students come to understand the kinds of research decisions that need to be made and how to arrive at them. I also wanted to create the type of classroom in which students could realize their own resources and learn about those of their classmates. I provided a basic framework for the course, which we followed with some modifications. It consisted of a set of readings that moved from critiques of mainstream psychology to articles describing how feminist scholarship would bring about change, and finally to some examples of exemplary feminist work. Against this theoretical backdrop, I planned for two research projects over the course of the semester. I selected the first one, an analysis of personal advertisements. Although I was reluctant to impose this choice, I felt it was necessary in order to be able to start work immediately. However, despite my selecting the topic, the students determined the parameters of the research. This study became more involved and time consuming than I had anticipated, and so our second project, interviewing, was shortened.

The interview topic, as well as procedures for the project, were selected within the class. This class could easily have been expanded beyond the semester allotted, to bring greater depth to each study.

Feminist critiques of traditional psychological research provided ideas for how we might structure our research projects. We explored the idea that peoples' lives are very complex and do not fit neatly into categories and therefore cannot adequately be understood by empirical methods that ignore context, complexity, and competing explanations. We also reflected on the role that the experimenter plays in any research. At every stage of the research process, decisions have to be made with clear potential for introducing biases into the work. How the questions are formulated, how the control group is selected, how the coding scheme is determined, and so forth, all reflect assumptions that influence the outcome. It is important to be aware of this and consider how women have often been portrayed in psychology: as passive, dependent, and in many ways less developed than men (Unger and Crawford, 1996; Sherif, 1979, 1992).

The first research project involved content analysis of personal ads, in which people seek a relationship by advertising in popular magazines, newspapers, and so forth. One goal of the study was to become aware of the expectations and requirements of and for women and men in differing contexts. We believed that these ads reflected societal expectations that would vary among subgroups and can be seen as both a reflection of what women value in themselves and what they believe promotes their cause in the eyes of others. We were interested, for example, to see if women were as likely as men to list professional achievements and education as assets or whether they felt it was more beneficial to present themselves in terms of physical characteristics. Personal ads presented a readily accessible source of data that could easily be studied in a situation with such limited time constraints.

The plan to study personal ads immediately required the class to make many decisions collaboratively. Initially, we collected advertisements from multiple sources: general newspapers and magazines, periodicals targeted at specific groups, ads on the Internet. We had access to periodicals representing input on various dimensions: urban-suburban, gay-straight, affluent or working class, local Philadelphia or geographically dispersed, and so forth. Our first decision was how to focus our initial analysis.

To aid in this determination, we visited the library as a class and explored what research had been done previously; we then made decisions about what we would need to read to do the research. In addition to reading research relating directly to our topic, we were also interested in ways of contextualizing our research, for example, in the area of stereotyping.

As we looked at possible sources, we discussed what we might want to pursue and why. This often led to my explaining why certain research might help to broaden our perspectives. The explanation enabled a kind of modeling of how to do research that would not exist in the traditional classroom setting. Analyzing personal ads is an area in which I had done no previous research, so I was reacting extemporaneously to possibilities. This factor seems somewhat unique; we were all looking at this material and grappling with it for the first time. It seemed to minimize the power differential—I was embarked on the same discovery process. Yet my previous research experience allowed me to be a guide, to offer insights.

Using the research we had found in our literature review, we were able to compare the coding schemes that had been used by others. As a group, we tried various schemes with our data and came to decisions about what would work and what sort of modifications we needed to make. Once we had created a workable coding scheme and resolved issues in using it, we jointly coded the ads from the *Philadelphia Inquirer.* We initially looked simply at the stated goal of the advertiser and compared men and women. What did people seek—romance, friendship, long-term relationship, etc.—and how did these goals vary by gender? From there we moved to a more complex analysis in which we examined what people offered as attributes about themselves and what they sought in a partner. These attributes might be status indicators such as education or financial situation; personality attributes such as sense of humor; interests; or such physical dimensions as weight or muscular development.

Having worked this far communally to provide a foundation, each student chose an additional, specialized periodical and focused on a theme of particular interest to her. The individual papers complemented the joint work that had been done and enabled comparisons among various special groups. The group process was thus enhanced as individual students contributed specific interests. This helped us look at patterns across a variety of groups—more than we could have done without breaking into subprojects. Thus there was continuous interplay: the group work laid the foundation for the individual projects, which in turn broadened the range that was covered and fed back into the collective information base.

The ads provided a window into the aspirations of numerous groups. By varying the source, one had access to differences in expectations by class, sexual orientation, and ethnicity. For example, during the semester philosopher Susan Bordo (1993) gave a talk on campus in which she discussed the pressures on ethnic groups to conform to a mainstream, white, middle-class vision of beauty. One of the groups she included in this category was African Americans. A student objected, stating that African

Americans were not subject to the same notions of beauty as were European Americans. The student hypothesized that African American women advertising in a mainstream magazine such as *Philadelphia* might be more likely to present themselves in terms of middle-class and white ideals of female beauty; however, women who advertised in periodicals with an African American audience might be dealing with alternative images—for example, less concern with being thin. She decided to pursue her hypothesis by analyzing the ads in these two types of periodicals. Thus, the ads provided a window for gauging differences in subgroups in the African American community.

For the second study, the selected data-gathering method was interviewing and the chosen topic was the educational experience in a women's college. For this project, we read theoretical articles on the nature of the interview (Franklin, 1997; Reinharz, 1992) and then during class designed and role-played interviews following different theoretical conceptions. Using categories designated by Franklin, students experimented with different interviewer stances, ranging from the interviewer maintaining her distance so as not to interfere with the flow of "true" information from the informant to an engaged relationship that leads to joint construction of meaning during the course of the interview. When role playing using these different interview approaches, students found that they were much more forthcoming if the interview permitted mutual exploration of a topic than if the interviewer assumed a formal stance and maintained her distance. These insights became valuable as students made decisions regarding their own interviewing projects.

We then jointly selected a topic and created guidelines for the interviews students would conduct. The interviews were designed to examine undergraduate experiences at a women's college. We were interested in whether students felt that a women's college provided a climate in the classroom and on campus that was perceived as beneficial. We had to decide how many interviews should be conducted and with whom (age, ethnicity, current students as opposed to graduates, and so forth). Students chose to conduct semistructured interviews in which they assumed an active role. In this way, they were able to create a degree of uniformity across interviewers. In their final analyses, class members were concerned with both the topic and the process: how they were able to facilitate the interviews and what they learned about student interests and experiences. They reflected on how they interacted with the interviewees and how that affected the process. Again, there was a critical interplay between form and content. Students experienced how their behavior, comfort level, and skill had an impact on the interview process.

The focus of the classroom was therefore collaborative. Much of the class time was devoted to working together and thinking through the research. This engendered a collective approach to research and allowed me to become a contributing member of the group. However, there were limits to working jointly. In each project, the final report was done individually. In this way, it reflected the interests as well as the work of each student. It also enlarged the depth of each project, adding new components to the overall topic. Students were able to take an aspect that was of interest to them and develop it. When the results were shared, everyone had access to how it was developed.

In addition to discussion of the class process, it is important to describe the relationships that developed and our understanding of how the content was developed. Any attempt at separating the process from the content or relationships that existed in the class is artificial because these three components are essentially intertwined. How the content arose and was approached resulted from the processes that were engaged in and the system of relationships that inhered. Yet, to describe the class, I must engage in this division. I do so knowing that it means separating what is intricately interwoven.

Relationships

Many levels of relationship existed within this class. Some arose from the nature of college instruction; others were stimulated by the particular design of the class. I think it is important to examine the benefits and limitations of the idea of collaboration and of democracy within the classroom. Although each situation brings its own particular instantiations, it is worth considering the interplay of roles in this classroom.

Collaboration and Authority Working Together

One of the important issues that consistently arises when talking about the collaborative classroom is how collaboration can occur given the power inherent in the role of the professor. One of the issues that has arisen for me in writing this chapter is the selection of pronouns. I keep moving between *I, we,* and *they*; *me, us,* and *them.* This is an indication of how much I feel the pull of simultaneously casting myself in two roles. Attempting this degree of collaboration was new for me—and perhaps even newer for the students. I felt that I was a part of the ongoing process, and at the same time I was clearly the leader. In an attempt to avoid dominating the process, I tried to set things in motion and then encourage students to proceed from there.

I ask myself, is it naïve to think of sharing power? Can one give away or share one's power? It is frequently explained that to think of eliminating power is naïve because society has invested the professor with authority—even in making it possible for her to create a classroom in this manner—and at the same time the institution requires from her things like grades that clearly reflect her power. Can the professor, then, in good faith, abjure this power? Yes, in some ways she can minimize her power. Students can play an important role in determining the direction of the course and participating in their own evaluations. They can be important in the day-to-day process of the course. Feminist classrooms typically create a relatively communal setting by placing students and the professor physically in a circle within the class, so there is no evident position of authority. On the other hand, the professor is not merely another member of the class. She has greater knowledge of the discipline and of how to facilitate a class. These attributes need not be looked at as representing a negative hierarchy; instead, they make it possible to model authority with grace.

When confronting this question, I was quite surprised. My remembered experience was of sharing power and authority; I experienced a wonderful sense of collaboration and sharing of the work in the class. After all, many decisions in the class were jointly made. I frequently looked to the expertise of the students as we chose what topics to consider and then created procedures. However, I was in charge of the class and felt the responsibility to move it along. It was precisely the looseness and the milieu of working things out that required my guidance. I had a sense of the shape of the semester and what I wanted to accomplish; I had to keep things moving in that direction. It was within that structure that students had choice and input. Thus, for example, student input affected the pace of the course and the directions that discussions and research took.

Institutional Realities

When evaluating classroom innovations, it is important to remember that certain realities are inherent in the institutional structure. Among these is the necessity of formal evaluation, the requirement for the professor to give grades to students. Again, power becomes an issue. Does the role of the evaluator interfere with collaboration? This has practical, not just theoretical, implications. Since one is presumably giving grades at various points throughout the semester, this issue of power is there, hovering over the class interactions. Since the professor has the power to grade, the collaborative process is potentially compromised to some extent. Further, grades can interfere with a process that depends on student participation.

Students can feel betrayed that their work, which often reflects their experiences, has not been sufficiently valued. Some begin to withdraw from classroom participation if they do not receive the grade they anticipate.

Clearly, then, power is a double-edged sword in these situations. In making the class interactive, you give students considerable power for determining the outcome. Once it is no longer mainly a function of how well you organize and prepare the classes but rather how willing students are to engage in a process, then you have indeed ceded much of this power. Student upset about grades can be somewhat ameliorated by (1) being very clear about criteria that are used for grading, (2) giving students an opportunity for self-evaluation that is considered when the grade is conferred, and (3) requesting evaluation and feedback of the course at both midsemester and the end of the term. One of the final assignments for this course was for students to write a self-evaluation reflecting their view of their own participation in the course and what they learned—and therefore what grade they believed they deserved. This allowed quieter students to demonstrate how they felt they had participated. Although I bestowed the final grade, I felt that this was a chance for students to have input and demonstrate what they felt they had contributed and learned. They were also asked to state which other students they had learned the most from in class, and to evaluate the class itself. I considered this input very seriously when giving grades.

Joint Experiences

In the collaborative structure of this classroom, complex relationships were formed that permitted diverse skills of the participants to become part of the process. Contrary to the traditional class, where the professor shows only her most polished side, I joined the students in the beginning stages of a new research project. As a result, I could not rely on a thorough grounding in a subject but instead showed my thinking as it developed. This was very different from a research group being supervised by a professor in her area of expertise. My expertise consisted more in how to approach the research than in knowledge about the specific topic. In this way, I modeled the process of working and making decisions. I did my thinking and figuring out right along with the students. Thus, when we did a literature search I too was encountering possibilities for the first time and sharing my reasoning with the students about what we might want to read and why. This is quite different from the process of planning readings for a class, or being familiar with a topic through my own research and reacting on the basis of years of experience. I found this interaction to be invigorating. I was challenged and stimulated by thinking like this, and I felt I was demonstrating something I could not teach in any other way. I looked forward to classes, and I think the students did too.

An interdependence existed in this class. Collaboration consisted of willingness on everyone's part to work together. It required active participation of all students. Clearly there is never equivalence; some are always more overt in contributing than others. However, there was surprising enthusiasm and involvement; people felt committed to the work we were doing. What was particularly interesting here were the many areas of expertise that appeared. People had special skills that allowed them to become leaders during particular segments. Thus, even though not everyone can easily participate in a theoretical discussion, individuals may have aptitudes that will surface in a class that calls on a variety of skills. For example, there was a student who was very clearheaded about coding. When we were attempting to come to decisions about how to use the coding scheme we had developed, this student was particularly good in making precise, reasoned decisions about how we should do it. Everyone respected this ability.

Collaboration took the form of mutual dependency. People stepped in to assume responsibility, and this happened without assignment. One student handled interlibrary loans; another created a spreadsheet for tabulating our data. Thus, we were all able to rely on each other to facilitate the process of the study.

Collaboration includes a rich but complex set of relationships. Working together collaboratively with a group of people who are coming together for the first time and without background experience in the topic requires facilitation, someone to guide the process. Presumably, the set of interactions would be somewhat different in each group, and one could predict the necessity of differing degrees of leadership coming from students; yet it seems that the professor is ultimately responsible for providing the structure that enables the collaboration to continue.

Content

"Changing what we teach means changing how we teach" (Culley and Portuges, 1985, p. 2). It becomes obvious that the reverse is also true: changing how we teach means changing what we teach. In a collaborative model, it is important for students to have input into what is taught, to make decisions about what they feel they need to learn. Their interests and responses focus the course to some extent and help to define the content.[2]

In looking at the concept of mastery in *The Feminist Classroom,* Maher and Tetreault (1994) consider how "pedagogy means the entire process of creating knowledge, involving the innumerable ways in which students, teachers, and academic disciplines interact and redefine each other in the classroom, the educational institution, and the larger society" (p. 57).

Among the ideas fostered is that what we know is constantly evolving and need not reside solely in the professor. If women's experiences become central, both the process and the content within the classroom are influenced.[3] Sometimes they are united so that, for example, one can study women's agency by becoming an active constructor of knowledge. Women's personal narratives (see Cottrell's Chapter Four in this volume) can become a way of illuminating a subject. They can also be used as building blocks to construct understanding of a situation and then extrapolate to develop a broader understanding of women's experiences in general. For this reason, feminist researchers frequently reflect on their own experiences (for example, Stack, 1997; and Datan, 1986) and use this reflexivity to inform their analyses.

This loosening of constraints inevitably leads to questions about the proper material for a class. Is there certain material that "must be covered"? How can ways of knowing that accept the intuitive and affective be introduced into the ongoing flow of the course? A class like this can be repeated but never replicated because each group constructs a different milieu and approaches situations in ways that are meaningful to them. For example, exploration of diversity arose naturally in this group but might not in another, or it might assume a different form. In making the class their own, it evolved in ways that reflected these particular students. Because the focus was on the process of creating knowledge rather than imparting it, the content would shift in certain ways with each group.

Additionally, the content became a learning of values and of behaviors. For example, the value of respect for others, reliance or mutual dependency, and active pursuit of one's intellectual interests develops from interacting with others and can never be learned through lectures. One has to be actively engaged. However, this is not to imply that there was not important content. We were dealing with an extensive feminist literature deeply concerned with how best to discover and represent women's experiences. We transformed major ideas from this literature into our own research, which helped us understand some aspects of women functioning in our society today.

What Did Students Learn?

This class veered from traditional classroom practice in several important ways. If the traditional model envisions the teacher-as-expert, whose role is to impart knowledge to a group of students, then this interactive and collaborative model is clearly a giant step away. If the goal of a class is to master a predetermined set of facts or knowledge, then again we veered away in our construction of knowledge. Yet I believe this class was successful for having just this distance from traditional expectations. Students experienced directly a large number of ideas relevant to women's lives and explored how social scientists can most profitably study them.

As described above, assuming mastery as a goal means an emphasis on learning how to learn—becoming sensitive to oneself as a learner becomes a significant goal. Becoming sensitive to oneself as a member of society is a different but critically important aspect of knowledge that can only be experienced through active engagement. I have heard the criticism, often voiced by other professors, that students learn more from professors than from each other. In response to that position, I return to the contrasting examples of teaching given at the beginning of the chapter. When students are presented with information without the opportunity to process it, they tend to remain at a certain distance from it. On the other hand, as they become actively engaged in the classroom process—for example, in performing all the processes involved in coding material—they learn because the issues become meaningful. There develops a complementarity between the content and the effects. Thus, students learn about how women function in society and have the opportunity to examine their own behavior. As they learn how women can become empowered, they experience their own empowerment through engagement. They also learn that there are multiple ways to understand an issue. The goal is not a single interpretation that can encompass all instances, but rather interpretation that allows for multiple perspectives.

Students were enthusiastic about this class and engaged with the process. They were able to draw on my expertise without my being in the position of the "banker" depositing knowledge. They responded to the opportunity for engagement by assuming responsibility and taking an active role in constructing understandings of the material. This is an investment I believe will mature.

NOTES

1. See, for example, Jayaratne and Stewart (1991), Parlee (1991), Fine and Gordon (1991), Riger (1992), Bohan (1993), Reinharz (1992), and Crawford and Marecek (1992).
2. One interesting example of this was designed by Vipond and Hunt (personal communication), in which an entire course was devoted to students designing its syllabus. This engaged them in doing extensive reading in cognitive psychology, deciding what the critical pieces were, and defending

those inclusions in the course. By the end of the course, students had read what they would read in a traditional course, but they had discovered it on their own and made decisions about the value of the work—instead of being told that it was foundational.

3. See Sebrechts, Chapter Two of this volume, for discussion of the impact of any minority group coming to experience majority.

REFERENCES

Bohan, J. S. "Regarding Gender." *Psychology of Women Quarterly,* 1993, *17,* 5–21.

Bordo, S. *Unbearable Weight.* Berkeley: University of California Press, 1993.

Crawford, M., and Marecek, J. "Psychology Reconstructs the Female, 1968–1988." In J. S. Bohan (ed.), *Seldom Seen, Rarely Heard.* Boulder, Colo.: Westview Press, 1992.

Culley, M., and Portuges, C. "Introduction." In M. Culley and C. Portuges (eds.), *Gendered Subjects: The Dynamics of Feminist Teaching.* Boston: Routledge and Kegan Paul, 1985.

Datan, N. "Corpses, Lepers, and Menstruating Women: Tradition, Transition, and the Sociology of Knowledge." *Sex Roles,* 1986, *14*(11/12), 693–703.

Davis, S. N. "Reading Together: Discourse in the Literature Classroom." In A. Barsch, G. Rusch, and R. Viehoff (eds.), *Empirische Literaturwissenschaft in der Diskussion.* Berlin: Suhrkamp, 1994.

Fine, M., and Gordon, S. M. "Effacing the Center and the Margins: Life at the Intersection of Psychology and Feminism." *Feminism and Psychology,* 1991, *1*(1), 19–27.

Franklin, M. B. "Making Sense: Interviewing and Narrative Representation." In M. Gergen and S. N. Davis (eds.), *Toward a New Psychology of Gender.* New York: Routledge, 1997.

Gross, P. *Joint Curriculum Design.* Hillsdale, N.J.: Erlbaum, 1997.

Homan, K. "Creative Teaching. Hazards of the Therapeutic: On the Use of Personalist and Feminist Teaching Methodologies." *Horizons,* 1997, *24*(2), 248–264.

Jayaratne, T. E., and Stewart, A. J. "Quantitative and Qualitative Methods in the Social Sciences: Current Feminist Issues and Practical Strategies." In M. M. Fonow and J. A. Cook (eds.), *Beyond Methodology.* Bloomington: Indiana University Press, 1991.

Kimmel, E., and Worell, J. "Preaching What We Practice: Principles and Strategies of Feminist Pedagogy." In J. Worell and N. G. Johnson (eds.), *Shaping the Future of Feminist Psychology: Education, Research, and Practice.* Washington, D.C.: American Psychological Association, 1997.

Maher, F. "Classroom Pedagogy and the New Scholarship on Women." In M. Culley and C. Portuges (eds.), *Gendered Subjects: The Dynamics of Feminist Teaching*. New York: Routledge, 1985.

Maher, F., and Tetreault, M.K.T. *The Feminist Classroom.* New York: Basic Books, 1994.

Parlee, M. B. "Happy Birthday to *Feminism and Psychology.*" *Feminism and Psychology,* 1991, *1*(1), 39–48.

Reinharz, S. *Feminist Methods in Social Science.* New York: Oxford University Press, 1992.

Riger, S. "Epistemological Debates, Feminist Voices." *American Psychologist,* 1992, *47*(6), 730–740.

Schniedewind, N. "Feminist Values: Guidelines for Teaching Methodology in Women's Studies." In C. Bunch and S. Pollack (eds.), *Learning Our Way: Essays in Feminist Education.* Trumansburg, N.Y.: Crossing Press, 1983.

Sherif, C. W. "Bias in Psychology." In J. S. Bohan (ed.), *Seldom Seen, Rarely Heard.* Boulder, Colo.: Westview Press, 1992. (Originally published in J. A. Sherman and E. T. Beck [eds.], *The Prism of Sex: Essays in the Sociology of Knowledge.* Madison: University of Wisconsin Press, 1979.)

Stack, C. B. "Writing Ethnography: Feminist Critical Practice." In M. M. Gergen and S. N. Davis (eds.), *Toward a New Psychology of Gender.* New York: Routledge, 1997.

Unger, R., and Crawford, M. *Women and Gender: A Feminist Psychology.* (2nd ed.) New York: McGraw-Hill, 1996.

8

ENCOURAGING PARTICIPATION IN THE CLASSROOM

Estelle Disch

SEVERAL YEARS AGO in my course on the sociology of gender, an entire seventy-five-minute class period passed in which not one woman spoke. Women constituted two-thirds of the class. I am fully aware that women and girls are less likely to talk than are men and boys in coeducational settings (American Association of University Women, 1992; Orenstein, 1994; Sadker and Sadker, 1994; Sandler, 1987), but I was not prepared for such an extreme illustration. There were dynamics occurring in the class that I believe might explain the women's silence, focusing on a man who repeatedly argued (unimpressed by facts to the contrary) that men really had less power than women. He frequently asserted that women filed false restraining orders to "get back" at men and that men's violence against women was no worse than women's violence against men. Once he attempted to convince the class that rapists got a raw deal in the criminal justice system. Although some women and men had challenged him at the beginning of the course, this group eventually gave up. While a couple of men in the class would still react nonverbally (as in rolling their eyes when he spoke), the women became silent and passive.

This situation provoked me to develop new means of communication with students in an effort to bring silenced voices, especially like those of

I would like to thank Rita Arditti and the editors of this volume for extending helpful suggestions to me as I developed this essay.

the women in that particular course, into the classroom discourse even when faced with a hostile environment.[1] In this chapter, I describe some strategies I have used that support the oral participation of *all* students in my classes. An effect of this has been the participation of women at a level more proportionate to their numbers. Since that day when the women were all silent, I have changed my teaching strategy to be more attentive to the unspoken messages in my classrooms. In particular, I have added weekly writing and short in-class responses to an array of community-building strategies that I have been using for many years.[2] All of these are described here.

My current teaching occurs in a public urban commuter university with twelve thousand students. The average age of the students is twenty-seven. About 55 percent of them are female; about 25 percent are people of color. Most are working class or middle class and were raised Catholic. A large proportion are the first in their families to attend college. As a white, fiftysomething, professional woman from a privileged Protestant background in a long-term relationship with a woman, I have very little in common with my students. Thus, in the midst of trying to get women and other silenced students to talk, I am simultaneously attempting to bridge a vast array of cultural gaps to establish communication with everyone in the class. My classes range in size from twenty-two to forty-five. I primarily teach sociology—sociology of gender and an internship in social services—plus a general-education diversity course for lower-division students. The students in my sociology courses are typically one-third male and one-third people of color. Those in my general education course are approximately half women, half men, and one-third or more people of color.

During my thirty years of teaching, I have used various combinations of the strategies described in this chapter in six different colleges, including private elite schools and public working-class schools, and have used them in classes as large as seventy students. In this chapter, I also discuss ways to adapt some of the strategies to large lecture courses (fifty or more students).

As a teacher, I try to create a productive and relatively safe learning environment in the classroom. Respectful discourse is paramount. Without it, too many people are afraid to join the conversation. Without it, the classroom discourse also tends to be dominated by people accustomed to public speaking and assertive argument—which leaves out the vast majority of women, most male students for whom English is not a first language, and many shy men as well.

Multicultural awareness is crucial to respectful conversation. By *multicultural* I refer to diversity of all sorts (racial, ethnic, class, religious, sexual, gender, age, and ability). As I attempt to build a sense of community in the classroom, I am continuously attentive to diversity, both in the syllabus and in how I call upon people to speak. I hope that within a relatively respectful atmosphere students can openly engage with each other about what they are learning.

The strategies described here are all designed to welcome a wide range of voices into the classroom discourse, whatever their message. Although I do not use all of these strategies in every class, I do use a substantial proportion. I have divided the strategies into two categories. The first has to do with establishing communication and relative safety right at the beginning of the course. I use all of these regardless of course content and am committed to spending a couple of classroom hours and a few administrative hours on this to get the classes off to a good start. The second category includes interactive strategies that can be used at any time during the semester. How I use these varies by subject, class size, and the level of the course.

Establishing Community and Safety

There are a number of strategies that can be used initially for building community in the classroom.

Ground Rules

Ground rules for discourse, including ways to disagree respectfully, can be very helpful in building community. Several of my colleagues develop ground rules with the class, convinced that the class has more investment in a list that they themselves generate. I personally hand out the ground rules, spend about five minutes on them in the first class, ask for additions in the next class, and request that students follow them. I include the ground rules in a handout entitled "Student/Teacher Rights and Obligations as I See Them," which has the discourse ground rules embedded in a section entitled "Human Rights/Human Obligations."[3] As I introduce this document to the class on the first day, I emphasize the helpfulness of confidentiality and request a nod from each person in the room as to whether they are willing to respect this before we begin. No one has refused thus far, but if they did I would simply point out that anything said in class was potentially public and would invite the people who chose not to agree to let us know if they changed their minds in the future. Under my definition of confidentiality, people agree to obscure the identities of people in the class when talking about the course to others.

Another aspect of the guidelines that I emphasize at the beginning of the first class is the importance of not sharing material about oneself that does not feel safe to share, to the extent people are able to predict that. I tell the class about an incident that occurred years ago on the first day of a sociology course, in which a woman introduced herself as an incest survivor, started to cry, and never returned to the class. I encourage people to remain silent when what is most pressing on their minds is something they don't feel safe sharing. Finally, I emphasize the fact that there are potentially many hidden diversities in the room of which we should be mindful, including the high probability that many people grew up in abusive families; have been victims of violence; are gay, lesbian, bisexual, or transgendered; have invisible illnesses or disabilities; or perhaps have religious or political views outside the mainstream.

During the second class, I ask students to propose additions to the ground rules, sometimes after discussing them in small groups. If there are any to which the class can agree, we add them. Occasionally there are one or two additions. Although I have never invited the class to delete items from the list, I suppose that this could be done during this discussion as well. Later in the semester, if the conversation becomes disrespectful, we can refer back to the guidelines, remind ourselves to follow them, and adapt them if necessary.

Icebreaker and Introductions

In the last four years, I have used an icebreaker focused on diversity that helps students meet some new people in the class and serves to help them look at where their attitudes about various differences came from. The point of this is to raise the issue of prejudice with a minimum of blame, as people get to look back at where they learned their attitudes—typically in systems of socialization over which they had little or no control as children. An example is, "Share with your partner your earliest memory of gender difference. Where and how did you learn about gender differences? What values were attached to what you learned?" In this exercise, people practice active listening in pairs as one person talks and the other listens. Each person in the pair gets a minute or two to answer the question. They switch partners for every new question. At the end of about half an hour, each person has met six or seven new people. This can be done in any size class and the questions can be tailored to the topic of the course. Even in a large lecture hall with fixed seats, people can talk with their neighbors and then do a minimum of moving around in order to meet a couple of additional people.

In the final pairing, I ask people to introduce themselves to each other in preparation for introducing the other person to the class. Prior to these introductions, I ask the class to generate a list of things they might like to know about each other. I emphasize that this is an opportunity to practice active listening, note taking, and oral presentation skills, and that it is up to the person whose turn it is to speak to say only what feels comfortable. Thus, for example, even though the class might be interested in knowing about disabilities, a person with a hidden disability who does not feel like coming out is free to remain silent on that issue. In a large class, these introductions can happen in smaller groups.

Learning Names

Given that it is nearly impossible to develop any effective sense of community without knowing people's names, I take this issue very seriously. I usually allow thirty to forty minutes of class time for doing this. Currently, I have two strategies for learning names. First, I make a name sign for each student and ask her or him to hang it over the edge of the desk for the first few weeks.[4] This helps me immensely. After looking at the name signs for a couple of classes, we play the "name game," which challenges all of us to actually memorize everyone's name. (I learned this game about twenty-five years ago and have no idea who invented it.) To do it, the group sits in a circle with everyone's name sign hidden. The first person to go says her or his own name. The next person says the first person's name and his or her own. The next person says all three . . . all around the circle. People at the end groan and laugh (I usually arrange to go last in this exercise). As we get toward the end, people who do it successfully frequently receive spontaneous applause. Anyone who has trouble with names can ask people to repeat their own names around the circle. I write on the board any names that seem difficult to pronounce or that have unusual spellings.[5] Once we complete the circle, we switch seats and allow time for several courageous volunteers to attempt to say all the names. In a large course (of more than, say, fifty), the name game is very difficult. In that case, I recommend using the name cards (perhaps throughout the semester) and encourage students to learn the names of the people with whom they tend to sit. I would address people by name during any question-and-answer interactions in a large lecture class, leaning on the name cards for my source of information.

Class List

With students' permission, I create a list of names, street addresses, phone numbers, and e-mail addresses to circulate to the class. I also collect this information for people who choose not to be on the list so that I can reach them myself if I need to. Usually all but a few students are willing to have their names circulated for purposes of networking, for finding out what happened if they miss class, and for group projects (when applicable). Circulating such a list might not make sense in a very large class; there, I might instead suggest that people exchange addresses and phone numbers with the people they tend to sit with. I would, however, collect such information for my own use. I usually set up e-mail distribution lists for each class, so that I can send out announcements or comments between classes to those having e-mail. This is a viable strategy in any size class, once the list is set up.

Interactive Strategies

In addition to these initial strategies, ongoing support for the classroom community can be fostered in several ways.

Structured Discussion in Small Groups During Class

Classroom discussion works best when people feel comfortable talking. A classroom process that offers people time to practice expressing their thoughts in smaller settings before opening the discussion to the whole class helps students clarify their opinions, reactions, and confusions. I require weekly short responses to the reading in most of my courses, which means that the vast majority of the students arrive in class having done at least some of the reading and having reflected upon it as well (see also Crawford and Suckle, Chapter Nine of this volume, for a discussion of weekly responses).[6] Thus, many students arrive in class with thoughts to share.

For the first half of the semester, I start most classes with students in groups of two, three, or four—perhaps for only five to ten minutes—addressing some aspect of the day's topic. If I am planning to lecture, I design questions for the groups that segue into the lecture. Sometimes I ask each group to report back to the whole class via a spokesperson. I ask the spokespersons to rotate, so that different people report back each time. I sometimes ask each small group to discuss a different topic, allowing students to choose which they would like to discuss in the small group.

This helps students meet various people in the class beyond the people with whom they typically sit.

If I want to discuss specific aspects of the reading with the class interactively, I frequently write a short ungraded quiz for students to answer alone and then in small groups.[7] I design the quiz to address the issues that I think are most important in the reading. As we go over the quiz and the class reports their answers, I am able to easily address what I want to cover. After working alone and then in small groups, a large proportion of students are usually ready to join the conversation when discussion is opened to the whole class. Students are enthusiastic about this. They seem to enjoy being "tested" without negative consequences and apparently appreciate the opportunity to discuss the answers together.

Short Assessment Techniques and Short Feedback

Many faculty think that if we teach something, the students learn it. But when we read papers or exams we are frequently shocked at the depth of misunderstanding of things that we believe we had made perfectly clear. A technique for finding out what students learn while simultaneously hearing from everyone in the class is to use one or more classroom assessment techniques (Angelo and Cross, 1993). I have successfully used variations on one of their techniques: the "one minute paper," which asks students to write briefly about what they understood or what they found confusing. This can be adapted to ask students to name what additional information they would like to know, what points they wish had been made in the discussion, or how they are feeling about what transpired in the class. These *anonymous* responses provide an opportunity for students who are afraid to publicly admit confusion, ignorance, or disagreement to have a voice in the discourse as the teacher reviews in the next class what students report.

I recently used a variation of the one-minute paper following a relatively volatile discussion on pornography in the course on sociology of gender and learned very useful information. In the classroom discussions about pornography, the focus had repeatedly drifted toward first-amendment issues, obscuring the opinions of many people who felt deeply troubled by pornography but were silenced in the conversation. In this case, I put together a short questionnaire on attitudes toward violent and nonviolent pornography that included a question asking for contributions to the conversation that had not yet been voiced. The results of the survey indicated that nearly everyone in the class was very troubled by violent pornography and almost everyone thought that something should be done about it. Their suggestions typically suggested censorship or public education. We would never have known this without the survey. Using this method, the students who had felt too shy to "fight the first amendment" were able to have their views known without engaging in what they felt would be a losing battle in class. The widespread agreement about the offensiveness of violent pornography was also illuminating and comforting to most of the class. In bringing the responses back to the class, I was able to give voice to the opinions of those who had felt silenced, while protecting their anonymity (including that of a couple of students who had come to my office to discuss this).

Midsemester Course Evaluation

I do a midsemester evaluation in every course I teach.[8] Students fill out an anonymous questionnaire, and in classes of fewer than thirty-five I typically hand one back to each person and we read them aloud together. In larger classes, I ask people to analyze them in small groups and report any recommendations or problems back to the whole class. This gives voice to everyone's opinion. I always provide a 10-point scale, asking how comfortable people feel about talking in small groups and large groups, and asking them also to check reasons why they are quiet when they are. Some of the options on the checklist include insecurity (shy in large groups, insecure speaking English), fear of being put down (fear of being judged negatively, already felt put down by a classmate, already felt put down by the teacher), not having done the reading, feeling out of place politically or as a minority in the room, etc. I analyze these responses using a show of hands, so that everyone can look at the pattern of comfort and threat. A close analysis of this scale helps me, and the class, understand where the insecurity lies and what kinds of hurt have already occurred. If anyone reports that they have felt put down by me, I apologize and invite whoever said that to come and tell me what I said if they have the courage to make themselves known (occasionally someone actually does so). This gives us an opportunity to acknowledge that the classroom is not equally safe for everyone, and to encourage respect. I also ask students what they as individuals can do to make the course better for themselves, what their classmates can do, and what I can do. There is inevitably a substantial group of students who request that the quiet people join the conversation. I cannot honestly say that the quiet people truly become an active part of the classroom conversation, but at least their reality is named, and many of their classmates invite them to join in.

If I were teaching a large lecture course, I would analyze the evaluations on my own and bring the conclusions back to the class, or invite a few students to volunteer to analyze them with me outside of class and perhaps ask the students themselves to report back to the class. I sometimes hand out the midsemester evaluation at the end of one class and process it in the next one so that I have a chance to read the forms before we discuss them together. Although I ask people to be respectful on the forms and let them know that we will be reading them together in class, occasionally someone writes something harsh ("I wish student A would talk less"). If I have some lead time I can think more carefully about how to handle any awkward situations that emerge.[9]

All of the interactive strategies just described can be employed quickly and relatively easily. Faculty concerned with coverage can therefore use them without sacrificing in-class time. Given that people seem to learn more effectively when not simply sitting passively in lectures and memorizing for tests, most of what is described here enhances learning since students are asked to reflect upon what they are experiencing in the course, in terms of both content and process. The strategies do, of course, involve time outside of the classroom, since they require careful faculty attention.

Group Projects

Collaborative learning seems to be one of the most effective learning methods for college students (Light, 1990; Matthews, Smith, and Gabelnick, 1996). Although a commuter school poses a big challenge to any sustained group work outside of class, I have developed limited ways of doing this with some success. I provide some class time for planning and allow students to work largely on their own outside of class. I give individual grades rather than team grades since I have not (thus far) been willing to dedicate the large amounts of classroom time to group projects that would be necessary if I were to require intensive teamwork.

One example of what I call a semicollaborative project is a multicultural literacy assignment that I use in an internship course in sociology (Disch, 1998). The goal of this assignment is to help future human service providers acquire research skills useful in quickly learning about a racial or ethnic group about which they know little or nothing, using resources available in most university libraries. By the end of this assignment, students are hopefully in a better position to ask appropriate questions and do some research. I assign students to groups and ask them to use what they learn to decide how best to help a hypothetical person in need of human services. I provide the hypothetical cases, and students are assigned to study a person or family that belongs to a racial or ethnic group different from their own. Students do research on their own but get together in class to apply their learning to the hypothetical case. During class time, the students divide the work of exploring various aspects of the particular group's culture and history. The students' task is to alert the rest of the class to the importance of cultural awareness in designing a strategy for learning more about the person's needs or for helping the person. Although in the past I have asked each person to present his or her findings to the whole class, these presentations could be made by one member of the team to shorten the presentation time.

Another group project I have found useful in a general-education course for first-year and second-year students is to create a fact sheet related to something that is not covered effectively in the course. Linking this to a library literacy assignment, I require that the fact sheet use at least one scholarly article, one book or encyclopedia, one piece from popular media on microfiche, and one Web source. I ask students to assess the reliability of their information as part of their fact sheets. The fact sheets are designed to enhance our understanding of a book we are reading.[10] Each team has to introduce its fact sheet to the class orally and is asked to be on call for further information as the topics come up in the book.

Relatively little time is involved for this exercise. We spend one class session in a computer lab in the library for a demonstration about the Web. During that session the students locate their Web sources and decide who will search out the other sources. Students meet in class for another twenty minutes comparing notes about what they have learned and deciding who will type up the findings into a two-page fact sheet. In this process, the students gather a lot of useful information, bond as a group as a result of our "field trip" to the library, and have a lot to add to the classroom discussion related to their topics. Everyone's input is important, and everyone's voice is heard. We have a very productive discussion of the reliability of sources as people compare scholarly articles to other kinds of print media.

Oral Presentations

Certainly a way to engage people in classroom discourse is to require that everyone give an oral presentation on something relevant to the course. On the other hand, most teachers know that oral reports can be deadly if not well prepared. I have worked this out in the sociology of gender course (typically a class of forty) by requiring short presentations (four minutes each) distributed throughout the last eight weeks of the semester. I require that the research paper for the course be completed by week six and then ask people to present what they learned when their topic (or a related one) comes up in the course. I provide guidelines for the oral presentations that emphasize the importance of keeping the class awake and engaged. I have also asked that the research papers address controversies in the field of gender studies, so we frequently have animated discussions following the presentations. Thus, rather than reading term papers alone in my office at the end of the semester, I have each student bring a small piece of that learning back into the classroom. In a large class, I might consider requesting abstracts from each student to distribute to the class, or ask people to present their findings to each other in small groups of others interested in that general topic. This past semester, the students expressed very strong interest in the reports, saying that they were learning a lot from their colleagues (though some of them regretted the time the reports took, since there was less time to discuss the reading, and a few hated having to do their own reports).

Disrespecting the Queue

As a facilitator of classroom discussion, I frequently call on people who have not yet spoken even when others are waiting to speak. I simply acknowledge that I am calling on that person next because she hasn't yet spoken. I recently had one hostile response to this, but ordinarily it works well.[11] Following the incident I described at the beginning of this essay in which no women students spoke, I phoned the first ten women students in the class whom I could reach during my office hour and asked them to participate more. I promised that I would do my best to call on them as soon as they raised their hands so that they would not have to sit waiting nervously for their turn to talk. The encouragement resulted in women talking about half the time for most of the remaining classes—a big improvement over that one depressing class session. Although the discourse was not particularly spontaneous, it was at least more gender-balanced.

Power and Grading

I ordinarily structure courses so that students have a lot of control over their grades by way of attendance (20 percent), weekly reading responses (10 percent), and sometimes self-evaluation (10 percent). I also typically assign a couple of pass-fail assignments that, if done, are almost impossible to fail (such as a visit to a gender-related agency off campus, or watching for gender messages during a thirty-minute TV program). I typically control about 60 to 70 percent of the grade. I own this power, provide clear grading criteria, offer feedback sheets on written work, volunteer to read drafts of papers, allow rewrites on at least one paper each semester, and sometimes do not count the lowest grade. Although I grade on attendance, I do not grade on participation. Occasionally I receive complaints about my attendance requirement, but not often.

Receptivity and Resistance

In general my students have been very receptive to these teaching techniques. The vast majority evaluate the courses positively, and even people who do not seem excited about learning from each other usually tolerate the process and seem to learn a lot anyway. I imagine that students who really cannot stand a highly interactive classroom in the context of a labor-intensive course either never sign up or are among the couple of students who drop the courses right away. (A few times, I have offered independent study to students who needed the course but just could not tolerate the interactive demands of the classroom.) The strategies described have helped me feel better about the teaching I am doing and the learning my students are doing. The vast majority of my students enjoy hearing others' ideas, genuinely like learning from each other, appreciate a classroom in which they can get to know people (this is especially important in a commuter school), and report that they take their learning out of the classroom and apply it to their lives—talking with friends, partners and families, sharing course readings, and making social sense of the difficulties they encounter as individuals.

In spite of this, I frequently encounter difficulties such as resistance to some of the material ("Social oppression can't be *that* bad"), men and women who are impatient with each other's experiences, and occasional women's studies majors who do not want to be in a class with men and do not want to study them. I sometimes need to manage cultural insensitivity or cultural conflict as well, since most of us harbor prejudices that can hurt others, even when we mean no harm. I also have experienced blowups in various courses that left me counting the minutes until the end of the semester and had me on the phone to colleagues trying to fix an unfixable situation.[12] In spite of occasional incidents like those, I have faith in these teaching strategies. Without them I imagine that the likelihood of classroom explosions would be much higher and the learning much less. As I currently handle classes, I can often spot the tension and address it before it gets out of control (as do Crawford and Suckle in the next chapter). For example, a couple of years ago I discovered via weekly reading responses that three white working-class men in my gender course each had experiences that they described as "reverse discrimination as a result of affirmative action." I was able to open conversations with them about what they had been through, offer career counseling where appropriate, and attempt to educate them about affirmative action from a position of empathy for their lost or postponed career goals. (They hoped to become police officers or firefighters and were going to have to wait longer than they wanted in order to get into those careers since people of color and white women were now in competition with them for jobs.) Rather than have this issue erupt in a volatile way in class, we addressed it calmly.

I greatly enjoy teaching and appreciate the wealth of experiences that my students bring to the classroom conversation. I am always learning, always challenged, and pressed to continue growing every time I design a new syllabus and start a new semester. I am nurtured by watching students become empowered by their learning and am inspired by the open communication that emerges as people who are usually silent find ways to use their voices.

NOTES

1. I have described this situation in more detail in Disch, E. "Gender Trouble in the Gender Course: Managing and Mismanaging Conflict in the Classroom." In E. Kingston-Mann and T. Sieber (eds.), *Against the Odds: Teaching and Learning at an Urban Commuter University in the New Millennium* (under consideration by publishers).
2. In reflecting on my own teaching in relation to the principles and strategies of feminist pedagogy and the suggested faculty responses to student resistance described by Ellen Kimmel (see Chapter Three of this volume), I think that I would qualify as a committed practitioner of feminist pedagogy in gender-mixed settings.
3. The first two sections of this handout relate to student-teacher rights and obligations. Students are frequently unaware of their rights to such things as a syllabus, clear course requirements, clear statements as to when written work and exams will be returned, etc. They are also frequently unaware of their obligations to do the reading before class, keep appointments with faculty, get to class on time, etc. I spell out many of these kinds of things and then discuss human rights and human obligations. Anyone wanting a copy of this handout can contact to me at the Department of Sociology, University of Massachusetts Boston, 100 Morrissey Blvd., Boston, MA 02125-3393 (phone 617/287-6256 or e-mail estelle.disch@umb.edu).

4. If you don't have time to make the name signs yourself, the students can make their own. However, I find that if I make them in bold print on my computer I can read them more easily, especially if the class is relatively large. The students also seem to appreciate that I have taken the time to make a sign for each of them. When I read the roll call the first day of class, I clarify pronunciation and ask what people want to be called in class. I then make the signs using the names or nicknames that the students prefer.
5. Occasionally while reading the class list on the first day, or during the name game, someone whose first language and name is not English will ask to be called by an Anglicized nickname. When this occurs, I check with them regarding what they really prefer and let them know that the class has the capacity to learn their real names if they prefer to use them. Then I work with the whole class to practice the pronunciation of the person's name. About half the time, the person prefers his or her own name and seems relieved to be able to use it in the class.
6. I require that these responses be turned in during class on the day they are due. I do not accept late submissions. I grade the responses pass-fail. If a student has obviously done the reading and addressed whatever question(s) I have raised, she or he passes. Students who have done some reading but do not address the question(s) have one week to rewrite the entry to my satisfaction. Students may skip several responses and still get full credit. For example, in a recent semester there were thirteen possible reading responses. Students who submitted ten passing responses received an A for this part of the course. Those submitting nine received a B, those submitting eight received a C, etc. The reading responses typically constitute 10 percent of the final grade.
7. Eric Mazur uses this technique in a large physics lecture course at Harvard University. In the middle of his lecture, he puts a single multiple-choice question on an overhead slide and asks students to answer it. The students then have one minute to convince another student sitting nearby that they have chosen the correct answer. He reports that after this short conversation, students who change their answers do so in the correct direction the vast majority of the time. A secondary effect of this interactive strategy includes higher attendance. See the videotape "Thinking Together: Collaborative Learning in Science," available from the Derek Bok Center, Harvard University, Cambridge, MA 02138.
8. See note 3 on the previous page to receive a copy of the midsemester course evaluation I use.

9. A few semesters ago someone did, in fact, request that a particular student talk less. I was able to call the student and alert her as to what was on the form and talk with her about her role in the class. She was not offended and had already figured out that she needed to talk less. Since there were forty students in the class, I had already decided to ask small groups to process the evaluations and report back. The student and I decided that it would make the most sense for me to distribute the questionnaire that included the comment about her to her small group so that she could address the comment directly with part of the class. Although this was obviously a breach of a random redistribution, I decided that under the circumstances it made the most sense.
10. The book in this case was *Coming of Age in Mississippi* by Anne Moody (1968). Students investigated several civil rights organizations and other issues, events, and people Moody refers to but on which she does not elaborate in depth (SNCC, NAACP, CORE, *Brown* vs. *Board of Education,* Jim Crow laws, KKK, Medgar Evers, Emmett Till).
11. The case of the hostile response was an unusual situation. A man in the class who talked more than anyone else, who frequently had his hand up, and who usually interrupted without raising his hand complained at the end of the semester that I had often neglected to call on him. He also accused me of bias against men.
12. I have written about three such incidents in the essay referred to in note 1 above.

REFERENCES

American Association of University Women Educational Foundation. *How Schools Shortchange Girls: The AAUW Report.* New York: Marlowe, 1992.

Angelo, T., and Cross, P. *Classroom Assessment Techniques: A Handbook for College Teachers.* (2nd ed.) San Francisco: Jossey-Bass, 1993.

Disch, E. "Multicultural Literacy Assignment." In T. M. Singelis (ed.), *Teaching About Culture, Ethnicity, and Diversity.* Thousand Oaks, Calif.: Sage, 1998.

Light, R. J. *The Harvard Assessment Seminars: Explorations with Students and Faculty About Teaching, Learning, and Student Life.* Cambridge, Mass.: Harvard University Graduate School of Education, 1990.

Matthews, R., Smith, B. L., and Gabelnick, F. "Learning Communities: A Structure for Educational Coherence." *Liberal Education,* 1996, *82*(3), 4–7.

Moody, A. *Coming of Age in Mississippi.* New York: Laurel, 1968.

Orenstein, P. *School Girls: Young Women, Self-Esteem, and the Confidence Gap*. New York: Anchor Books, 1994.

Sadker, M., and Sadker, D. *Failing at Fairness: How Our Schools Cheat Girls.* New York: Simon & Schuster, 1994.

Sandler, B. R. "The Classroom Climate: Still a Chilly One for Women." In C. Lasser (ed.), *Educating Men and Women Together: Coeducation in a Changing World.* Urbana: University of Illinois Press, in conjunction with Oberlin College, 1987.

9

OVERCOMING RESISTANCE TO FEMINISM IN THE CLASSROOM

Mary Crawford, Jessica A. Suckle

THE IDEALIZED FEMINIST CLASSROOM sounds like a wonderful place, a collaborative laboratory in which students and faculty coconstruct and deconstruct research and theory on women's experience. Because teacher and students are active and interdependent agents in knowledge production, the outcomes are excitingly unpredictable. Within the feminist classroom, all voices are heard and respected. Moreover, the power relations between students and faculty are opened up for analysis. Power may be questioned, shared, even given away (Kimmel and Worell, 1997; Weatherall, forthcoming).

Because many of us who teach feminist studies received our own formal education largely in traditionally hierarchical and authoritarian classrooms, providing an alternative pedagogy for our students seems a valuable gift to give the next generation. Thus we may be surprised, even shocked, to discover that students do not always respond to our efforts. In fact, they sometimes react to feminist theory, research, and teaching strategies with hostility, resistance, and rejection.

In this chapter we (MC, a psychologist with more than twenty years' teaching experience, and JS, a doctoral student in social psychology) explore resistance in the feminist classroom. We begin by describing some of the forms that resistance takes. Contending that resistance cannot be understood without asking how students benefit from it, we explore its dynamics. Further, we describe active strategies for classes in the social sciences and the humanities. Finally, we describe how to make the learning process more collective and less individualized, allowing for a cumulative effect that dissipates resistance.

Resistance: A Few Illustrations

Resistance to feminism in the classroom takes many forms, from covert to overt, from passive to active (Dunn, 1987; Kimmel, Chapter Three of this volume). We briefly illustrate resistance as it has been experienced by ourselves and reported by other feminist teachers.

Refusing to Engage with the Ideas and Discussion in the Classroom

In a discussion of homophobia within a gender and communication class, students professed a willful ignorance about the topic ("I don't need to understand this since I don't know anyone or choose to know anyone who is homosexual or lesbian" [Anderson and Grubman, 1985, p. 228]). Judith Anderson and Stephen Grubman suggest that rather than expressing homophobic or sexist views overtly, students often refuse to engage in interaction, responding to the instructor's attempts at generating discussion with "absolute silence."

Minimizing

In this form of denial, students may dismiss the instructor's issues as trivial or irrelevant. In a gender and communication course, they insisted that sexist language (using "generic" masculine pronouns, *Mrs.* versus *Ms.*, *chairman, authoress,* etc.) had little effect in shaping gender expectations (Anderson and Grubman, 1985). In our own psychology classes, minimizing often takes the form of dismissing research as "ancient history" if it was not published within the last year or two ("So what if this study showed women earning 24 percent less for equivalent work? That was 1994—things have changed since then!").

Anger

Janice Wolff (1991) has written about her experience of teaching an English composition course for first-year students in which she assigned short essays by Rosalind Coward ("Let's Have a Meal Together") and

Lucy Gilbert and Paula Webster ("The Dangers of Femininity"). The students vehemently and passionately attacked the essays and the writers, describing them as "very offensive," a "bunch of baloney," "totally ignorant," and "absurd and annoying." According to the more vocal students, feminist ideas "got old fast" and "sent my blood pressure sky high."

Consider this response to Gilbert and Webster's essay:

> The whole essay . . . was a joke but since this is only a one-page essay and I'm a male I'll react to Lucy and Paula's ridiculous ideas about masculinity. It must be that the only guys these two clowns ever see are at crummy bars or on Days of Our Lives. . . . Their depiction of the Real Man amounts to a creature below Rocky on the evolutionary chain. . . . I'm getting madder and madder the more I think about these fools. I'd like to know how this pathetic excuse for an essay made its way out of the National Babbler and found itself in a college textbook [Wolff, 1991, p. 486].

Having occasionally been on the receiving end of similar invective, we remember that heart-sinking moment as one encounters such a reaction to an assigned reading. In Wolff's experience, the overtly hostile reactions come from men. She notes that their resistant writing is "loud and lewd" (1991, p. 491). Women who resist are politer and tentative. Thus, the writing of women and men alike reflects and reenacts their gendering. In our own classes in the psychology of women, in which there are four or five women students for every man enrolled, we have not observed reliable gender differences in ways of expressing resistance in writing.

Blaming the Teacher

Ellen Kimmel (in Chapter Three of this volume) suggests that many students experience conflicts over the feminist (female) teacher's behavior, expecting her to nurture and mother them and at the same time resenting her power. Moreover, students may resent the presence of feminist theory and research in the classroom, believing that feminism is "biased" and "political" while other, more familiar perspectives are ideologically neutral. It is not uncommon for these resistances to be expressed in negative student evaluations. Consider two complaints from evaluations of a first-year course in composition and introduction to literature, reproduced verbatim:

> "I feel this course was dominated and overpowered by feminist doctrines and ideals."

> "My professor has one distinct and overburying [sic] problem. She is a feminist and she incorporates her ideas and philosophy into her grading scale. . . . I think the University should investigate this class and compare the scores of the males in the class with the females. It is my belief that among males that we are getting lower grades because of our sex" [Bauer, 1990, p. 386].

Because they fear feminism, these students create a "cultivated distance" from the authority of the feminist teacher, an authority they identify with an "alien, radical, and threatening political position" (Bauer, 1990, p. 386). The professor may be judged to be a lesbian, a man-hater, or someone who has it in for men (Atwood, 1994; Bauer, 1990; Deay and Stitzel, 1991). If students attribute feminist theory to personal bias, they can discount feminist ideas more easily (Atwood, 1994).

This form of resistance sustains the alienation of the traditional classroom. By keeping the teacher firmly in place as the "other," students avoid the responsibility and radical potential of an open, collaborative approach to learning. Of course, resistance expressed in formal student evaluations or negative comments about the teacher can have significant effects and may provoke defensiveness on the part of the teacher. It can also jeopardize the academic future of untenured faculty.

Acting Out

Although overtly hostile behaviors in the classroom are probably rare, they are memorable because of the strong feelings of fear and vulnerability they evoke. I (MC) remember one student slamming his fist on the desk, kicking a chair over, and shouting his displeasure over receiving a low exam grade.

Another form of acting out occurred when a student insulted the women in his class. We often schedule a "Women's Creativity Day" immediately following the unit on violence against women. Students are asked to bring to class something meaningful to them that was created by a woman. Placing chairs in a circle, we share the objects and their stories. The majority of students bring objects created by someone in their circle of family and close friends, objects that have a deeply personal meaning to them. The group then discusses the characteristics of the objects, their commonalities, and the broader issue of women's creativity within patriarchal constraints.

By illustrating women's agency and generativity, this exercise allows for healing from the feelings of vulnerability and oppression evoked by learning about violence against women. The exercise has been a positive experience for all, except for one incident with a very resistant male student, who announced that "most of the stuff here could have been made by a monkey." Confronted by the instructor (MC) after class, he seemed to understand how demeaning his remark had been. However, at the start of the next class, and in full view of all, he angrily demanded class time to "apologize" and expand on his views about women and art.

Acting out is not restricted to those who hold antifeminist views or resist female authority. Because feminist students are accustomed to political protest, dissent among feminist factions can lead to overt actions: "During a particularly emotional moment in debates on whether white women can fully understand racial oppression and, in a similar vein, whether men can contribute to the development of feminist knowledge, dissent led to a handful of students walking out in protest. . . . These students questioned who can speak about, or on behalf of, others. . . . Included in this disavowal of knowledge disconnected from experience was my authority as an academic 'expert.' After all, what could someone with my privilege and identity know about the actual lives of the poor and underprivileged, of women of colour . . . ?" (Currie, 1992, p. 347).

Resistant Students: Who and Why

What are the reasons for student resistance to feminism in the classroom? First, the students enrolled in our classes today are quite different from those of one or two decades ago. When feminism first infiltrated the academy, *students* were the vanguard: demanding women's studies courses and programs, arguing for inclusion of women in the curriculum, and insisting on being taught by women (Kimmel and Worell, 1997). Today, many students are skeptical of feminism and of courses that incorporate its theories and knowledge base. Some believe that feminism is unnecessary because equality has been achieved (Deay and Stitzel, 1991; James, Chapter One of this volume; Wolff, 1991).

As students' ability to perceive problems inherent in the social structure increases, resistance may stem from fear of failure. In this case, resistance serves as protection against being overwhelmed. To open one's eyes means becoming aware that the entire social structure in which we live has to be changed. To take on the challenge of changing this structure is laborious, demanding, and formidable (Atwood, 1994).

I (MC) have been teaching psychology of women since 1975, and I have seen a distinct increase in conservatism, ambivalence, and detachment from the women's movement in my own classes over the past two decades. Attitudes toward feminism become apparent on the very first day of the course. Two decades ago, a majority of the students would endorse feminism at the outset; in the 1990s, there are seldom more than two or three brave souls (usually women's studies minors) who admit to feminist tendencies. To the others, feminists are angry, man-hating radicals left over from the 1970s.

The students in our classrooms are different from those of the 1970s not just because of the *Zeitgeist* but, ironically, because of the success of women's studies. From its grassroots origins, women's studies has become thoroughly assimilated into the academy. Its growth has been dramatic: in only two decades (1970–1990) 623 women's studies programs were established in the United States, according to the National Women's Studies Association.

Assimilation has come about through a process of connecting women's studies to the core values and goals of the academy (Crawford and Biber, 1994). Introductory courses in women's studies experience large enrollment growth when they are designed to meet general education requirements, interdisciplinary "breadth" criteria, or writing-emphasis credit in line with institutional mandates. Thus, our classrooms, especially at the introductory and intermediate levels, are likely to be filled with students whose primary goal is to "get a requirement out of the way." Not only are these students unlikely to learn much but they may prevent others from learning as well (Orr, 1993). Group pressures toward conformity can spread the influence of resistant students, making the classroom climate intolerable.

For both of these reasons, then—declining feminist sensibilities among the young and assimilation of women's studies—the women's studies classroom is increasingly a site of resistance. Faculty, not students, are now the vanguard in feminist studies—a problematic situation since feminist pedagogy rejects the model of the all-knowing instructor educating the needy masses (Kimmel and Worell, 1997). The task of feminist educators is to work with the students we have, resistant though they may be. We must seek to understand the sources of their resistance and find creative ways to open their minds to critical feminist thinking.

The Gendered Dynamic of Resistance

Does resistance take different forms in male and female students? Curiously, few feminist teachers have written about gender and resistance, although there are important gender-related issues to explore. In this chapter we look at the sources of resistance in male and female students separately, and then at the gender dynamics of feminist classrooms.

Men's Resistance: The Contradictions of Masculinity

Some men, having little experience and few models for egalitarian relationships with women, fall into dysfunctional stances in the classroom. Renate Klein (1983) described three: the "Expert," the "Ignoramus," and the "Poor Dear." The Expert, in his own opinion, knows more than the other students (and maybe the teacher too) about the "objective facts and figures" needed to enlighten women. He wants to save us from the horrors of "reverse sexism" or "male bashing." In the guise of "helping," he may seek to manipulate and control.

The Ignoramuses "inform us quite frankly that they don't have a clue what WS (and feminism) is all about, and would we please tell them" (Klein, 1983, p. 417). Like the white racist who expects people of color to educate him or her, the ignoramus is happy to accept the time and effort of women on his behalf. He rejects the notion of exploring his own internalized sexism and his ignorance about feminist research, and in this rejection his underlying contempt for women becomes apparent.

The Poor Dear "confides in you how really deeply awful it is to be a member of the dominant group" (Klein, 1983, p. 417). Appealing to the nurturing and compassionate feelings of the women in the class, the Poor Dear asks for help in understanding his own sexism. Once he engages the women in helping him, he quickly assumes a dominant position. The topic shifts from women's lives to *his* oppression as an oppressor, and he claims the verbal space and time of the classroom for an analysis of his wounded feelings.

The likelihood that a woman (and perhaps one who is not straight and not white) is in charge, the unconventional teaching methods, and the woman-centered curriculum of the feminist classroom all provide potential challenges to male students steeped in conventional masculinity and gender relations. Their resistance is not a superficial artifact of any one of these factors. It cannot be deflected by changing a particular teaching strategy or adding a "male viewpoint" to the readings. Instead, it reflects the very real threat that feminism brings to men who have been socialized to our culture's norms of masculinity (Orr, 1993).

Men in women's studies classes need to become aware of their complicity in a culture that subordinates women—how their taken-for-granted male privilege contributes to problems that are perceived as "women's issues." This is a difficult and painful process (Lewis, 1990; Mahlstedt and Corcoran, Chapter Eighteen of this volume).

Deborah Orr (1993) develops a compelling theoretical argument for pedagogical praxis based on helping male students learn to perceive the contradictions in their lived experience of masculinity—how they are simultaneously "oppressor" and "oppressed." This opens the way to a process of conscientization (Freire, 1970), in which their unconscious and contradictory experience of masculinity is made conscious.

Drawing on the work of Michael Kaufman (1987), Orr (1993) examines the contradictions of contemporary Western masculinity. A masculine self-identity is one centering on domination, control, autonomy, and instrumental power, but the daily lived experience of most men contradicts this ideology. Rather than being "on top," they must accede to the demands of a society that is hierarchical, bureaucratic, and conformist. Only in the home—and at the cost of authentic relationships with women and children—can they exercise limited power and control. The resistant young man in the classroom can be understood as "not only sexist, an oppressor, and a disrupter of the classroom, for he is often all of these, but also as radically oppressed himself. . . . The resisting male student, then, is one who has paid a high price (all that is identified ideologically as 'feminine') for his masculinity, but he also perceives the cost of giving up masculinity as great—the power and privilege that he is promised and that he, however naively, believes will be his" (Orr, 1993, p. 245).

Men are here to stay in women's studies classes, a consequence of the successful assimilation of women's studies into the mainstream curriculum. Their resistance is psychologically complicated and often well shielded from their own insight. Dealing with it may mean that they receive a disproportionate amount of the feminist pedagogue's attention and support (Klein, 1983).

To this dismal prospect we add a note of optimism. Not all men who explore women's studies are resistant. Some are what our women students call "the good guys." Perhaps they were raised in feminist households, by parents in an egalitarian marriage, or by single mothers whose hard lives made the student prematurely aware of gender inequities. Some are brought to our classes by sisters, lovers, or friends who have urged them, "Take this course, it really opens your eyes!" For these men, loyalty to a particular woman can be the beginning of a feminist transformation. Other men may have experienced sexual violence or abuse from other men, or prejudice and discrimination based on racialization, ethnic identity, or disability; some are aware that their sexuality sets them apart. Their personal experiences of oppression can provide a basis for men's solidarity with women. Lastly, even in the apolitical 1990s there may be a few who understand feminism as integral to a broader human-rights agenda (Stoltenberg, 1989; Crawford, McCullough, and Arato, 1983).

Although we have experienced hostility, disruptiveness, and rejection of female authority from some men in the classroom, we have also taught men who carefully (and voluntarily) limited their own speaking time, who unashamedly spoke of their fathers' absence and their mothers' struggles, or who were capable of interrogating their own privilege.

Women's Resistance: The Politics of Hope

Feminism can be threatening to women because it "challenges the everyday lives they have learned to negotiate" (Lewis, 1990, p. 471). For the most part, students are individualistic, heterosexually centered, and optimistic about the economic and social benefits of a college degree. They want to *join* the power elite, not deconstruct it (Atwood, 1994). When feminist teachers point out gender injustices, they may chastise us for viewing women as "victims." They may defend against our knowledge by claiming that "women are their own worst enemies" or "times have changed."

The classroom dynamic can be painful for all. My (MC's) students, for example, insist that "times have changed" and the wage gap is ancient history, although recent data indicate otherwise. When a spontaneous discussion of "equal pay" arose, we looked up the statistics. White male high school graduates earn about $27,000 per year on average, while white female college graduates earn about $30,000—in other words, by investing in four years of higher education, a white woman can expect to earn about $3,000 more annually than a white man who does not make that investment. Moreover, Hispanic women with a college degree earn about $9,000 a year more than those without. For African American women, the difference is about $8,000, and for white women, about $10,000. For white men, in contrast, a college degree increases annual earnings by about $15,000—a premium of more than 50 percent over all women (Unger and Crawford, 1996).

My students' realization that their male classmates, graduating with nominally equivalent degrees, would have a premium payoff for their educational investment was painful and depressing. There can be a certain mildly sadistic pleasure for the instructor in forcing students to confront their disadvantage. Perhaps we try to justify it with the belief that the truth will make them free. When this spontaneous discussion of wage inequity arose, I was glad for the "teachable moment" and sure that the students should be helped to see that their college degree is no protection from sexism. However, I soon began to wonder about the effects of this knowledge. Most of my students are working twenty or more hours a week to stay in school; some commute long distances and/or juggle family responsibilities. They must ask themselves sometimes why they are struggling so hard, and they must be tempted to take an easier route, earning money now rather than going deeper into debt. Surely the goal of feminism is not to take away hope. If we feminist teachers who could be their main source of support and empowerment participate in depriving them of a reason to pursue their goals, our students may well reject us and all we represent.

Our students' orientation to pleasing men and staking their identity on relationships with men is another source of threat and conflict in the feminist classroom. They are quick to ask teachers, invited speakers, and other women in authority, "Are you married? Do you have children?" These questions reflect their unspoken knowledge that their interest lies both within and against the dominant group (Lewis, 1990). They also reflect a need to believe that one can embrace feminism, autonomy, and careerism without sacrificing marriage and family. This dynamic can contribute to silencing bisexual and lesbian students, to whom the costs of not presenting oneself as feminine are salient.

We need to acknowledge that endorsing feminist views—or simply failing to display "appropriate" enactments of femininity—makes women more vulnerable to psychological and physical violence:

> We cannot expect that students will readily appropriate a political stance that is truly counter-hegemonic, unless we also acknowledge the ways in which our feminist practice/politics *creates,* rather than ameliorates, feelings of threat: the threat of abandonment; the threat of having to struggle within unequal power relations; the threat of psychological/social/sexual, as well as economic and political marginality; the threat of retributive violence—threats lived in concrete embodied ways. Is it any wonder that many women desire to disassociate from "those" women whose critique of our social/cultural world seems to focus and condense male violence? [Lewis, 1990, p. 485].

We feminist teachers need to be careful not to strip away students' only insulation against the cold realities of patriarchy. Their reaction to our stripping away illusion is probably the source of many student complaints that feminists see women only as "victims." With this assertion, they challenge us to provide an alternative vision that can sustain and empower them through the tough times they suspect lie ahead. They need to sustain hope, and they reject analyses that do not offer it. They are right: at the least, if we participate in exposing their illusions then we have a responsibility to offer new sources of strength in return (Atwood, 1994; Bauer, 1990; Lewis, 1990).

Most simply, we can teach that change is possible, and we can analyze the social and political conditions that reduce gender inequities. Further, we can offer a vision of *collective* change; "political commitment—especially feminist commitment—is a legitimate classroom strategy and rhetorical imperative" (Bauer, 1990, p. 389).

Gender Dynamics in the Classroom

The different sources of resistance in women and men lead to complicated gender dynamics in the classroom. Women sometimes protect their male peers, openly worrying and wondering about what the men are thinking, whether their feelings might be hurt by feminist perspectives, and whether they may feel silenced. A common behavior is to ask one of the men for "the male viewpoint." Magda Lewis (1990) suggests that this reflects women's internalized roles as caretakers. It probably also reflects the risks we discussed above; refusing to display "feminine" nurturance has its costs.

Women students sometimes persist in wanting to give authority and centrality to the minority of students who are male. In these cases, I (MC) sometimes use gentle humor. I ask if any of the women have ever been in a class in which they were a minority. Usually, there are several. I ask them to describe their experiences. Were the men careful to ask for their perspective? Did they worry openly about whether the women were comfortable and felt welcomed? Did they fear that any of the course material might offend the women? That these possibilities seem so ludicrous makes the point more effectively than a lecture: it is not the responsibility of women to protect men in the women's studies classroom.

Classroom dynamics can be analyzed by the class for pedagogical purposes. One technique I use is to set aside twenty to thirty minutes of a class at about the fourth or fifth week of the semester for a discussion of process. Because this is a new experience for most, I begin by illustrating the meaning of process by raising a few process questions: Are you satisfied that your voice is heard in this class? How would you characterize the interactions among students? Are we respectful of each other's views? Is class time shared, or dominated by a few? Then, seated in a circle, each person writes one comment about the class process on an index card, anonymously. I shuffle the cards, pass them around the circle, and each student reads the card received. This technique protects anonymity, ensures that every voice is heard, and opens up a discussion of what the class is like and how we would like it to be: a discussion framed in the students' own words. It is usually quite useful in helping me spot process issues that I might have overlooked. Moreover, it demonstrates to students that I care about how they behave in my classroom and how others behave toward them.

Proactive Strategies for Overcoming Resistance

Throughout this chapter, we have mentioned several active strategies for directly engaging resistance. In this section, we describe proactive strategies we use in our psychology of women class that allow students to generate feminist knowledge on their own, rather than receiving it from an authority figure.

Deconstructing Stereotypes

Students may hear their teachers talking about various forms of oppression or gender bias yet believe that these descriptions are exaggerated, that they themselves are removed from such incidents, or that sexism has been eliminated. Students are more likely to connect to information about stereotyping if they determine its existence for themselves. Reading a romance novel and rewriting a fairy tale are two assignments we use to help students think critically about stereotypes.

For the romance assignment, students are asked to individually select and read a Harlequin-type romance novel. Most, if not all, students know about these books, and some have been known to admit they read them. Students then write a paper, examining the principles displayed by the characters in their roles and the plot, as to how men and women should act, particularly in heterosexual love relationships. In addition, students are asked to comment on the popularity of this genre among women readers and authors.

A class discussion of this project is important. Because each student has read a different novel, each has an analysis of stereotyping that differs from the work of the next student. Discussing their conclusions as a group helps reaffirm their original analysis. In addition, students collectively examine the prevalence of sexual coercion in this genre, the lack of birth-control methods or concern about sexually transmitted diseases, and the sexual experiences of male and female characters within these books. At the end of the discussion, students explore the idea that the stereotypes concerning romance have an impact on how people construe events. Evaluations of the romance novel project reveal strong positive reactions to the assignment (Crawford, 1994).

The second project, rewriting a fairy tale, also elicits positive results. Students are directed to choose any fairy tale they wish and rewrite it so the person who saves the day is female. They are advised to keep the original moral in mind and to keep the story believable.

Although the directions appear simple, students soon learn that providing for female agency within their stories is difficult. Simply switching the gender roles rarely suffices. As research shows, identical behavior can have very different meanings depending on whether the actor is a man or a woman (Unger and Crawford, 1996). In the case of fairy tales, this often means that role-reversal stories are ridiculous and implausible. Think of a male Snow White, for example.

Other fairy tales serve to *decrease* female agency when roles are reversed. An excellent example is "Rumpelstiltskin." Although initially the heroine enlists the help of a "strange little man" to save her life, in the end she outwits him. Reversing the roles leads to a woman who is outsmarted and overcome in the end by a man. Although this scenario is quite believable, such a story does nothing to break traditional stereotypes of women.

What kinds of story do students write? The women characters take active instrumental roles, bravely wielding swords as well as intellectually wielding words. Instead of a damsel in distress being saved by a handsome stranger, we have found princesses rescuing princesses, which challenges the institution of heterosexual marriage. Men and women no longer meet, fall in love, and get married within the last two sentences of the story; now they are meeting and becoming friends. Sometimes love follows, and sometimes it does not.

Our modernized Cinderella has also aspired to be more than a decorative princess. She has done everything from obtaining a Ph.D. to starting and chairing a corporation (selling—what else—glass slippers!) to finding a cure for breast cancer. As for marriage, sometimes she does, sometimes she does not, and—reflecting today's marital trends—sometimes she does and then gets a divorce.

As with the romance project, we have a group discussion to explore comments about this assignment. In written evaluations, many students voice their disbelief at the difficulty of the assignment. Many admit that they had never realized how prevalent the traditional stereotypes were in their beloved fables: "I enjoyed doing the project, and luckily, my paper was a success—but it was hard! These gender roles are so ingrained in our lives, it was difficult to rearrange them—especially without having a 'wicked witch' or 'evil stepsister' still in the story. Now when I see a movie like *A Little Princess* (I work at a day care center), I *cringe.*"

Some students also experienced the empowerment of creativity. Said one: "The coolest result of this paper for me was, when I wrote and read my paper about this strong, triumphant girl, I felt *empowered*! I could totally see the effect—motivationally and otherwise."

These assignments actively and engagingly help students gain understanding of the cultural impact of gender and how sexual scripts are shaped. The fairy tale in particular engages their creativity in producing an alternative vision.

Interview

As the semester comes to a close, another good, hands-on assignment ties together the material learned throughout the course while serving to connect the material learned to the real world: asking students to interview a woman in their lives.

Students are directed to interview any woman they admire, so long as the woman is not a student. Although a list of interview questions is provided, students are advised that it is merely a guide. In addition, they are asked to reflect on the interviewee's answers and how they coincide or conflict with the information learned in class.

Some students choose to interview professors and employees; others interview their mothers (see Howe, 1989). Thus, the interview process may serve to personalize and integrate the information taught in the course.

Weekly Check-Ins

Often, while reading the text, students come across information that sparks a strong response. Weekly check-ins can serve as an outlet when such responses occur. This is a one-page assignment in which students must answer three questions pertaining to the reading material: What was something they learned or agreed with? What did they have trouble understanding or disagree with? What topics would they like to see discussed in class?

There are many benefits to this type of class requirement, but it is particularly helpful in the case of negative reactions or cognitive dissonance. Without the opportunity to express their thoughts on a particular topic, students may refuse to believe the information to be true. Although some students are bold enough to speak in class, many are wary of directly confronting the professor face-to-face. Writing allows the students an alternate voice to use in order to be heard.

Check-ins can also serve to build rapport with students. As they constantly receive feedback on check-ins, students come to believe that their opinion matters. As a result, they are more likely to approach the professor with personal and sometimes painful questions. I (JS) was approached by one student who needed to talk about an experience she was finally able to label as rape; another revealed that her brother had recently been raped. Additionally, both authors had recently talked with a student whose roommate was terrified to end a relationship with an abusive boyfriend. We are not counselors, but we provide a comfortable space for those who need to be heard yet do not know who to turn to first.

Finally, it is useful for the professor to know what topics students are having trouble understanding or accepting. Strong reactions in class can sometimes take the teacher by surprise, particularly if there is no warning. Often, the reactions given in class are expressed earlier in the students' check-ins. Answering the challenge expressed in the check-in allows the professor to think about the question and give the best possible answer in writing. Therefore, this assignment not only saves time in the classroom but it also creates a positive climate for everyone.

Students resist feminist ideas if they appear to be imposed on them. If students and their teachers actively collaborate in creating meaning, resistance often dissipates and learning can begin.

REFERENCES

Anderson, J., and Grubman, S. "Communicating Difference: Forms of Resistance." In M. R. Schuster and S. R. Van Dyne (eds.), *Women's Place in the Academy: Transforming the Liberal Arts Curriculum.* Totowa, N.J.: Rowman and Allanheld, 1985.

Atwood, J. "Good Intentions, Dangerous Territory: Student Resistance in Feminist Writing Classes." *Journal of Teaching Writing,* 1994, *12*(2), 125–143.

Bauer, D. M. "The Other 'F' Word: The Feminist in the Classroom." *College English,* 1990, *52*(4), 385–396.

Crawford, M. "Rethinking the Romance: Teaching the Content and Function of Gender Stereotypes in the Psychology of Women Course." *Teaching of Psychology,* 1994, *21*(3), 151–153.

Crawford, M., and Biber, M. "Developing a Women's Studies Program: General Strategies and Practical Tactics." *Furman Studies,* 1994, *36,* 51–57.

Crawford, M., McCullough, M., and Arato, H. "Attitude Change in Women's Studies Courses: A Field Study." Paper presented at the National

Women's Studies Association Conference, Columbus, Ohio, June 1983. (ED 250 233)

Currie, D. H. "Subjectivity in the Classroom: Feminism Meets Academe." *Canadian Journal of Education,* 1992, *17*(3), 341–364.

Deay, A., and Stitzel, J. "Reshaping the Introductory Women's Studies Course: Dealing Up Front with Anger, Resistance, and Reality." *Feminist Teacher,* 1991, 6(1), 29–33.

Dunn, K. "Feminist Teaching: Who Are Your Students?" *Women's Studies Quarterly,* 1987, *15*(3/4), 40–46.

Freire, P. *Pedagogy of the Oppressed.* New York: Seabury Press, 1970.

Howe, K. G. "Telling Our Mothers' Story: Changing Daughters' Perceptions of Their Mothers in a Women's Studies Course." In R. K. Unger (ed.), *Representations: Social Constructions of Gender.* Amityville, N.Y.: Baywood, 1989.

Kaufman, M. (ed.) *Beyond Patriarchy: Essays by Men on Pleasure, Power, and Change.* Toronto: Oxford University Press, 1987.

Kimmel, E., and Worell, J. "Preaching What We Practice: Principles and Strategies of Feminist Pedagogy." In J. Worell and N. G. Johnson (eds.), *Shaping the Future of Feminist Psychology: Education, Research, and Practice.* Washington, D.C.: American Psychological Association, 1997.

Klein, R. D. "The 'Men-Problem' in Women's Studies: The Expert, the Ignoramus, and the Poor Dear." *Women's Studies International Forum,* 1983, 6(4), 413–421.

Lewis, M. "Interrupting Patriarchy: Politics, Resistance, and Transformation in the Feminist Classroom." *Harvard Educational Review,* 1990, *60*(4), 467–488.

Orr, D. J. "Toward a Critical Rethinking of Feminist Pedagogical Praxis and Resistant Male Students." *Canadian Journal of Education,* 1993, *18*(3), 239–254.

Stoltenberg, J. *Refusing to Be a Man.* Portland, Ore.: Breitenbush, 1989.

Unger, R., and Crawford, M. *Women and Gender: A Feminist Psychology.* (2nd ed.) New York: McGraw-Hill, 1996.

Weatherall, A. "Exploring a Teaching and Research Nexus as a Possible Site for a Feminist Methodological Innovation in Psychology." *Psychology of Women Quarterly,* forthcoming.

Wolff, J. M. "Writing Passionately: Student Resistance to Feminist Readings." *College Composition and Communication,* 1991, *42*(4), 484–492.

PART THREE

TRANSFORMING MATH AND SCIENCE

TEACHING MATH AND SCIENCE more effectively is on the national agenda. The most conspicuous evidence for this fact is the continuing increase in the national budget for teaching and research in the sciences, and the proclamation of the 1990 Governors' Conference (which the president endorsed) that *by the year 2000, U.S. students will be first in the world in science and math achievement*. Part of a manifesto that identified ten equally ambitious national educational goals, this prioritizing of science education gave urgency to expanding the talent pool and to retaining those who would be recruited into the math and science enterprise. Expansion of the talent pool would require encouraging traditionally underrepresented groups—most notably women and minorities—to enter the technical disciplines. That in turn would entail adopting better and more productive teaching strategies and transforming the exclusive culture that has prevailed in at least some of the scientific and technical disciplines.

The new national prioritizing of math and science has served as symbol and as substance in the transformation of college curricula in math and in sciences. The recognition of American students' serious underperformance in these disciplines, relative to their international peers, provided the impetus for this new resolve. But the decision to expand the talent pool by encouraging and retaining in the pipeline women and other underrepresented groups required more than curricular change. It required a cultural change—most vividly reflected in a change of metaphors. Rather than seeking to *weed out* the underprepared from the scientific garden, math and science faculties had to consider ways to better *cultivate and propagate* the young plants in their garden.

They began by examining curricula. Some fields—most especially math and biology—became the first to expand hands-on opportunities for students, and to establish collaborative frameworks for all work between faculty and students. Other disciplinary areas were slower in implementing curricular overhaul and have yet to implement global reform.

The three chapters in Part Three provide strategies for maximizing the effectiveness of math and science education for women. Chapter Ten outlines an intervention that reaches into the precollege population and plants the seed of interest in historically forbidding fields of study within a selected group of adolescent girls. Interventions are needed before college if sciences are realistically to become a choice for high school girls to make when they enter college. Rebecca Pierce and Mary Kite's chapter shows the role that colleges can play in setting both academic and career expectations among precollege students, and in encouraging those who do not see themselves as scientists to start doing so.

By the time of early adolescence, intimidation has often replaced the original excitement and wonder of doing science. Hence, this is a critical stage for an intervention if even the possibility of studying science is to be preserved. The program at Ball State University features elements that are crucial in encouraging underrepresented groups in these disciplinary areas. First, the program models the collaborative dynamic that scientific research and study depend upon. Second, it offers role models as well as mentors to initiate the adolescents into science, mathematics, and engineering. To reinforce the relationship between studying a discipline and applying this knowledge in the professional context, explicit career information is imparted to the adolescent participants. As Jacquelynne Eccles's research (1989) has underscored, it is especially important for girls to recognize the social relevance, or validity, of studying math and science. Doing well academically in these fields appears insufficient to motivate females to pursue them in higher education. A program such as this one reinforces the social applicability and utility of the sciences, while igniting the spark of wonder that hands-on science experience provides. This intervention program for adolescent girls recognizes the fact that interest in and pursuit of science can be cultivated through exposure. Scientists are not only born; they can be trained.

In Chapter Eleven, Mary Harris and Candace Schau outline how an important gateway course, statistics, can be transformed from a hurdle into a pathway and can serve the needs of women effectively. The natural sciences and the social sciences require knowledge of statistical methods; hence, an indomitable statistics course can have a profound effect on the choice of major that students make. Recognizing the diversity of perspectives that students apply to the study of statistics is crucial to effective teaching of this discipline. Moreover, the singular importance of statistics to the educational choices of all students makes the attention given this course particularly consequential for a broad spectrum of students.

Chapter Twelve describes the holistic cultural reform that can take place in a physics department. A traditionally male discipline, with one of the smallest women-to-men graduation ratios of any science (4 percent compared to 30 percent for mathematics and 50 percent for biology), physics too can be transformed to become a highly popular major for women. Even those students who never considered physics as a possible major before enrolling at Bryn Mawr College came to view it both as interesting and accessible to women. The strategies proffered in Neal Abraham's chapter make clear that alchemy is not responsible for the transformation; rather, it is a broadly based pedagogical reform that transcends both disciplinary and classroom boundaries and affects the entire departmental environment. At the heart of the transformation lies the crucial component of mentoring in all of its manifestations in the lab, as much as in the lunchroom.

The specific programs that are detailed in Part Three can be replicated in their entirety or, more usefully, viewed as types of solutions to a broad range of challenges that teaching math, science, and technology present. Either way, may a thousand transformed flowers bloom!

REFERENCE

Eccles, J. S. "Bringing Young Women to Math and Science." In M. Crawford and M. Gentry (eds.), *Gender and Thought: Psychological Perspectives.* New York: Springer-Verlag, 1989.

10

CREATING EXPECTATIONS IN ADOLESCENT GIRLS

Rebecca L. Pierce, Mary E. Kite

AS THE TWENTY-FIRST CENTURY approaches, our nation has become aware of changes in economic, social, and technological needs that require a great number of people who are trained to fulfill those needs.

Why Science and Mathematics Matter

Mathematics and science are at the core of producing a scientifically literate citizenry. Both are essential for all people to meet the demands of the global marketplace and the rigorous demands of a technologically advanced society (Hollenshead and others, 1996).

One obvious way to meet these demands is to increase the numbers of women and minorities who pursue careers in science, mathematics, and engineering. Although women are fairly well represented in the biological sciences at undergraduate and graduate levels, for most other science-related disciplines the number of degrees granted to women does not approach equity with that for men (Hollenshead and others, 1996). At

Correspondence should be sent to the first author at the Department of Mathematical Sciences, Ball State University, Muncie, IN 47306. Because of her untimely death, Bernadette Perham, one of the original codirectors of Calculate the Possibilities, was unable to see the project carried out. We dedicate this chapter to her life and work.

the bachelor's level, women represent approximately 16 percent of engineering graduates and 28 percent of computer science graduates; these percentages approximate the number of women who obtained graduate degrees in those fields. Although women are earning both undergraduate and graduate degrees in record numbers, they continue to be underrepresented in most science-related disciplines.

During the long post–World War II and cold-war periods, science research emphasized national defense. Today we face a world in which science and technology are necessary more for reasons of global competition (National Science Foundation, 1997). The societal value placed on science and engineering has shifted and will continue to do so. As more people from underrepresented groups join the scientific community, they bring with them different perspectives on the scientific process. Feminist researchers, for example, may see the traditional approach to science as limiting in that it considers issues out of context. In contrast, feminist researchers are often concerned with events as they occur in their natural context (see Rabinowitz and Sechzer, 1993). The topics worthy of investigation may also change as diversity is achieved. Ethnic minorities may focus on how health issues differ for some societal groups, women may call for research on breast cancer and women's heart disease, and gay men and lesbians may examine how antigay prejudice affects their mental and physical well-being (see Hare-Mustin and Marecek, 1990; Unger and Crawford, 1996).

American science must respond to these current pressures and future hopes. As a nation, we have tremendous resources, notably the diversity of our people. Tapping into this diversity is crucial, and doing so can add new ideas, perspectives, and ways of thinking to science and its applications (National Science Foundation, 1997). Although we believe all types of diversity are critical to scientific advancement, this chapter focuses on women and the importance of encouraging them to pursue science-related careers. We believe doing so offers a benefit to the women themselves, personally as well as economically, and also to science and engineering by introducing new perspectives on problem solving and advancement.

We describe a program that encouraged Indiana high school girls to consider science, mathematics, and engineering careers. In Indiana, disproportionately low numbers of girls are entering undergraduate studies in these disciplines. This is true despite the fact that they performed at least as well as the boys in mathematics (Sullivan, 1993). In addition, "the occupations that Hoosier girls say they want to pursue continue to be mostly traditional and predictable, although they have made in-roads in some nontraditional fields" (Sullivan, 1993, p. 6).

Why Women Are Not Becoming Scientists

Although a detailed summary is beyond the scope of this chapter, the literature on boys' and girls' school experiences points to clear, gender-based inequities (American Association of University Women, 1992; Sadker and Sadker, 1994). The AAUW report, based on an assessment of self-esteem, educational experiences, interest in math and science, and career aspirations of girls and boys age nine to fifteen offers compelling evidence that girls are not receiving the same quality, or even quantity, of education as boys. Such experiences are exemplified by the memories of a high school teacher in her early forties. She writes:

> I probably would have been an engineer if I had been given the opportunity. Well, maybe *opportunity* isn't exactly the right word, because nothing really prevented me, but nobody encouraged me, either. . . . I always liked science and did well in it, but none of my counselors mentioned engineering or being a chemist or any science career except teaching. I think they mentioned those careers to the boys who were good at science, but not to the girls. They steered us toward teaching. That's just the way it was, and I'm not sure how much it has changed [Brannon, 1996].

In response to these charges, the AAUW offers specific strategies designed to effect change in girls' school experiences. Relevant to our program, the AAUW proposed that "local schools and communities must encourage and support girls studying science and mathematics by showcasing women role models in scientific and technological fields, disseminating career information, and offering 'hands-on' experiences and work groups in science and math classes" (1992, p. 7).

We believe "Calculate the Possibilities" implemented this strategy and addressed a critical need.

Overview of "Calculate the Possibilities"

"Calculate the Possibilities" was a four-week summer residential program for Indiana high school students who had completed grade ten or eleven. It had a dual focus of career awareness and skill development in the areas of science, engineering, and mathematics (SEM). The program increased awareness about careers in SEM, introduced the participants to SEM role models, fostered collaboration with SEM mentors, and encouraged them to pursue an SEM career. Figure 10.1 illustrates the essential components of the program. It was funded by the National Science Foundation (NSF) and Ball State University (BSU).

Program Directors and Consultants

Bernadette Perham, professor of mathematical sciences at BSU, and Rebecca Pierce, associate professor of mathematical sciences at BSU, were codirectors of the project. (Because of her untimely death, however, Perham was unable to see the project to completion.) Five women faculty served as SEM mentors, each meeting with four or five of the young women to work on discipline-specific projects. They were Nancy Behforouz, professor of biology, Mahfuza Khatun, associate professor of physics and astronomy, Jayanthi Kandiah, then assistant professor of family and consumer sciences, Mary Kite, then associate professor of psychological science, and Patricia Lang, associate professor of chemistry. Ellen Mauer, BSU's coordinator of career counseling, served as the career consultant and assisted the young women in exploring their career objectives and goals.

Figure 10.1. Introducing Young Women to Science, Engineering, and Math (SEM) Careers.

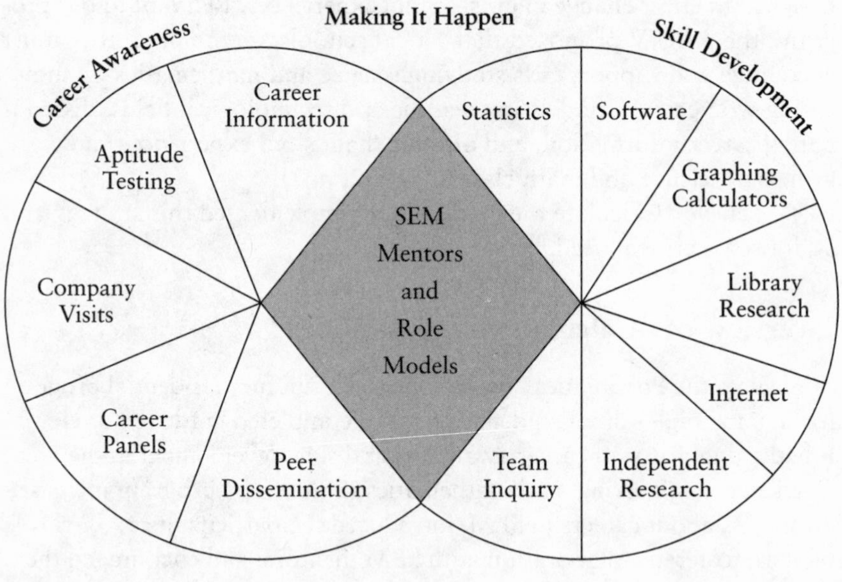

Selection of Participants

Students selected for this program had completed either their sophomore or junior year in high school by the beginning of the residential program. Applicants were required to have completed the following courses: algebra, geometry, and at least one laboratory science course (biology, chemistry, or physics). GPA requirements were at least 3.0 (on a 4.0 scale) in mathematics and science courses and an overall GPA of at least 2.75.

The group of applicants (thirty-four juniors and forty sophomores) came from every sector of the educational system; 83 percent attended public high schools, 10 percent parochial, and 7 percent private. The geographic and demographic goals of the program were met. The program participants' hometowns represented the whole state of Indiana. Ten juniors and fourteen sophomores were selected, representing inner-city, rural, affluent-public, private, and parochial schools. Although young women of color and Hispanic backgrounds participated, the participants' ethnicity was primarily Caucasian, reflecting the ethnic makeup of the state of Indiana.

The participants' GPAs exceeded the requirements. As a group, overall GPA was 3.78 and mathematics and science average GPA was 3.75. In addition, the group had numerous extracurricular accomplishments: one played on the boys' golf team and had made the all-state finals, another was a winner in the state swimming competition and had a goal of competing in the next Summer Olympics, several played competitive softball, about half belonged to some form of organized singing group, and several played musical instruments.

Living Arrangements

The program participants arrived for the four-week program in June 1996. They lived on campus during the program, leaving if they wished for weekends. The dormitory was staffed by four female counselors. Three of the counselors were graduate students completing M.A. degrees in psychological science. The fourth counselor was an undergraduate secondary education mathematics major who lacked only student teaching in completing her degree. All the counselors had relevant experience, having previously served as residence hall assistants or camp counselors.

Dorm living was a new experience for all of the program participants, and the counselors made their transitions easy. Each counselor was responsible for a group of six young women and had a room within close proximity of the group. Room assignments were made so that the participants' living group did not overlap with their assigned SEM group. The counselors kept track of the young women after hours, got the women to meals on time, made sure curfews were met, kept the peace when necessary, and planned a few informal parties.

Bringing high school girls to a college campus raised a number of issues that college faculty often do not consider. College students are generally considered to be adults who can make reasonably mature decisions about their schedules and activities. Moreover, although colleges and universities are, of course, concerned about student safety and well-being, the issues are more complex and vivid with high school girls. Several of our program participants were away from home for the first time. Because the campus was in summer session, the young women would have opportunities to meet college students who, in turn, might expose them to experiences beyond their level of maturity. Unlike the average college professor, we believed we *did* need to fulfill the role of *in loco parentis*. For that reason, we believed it essential to have strict curfews, strict rules about whom the program participants could spend time with, and a busy schedule.

The counselors played an essential part in maintaining a high level of enthusiasm outside the course work and were sought out by the young women for information about college life. These four served as younger role models for the participants as each discussed their plans for the future (law school, high school mathematics teacher, clinical staff psychologist, and additional graduate school). We were extremely pleased to have four highly mature, enthusiastic dorm counselors.

Goals of the Program

After the families had left on the first day, the young women were acquainted with the schedule for the first week and informed in detail about the goals of the project:

- To increase awareness about careers in science, engineering, and mathematics
- To introduce participants to SEM role models on the job
- To have participants collaborate on a research project with SEM mentors
- To have a positive impact on the participants' choice of an SEM career

The participants' responsibilities were also conveyed:

- Creating a portfolio of career information
- Formulating and carrying out a plan to disseminate information on SEM careers and job opportunities with their home school peers and other friends
- Completing a career assessment
- Acquiring skill in the use of a spreadsheet, a graphing calculator, and the Internet
- Engaging in a research project led by the SEM mentor to gain hands-on research experience
- Sharing the research experience with the other participants and the SEM mentors
- Defining and/or independently completing related research work at their home school
- Attending, with their home school resource teacher, a followup day on the BSU campus
- Presenting results of their independent research orally to home school peers and faculty
- Submitting written research work for outside review

Initial reactions to these responsibilities were positive, but the young women were also somewhat overwhelmed and hesitant—expecting perhaps more of a "camp" atmosphere despite being sent detailed instructions about the program beforehand. Much of this was alleviated by reassuring the women of their past accomplishments and reminding them that they had been selected from a larger pool of applicants. Distributing the TI-92 graphing calculators and receiving some instruction in their use also helped to get them thinking and realizing their own potential as they quickly and easily conquered this new technology.

Summary of Activities for All Participants

The program had a structured daily schedule. On Wednesdays, a chartered bus transported all the young women and author Pierce (as project director) to companies for site visits. These trips required most of the day because of the distance to the companies. The bus left around 7:15 A.M., just after breakfast, and returned by late afternoon. As one might imagine, the early-morning departures made for some interesting activities on the bus, as the young women might not be completely ready for the day! Often new hairstyles would appear by the time we reached our destination.

The July Fourth holiday fell on a Thursday, so the participants were required to stay through that holiday. As a change of pace, the participants were allowed to sleep in on the holiday itself. Late morning and early afternoon included activities such as swimming, a softball game, and attending the local fireworks. The dorm counselors and SEM mentors also participated in these activities. This one day of extracurricular activities provided time for the participants to view the project director and SEM mentors in a much different light and added a new dimension to their frame of reference of "who scientists are."

Because most of the women did spend weekends at home, the first couple of Sunday evenings were especially difficult for them. Leaving family and home, realizing at times that they *wanted* to leave family and be with new friends, and facing another week of challenging work were difficult. However, each Sunday after their return to campus a specific group physical activity, such as bowling, got the group back to its cohesive structure and refocused the participants to the program.

Career Opportunities

An emphasis on SEM careers was a significant part of the summer workshop. A variety of efforts were made to acquaint the participants with women who have SEM careers and have the participants investigate their own interests and abilities.

COMPANY VISITS. Through career seminars, company site visits, and panel discussions, the participants learned about careers and job opportunities: what they require and how they are achieved. The young women visited and took planned tours of major Indiana companies, where they interacted with professionals in pharmaceutics, medical care, manufacturing, engineering, natural resources, and quality control. The visits took place on business workdays, and the young women were informed of the need for appropriate dress. For the most part, they did well in judging what was appropriate and inappropriate for the various companies.

Each company site visit offered a different perspective. Every effort was made to provide female role models at the facility. The first visit was to Delphi Energy and Engine Management Systems, a manufacturing company associated with the automobile industry. Besides a plant tour, the young women had an opportunity to talk with two female engineers, one a generator engineer and the other a design analysis engineer. In addition, female coop students shared information about their experiences at Delphi. Although prior to this company visit several of the participants were sure they wanted to be engineers, most commented on the noise and dirtiness. It was evident after this visit that the girls needed advice about how to interact and ask questions on these one-day visits since it would be their only time to do so; this advice made subsequent visits livelier.

The following week's visit to Eli Lilly, an Indianapolis-based pharmaceutical firm, allowed the women to observe male and female scientists in their labs. Specifically, they interacted with a molecular biologist, a chemist, and a biologist testing a new heart apparatus on live animals. This major corporation and the Lilly Corporate Center were fascinating and a bit overwhelming for some. However, all were impressed by the wealth of resources and the campus. That afternoon, they also visited the National Institute for Fitness and Sport and James Whitcomb Riley Hospital. At these facilities, they met with a sports nutritionist, a diabetes researcher, a pediatric dietitian, a neonatal-pediatric dietitian, and a professor of nutrition from the Indiana University Schools of Allied Health Sciences and Medicine, Indianapolis. All were enthralled by these professionals, and they felt very comfortable asking questions of them.

On the third Wednesday, the group visited the Indiana Department of Natural Resources (DNR) at the Indiana Government Center. After a tour of the grounds and buildings, the young women met with a group of female scientists employed by the DNR. The group included a lake and river enhancement biologist from the Division of Soil Conservation, a nongame supervisor from the Division of Fish and Wildlife, and a landscape architect from the Division of Parks and Reservoirs. The women shared information about their careers and the paths that had led them to their current positions. They talked specifically about "making it" in a mostly male-dominated arena. After lunch, the young women visited Summit Lake State Park and met a very young naturalist who was completing an undergraduate degree in biology. Because she was nearly the same age as the young women, this made for a lively interaction and some direct questions about salary and availability of positions. It was evident the young women felt very comfortable at this site; several left saying, "This is what I want to do, no doubt about it!"

For the final week, the group visited the Ball Corporation Metal Container Operations Packaging Laboratory and a local 3M manufacturing facility. Ball Laboratories employs women and men who have degrees in biology, chemistry, food science, and metallurgical engineering. The young women were amazed how these and other technical disciplines are absolutely required in manufacturing everyday items such as glass, metal, and plastic containers. At the 3M plant, the young women experienced a rude awakening. Three engineers, two older males and one younger female, conducted tours of the plant, which produces and cuts all types of tape. Overall, the visit was positive and presented (in the young women's opinion) a more desirable working environment than Delphi. However, a comment from one of the male engineers was the center of conversation on the bus trip home. In describing the many types of tape made at the facility, the older man said, "Here's one each of you will become acquainted with when you diaper your babies!" Until this visit, the group had not really experienced any outright chauvinism and was in an uproar over the comment. Most felt it was very presumptuous for him to assume they would be diapering babies—not that they did not plan to have them, but that they believed their husbands would be the ones doing the diapering. A very beneficial discussion followed about how far we still are from equity in the workplace and in society in general. The speaker had shared that he was a father of two girls, and many of the program participants commented that they felt very sorry for his daughters.

CAREER EXPLORATION AND GOALS. BSU's Mauer met four days a week with all twenty-four participants and assisted them in exploring their career objectives and goals. She administered and interpreted the results of a career assessment battery that examines skills, interests, and abilities and provided a listing of occupations that matched the participants' career interests. The career-counseling process consisted of a six-step program with sessions on self-assessment, career research and occupational information, tentative decision making, experiential learning, decision making and implementation, and reevaluation. The self-assessment phase included specific activities related to skills, values clarification, interests, and personality variables. The young women took the Myers-Briggs Interest Inventory (Myers and Myers, 1993) and used the *Career Choices Workbook and Portfolio* (Bingham and Stryker, 1990).

Creative Problem Solving

In the context of creative problem solving within a variety of SEM areas, the young women acquired skill in the use of a spreadsheet (Microsoft Excel), word processing software, and the TI-92 graphing calculator. They were aided in the computer laboratory by technologically literate undergraduate and graduate assistants; the young women's mathematical understanding and problem-solving abilities were addressed in daily technological sessions. Each week, a topic in mathematics was used as the basis for learning about technology. The topics covered were algebra, geometry, and statistics. Both written and hands-on activities and experiments were used to present material in these areas.

Using statistics and technology to support future research efforts was also emphasized. In collaboration with an SEM mentor from BSU, each young woman gained hands-on research experience in a university laboratory setting. She also independently completed a final report at her home school with the support of an onsite resource teacher and her university mentor.

Discipline-Specific Programs

The young women were selected to do collaborative research in one of several areas: biology, chemistry, nutrition, physics, or psychological science. From the pool of applicants who met the program requirements described earlier, the SEM mentors and codirectors selected students for their discipline-specific program based on personal statements and self-indicated interests.

The SEM groups met in the afternoons four days a week. Each mentor planned and developed activities for her specific discipline. Working in groups of four or five, the young women gained exposure to the scientific method of inquiry and to various laboratory techniques. The SEM mentors introduced the young women to the library as a resource for research and showed them how to go about a literature search for writing scientific reports and research proposals within the context of their collaborative research projects.

In biology, Behforouz introduced the theoretical basis of life and practical approaches to deriving and presenting experimental data. During the hands-on program, the students learned about and analyzed the characteristics and nature of proteins, enzymes, and nucleic acids. In addition, the students performed antigen-antibody reactions in gels, examined whole blood under the microscope, and performed a differential white cell count. Using more complex experimental protocols, the group used plasmids to transform bacteria and conducted digel electrophoretic fingerprinting of the DNA plasmids. The overall intent was to introduce the small group to both the breadth of biology and the technical aspects of doing biological science.

In chemistry, Lang introduced her group to laboratory chemistry techniques. Specifically, they learned about thin-layer chromatography and infrared microspectroscopy. The group first replicated a recently published experiment in which microscopic amounts of dyes were separated on a zirconia-coated slide and then detected using a microscope coupled to an infrared spectrometer. The students learned how to prepare solutions and chromatography plates, how to read the scientific literature, and how to run a research-grade spectrometer. Gradually, the young women were introduced to many of the theoretical aspects behind the experiments and instrumentation. They began to understand how a scientist considers, evaluates, and controls the mass of variables that pop up in a complex experiment. This group constructed a twenty-minute presentation on their research, which they gave to the chemistry department faculty, graduate students, and other summer researchers at BSU.

Kandiah's nutrition group studied the correlation between fat and calcium intake among college students. This group first collected data on their own attitudes and conduct regarding nutrition. Next they studied approximately fifty BSU female students who had not previously taken nutrition classes. Three-day diet and food records were collected before and after nutrition education. The group analyzed the data using Nutritionist IV computer software.

In physics, Khatun's students studied basic analog and digital electronics. They attended a series of lecture and problem-solving sessions on circuit theory and became familiar with electronic components, devices, and equipment. They conducted experiments that included working with multiloop circuits (series and parallel), AC circuits, measurement of capacitive reactance, power supply rectification and filtering, use of audio and operational amplifiers, integrated circuit signal generators, and basic logic gates.

Kite's psychology group read and discussed articles about the psychology of gender. In particular, they considered how this topic could be researched and what issues scientists in this area must consider. Much of this was guided by Caplan and Caplan's book *Thinking Critically About Research on Sex and Gender* (1994). As they learned about research methodology, the participants prepared to collect their own data, using a reaction-time measure to assess women's and men's self-descriptive traits. It was expected that men would respond more quickly to male stereotypic traits and that women would respond more quickly to female stereotypic traits. Although the results were not statistically significant, the young women learned how to collect psychological data and were introduced to the ethical issues one must consider when studying people.

GROUP PRESENTATIONS. On the final day of the program, the five research groups each gave an oral presentation of its research results to the other participants, the codirector of the program, and the SEM mentors.

It was an exciting afternoon. Each group presented its results uniquely, using a variety of presentation techniques to convey the essence of the students' work. The enthusiasm and pride in what they had accomplished within a short four-week period came shining through. The entire group of participants showed their appreciation to the dorm counselors, the SEM mentors, and the program directors by presenting them with plaques of appreciation. In addition, everyone received certificates of achievement, T-shirts, and a group photo. Although the general atmosphere was happy, an underlying sadness was present as well; leaving friends and mentors was difficult. The young women were ready to return home, but they also expressed a desire to return soon and continue the program.

Introducing Other Role Models

The codirectors believed it was important to involve as many women role models as possible in the summer workshop. Several strategies were employed to provide opportunities for the participants to interact with science and math professionals.

E-MAIL PEN PALS. Participants in the psychology group were assigned two successful women psychologists with whom they could correspond. (These women were asked in advance whether they were willing to participate in this aspect of the program.) To the extent possible, the young women were matched with the psychologists based on mutual interests. The young women wrote their pen pals and asked questions about the psychologists' careers. If the psychologist agreed, responses were shared during psychology group meetings. This allowed the young women to learn more about women in psychology, their career paths, and their interests.

GUEST SPEAKERS. The SEM mentors incorporated interactions with additional professionals, other faculty, and pertinent visitors. These exposures to other mentors varied across the disciplines. For example, psychologists from BSU talked to the psychology group about their own careers in psychology. These talks were informal; many shared their personal story of how they came to be involved in the discipline. Some demonstrated research equipment and explained the details of particular experiments. One goal was to introduce students to the breadth of psychology and to disabuse them of the notion that all psychologists are clinicians. A second goal was to provide a variety of role models for the young women.

Additional guest speakers also talked briefly about their careers and background during the technology sessions. Among those making presentations were an actuary, a computer scientist, a statistician, and a science educator (the director of gifted education and talent development at BSU).

During the last week of the program, Mauer hosted a career and family panel for the participants. A panel of women, including a family physician, a lawyer, a clinical psychologist, and a teaching nutritionist, informally shared information about their career paths and the balancing act required to keep career and family going. These personal stories were enlightening and helped the participants think about decisions for their own lives.

Follow-Up Activities

The following fall, the participants and their home school resource teachers returned to spend a day on the BSU campus with the BSU program staff. At this time, the resource teachers received the training needed to support the research efforts of their respective students. The resource teachers became acquainted with the research techniques and technology used by the young women in the summer research projects.

The five SEM groups met with each mentor and discussed the participants' progress to date. Additional instruction was given as needed, and first drafts were collected from the participants. Each young woman also provided her plan for sharing career information with peers. The group came up with a variety of ideas for this process, including visiting a middle school class, making a presentation in a high school chemistry class, preparing an all-school display, and visiting a local Girl Scout troop.

Evaluation of Program

This project was designed to help young high school women assess their career direction and become more aware of the role of women in the sciences. Several evaluation instruments and activities measured the program's success, including changes in the participants' thinking with respect to their own careers and the effectiveness of particular aspects of the program. Specific evaluation strategies included a career commitment inventory, an overall project evaluation form, evaluation of company visits and career activities, and focus groups for mentors. Overall, the program was very well received by participants. Detailed findings are described in the next subsections.

VOCATIONAL INVENTORY. At the beginning and end of the project, participants were asked to complete the inventory *My Vocational Situation* (Holland, Daiger, and Power, 1980), which is widely used in determining career awareness. The range of possible scores on the inventory is 0 to 18. A score of 13 or above indicates the student is fairly clear about her career path. A score of 9–12 indicates the student may feel anxious about career choice; lack the confidence needed to pursue goals; or need more information about the world of work and about her own values, skills, and interests. The scores for the group were significantly higher on the posttest ($M = 12.09$) than on the pretest ($M = 9.47$), $t\ (22) = -5.12$, and $p < .05$, indicating that overall participation in the project increased clarity about career direction. (Twelve of the twenty-three students who took the posttest scored 13 or above, compared to 7 on the pretest.)

EVALUATION OF COMPANY VISITS. Ratings of increased awareness of SEM careers were highest for the visit to Eli Lilly across all visits, but overall 77 percent reported that the visits increased career awareness. As to whether the company visits increased their awareness of women's careers in science, ratings of Ball Corporation and Riley Hospital were highest (greater than 90 percent agreement), followed by Eli Lilly, the state DNR, and Summit Lake (greater than 80 percent agreement). The two manufacturing firms, Delphi and 3M, received much lower agreement levels (55 percent and 22 percent respectively).

EVALUATION OF CAREER ACTIVITIES. The specific sessions addressing career activities were also evaluated at the end of each week. Ninety-one percent of the respondents agreed or strongly agreed that they were pleased with the weekly career activities. About 87 percent of the participants agreed or strongly agreed that the goals of the weekly activities were clear to them.

OVERALL WORKSHOP EVALUATION. Results from the overall summer workshop evaluation indicated that the program was very successful. At least 80 percent of the respondents strongly agreed that the workshop familiarized them with "the skills, interests, and abilities needed for success in science, engineering, and mathematics" and provided them with career information they can share with their peers. More than 90 percent strongly agreed the workshop introduced them to role models in science, engineering, and mathematics. However, only 23 percent strongly agreed the workshop "helped me get ready to write a report." Fifty-nine percent agreed with this statement and 18 percent (four respondents) were neutral with respect to this statement.

The participants provided positive and negative open-ended comments on the summer workshop evaluation. These responses were categorized, with percentages representing the number of participants who mentioned each category. If participants mentioned more than one category, each was counted. On the positive side, the participants most often mentioned liking career class, the SEM groups, and the other program participants (41 percent mentioned each of these categories). Even though comments were anonymous, surprisingly few were negative. In fact, the only consistent complaint was the lack of free time, mentioned by 32 percent of the participants. In response to the question, "What did you like most about the summer workshop?" the positive comments included:

- Everything! This was the best learning experience! I learned about researching science and that it is fun and interesting. I learned women have a place in this world and a right to work for it.
- Everything that we did benefitted me in some way, so I can't really say what I liked best. I feel as though I'm going home a much more developed person and I owe it all to this program.
- I got to learn about what the future may hold in science, engineering, and mathematics with a group of interesting peers.
- I liked how all of us got along so well. It seemed like a family.
- In biology, there were so many opportunities that people my age never get to follow through with. I never thought I'd be this lucky. I feel better about myself and getting a job, knowing every one of us is scared. [The program] gave an insider perspective rather than them just coming to us.
- I liked the fact that we were encouraged to go for our dreams and not let ourselves be discouraged by any male chauvinist person. I liked that we had the opportunity to get anything out of this that we wanted. I liked the fact that we were encouraged to be well-rounded, not just excelling and concentrating in one area and forgetting others that are equally important to a successful life.
- The visits have shown me that women still have a long way to go to be equal. I liked working with the mentors. Their experiences and stories have been very helpful in ways that are impossible to describe. It shows scientists can be real people.

INFORMATION FROM SEM MENTORS. The SEM mentors participated in four focus groups and completed an open-ended questionnaire. The focus groups gave the mentors a chance for problem solving and reflection. Overall, the mentors believed that the students were challenged by their sessions with them and that the students responded well to the mentors' expectations. The mentors' written comments indicated they believed the program was very successful in accomplishing its goals.

LIMITATIONS. One of the goals of the SEM program was to address diversity issues in science. Although our SEM mentors and speakers provided diverse role models, we were disappointed that the program did not attract a diverse group of participants. In retrospect, we might have recruited more proactively from high schools with ethnically and economically diverse populations. The benefits to the participants and the faculty would have included a wider perspective on the issues young women face in making career decisions. For example, students from less advantaged areas of the state could discuss how these economic issues limit the resources available to them in their current settings. Latinas might have described the lack of role models for them in Indiana. Because so much information was shared informally among the young women, having interactions with others from different backgrounds would have benefited them immeasurably. Similarly, the faculty participants would have benefited from interacting with a more diverse group. The majority of our students represent a white, middle class, Midwestern population. We believe our worldview would have been expanded by the opportunity to teach a broader cross-section of the population. Finally, a diverse group of participants might have led us to focus on how science is limited by a traditionally masculine focus. Addressing these assumptions was difficult with young women from similar backgrounds. Diverse voices might have called attention to how the world has changed since we, ourselves, went through the process of becoming scientists.

Summary

The thoroughness of the evaluation instruments provided a great deal of information that can be used to help plan future projects of this kind. Looking over the results of all the assessment activities, we conclude that the program was well thought out, well executed, and very successful in accomplishing its purposes.

We believe participation in the program enriched the lives of twenty-four Indiana high school girls and the twenty Ball State University faculty and staff who were involved in the program. We are interested in following the participants, many of whom are headed for college this fall. Author Pierce plans to conduct such a follow-up and hopes to learn more about the impact of the program on their career choices. Few high school (or college) students receive the attention and mentoring provided through

"Calculate the Possibilities." We have no doubt the experience influenced the participants' lives. We know it influenced our own. We look to a future in which more such programs are available to a wider range of students.

REFERENCES

American Association of University Women. *The AAUW Report: How Schools Shortchange Girls, Executive Report.* Washington, D.C.: AAUW Education Foundation, 1992.

Bingham, M., and Stryker, S. *Workbook and Portfolio for the Text: Career Choices: A Guide for Teens and Young Adults.* Santa Barbara, Calif.: Academic Innovations, 1990.

Brannon, L. *Gender: Psychological Perspectives.* Needham Heights, Mass.: Allyn & Bacon, 1996.

Caplan, P. J., and Caplan, J. B. *Thinking Critically About Research on Sex and Gender.* New York: HarperCollins, 1994.

Hare-Mustin, R. T., and Marecek, J. (eds.). *Making a Difference: Psychology and the Construction of Gender.* New Haven, Conn.: Yale University Press, 1990.

Holland, J. L., Daiger, D. C., and Power, P. G. *My Vocational Situation.* Palo Alto, Calif.: Consulting Psychologists Press, 1980.

Hollenshead, C., and others. *The Equity Equation: Fostering the Advancement of Women in Science, Mathematics, and Engineering.* Ann Arbor, Mich.: Center for the Education of Women, 1996.

Myers, P. B., and Myers, K. D. *The Myers-Briggs Type Indicator.* Palo Alto, Calif.: Consulting Psychologists Press, 1993.

National Science Foundation. *Women and Science: Celebrating Achievements, Charting Challenges.* Arlington, Va.: National Science Foundation, 1997.

Rabinowitz, V. C., and Sechzer, J. A. "Feminist Perspectives on Research Methods." In F. L. Denmark and M. A. Paludi (eds.), *Psychology of Women: A Handbook of Issues and Theories.* Westport, Conn.: Greenwood Press, 1993.

Sadker, M., and Sadker, D. *Failing at Fairness: How America's Schools Cheat Girls.* New York: Scribner, 1994.

Sullivan, A. "Gender Report." *High Hopes, Long Odds.* Indianapolis: Indiana Youth Institute, 1993.

Unger, R., and Crawford, M. *Women and Gender: A Feminist Psychology.* New York: McGraw-Hill, 1996.

11

SUCCESSFUL STRATEGIES FOR TEACHING STATISTICS

Mary B. Harris, Candace Schau

STATISTICAL THINKING is needed for effectively completing tasks both in and outside of the workplace. These tasks may include, for example, evaluating the claims made for the effectiveness of prescription drugs and herbal remedies, understanding the results of political polls, interpreting the results of children's test scores, and creating policies from research results. To meet these needs, increasing numbers of undergraduate and graduate programs require successful completion of at least one statistics course. Even when not specifically required, introductory statistics is often included as an option to fulfill a mathematics "group" requirement for graduation (Oathout, 1995).

Teaching these courses is always a challenge. Between the two of us, we have probably taught one hundred statistics classes over the years, and almost every one has included students who were uneasy, uncomfortable, and uninterested, at least on the first day of class. Moreover, almost every course has had a predominance of women students, a situation that appears to be typical in statistics classes. Indeed, virtually every article we reviewed for this chapter that reported the numbers of women in the statistics classes studied indicated that women outnumbered men, as is now the case in post-secondary education in the United States generally. Although it is not obvious that the difficulties in studying statistics are different for women and men, it is clear that statistics education at the college level is often not productive and that women students are disproportionately affected by this education.

In this chapter, we concentrate on statistics education at the college level. We summarize the literature related to women and math; women and statistics in college, including statistics performance and attitudes toward statistics; and two cognitive models relevant to learning statistics. We then discuss a number of topics relevant to teaching college statistics: the overall approach for the course, structural and organizational issues, presentation of numbers and formulas, computers and technology, process issues, recommended study strategies, counseling and advising, sexism, and classroom assessment. Finally, we provide some overall conclusions. Readers who want a more detailed review and a greatly expanded reference list are requested to contact us.

Women and Math

Based on the large body of K–12 mathematics research, three related areas in mathematics education have potentially important implications for statistics education: experience with mathematics, mathematics achievement, and attitudes toward mathematics.

Gender and Mathematics Experience

There is clear evidence that more males than females elect to take mathematics courses, particularly higher-level mathematics courses, a pattern that continues throughout postsecondary education. Males also engage in more mathematics activities outside of school, even when compared to females who are high achievers in mathematics (see for example Kimball, 1989).

Gender and Mathematics Achievement

Folklore, often reinforced by the media, suggests that males outperform females in mathematics and related tasks. Discussions (and arguments) about gender differences in mathematics have an extensive history, accompanied by an impressive amount of research. Recently, feminist researchers as well as others have studied this issue using newer sophisticated analysis techniques such as meta-analysis, a secondary analysis method that quantifies gender differences across primary research studies.

Findings from this research differ depending on how mathematics achievement is measured. The two most common measures are standardized test scores and course grades. Since the greatest body of research by far uses test scores as the outcome measure, most meta-analyses do also (for example, Hyde, Fennema, and Lamon, 1990; Linn and Hyde, 1989). Several conclusions have emerged from these studies:

- In the general population, females and males perform about equally well on measures of mathematics achievement.
- Increasing selectivity is associated with increasing mean gender differences favoring males; in general, this finding means that a moderate male advantage exists for college-bound and college students and gifted students.
- These differences are associated primarily with problem-solving and reasoning tasks and the content areas of geometry and calculus (not in algebra or in understanding mathematics concepts); there is some evidence that females are better than males in computation.
- The largest mean gender differences are often found by using the SAT-M test.
- Males' mathematics scores are more variable than are females'.
- There is much more mathematics score variability within each gender than between females and males.

Mathematics performance also can be assessed using mathematics course grades. Most commonly, females earn better grades in junior high school, high school, and college than do males (see Kimball, 1989, for a summary of this work).

Gender and Attitudes Toward Mathematics

The technique of meta-analysis has also been fruitfully applied to examining mean gender differences in attitudes toward mathematics. Studies on this topic (Hyde and others, 1990; Linn and Hyde, 1989; Pajares, 1996) lead to two generalizations. First, on average males hold more-positive attitudes toward mathematics (including their own competence and interest in mathematics) than females at the high school and college levels but not at earlier levels. Second, for both genders mathematics attitudes, including for example affect and confidence, become increasingly less positive from the end of elementary school at least through high school.

Relationships Among Mathematics Experience, Achievement, and Attitudes

A great deal of research shows that these areas are interrelated. On average, positive attitudes toward mathematics are associated with higher achievement and continued enrollment in mathematics courses, once students are given a choice about enrolling. Two of the strongest and most consistent variables affecting mathematics achievement are continued enrollment in mathematics courses and past mathematics achievement (Pajares, 1996).

Women and Statistics in College

Who takes statistics courses in college and graduate school? National numbers are not readily available. At our university, the percentages of undergraduates by gender and ethnic group membership enrolled in introductory statistics courses are comparable to the overall percentages enrolled in the institution. This pattern, at least for gender, appears to be the case at other institutions too.

We believe that one student group is frequently missing from general introductory statistics courses, certainly at the graduate level and often (but not always; see Oathout, 1995) at the undergraduate level: students majoring in mathematics or the physical or biological sciences. These students tend to either have no statistics requirement or take a specialized introductory course in their own department. Traditionally, students majoring in these fields have tended to be non-Hispanic white males. The usual introductory statistics courses, then, often do not include the group that traditionally has scored highest on mathematics tests. The absence of this group means that many of the students found in introductory statistics classes are (and often consider themselves to be) average or poorer achievers in mathematics.

Gender and Statistics Achievement

There is a growing body of research attesting to statistical and probabilistic misconceptions held by students of all ages, as well as by adults. Derry, Levin, and Schauble (1995) cite study after study that demonstrate this problem. They conclude that people do not use statistical reasoning effectively; unfortunately, this conclusion often holds even after exposure to instruction in statistics. Some research evidence, however, does indicate that teaching and training interventions can (but do not necessarily) increase people's ability to reason statistically about everyday problems.

Until the recent advent of the advanced placement test for statistics, no standardized tests to assess statistics achievement existed, so gender differences in statistical achievement using standardized test scores could not be explored. Studies that measured statistical reasoning, using instruments developed specifically for research purposes, either failed to test for gender differences (sometimes because too few males existed in these college samples to allow inferential tests) or found no gender differences.

Some research has explored possible gender differences using in-class test scores or overall statistics course performance. Schram (1996) used meta-analysis to synthesize the results from thirteen studies containing eighteen samples of college students. She concluded that (1) females earned higher grades and more total course points in statistics classes than males (seven samples), (2) females and males achieved equally when scores from a single exam were used to measure achievement (nine samples), and (3) males outscored females when a series of exam scores was used (only two samples). Unfortunately, her conclusions, especially the last one, are very tentative because of the small number of research studies and samples available.

Gender and Attitudes Toward Statistics

Most of the measures used to assess students' attitudes about statistics are paper-and-pencil Likert scales in a survey format designed for postsecondary students. Many of them include items or scales that measure college students' attitudes on three general topics: positive and negative *affect* associated with statistics; their own competence (*cognitive competence*) in understanding statistics; and the *value* of statistics, often in both personal and professional settings.

After reviewing these surveys and considering postsecondary research and instructional assessment needs, Schau developed the Survey of Attitudes Toward Statistics (SATS) to measure four aspects of postsecondary students' statistics attitudes: the three mentioned above plus attitudes about the *difficulty* of statistics as a subject. The SATS is the most carefully constructed of the surveys purporting to measure attitudes about statistics; it is the only one whose scale structure has been validated using confirmatory techniques (Dauphinee, Schau, and Stevens, 1997; Schau, Stevens, Dauphinee, and Del Vecchio, 1995).

Research using the SATS (Schau, Dauphinee, and Del Vecchio, 1992) found that beginning statistics students had slightly positive attitudes about their cognitive competence regarding statistics and the value of statistics. Their affective attitudes were neutral, and they believed that statistics would be slightly difficult. Other researchers using other surveys have tended to find similar results (for example, Elmore, Lewis, and Bay, 1993).

Most studies examining attitudes about statistics have not examined possible gender or ethnic differences. Research that has examined gender differences has either not found them or found slightly more positive attitudes in males.

Relationships Among Statistics Attitudes, Achievement, and Course Persistence

We believe that attitudes, achievement, and persistence influence each other in statistics education in ways similar to those found in mathematics. That is, we believe that persistence in statistics education and past statistics achievement have strong and positive effects on current statistics achievement and that positive statistics attitudes are related to both.

Research evidence supporting this interpretation is not yet well established. Some of the research that does exist suggests a small-to-moderate positive relationship between some aspects of attitudes and course achievement in statistics at the postsecondary level. Moreover, attitudes measured at the end of courses tend to have higher relationships with achievement than those measured at the beginning, as might be expected.

Some studies have used multiple-regression approaches to examine the relationships of many variables taken together (including attitudes) with achievement. These analytic approaches and variable sets are widely divergent, making generalizations and summaries difficult (see, for example, Elmore, Lewis, and Bay, 1993).

We have located only one study that examined the relationship between attitudes and persistence. Del Vecchio (1994) found that introductory statistics students who reported more confidence in their ability to do statistics were more likely to complete their course with a passing grade. This relationship was more than twice as strong for females as for males.

Self-Efficacy and Statistics

The issue of cognitive competence leads directly to the theory of self-efficacy, most clearly articulated by Bandura (1997), who has suggested that specific self-efficacy beliefs about one's competence in particular areas affect level of motivation and performance in a wide variety of domains. These self-efficacy expectations are, in turn, influenced by a number of variables, including mastery experiences, observation of others, verbal persuasion, physiological states, and moods. Both Bandura (1997) and Pajares (1996) provide substantial evidence that very specific contextualized measures of self-efficacy are much better predictors of performance than are more global measures. Teaching procedures that reduce statistics anxiety, encourage mastery of individual skills, and lead to recognizable success experiences should serve to directly increase self-efficacy beliefs and thus increase statistics performance both directly and indirectly.

Cognitive Models of Statistics Learning

There are many models of cognition and learning that can be fruitfully applied to statistics education. In this chapter, we briefly describe two of them: a mental-network model based on schemas and a metacognitive model. Although educators and researchers have applied these models to mathematics education (and we emphasize those conceptualizations here), much less work exists that explicitly relates them to statistics education.

Mental-Network Model

One set of theories suggests that students form and use mental networks (or cognitive structures) as they learn and think. The schema is an important concept in many of these theories (Skemp, 1987). Marshall (1995) suggests that a schema is a mental storage mechanism that is structured as a network of knowledge. Thus, schemas contain both concepts and connections among the concepts. All but the most basic schemas are built on other schemas that are interconnected. According to this model, then, expertise in statistics means possessing a rich, accurate, and relevant set of interconnected schemas and schema components (Schau and Mattern, 1997a, 1997b).

Students enter statistics classes with schemas developed during previous experience with situations they view as relevant to statistics (for example, prior mathematics courses, or newspaper articles reporting research results). Assessing the existence and accuracy of relevant foundational schemas when students first enter a statistics class can help them understand their strengths and weaknesses at that point. As students are exposed to statistics problem-solving situations, they form statistics schemas by abstracting what to them are the most relevant features from these problems and then either connecting these features into existing schemas or creating new schemas. With increasing expertise in statistics, three related processes occur: their schemas gain accurate components, the components and schemas themselves become more interconnected, and the interconnections become more appropriate (Schau and Mattern, 1997a, 1997b).

As those of us who have taught statistics know, students often develop statistics schemas that are inaccurate. Students who either do not possess prerequisite schemas or possess inaccurate prerequisite schemas (misconceptions) are likely to develop inaccurate statistics schemas or none at all, which sometimes leads them to just "give up" (Skemp, 1987). Moreover, even if students possess the necessary prerequisite schemas, the problem-solving tasks we use in our classes may actually impede accurate statistics schema formation. Three circumstances commonly found in statistics (and many other) courses interfere with this process. First, because of time constraints, students may not experience enough tasks to be able to abstract the needed relevant common features. Second, the tasks that they do experience may lack these features. Third, tasks may have many features in common, making it difficult for students to distinguish those that are relevant from those that are not. As instructors, we need to carefully select the problem-solving tasks we use in our courses and design instruction to help students identify the important features of these tasks.

In solving statistics problems, students can create a mental model by abstracting the important components of the problem and matching them to their existing schemas. This approach works well if the student possesses relevant, accurate, and accessible schemas. However, if students do not possess relevant and accurate schemas or if they do not or cannot access them, they may attempt to form their mental models through trying to recall the appropriate formula. As Skemp (1987) suggests in discussing mathematics problem solving, this approach becomes increasingly difficult as more and more formulas are encountered. Of course, there are also many problems that cannot be solved by using a single formula.

Metacognitive Models

At its core, metacognition refers to thinking about one's own thinking. Schoenfeld (1987) and others (for example, Paris and Winograd, 1990) have identified three related and important aspects of metacognition, which we have applied to statistics education: (1) the accuracy of students' knowledge about their own statistical thinking, (2) students' control of their thinking about statistics, and (3) the impact that students' attitudes about themselves and the discipline of statistics have upon their thinking. We believe that statistics education should help students develop in all three of these areas.

In our experience, many students enter postsecondary statistics courses with relatively poor metacognitive skills. That is, they are not able to accurately evaluate their thinking processes, do not engage in adequate cognitive self-control, and have beliefs that interfere with good problem solving. Of course, they have found approaches and strategies that work in their other classes (a common one is memorizing formulas and definitions), but these approaches often do not work in statistics courses.

Schoenfeld's work on metacognition and problem solving in mathematics education (1987, for instance) seems directly generalizable to these statistics students. In his work, he found that experts who are engaged in a mathematics problem-solving task usually spend the majority of their time analyzing the problem at hand and planning their solution strategies. They spend less time actually implementing their solution strategies, frequently evaluate their progress in solving the problem, and abandon or revise solution strategies that do not work. This pattern is in direct contrast to novices' problem-solving activities in mathematics (and to what we have noticed in many statistics students). Novice students spend little or no time thinking and most or all of their time implementing one (and often only one) solution strategy. If the strategy they pick is an incorrect one, they either run out of time or give up.

Other aspects of statistics education that fit into a metacognitive model are attitudes toward statistics, as discussed earlier in our chapter, and attributions for success and failure on mathematical and statistical problem-solving tasks. Weiner's theory of attribution (1986) postulates that students attribute success and failure on academic tasks to one of four causes: their innate ability (which is internal to the student and cannot be changed easily), effort (internal and changeable), task difficulty (external to and not controlled by the student), or luck (external and not controllable). As statistics teachers, we want students to attribute their failure to lack of effort (they can try harder next time), not to lack of innate ability, hard tasks, or bad luck.

There are gender differences in these attributions. Males, more than females, attribute their successes in mathematics tasks to ability, while females (more than males) attribute their successes to effort. More than males, females attribute their failures to lack of ability or to task difficulty, neither of which they can control. These gender differences exist at all levels of mathematics achievement; however, as achievement levels increase—perhaps reflecting a transition from novice to expert—both genders attribute success more to ability, and failure more to lack of effort.

Many teachers and researchers believe that metacognitive skills and processes can be taught (Paris and Winograd, 1990; Schoenfeld, 1987), although they do not agree on how to teach them. Suggestions include direct teaching of strategies, using cooperative problem-solving groups (small groups as well as the class-as-a-whole approach), evaluating videotapes of novice problem solvers, modeling problem solving of new (not "canned") problems by the instructor, and developing apprentice-type programs and experiences for students (see Pierce and Kite's Chapter Ten in this volume). Many of the suggestions we provide in the next section of this chapter follow directly or implicitly from metacognitive theories.

Issues in Teaching Statistics

There are a great many issues to consider in designing and teaching statistics courses. In this section, we review some of them and provide suggestions for teachers based both on the research and theory discussed earlier in this chapter and on our own experiences in the classroom.

Overall Approach to Statistics

One of the issues in teaching statistics is how one should approach the overall topic. Statistics may be taught as a branch of mathematics or as a tool for use in work and life. When taught as mathematics, instructors may emphasize derivation of formulas and understanding of the mathematical underpinnings of statistical equations and procedures. They may emphasize probability theory as the basis of inferential statistics and spend a substantial portion of the course explaining the underlying laws of probability, discussing a number of theoretical probability distributions, and teaching the formulas for computing probabilities for different distributions. They may also use what students often call the "plug-and-chug" approach (Oathout, 1995), which teaches students how to substitute numbers into a formula with the goal of "correctly solving" problems. Proponents of the plug-and-chug approach typically go one step further, requiring students to compare their solution to a table and to label their answer as "statistically significant" or "nonsignificant."

A growing number of statistics instructors believe that the mathematics approach is inadequate and often does not lead to learning that lasts once the course is completed. The mathematical and probabilistic emphasis is too difficult and too abstract for the majority of introductory statistics students. More important, even for those students who understand all the nuances it fails to teach students skills that are useful in evaluating statistical claims (in their professions and their daily lives) or for answering empirical research questions. The same is true for the plug-and-chug method.

Instructors who teach statistics as a tool for professional and daily life (including the two authors) use a variety of approaches. The global goal, however, is to help students develop statistical reasoning skills that are useful to them outside of school. Instructors holding this goal try to stress the value and importance of statistical knowledge. For example, we teach introductory statistics courses to graduate students in our College of Education. In these courses, we focus on real-life uses (and misuses) of statistical analysis and constantly relate the techniques we discuss to research issues. We try to provide relevant, realistic examples from research of how statistics can be used and misused in attempts to answer research questions. We frequently ask our graduate students to generate examples of research questions or data and to think about how statistical procedures can be used to answer these questions.

Structural and Organizational Issues

Many instructors—and we are among them—feel that a high degree of structure is an asset for most statistics classes. Although we recognize that some graduate courses with little in the way of an outline may provide a kind of spontaneity and freedom to pursue independent ideas that can be exciting and motivating for students, we believe that statistics classes work best if there is a reasonably detailed syllabus with a coherent, organized structure. Students seem to appreciate the use of outlines; clear expectations for assignments, tests, and grading; and a clearly organized presentation of topics during each class. This structure by no means precludes bringing in articles from current newspapers, leaving room for student questions, and providing for assignments that permit creativity on the part of the students. However, having a clear structure with a planned schedule and explicit expectations seems to reduce student anxiety, encourage frequent studying, assist in developing students' metacognitive skills, and lead to better performance.

Presentation of Numbers and Formulas

We both agree that many students in introductory statistics classes are afraid of numbers and arithmetic more than of statistics per se. We disagree on the best way to handle this issue. One of us finds that solving many problems by hand using computational versions of statistical formulas helps students. The other minimizes computation and emphasizes the conceptual meaning found in the definitional formulas covered in most introductory statistics courses. For computational problems, both of us believe that, at least at the beginning, using numbers that are small, integers, and meaningful allows students to follow the calculations better. Step-by-step examples with every intermediate step described are useful for most students. Similarly, multiple carefully crafted examples and problems are helpful, since generalization is not automatic. In fact, we often find that students request more problems, and we suggest that a number of simple computational problems be made available to students for each concept covered, so that those who want practice in working through examples by hand can get this experience and develop a sense of self-efficacy. However, we acknowledge that there are others who feel that working through formulas with small, artificial data sets is unnecessary in an age of computers.

Computers and Technology

One issue that instructors in introductory statistics classes face is the extent to which computers are used by the students. The current literature strongly and consistently recommends their use, and we agree. However, the extent of computer use should depend on the goals of the course; it clearly does depend on the extent to which computers and software packages are available for the students. We agree that computer analyses should be used for examples and demonstrations, even if students are not taught how to use the particular computational packages themselves. However, computer use does not always affect statistics learning; Stephenson (1990) found that students who were randomly assigned to learn and use a computer statistical package performed no differently on their exams than those who were not assigned to use it.

A related issue is use of technology (overheads, slides, videos, multimedia, the Internet) for presentations. Although it seems logical that such technological innovations would lead to better understanding—and instructors have recommended their use—there is little definitive research on their effects.

Process Issues

Traditionally, postsecondary statistics courses (especially those offered to large classes) have been taught using varying amounts of lecture, questions asked by class members and answered by the instructor, and discussions led by the instructor. These techniques work well for some aspects of learning, but researchers and teachers have suggested a variety of other approaches aimed at helping students construct their own understandings of statistics (content, processes, and attitudes). Assessment is often naturally built into the activities used to implement these approaches. There is theoretical justification for each of these kinds of technique, as well as some research evidence that they are effective and lead to additional positive student outcomes.

One set of techniques uses examples from professional or personal life as the basis for problem-solving tasks. These techniques are designed to be authentic; that is, instructors who use them expect that they have relevance to students outside of school, in "real" life (Colvin and Vos, 1997). They are designed to encourage students to develop good mental statistical models for approaching tasks similar to those they will experience in their lives and to develop positive attitudes about the value of statistics in real life and about their own competence in using statistics. With this approach, students may collect and analyze their own data, use existing data sets, participate in real-world problem simulations, or evaluate examples from the media such as newspaper articles and television commercials.

A second group of techniques focuses on cooperative learning groups (see Davis, Chapter Seven of this volume), in which students work together on course work, project work, and teaching and problem solving. Steinhorst and Keeler (1995) provide examples of additional ways to involve groups of students in active, conceptual learning. These authors, and others (such as Oathout, 1995), suggest that using cooperative groups leads to greater student satisfaction, less anxiety, and an increased sense of self-efficacy. There is evidence, however, that a significant number of students do not like cooperative work (Oathout, 1995).

Study Strategies

Along with other authors (see Oathout, 1995), we advocate recommending specific study strategies to the students in the class. The following suggestions (Harris, 1998) are the most important ones we make to students:

- Study frequently, at least several times per week.
- Read over the relevant material in the textbook before going to class; then reread it after class.
- In working problems, try not to look at the answer first.
- Before doing a problem, estimate what a reasonable answer would be; check your computed answer against this estimate.
- If possible, study with someone else. Try to teach a concept to someone else.
- Make up problems and examples of the concepts that come from your own experiences.
- Keep a list of your mistakes and the things you frequently forget or find difficult.

- Every few weeks, look back at the materials that have been covered previously. Think about how those materials do or do not relate to the materials currently being covered in class.
- Think about the underlying concepts in assigned work, and try to identify the essential features of the problem or task.
- Analyze assignments and plan possible solution strategies before beginning any computations. You might rewrite the assignment in your own words, draw a picture or diagram, underline the essential features, or list possible strategies.
- Do assignments well before they are due, and go back to them before handing them in.

Counseling and Advising

Oathout (1995) reported that good, caring, supportive instructors who alleviated students' anxiety by reassuring them that they could succeed, who empathized with students' difficulties and were receptive to questions, and who were accessible outside of class could influence students to persist in the face of obstacles. It is possible that such a supportive environment works by encouraging students to attribute their failures to temporary, external causes (such as insufficient effort and persistence) rather than to stable, internal ones, such as lack of ability (Weiner, 1986).

Sciutto (1995) has suggested a number of specific activities to help reduce anxiety: an icebreaking exercise in which students indicate what a class in statistics is like, the use of humor, the use of personalized examples, and a student-generated data set. We suggest also that readiness to share the instructor's own struggles when a statistics student, discussion of common errors and difficulties, and willingness to listen to individual stories can help make students more comfortable in the class.

Gender Issues and Sexism

It should go without saying that no class at any level or in any subject should be taught by a sexist instructor. Presumably, knowledge of the relevant research dispels any notions that women in statistics classes are less able to understand the content or that they perform more poorly than men (Schram, 1996). Nevertheless—from the generic *he,* to use of male sports analogies—it is easy to think of examples in which the content of statistics classes may be slanted in ways that cater more to the interests of the male students in the class than to the females. As an alternative, Kellermeier

(1994) has suggested how a statistics class can serve to introduce feminist examples and issues to the students by incorporating gender issues into the content of the class. We would add that female instructors in this traditionally masculine domain have an important opportunity to serve as role models for the men and women in their classes.

Classroom Assessment

Students learn what is important in a discipline, and how to engage in learning in that discipline, through the kinds of assessment used to assign grades (Hubbard, 1997). If statistics teachers test students using items that require mostly memorized facts, students learn that statistics is a large collection of isolated facts that must be memorized (and forgotten as soon as they walk out of the classroom). If students are tested for their skill in choosing *the* correct answer, they learn that every statistics problem has one and only one correct answer. If students are evaluated for their skill in solving a variety of short word problems, they learn that statistics problems are well defined, brief, and quickly soluble. These illusions form the basis for metacognitive beliefs that interfere with learning the kinds of statistical skill that we desire in our classrooms.

As instructors, our theories about what students should understand and be able to do should drive the design of our assessments (Begg, 1997; Colvin and Vos, 1997). Moreover, assessment should be an integral part of instruction, not an add-on used only to evaluate students and assign grades (Colvin and Vos, 1997). An integrated assessment system in statistics education should include measures that assess what students can and cannot do, as explicated in the goals for the course. These goals should be available and understood by students and instructors alike (Begg, 1997; Colvin and Vos, 1997).

Statistics assessments should be used for two broad purposes, formative and summative (Begg, 1997; Jolliffe, 1997). When used formatively, good assessments can give students and instructors information about how well the course is proceeding and what revisions need to be made. When used summatively, good assessments encourage students to develop their metacognitive skills and schemas; they allow instructors to accurately award the grades they are required to give. For both these purposes, it is important to use various types of assessment tasks (Colvin and Vos, 1997). A number of alternative kinds of assessment can be used to supplement or replace traditional "objective" test items or short word problems (Hubbard, 1997). These include, for example, short essays; oral presentations; projects; portfolios; analysis and evaluation of research reports; and concept maps, flow charts, and other visual representations of learning (Begg, 1997; Jolliffe, 1997; Schau and Mattern, 1997a, 1997b). Many of these assessment tasks can be completed by individuals working alone or in groups. Of course, each type of assessment always should relate back to course goals, and the goals should be measured in the simplest effective way possible.

In addition to evaluation of achievement and learning, it may well be worthwhile to have students complete and score a statistics attitude survey such as the SATS, especially in introductory courses. Students can then use this information to evaluate their own attitudes and seek help at the beginning of the course if these attitudes might cause problems with their learning. Another potentially useful type of attitude-related assessment task is use of learning logs, in which students can record their feelings about their statistics learning (Begg, 1997).

Summary

It appears that there are few differences between females and males in attitudes toward statistics and in statistics achievement. We know that good statistics instruction can improve general statistical reasoning for both genders. However, poor teaching with inappropriate course goals succeeds only in convincing students that statistics is painful and useless to learn. We recommend that instructors think about what they want their students to learn how to do and then begin to revise their courses to move in a direction of effectively accomplishing those goals. There is no guaranteed method to improve statistics learning, and it is likely that different methods are maximally effective with different students. Still, statistics instructors can consider the suggestions contained in this chapter and try the ones that appeal to them. We expect that most work for at least some students, but some may not. They all take time to design, implement, and evaluate. Nevertheless, each attempt moves us closer to creating statistics courses that will have a positive impact on our students' lives once they no longer are our students. We believe that this outcome is worth the effort.

REFERENCES

Bandura, A. *Self-Efficacy: The Exercise of Control.* New York: Freeman, 1997.

Begg, A. "Some Emerging Influences Underpinning Assessment in Statistics." In I. Gal and J. B. Garfield (eds.), *The Assessment Challenge in Statistics Education.* Amsterdam, Netherlands: IOS Press and International Statistical Institute, 1997.

Colvin, S., and Vos, K. E. "Authentic Assessment Models for Statistics Education." In I. Gal and J. B. Garfield (eds.), *The Assessment Challenge in Statistics Education.* Amsterdam, Netherlands: IOS Press and International Statistical Institute, 1997.

Dauphinee, T. L., Schau, C., and Stevens, J. J. "Survey of Attitudes Toward Statistics: Factor Structure and Factorial Invariance for Females and Males." *Structural Equation Modeling,* 1997, *4*(2), 129–141.

Del Vecchio, A. M. "A Psychological Model of Statistics Course Completion." Unpublished doctoral dissertation, University of New Mexico, Albuquerque, 1994.

Derry, S., Levin, J. R., and Schauble, L. "Stimulating Statistical Thinking Through Situated Simulations." *Teaching of Psychology,* 1995, 22(1), 51–57.

Elmore, P. B., Lewis, E. L., and Bay, M.L.G. "Statistics Achievement: A Function of Attitudes and Related Experiences." Paper presented at the annual meeting of the American Educational Research Association, Atlanta, Apr. 1993.

Harris, M. B. *Basic Statistics for Behavioral Science Research.* (2nd ed.) Boston: Allyn & Bacon, 1998.

Hubbard, R. "Assessment and the Process of Learning Statistics." *Journal of Statistics Education* [online], 1997, *5*(1). Available by e-mail at archive@jse.stat.ncsu.edu; message: "send jse/v5n1/hubbard."

Hyde, J. S., Fennema, E., and Lamon, S. J. "Gender Differences in Mathematics Performance: A Meta-Analysis." *Psychological Bulletin,* 1990, *107*(2), 139–155.

Hyde, J. S., and others. "Gender Comparisons of Mathematics Attitudes and Affect: A Meta-Analysis." *Psychology of Women Quarterly,* 1990, *14*(3), 299–324.

Jolliffe, F. "Issues in Constructing Assessment Instruments for the Classroom." In I. Gal and J. B. Garfield (eds.), *The Assessment Challenge in Statistics Education.* Amsterdam, Netherlands: IOS Press and International Statistical Institute, 1997.

Kellermeier, J. "Women's Studies in a Statistics Classroom." *Feminist Teacher,* 1994, *8*(1), 28–31.

Kimball, M. M. "A New Perspective on Women's Math Achievement." *Psychological Bulletin,* 1989, *105*(2), 198–214.

Linn, M. C., and Hyde, J. S. "Gender, Mathematics, and Science." *Educational Researcher,* 1989, *18*(8), 17–27.

Marshall, S. *Schemas in Problem Solving.* Cambridge, England: Cambridge University Press, 1995.

Oathout, M. J. "College Students' Theory of Learning Introductory Statistics: Phase One." Paper presented at the annual meeting of the American Educational Research Association, San Francisco, Apr. 1995.

Pajares, F. "Self-Efficacy Beliefs in Academic Settings." *Review of Educational Research,* 1996, *66*(4), 543–578.

Paris, S. G., and Winograd, P. "How Metacognition Can Promote Academic Learning and Instruction." In B. F. Jones and L. Idol (eds.), *Dimensions of Thinking and Cognitive Instruction.* Hillsdale, N.J.: Erlbaum, 1990.

Schau, C., Dauphinee, T., and Del Vecchio, A. "The Development of the Survey of Attitudes Toward Statistics." Paper presented at the annual meeting of the American Educational Research Association, San Francisco, Apr. 1992.

Schau, C., and Mattern, N. "Assessing Students' Connected Understanding of Statistical Relationships." In I. Gal and J. B. Garfield (eds.), *The Assessment Challenge in Statistics Education.* Amsterdam, Netherlands: IOS Press and International Statistical Institute, 1997a.

Schau, C., and Mattern, N. "Use of Map Techniques in Teaching Applied Statistics Courses." *American Statistician,* 1997b, *51*(2), 171–175.

Schau, C., Stevens, J., Dauphinee, T. L., and Del Vecchio, A. "The Development and Validation of the Survey of Attitudes Toward Statistics." *Educational and Psychological Measurement,* 1995, *55*(5), 868–875.

Schoenfeld, A. H. "What's All the Fuss About Metacognition?" In A. H. Schoenfeld (ed.), *Cognitive Science and Mathematics Education.* Hillsdale, N.J.: Erlbaum, 1987.

Schram, C. M. "A Meta-Analysis of Gender Differences in Applied Statistics Achievement." *Journal of Educational and Behavioral Statistics,* 1996, *21*(1), 55–70.

Sciutto, M. J. "Student-Centered Methods for Decreasing Anxiety and Increasing Interest Level in Undergraduate Statistics Classes." *Journal of Instructional Psychology,* 1995, 22(3), 277–280.

Skemp, R. R. *The Psychology of Learning Mathematics.* Hillsdale, N.J.: Erlbaum, 1987.

Steinhorst, R. K., and Keeler, C. M. "Developing Material for Introductory Statistics Courses from a Conceptual, Active Learning Viewpoint." *Journal of Statistics Education,* 1995, *3*(3), 1–12.

Stephenson, W. R. "A Study of Student Reaction to the Use of Minitab in an Introductory Statistics Course." *American Statistician,* 1990, *44*(3), 231–235.

Weiner, B. *An Attributional Theory of Motivation and Emotion.* New York: Springer-Verlag, 1986.

12

MENTORING THE WHOLE LIFE OF EMERGING SCIENTISTS

Neal B. Abraham

MENTORING UNDERGRADUATE SCIENCE MAJORS is often taken to apply to the one-on-one relationships that are formed between thesis students and faculty members, usually entailing extended conversations and interactions for a summer, an academic year, or several years at most. The focus is often on career advice and encouragement. By contrast, in this chapter I describe a complex mixture of mentoring activities developed and refined over the last twenty years by the members of the physics department at Bryn Mawr College,[1] including some things that are not traditionally thought of as mentoring. These range from early activities in recruiting new students, through strategies in introductory and intermediate courses, to internships and research experiences and career counseling. These programs have brought Bryn Mawr, a liberal arts college for women that awards approximately three hundred bachelor's degrees each year (with small Ph.D. graduate programs in twelve of its twenty-seven

Adapted from a presentation at the American Association of Physics Teachers and the American Physical Society (AAPT/APS) Physics Department Chairs Conference, May 1997; earlier versions printed in the APS *Forum for Education Newsletter,* Summer 1997, pages 4–7; and *Bryn Mawr Now,* Fall/Winter 1997–98, pages 4–5. Earlier versions with pictures and data are available on the APS Website (http://www.aps.org) and the Bryn Mawr College Physics Department Website (http://www.brynmawr.edu/acads/Physics).

departments and programs), to numerical leadership nationally in producing women physics majors.

This opening summary could also be the conclusion: What works? Many things work, but no particular thing chosen in advance is likely to work for every student. To find something that will work for a new student entering the program, the successful old programs and interventions often need to be repackaged, personalized, and invigorated with energy and compassion. To make the task more interactive (and more difficult), what works most successfully one year often does not work at all the next. Successful programs are often forgotten by the same students from one year to the next as the students mature and as individual needs and local contexts change. My advice to myself and to others is that we must listen carefully to the students themselves, act thoughtfully, assume nothing, and bring a renewed personal and friendly touch to the task over and over again.

It is well documented that a disproportionate share of students earning bachelors degrees in physics (and in mathematics and science more generally) from underrepresented groups come from colleges and universities whose student populations have substantial numbers of students from those groups. Additional facts are that:

- Predominantly undergraduate colleges and universities have a disproportionate number of physics majors.
- Research and career internships help to attract and retain students.
- Informal and formal peer teaching nurture confidence.
- Teamwork and human-scale faculty members can have an immense impact on the social rewards of doing physics.
- There is a synergistic effect of student peers sharing their academic pursuits.[2,3]

That institutions serving traditionally underrepresented minority groups carry out their tasks with a certain missionary zeal also contributes to their success. But I think that a close look at these successful programs offers insights that can benefit most students in many different kinds of institutions. Indeed, this has been the consistent message in the studies and findings of Project Kaleidoscope of what works best in undergraduate mathematics and science education. The programs leading to this success can be accomplished on many other campuses, and they turn out to be equally valuable for women, men, and members of underrepresented groups.

The Bryn Mawr College Physics Program

The *New York Times* in November 1995 and *Physics Today* in August 1996 touted the numerical strength of the physics major program at Bryn Mawr. Let me review some of that strength in numbers and diversity. Approximately 40 percent of the undergraduate students take introductory physics in one of four different courses; about 30 percent of the graduates take their degrees in mathematics or science; and, over the last two decades, the number of physics majors has grown steadily. From 1995 to 1998, nearly 5 percent of the graduates took their degrees in physics, practically one hundred times the national average for women as a percentage of the women in the graduating class. In 1995, Bryn Mawr's total of ten women physics majors was surpassed only by Harvard's fifteen and MIT's twelve.

That some form of this success has been going on for quite some time is evident from other statistics: twenty years ago, more than 5 percent of the women listed in the APS directory had received one of their physics degrees from Bryn Mawr; Bryn Mawr graduates are on the faculties of physics and/or astronomy in departments at Michigan, MIT, Connecticut, and Rice; they work at Goddard, Lucent, Bellcore, NIST, NRC, and JPL, among others; and one such graduate is the director of the physics program at NIST in Gaithersburg. In 1993, four of the twenty women elected Fellows of the American Physical Society were Bryn Mawr graduates. In recent years about 1–2 percent of the 150 women earning Ph.D.s in physics each year earned A.B. degrees from Bryn Mawr and a similar number earned Ph.D.s in related fields (astronomy, astrophysics, materials science, chemical physics, physical chemistry, engineering, and medical physics, among others). But these represent barely a third of recent Bryn Mawr College physics majors; others are successfully pursuing medicine, law, or high school and secondary school teaching or are working in science museums, industries, or research labs. In 1997, the department graduated fifteen physics majors—five of them double majoring in other departments: mathematics (3), biology (1), philosophy (1)—and an additional thirteen graduated in 1998, with double majors in mathematics (2), astronomy (1), and biology (1).

My colleagues and I at Bryn Mawr believe that the steady surge in the number of majors is tied to a mixture of factors: recruiting, advising, improved introductory course teaching strategies, encouragement of intermediate work, research opportunities, and the large number of synergetic relationships that these women form with each other. Many of these features are part of what we might call "generalized mentoring."

So, what do I mean by *whole-life mentoring*? The answer is that we must seek to intervene and provide counsel, comment, and insight at each stage of a student's thinking about physics. This is all the more necessary because today's physics undergraduates are clever and attentive. They have read the publicity about the employment malaise, they have heard about long hours and difficulties in balancing the demands of families and careers, and they have heard about and experienced both the abstract and the rote courses that differ from science as practiced and the arcane testing hurdles.

At Bryn Mawr, the mentoring process starts early, at the stage of helping the admissions office during recruiting with posters, scripts for tour guides, handouts for students and their families, and individual conversations and correspondence with prospective students. We work informally with all students who want to take physics, entice some to take physics earlier, convince others to take physics at some point, recognize good work, and encourage good students to continue. We provide a rich set of educational, learning, and teaching experiences (both those in formal class and lab settings and those in informal consultations with faculty and fellow students). We affirm a variety of learning styles and ways to demonstrate mastery; encourage and arrange internships and research experiences throughout the four years of the undergraduate experience; counsel for pursuit of a wide variety of careers; and, at each level, demand excellence and insist on involvement. We encourage all students uncertain about their preparation in physics to consider taking a departmental placement exam, which serves as a basis for assessment and counseling about starting points in the curriculum. We also work hard to make early contact with those qualifying for advanced placement by external AP exams or International Baccalaureate degrees, since some of those students are daunted by the academic maturity that is expected in sophomore courses.

There are also many misconceptions about the nature of physics with which we must deal. From AP courses or conversations with siblings at other colleges or universities or with parents who are teachers of science and engineering, some especially strong students often have a definite idea that physics is what is contained in the text, formulas, and problems in an introductory engineering physics textbook. Others became enamored of physics through their experiences with conceptual courses and believe that the practice of physics is unfettered speculation about the birth or death of the universe. Some believe that physics is only writing essays; others wish to become physicists to avoid writing essays. For each student, on her own terms, we must address the rich variety of skills and experiences that are most useful in shaping a physicist. Some must be encouraged to be less cautious, some must be encouraged to be more disciplined, and all must be encouraged to set high expectations for themselves.

Mentoring Through Designing Introductory Courses

To mentor the whole life of a student, one must stay in contact with each student in an individual setting during the critical first year of college experience. This requires getting to know enough of her past preparation, her present anxieties, and her aspirations for the future to provide advice and support. Our experience is that waiting to talk to those who spontaneously enroll in the second-year course reduces potential majors to a third or less of those who might have continued successfully.

We have tried various designs for our introductory courses, and many of these designs are important parts of the mentoring process. We have found that our introductory courses are most successful if they have a minimum of prerequisites; if they have a combination of applications (especially laced with demonstrations and laboratory explorations) and emphasis on conceptual understanding; and if students are encouraged to talk, write, discuss, and think about physics in more than chalkboard presentations, formalized homework problem solving, and textbook-based memorization and regurgitation. Sometimes we use a conceptual and thematic approach. Sometimes we require oral reports and diary entries on articles about scientific current events or science policy. It has not been necessary to use all of these techniques, but it is clear to us that conventional lecture, lab, and assignments are less effective without them.

Classroom demonstrations often seem to be distracting and inconclusive in large classes, but we are convinced that they have an important pedagogical value as a supplement to textbook descriptions and illustrations, blackboard sketches, and professorial narratives. We find that using lecture demonstration apparatus for lab experiments and using conventional laboratory equipment for classroom demonstrations gives students a sense of continuity and participation that improves their mastery. We have found it particularly effective to use demonstration apparatus in the laboratories for "conceptual labs" (the "instructions" might be *Take this miscellaneous collection of apparatus, figure out some interesting phenomena, measurements, and questions, and write us an essay about the issue and the evidence*).

Some of our labs are relatively conventional, but we often try to see that they have a twist. Ours are rarely "prove the theory by experiment," or "fit the theory to the experiment," since some aspect of the idealized problem is tampered with to give anomalous experimental results. The student teams and the teaching assistants and instructors then search for explanations, reducing the activity of a larger class to groups of only two or three investigators. We also try in lab to have different subgroups of students doing different things—a design that is hard on instructors but challenging for the students. The lively discussions in lab are a way to establish trust and rapport, which facilitate other mentoring activities.

It is important to build and sustain student confidence, especially in the introductory courses. Some students focus on the 10 percent of wrong answers on a test and do not recognize our endorsement or their mastery implicit in a 90 percent correct score on the exam. Encouragement can be delivered privately through written comments (on homework and exams) and in person. Neutral colors for grading and comments may help to deliver the message (red is often taken to be harsh and critical despite the actual encouragement of the words). Another feature that we changed about a decade ago was our previously common practice of "challenging exams," designed, we told ourselves and our students, not to demoralize but to indicate the level of mastery we expected—a level most students eventually reached. Nonetheless, these exams provided discouraging feedback to students, and they provided very little indication to students of their growing mastery. Awakened by a visit and report of the Committee on the Status of Women in Physics (CSWP), we have since chosen to use a different testing strategy, with a wide range of questions (that may be answered by examples, definitions, illustrations, and explanations, as well as conventional problem solving) and choice in most sections, so that the emphasis is on what students know rather than on their ability to do a very small and necessarily unrepresentative subset of problems.

Many of us have taken to using short office meetings in which we return one-hour or midterm exams to students to have a chance to offer a few comments or words of encouragement or interpretation of the significance of their tests or assignments. This provides an important supplement to the always-positive benefits from quickly returning exams with comments and explanations. Prompt debriefing also helps to make testing and test reworking a part of the learning experience. Sometimes we approach students in lab or in the corridors to assure them that they are doing well enough to major. In short, we find that the best way to expand the pool of majors beyond the "hard core," self-selected, and hard-to-deter is to provide individual advice and encouragement—mentoring at a time that we had often neglected previously.

Curricular Advice and Opportunities for Students

The faculty members in the department share the tasks of helping students plan their curricular choices. Our major program is probably more enticing because there is room for choice among the curricular offerings and because substitution of other advanced math and science classes is permitted. We frequently find ourselves helping individual students rearrange their future plans (at least their curricular plans); I suggest that it is not enough to offer this service once a year, or even once a semester, because students benefit most from this kind of advice in those quiet crisis moments of indecision or choice. It is not clear whether it is the choices we offer, or the frequent discussions and advice that choice necessitates, that have the greater positive impact.

We have made some interesting mentoring-related choices about our intermediate and advanced curriculum. One goal is to provide a rich set of laboratory experiences; each student in our intermediate electronics course has a bench with a full set of apparatus. Although the students are encouraged to cooperate, visit each other's benches, and ask questions and share answers, no one makes the experiment work (no other hands are on the knobs and dials) at each bench except the student herself. This may make some things slower, but it builds the student's confidence over the semester that she can operate oscilloscopes, design circuits, and analyze data. Other labs emphasize teamwork; some labs involve one-week projects, and some are multisession projects (laboratory courses may meet three afternoons a week) with freedom for students to explore alternatives. Many labs are well equipped with research-grade investments that introduce students to sophisticated technologies and research styles and strategies, which students may see again in research projects. When labs run late, we often take twenty-minute breaks for tea (faculty-supplied) and snacks (student-supplied). Conversations are wide-ranging and vigorous and help to build camaraderie. The lost time is more than made up in the added efficiency that a break and a little sugar can provide.

In our junior-and-senior-level curriculum, we teach most courses in alternate years, in a coordinated program with nearby Haverford College's physics department, so that most courses are offered every year at one campus or the other. Haverford's number of physics majors is about the same size as ours, though their majors are predominantly male as is typical in coed schools. If students choose to mingle, these alternately offered courses foster a coeducational environment and a wider variety of instructors. Some students enjoy the cross-registrations. Conversely, others find them laden with added competitive pressure, and even a formal distance of as little as a mile (despite frequent shuttle bus runs) is enough for some students to detach themselves from a student and faculty network of teamwork and support, significantly depressing their performance and confidence. Beyond the commingled courses, we also emphasize in upper-level courses that work and material are not simply defined by texts and in-class presentations. We use library reserves and frequently ask students to prepare written or oral reports on supplemental topics. Coaching each student through preparation and exploration of a report from current research literature or electronic sources is an added way to build confidence. Once a student has mastered something for presentation to her peers, she gains an added sense of accomplishment that goes beyond presenting it to the faculty member for a grade. In addition, training each student to be a skillful listener and questioner of her peers gives a further confidence burst.

Nonetheless, both because of numbers and on principle, we have resisted merging our second-year courses with those taught at Haverford. Experience teaches us that confidence is fragile for some women physics majors, and the added pressure and competition in larger and coed classes in the first two years contribute to a noticeable reduction in the number of women majoring in physics. We also find that students must learn to use office hours, plan ahead to work on problem assignments, and develop teams for initial out-of-class discussions. Smaller sophomore year classes make it easier for the faculty member to meet regularly with each student, invite her for midcourse assessments, and help her make adjustments in the critical year in which she decides on her major.

Research Opportunities and Internships for Students

We also have a vigorous program of student research opportunities during the academic year and in the summer. Thanks to a complex network of successful fundraising, Bryn Mawr supports thirty to fifty students doing summer research in mathematics and the sciences. Nonetheless, our population of science majors far exceeds our ability to offer them on-campus summer internships. Hence we have a vigorous program to encourage students to look for research internships in industry and government labs and at other colleges and universities. In physics, one faculty member is designated to advise students about such job hunting, and much of the fall is spent in helping students identify options and prepare resumes that emphasize their interests and practical experiences in computing, electronics, and instrumentation. We find it helpful to most students that they do summer research on campus early in their four years (after the first or second year) so that they have skills and experiences (and detailed letters of recommendation) to help them qualify for highly competitive positions after their junior year. This process provides mentoring opportunities, including counseling each student to help her gain an appreciation for the generalized value of the specific class projects or lab experiences she might have had.

For research at undergraduate colleges, encouraging students to take summer internships after their junior year can be a sacrifice for ongoing research programs, since to prepare a student one often invests a summer or more in intensive supervision of an apprentice so that a second summer is more productive. However, we have found that students gain considerable maturity and confidence from working with those who had not taught them elementary subjects, and from returning to campus with summarized accomplishments that their local mentors had not seen pass through foibled stages. This choice is therefore not one that every department or faculty member may wish to emulate, particularly at primarily undergraduate institutions with fewer students; but we feel the efforts to find placements for juniors, some seniors, many sophomores, and a few freshmen have paid off in better, stronger, and more confident majors.

A consequence of these systematic efforts is that most juniors and many seniors find summer positions off campus, so our employment opportunities are available also to sophomores and some freshmen. I think we have clear evidence that early opportunities to do science-related research are among the best forms of encouragement to students to continue to do coursework toward completion of a physics major. The college has extended this to offering academic-year research internships to specially selected first-year students. The mentoring opportunities that emerge informally during early research experiences are many. We also have formalized programs in the summer that include seminars on faculty research and brown-bag discussions about science topics and science careers. The summer program ends with a gathering of all students and faculty for a series of oral presentations. Then in the early fall, all students who did summer research give talks about their work, open to all physics students and following a pizza party. In recent years, we have needed two long evenings for all of the students to report about their experiences and their results. These sessions are not only fun and interesting but they also do a good job of encouraging first-year and second-year students to apply for such programs.

Our academic-year student research program has also grown and evolved. We ask interested students to talk with each faculty member to gain an idea about on-campus research opportunities. We ask students to apply to the department, indicating their choices, and then we assign students after departmental discussions, thereby helping faculty members balance their desires to be supportive and encouraging of eager students with practical issues of time management and student needs. We have often had trouble getting students to complete thesis writing on time at the end of a yearlong project, but this has gotten easier since we moved from a single end-of-the-year report to an alternative pioneered by our chemistry department. We now have students who are doing research give oral reports at the end of the fall semester, which requires them to work through a formulation of the background, motivation, and goals for their ongoing work. This sometimes-painful process, compelled midway through the project, makes it far easier to begin writing introductory and background chapters of a thesis early in the spring semester. We then join with the chemistry departments of Bryn Mawr and Haverford for a student poster session in a public forum late in the spring semester. This is a good opportunity for the students to see the work of their peers and for underclass students to learn more about on-campus research opportunities. It is also a good time for faculty and students to mingle and learn of the career choices of the seniors.

Faculty Apprentice Opportunities for Students

We also have a program sponsored by college funds to "apprentice" students as faculty members, so that they can see more facets of the whole life of a faculty member. In this program we are encouraged to help the students participate in the design and uncertain phases of a research project, in assessment and ordering of equipment from suppliers and apparatus from the instrument shops, and in regular reassessment of goals and accomplishments. Some argue that it is important to make an undergraduate research project "successful" or "conclusive." Instead, we have found that it is equally valuable for students to have some insight into the doubts, despair, and indecisions that are natural parts of our professional lives. We have a similar program for teaching apprentices and involve those students in preparing and assessing assignments, examinations, and class presentations.

Giving students teaching opportunities is another form of mentoring. Coaching of and working collegially with student teachers helps give them perspective on learning and pedagogy. Students working as laboratory teaching assistants, tutors, monitors of a physics clinic for problem solving, graders, or in any facet of the program have an opportunity to see others making progress in their mastery. The students mentor each other across the four years of their work. They seek advice and guidance from each other; they work together in teams both as students and as teachers. Much is made in many places of the importance of role models, and we have found in the educational environment that one of the most important forms of role modeling is having peers, or near-peers, fill the pipeline of success. When a student can see a role model at every level of success, she is hard pressed to make generalizations about gender-related difficulties, and she encounters many encouraging glances and words that suggest she may soon be like them.

Mentoring Through Advising Materials and Visitors

Another way to mentor is to provide advice in a variety of media; printed handbooks, posters, and Websites are among the ways we try to make information available. Our brochures, posterboards, and Website range over such topics as careers, preparing for teaching, preparing for the GREs, announcements of where recent graduates are working, and advice on how to plan for different and flexible futures. We update them often and discuss them with students over pizza and soda in the evenings. We also frequently mix with students to discuss time and stress management, review our curriculum, and have meals with our colloquium speakers. Our evening (dinner-time) speaker program held in the cafeteria sideroom has been most successful in drawing students and has given them the opportunity to dine with other physicists. We have found that our own contacts, alumnae, and the CSWP speakers list give us a nearly inexhaustible supply of women with diverse careers, talents, topics, and stories. One way to mentor your majors is to recruit others to share in the mentoring!

However, we rely less on infrequent visits by outside women than on the daily support networks that develop among students within the department. Programs and facilities range from a "majors' room" with computers and lockers; lock-and-key access to kitchenette, computers, and classrooms; desks in research labs for students doing research; mailboxes for messages; placing homework solutions in the conference rooms as well as in the more distant library; and a student-run evening physics clinic for answering questions. With a little luck and lots of synergy, our majors have come to think of the physics department as the place where they can and will find each other for teamwork or companionship, for problem solving or relaxation, daytime, nighttime, and weekends. They mentor each other as much as we mentor them—indeed, sometimes even more.

There are other little touches that give *whole-life* added meaning. Bulletin boards in the department corridors contain information about new science, women in science, summer jobs and careers, and activities of current majors and alumnae. The students design T-shirts, celebrating such things as "women in classically forbidden regions" and "strangely attractive women," demonstrating their scientific humor and their awareness of their unique participation as members of an underrepresented group in physics. The majors often organize field trips to industrial, university, and national labs, and we arrange class schedules to support these trips.

Mentoring Advice

Let me also reiterate an earlier point that makes the task for all of us much more difficult when it comes to mentoring. Our students are agile and active readers; they listen well, and they hear our code words and our occasional despair. Every word about job shortages, the absence of women, "chilly climate"-style discrimination in laboratory work and research groups, hiring crunches, horrors of graduate school teaching, difficult working conditions for teaching assistants, and competitive testing and grading practices is heard and magnified. We must work hard to spread reality, and we must caution students when it is appropriate to do so. One of the reasons we post and report on our alumnae career paths is to assure current students that employment options remain open. We must counsel students against applying to some graduate schools where teaching is abysmal or where the expectations are for one prior year of graduate-level work (an inappropriate standard but one that is not uncommon when master's-level foreign students and advanced-placed undergraduate majors at research universities might gain that qualification). Poor teaching in graduate-level courses is not a secret, so it behooves graduate schools to invest in burnishing their programs and thereby their reputations.

Summary

I suggest that mentoring has three primary tasks: giving honest advice, instilling confidence, and leaving room for growth. Among the best ways to do this:

- Share secrets of successful teaching and learning strategies.
- Validate student mastery and career choices.
- Ensure a personal and socially supportive atmosphere.
- Be aware of the fragility of success.

Perceptions are reality. What you meant or thought you had done is irrelevant if it contradicts the stories students have in their own minds.

Such classic attributes of the chilly climate as low expectations, mindless assignments, or sexist (racist) attitudes or remarks can destroy careful plans and good intentions; each of us must be forever on guard to encourage and support. One misstep—not only remembered but quoted or retold and embellished for shock value or emphasis or outrage—may destroy the atmosphere for a generation of students (two to four years). Become accustomed, in your conversation and examples, to using pronouns and career choices that reflect your students' interests and that clearly reflect the diversity of students. One of the simplest rules is to eschew use of male pronouns as "generic" or "gender neutral." Make yourself say it until it just comes naturally: "The scientist . . . , she . . ." or "The engineer who describes her work . . ." or other such phrases you might rehearse. Avoid making allusions to the nonscience community (such as parents, siblings, and friends) that use gender-specific language (mother, grandmother, sister, girlfriend). Avoid using analogies or activities (sports, car mechanics, cooking) that are familiar to only some of the students in a way that gives them an advantage—though you might easily draw on student expertise with some activity to explain or illustrate a sensation, a learned experience, or a developed intuition. In short, be aware of all of the pitfalls of the chilly climate, identify with all students in your class, and see and hear yourself through their eyes and ears as much as possible.

Finally, for good and effective mentoring, keep asking, keep trying, and keep listening. Expect to have to do things differently each and every time. Each new student benefits most from energetic and personal mentoring, not from generic goodwill.

NOTES

1. Over the course of twenty years, the major contributing faculty members have been Rosalie C. Hoyt, retired; John R. Pruett, retired; Alfonso M. Albano, currently chair (aalbano@brynmawr.edu); Peter A. Beckmann; Mary E. Scott; Teymour Darkhosh (now at St. Mary's College); Michelle D. Shinn (now at Jefferson Laboratory); Elizabeth C. McCormack; Aurora Vicens (now at the Universitat de les Illes Balears, Spain); and Charles Samuels.

2. David Davis-Van Atta, Sam C. Carrier, and Frank Frankfort, "Educating America's Scientists: The Role of the Research Colleges," a report prepared for a conference on "The Future of Science at Liberal Arts Colleges," held at Oberlin College, Oberlin, OH, June 9–10, 1985 (Office of the Provost, Oberlin College, Oberlin, OH, May 1985); Sam C. Carrier and David Davis-Van Atta, "Maintaining America's Scientific Productivity: The Necessity of the Liberal Arts Colleges," prepared for the second conference on

"The Future of Science at Liberal Arts Colleges," held at Oberlin College in June 1986 (Office of the Provost, Oberlin College, Oberlin, OH, Mar. 1987).

3. "What Works: Building Natural Science Communities: A Plan for Strengthening Undergraduate Science and Mathematics," Vol. 1 and Vol. 2 (Project Kaleidoscope, Washington, D.C., 1991) pkal@pkal.org.

PART FOUR

CHANGING INDIVIDUAL EXPECTATIONS

THE CLASSROOM IS CERTAINLY NOT the only locus of change in higher education. In Part Four, we consider three kinds of structured interactions that take place at least partly outside the college classroom: mentoring disadvantaged high school girls, building and maintaining relationships between advisors and students of color, and teaching women self-defense strategies. We look at how the interactions taking place in these less conventional settings can have enormous effects on reducing student alienation, developing feelings of belonging and entitlement, creating a learning community, and increasing self-efficacy. Though the word *mentoring* appears in only one of the three titles in this part, all the chapters are about guiding women along new pathways and helping them come into their own power and strength.

Mentoring, Roxana Moayedi writes in Chapter Thirteen, has often been constructed in individualistic, careerist terms: if their individual deficiencies can be remedied by guidance from a successful mentor, women and people of color can achieve educational and workplace equity. The benefits of the mentoring interaction are presumed to flow in one direction: downward in the status hierarchy. This model of mentoring allows the mentor to bask in rescuer fantasies and to take credit for good works without conceding any of his or her own privilege. Moreover, it functions to obscure structural inequities of classism, racism, and sexism.

Moayedi set out to create a different, more reciprocal kind of mentoring. Her target group, inner-city Hispanic immigrant high school girls, certainly stood to benefit from mentoring relationships; Hispanic girls are the least likely of any major ethnic group to attend college. However, Moayedi structured her program so that the mentors—college students—had the opportunity to learn about the sociology of race and class and to see firsthand the effects of class and ethnic backgrounds on their mentees' opportunities. She writes eloquently not only about the positive effects on the high school girls and their families but also about how the college student mentors grew from "rescuers of the disadvantaged" to allies and advocates for change.

A similar focus on the dynamics of change characterizes Chapter Fourteen, by Susan Murphy, Sharon Goto, and Ellen Ensher. In this case, the interaction under study is between advisors and advisees. Advising is a critical point in education, one that can be a site of support and a source of learning for both parties. With the increasing numbers of women of color entering higher education, advisor-advisee relations that cross cultural divisions are becoming more frequent. Both parties in these relationships may bring with them stereotypes about the other, and first impressions are very important. Moreover, both parties may make culturally specific assumptions about how such a relationship should be developed and sustained.

Many constructs have been developed to broadly categorize cultural differences; individualistic-collectivist is perhaps the best known example. Murphy, Goto, and Ensher remind us that despite the validity of generalizations about culture, situation and context are also very important—no one, for example, is *always* collectivist or individualistic. Moreover, group classifications in use in North America, such as "Asian" or "Latino-Latina" are generalizations; subgroups within these designations (for example, Vietnamese and Taiwanese) may have very different experiences of immigration and level of acculturation. If an advisor relies on group membership alone in trying to understand an advisee, developing an authentic relationship can be impeded. The authors illustrate how advisors' knowledge of their students' cultural backgrounds must be integrated with knowledge of the individual advisee at every stage of developing and maintaining an advising relationship.

Mentoring and advising are dyadic relationships, in which two individuals jointly create an environment for learning. By contrast, in Chapter

Fifteen Glenda Russell and Kari Fraser explore a group setting for fostering women's development. The setting is a self-defense course, Model Mugging, which teaches both physical skills and psychological strategies for coping with the threat of violence. Model Mugging is designed to move women from fear-governed behaviors (paralysis or avoidance) to empowerment and self-efficacy.

Prohibition of anger and aggression for women is among the most powerful gender controls in contemporary society. Moreover, women are encouraged by countless media depictions to believe that they will be unable to respond effectively should they be physically or sexually assaulted. How, then, can an educational intervention succeed in disrupting these gendered norms and images? The effectiveness of Model Mugging, as revealed in Russell and Fraser's interviews with graduates, stems from creating a safe environment and providing a clear structure. Perhaps most important, the pedagogy is tailored to the learner's strengths, both physical and psychological.

Moving women from fear to empowerment through self-defense training can be taken—literally and metaphorically—as a model for developing self-efficacy in other settings. Indeed, participants in the program report that their newly acquired skills generalize to very different situations at work and in relationships. Russell and Fraser use their analysis of the structures and processes involved in Model Mugging to create general principles for optimizing learning environments for women.

In all the works in Part Four, learning is conceptualized as reciprocal. Mentors learn from and about those they mentor. Advisees learn from their advisors, but advisors too must learn about the realities of people from diverse cultural backgrounds. Women learn not only from designated instructors but also from each other as they confront their fears of victimization. In all these instances, as Russell and Fraser suggest, women have chosen to "identify with other women around their power rather than their vulnerability. Learning environments that reinforce women's strength support women in seeing themselves as competent, capable, and able to protect their interests proactively rather than simply reacting to the behavior and expectations of others."

13

MENTORING A DIVERSE POPULATION

Roxana Moayedi

OVER THE PAST TWO DECADES numerous reports have suggested that mentoring is an important part of an individual's career and workforce development. These reports, however, focus their attention on the importance of mentoring as a tool for social integration into the "organizational culture" of academia or the workplace. This chapter presents a new focus, a case study of mentoring as a feminist pedagogical technique, to teach about the intersection of race, class, and gender. The pilot course, titled "Mentoring and Diversity," was taught at Trinity College in Washington, D.C. This report provides an overview of mentoring programs in institutions of higher education, includes a description of Trinity College's mentoring program, and presents recommendations for future implementation of such a program.

Review of the literature and past research on mentoring suggests three facts: everyone who makes it has a mentor; it is especially important for women (Bova, 1995; Halcomb, 1980; Kim, 1995; Merriam, 1983; Missirian, 1982) to have mentors because of the obstacles they often face in career advancement; and yet mentor pools are largely composed of white males. The lack of available female mentors (Cook, 1979; Sheehy, 1976; Shapiro, Haseltine, and Rowe, 1978) is particularly disturbing in

The author gratefully acknowledges editorial advice and support from her colleague and friend, Norma Nager.

light of research indicating that same-sex mentoring relationships are most productive (Goldstein, 1979; Tidball, 1973). Research also indicates that early experience with the protégé role is linked to willingness to assume the mentor role later (Carden, 1990; Phillips-Jones, 1983).

Diagnosing mentoring as an important organizational skill (part of the game that women must learn to play to survive in organizations) has prompted various institutions of higher education to develop formal mentoring programs for their female and minority students (Bell and Drakeford, 1992; Dickey, 1996; Association of American Colleges, 1991; Redmond, 1990). These very popular programs usually involve matching a junior or senior college student with a successful career woman working in the field in which the protégé is interested. The personal ambition of the protégé is the focus of the mentoring relationship. Mentors are seen as experts who socialize their protégés into the "rules of the game" and provide job contacts in the future. Establishing mentoring programs has become particularly popular as a tool for increasing the number of women and minorities in nontraditional fields such as mathematics and science (Atkinson, 1991; National Science Foundation/ACM, 1992; Pearl and others, 1990). The career model of mentoring is designed to help women and minorities "catch up" with white men. Mentoring programs with a community focus, in which college students become mentors to at-risk elementary or secondary school students, are often limited to tutorial services for developing basic skills.

A latent function of the career model of mentoring is to reinforce an elitist and individualistic lesson. The unintended message to students is that if these successful women and minorities can achieve career success in the face of obstacles, it must be simply faulty socialization, lack of motivation, or other individual deficits that keep more women and minorities from attaining the same heights. Students fail to see the larger social system in which the struggles of all women and minorities—whether successful or not—take place.

In a community-service-oriented mentoring program, like most community service projects, students are supposed to learn from their experiences. However, we know that learning from experience is neither easy nor automatic. In the absence of any activities designed to facilitate learning, students often learn nothing or learn the wrong lesson. Mentors who participate in community-service projects are often motivated by a sense of charity, usually rooted in their religious faith. Others see it as an opportunity to link their college experience to future job opportunities. Usually, the only outcome reported by the mentor is the personal satisfaction of helping those who are less fortunate. Again, like most community-service projects, the mentoring relationship does nothing to challenge students' stereotypes of disadvantaged people, and at worst it encourages victim-blaming attitudes.

In response to these shortcomings, Trinity College proposed to develop a course titled "Mentoring and Diversity," to combine a structured mentoring program with classroom learning. Trinity is a Catholic liberal arts college for women. Because it is an urban college, the student population is quite diverse. The general curriculum is interdisciplinary, focusing on development of leadership values and skills; thus the course is designed to be interdisciplinary. The semester discussed here was taught by a team of sociology and chemistry faculty members. The academic section of the course focused on review of literature and mentoring, as well as on exploration of race, class, and gender scholarship; the theme of women in mathematics and science was emphasized. The mentoring component was designed to match Trinity students who would be mentors with female students from two high schools. One group came from Bell Multicultural High School, which is an inner-city D.C. public school and a model of multicultural education. Eighty percent of Bell students are Hispanic and recent immigrants from disadvantaged backgrounds. The smaller group came from Paint Branch High School, which is located in a middle-class suburban area of Maryland. The participants from this latter group were in a parent-sponsored organization at their high school that encourages young women to pursue careers in math and science.

It was hoped that the students from Paint Branch would be mentored by Trinity students majoring in math and science. High school students were expected to attend four workshops focusing on diversity training, development of leadership skills, and exploration of careers in math and science. They also were expected to "shadow" their mentors for two half days, attending classes and having meals at Trinity. In addition to these structured activities, mentors were required to meet with their partners in between events (see Table 13.1).

Another unique feature of this program was the inclusion of mothers of the high school students. The mothers were expected to participate in a campus open house and a tour at the beginning of the project, and to attend a leadership conference in the middle of the semester. In this conference, successful African American and Hispanic women gave presentations on their commonalities as well as their unique experiences in the workplace. The primary objective of the conference was to challenge students' and other participants' stereotypes and misinformation about their own group as well as members of other ethnic groups. In the process, we hoped that their recognition of common themes in Hispanic and African

Table 13.1. "Mentoring and Diversity" Course Activities and Participation Design.

Event	Participation: Trinity Students	Participation: High School Students	Participation: Parents
Diversity training (conducted by National Coalition Building Institute)	x	x	
Reception (tour of Trinity campus)	x	x	x
Shadowing	x	x	
Workshop on development of leadership skills (conducted by WOW)	x	x	
Shadowing	x	x	
Second leadership workshop (conducted by WOW)	x	x	
"Gentle Heroism: Women's Experience in the Holocaust" (presented by Mayrana Goldenberg, chair, women's studies, Montgomery College)	x		
Community service and student activism (presented by Trinity students)	x		
2nd annual Leadership Symposium	x	x	x
Women in mathematics and science: naval research	x	x	
Final reception and awards ceremony (with students and parents)	x	x	x

American work experiences would lead to strategies for forming multicultural alliances. The mothers also were to participate in an awards ceremony at the end of the semester. For the majority of the Bell students and their mothers, this would be their first time on a college campus.

The program was initially designed to establish a formal mentoring relationship between college women and at-risk Hispanic high school students. The Paint Branch students were added to the project to give a math-and-science focus to the project and thus increase the likelihood of obtaining funding for it. This component would allow identification of the specific barriers to math-and-science achievement experienced by women and minority students.

What was the rationale for targeting low-income girls and their mothers? According to the Census Bureau, in 1990 among all women of color, Hispanic women had the highest drop-out rate of any group in high school and were identified as the students most at risk. They also had the lowest enrollment rates on college campuses. In 1990, about one in twelve Hispanic women had completed college, compared to one-fifth of white women, one-eighth of African American women, and one out of eleven Native American women. According to Tinajero (1991), the most significant factor determining whether Hispanic females enter college is their mother's attitude and encouragement of postsecondary education. Given the low enrollment rate of Hispanic females in college, the number of mothers who would be able to actively model educational and career aspirations for their daughters would be very small. There is, then, a need to make mothers partners in the postsecondary experience for Hispanic female students.

Expected Outcomes

Shrewsbury (1987) suggests that feminist pedagogy is characterized by three concepts: community, empowerment, and leadership. These were the general goals both for the structured activities and for our classroom. We hoped to create a community of learners (mentors, protégés, and teachers) who learn and practice leadership skills and feel empowered by these experiences. In line with these general goals, we developed more specific expected outcomes for the participating high school girls:

- Encouragement to complete high school education and raise their expectations of attending college
- Exposure to higher education and various professional careers, particularly in math and science
- An increase in mothers' commitment to their daughters' education by involving the mothers in the mentoring process

For Trinity students, we hoped to use mentoring relationships as a pedagogical tool to encourage three additional outcomes:

1. Develop a deeper understanding of difficult and complex issues related to race, class, and gender. Specifically, we hoped they would gain awareness of individual and organizational factors that encourage female participation in careers in math, science, and technology.
2. Develop mentoring skills.

3. Encourage mentors and protégés to recognize the significance of such mentoring relationships so that they would want to be mentors in the future; this was our long-term goal.

Project Implementation

Sixteen Trinity college students enrolled in the course. None were mathematics or science majors. Despite our efforts, we failed to recruit any math or science majors to act as mentors. This was due to the small number of students in these majors as well as scheduling conflicts. Among sixteen students, four were Hispanic, one African American, one Chinese American, and one from Indonesia. The remainder were of European descent.

A Bell High School counselor, appointed by the Bell principal, selected ten students from that school. She described them as motivated students who "needed a push" to consider going to college as a real possibility; they were in grades eleven and twelve. All were recent Hispanic immigrants except one, who was Vietnamese.

The Trinity College science faculty member, who was a parent advisor of the Paint Branch Science Club, selected six students. They were all tenth graders, five white and one Chinese American. Lack of support by the Paint Branch principal resulted in sporadic participation on the part of these students. We had hoped that the mentoring relationship between Trinity students majoring in math and science and Paint Branch students would provide the raw material to counter the American myth about who can do math and science, which emphasizes the importance of innate ability. Rather than presenting theory and research information, the learning process for the course was designed to be reality-based and active. However, a number of factors, including the absence of any math and science mentors and sporadic participation by Paint branch students, made it necessary to cover this topic with the more traditional method of class presentations and discussions. Although Paint Branch students' interest in careers in math and science went unused, as the following section shows, their middle-class background became an unexpected pedagogical tool for exploration of the impact of social class.

Project Impact

The major challenge of this kind of experiential format is the unpredictability of the outcome and how to best use the outcome to teach about race, class, and gender. In our case, the ethnic and social class diversity among mentors and mentees created a learning context for Trinity students. Their diversity provided the context for exploration and discussion of race and class in shaping options and influencing their behavior as women.

The semester began with a review of the literature on mentoring, discussion of the nitty gritty of being a mentor, and match-up of Trinity students with their mentees. We discussed research findings on the benefits of same-sex (and same-race) mentoring relationships, particularly for minority women (Dreher and Cox, 1996; Jackson, 1996; Kalbfleisch and Davies, 1991; Wilson, 1992). We agreed, as a class, that since it was practical, and diversity was the theme of the class, cross-race or cross-ethnic mentoring relationships should be encouraged. However, we still gave students the option of choosing a protégé from either Bell Multicultural or Paint Branch High School.

This discussion triggered an intense argument outside of the classroom between a group of Hispanic and white students who both wanted to have Hispanic mentees. The Hispanic students suggested that their white classmates could never develop as strong a mentor-mentee rapport as they themselves could based on their common ethnic background. The white students angrily argued that compared to their middle-class Hispanic classmates, such painful experiences as coming from a working-class background or being rape victims would make them equally good partners for these underprivileged Hispanic girls. We recognize that both groups perceived Bell students as victims and were competing for the role of the rescuer. After a few private meetings with the students, the discussion was brought into the classroom.

This episode was used to bring to life some of the assigned readings in Andersen and Collins (1995). One of the main points made by those authors is that race, class, and gender do not create automatic connections. Sharing common enemies or victim status cannot be the reason for solidarity. The readings and classroom discussions made it clear that *partnership in misery does not necessarily produce partnership for change.* The conclusion was reached in the class that, to be an effective mentor or ally, it is more important to be able to see the world through the partner's eyes, develop compassion, and be able to act on behalf of the partner. The definition of a good mentor that emerged from our discussion was not the traditional idea of mentor-as-expert but rather mentor-as-ally or advocate who will be there for the partner and support growth and change. Clarification of the role of the mentor was significant in light of the discomfort expressed by the majority of the Trinity students about assuming the position of the all-knowing expert.

At the beginning of the semester, all mentors were asked to write anonymously about their expectations and fears of participating in the project. A majority (80 percent) expressed discomfort with the idea of being perceived as an expert by their protégé. The second most common anxiety expressed by the Trinity students was that they might fail to develop a relationship with their partner and thus would fail to make a difference in the partner's life. Defining mentor as ally or advocate allowed for cross-race and cross-ethnicity mentorship and also made assuming the role more comfortable for Trinity students.

Our mentoring program provided many unique opportunities to challenge and combat stereotypes held by Trinity students about people of color and their situations. For example, all the mentees and their mothers were invited to an introductory reception held at Trinity College. Though all the Paint Branch students attended the reception with their mothers, only one mother of a Bell Multicultural student attended the reception with her daughter. Trinity students were required to write a reflective paper after each event, but only one student noted the discrepancy in mothers' participation as significant in her reflection.

The issue was raised in class. Students were asked whether they thought that social class was a factor in the discrepancy. They tried to dismiss it as an individual choice or lack of assimilation on the part of the mothers who did not attend. One student said that "these mothers [recent immigrants] did not realize that attending school activities was important and that this program is teaching Bell students that they should attend school activities for their children in the future." Information received from counselors at Bell High School was used to challenge Trinity students' stereotypes and misinformation. It was suggested that some of the parents might not be here in the United States, and other parents might have been working or could not afford to pay for a babysitter. The one Vietnamese couple wanted to attend the reception but communicated to the Bell counselor that they felt uncomfortable and embarrassed since they do not speak any English. This incident helped Trinity College students understand how the social structure of inequality contributes to different life chances and choices for people of various races and class backgrounds.

Other incidents highlighted the privileges that exist in the system for white, middle-class, and upper-class people while people of color and/or from lower-class status face disadvantages. During a grassroots leadership workshop attended by high school mentees, students were asked to suggest social problems and solutions. The passion and anger of the Bell students made the condition of their school the main focus of the workshop. They said that although their school is a D.C. public school it does not have a cafeteria or a gymnasium. They talked about various actions they had taken as a community to get these facilities installed. Students blamed Bell students' apathy for their failure to obtain the needed facilities. The discussion focused on different courses of action the Bell students should continue to take, such as demonstrations in front of the office of the superintendent of D.C. public schools, or contacting the media. One of the continuing education students from Trinity raised an interesting question. She said that neither her white, middle-class children nor the Paint Branch students who were sitting there had to go to the streets to demand basic facilities for their schools; she wondered why we were asking Bell students to do so.

Through this incident, the students learned that instead of blaming the victims (that is, the Bell High School students) for their lack of activism, they should examine the social contexts in which disadvantaged people are educated. They came to appreciate the frustration, anger, and courage of the Bell students who were demanding basic services.

Overall evaluation of student journals and their final reflective papers suggested that the combination of mentoring activities, workshops, readings, and classroom discussions contributed to the effectiveness of the course in raising consciousness about issues related to race, class, and gender. The mentoring component of the course allowed Trinity students to listen to people who have been silenced, by placing those people's stories in the center. It allowed the students to hear authentic voices of low-income immigrant girls directly, and in their own terms, rather than being interpreted through the lens of the dominant culture. Their voices helped make clear the multiple nature of reality for people of different ethnic, racial, and social-class backgrounds.

It was very rewarding to see some of the Trinity students move beyond seeing Bell students as victims. Their condescension and desire to act as savior was transformed into respect for the Bell students' strength and resilience in spite of the difficulties they face as women and minorities. One Trinity student wrote, "when we are able to share our feelings, our struggles, we are able to move on and realize that we are not alone. Just as my mentee realized she is not alone in certain struggles and she need not be ashamed. And she need not be a victim, rather a survivor. But above all she must see the beauty inside her, and the power she possesses; the power we all possess."

Another Trinity student, who came from the Dominican Republic, wrote this about her partner: "We are both very strong women who accept challenges, but she is already in charge of her life independently. Even when I am acting independently from my parents (e.g. I do not ask my mother for money), they still pay for my college tuition. In my subconscious, I know that if I need money, my mom would help me. My friend Elisabeth has nobody to count on. She came here with nothing in her pockets to start a new life from the bottom. That is why I have learned more from her."

A number of students wrote in their final reflective papers that they can no longer look at their environment without seeing things through the lens of race, class, and gender. One of the white students wrote, "This course has been an eye opener for me in the sense that I have never really sat down and thought about racism or sexism before. But with this class it seems I am seeing examples of them everywhere." An African American–Mexican student expressed similar views: "Entering this course I thought that I practically know everything there is to know about my environment. I found that my views changed, from the way I view my own culture to the way I deal with others." She wrote that learning about the constraints that racial and sexual barriers imposed on women of color was "scary for me because I know that it will be really hard. This course was like a serious reality check for me. Being what I am I was not exposed to the privileges that the Caucasians are exposed."

Some wrote that the course had contributed to their personal growth or spiritual journey by encouraging self-reflection, which led to a deeper understanding of their place in society and a sense of activism. As an example, one student wrote:

> I never realized that I live with privileges that are not God-given rights while others are suffering because of my luxuries. And at the same time I could identify with oppressed people because of my gender. This has left me very perplexed as to what to do. The "poor me" syndrome is wielding its head when I think of the no win situation that many people like myself and others less fortunate than I live with. It frustrates me to find that there is no easy solution for elimination of the oppression that I live with. How do I begin to give up what I have been socialized to believe is essential to survival?

She concluded her paper by declaring, "I can be an activist and I can make much needed change in this society with the help of the others."

Project outcome goals for the high school students included encouraging minority high school girls to learn about and to attend college. We were quite successful in achieving these goals. The program demystified college life for these schoolgirls. In our final interviews with them, we asked how they felt they had benefited from this program. They mentioned being introduced to college life and having the opportunity to meet real-life college women as the most important benefit of the mentoring program. Many of the Bell students stated that before participating in the project they had not known anybody who attended college; their perceptions of college life came from watching TV. The Vietnamese student commented that her mentor was the first white person she had gotten to know personally. A number of them mentioned that before the program they had never thought about going to college, but it made them think that college is an attainable goal. Three of the mentees are now attending Trinity College.

The high school girls mentioned other benefits in their interviews. They said that the program gave them the opportunity to learn and expand their minds. They believe that being around all females gave them a "feminine perspective"; one can assume they meant "feminist perspective" because they said it empowered them to think that anything is possible.

Mentors and mentees were asked to provide feedback on how to improve the program. Trinity students unanimously suggested dropping the math-and-science component and making it a separate course. They said we attempted to cover too much in too short a period of time. They complained that it is quite a challenge to deal with the complexity of race, class, and gender in one semester. They also suggested that we not include students from Paint Branch High School in our future mentoring programs because these students were already college-bound and had parental support and the financial means to attend college. They believed that minority students from disadvantaged backgrounds are the ones who would benefit most from the mentoring relationships.

Both mentors and mentees suggested that mentoring should have been a greater focus of the class, and we should have had more structured mentoring activities and contact hours. Both groups thought that shadowing experiences were the most beneficial in demystifying college experience. By attending classes with their mentors, Bell Multicultural High School students discovered that attending college was something well within their capabilities. A few Trinity students suggested that mentors should have shadowed their partners in their school and home environments so as to develop better appreciation of the mentee's reality.

Recommendations for Elaboration

In many ways, this course was very successful. With further expansion of its components and some reorganization, it can be an even better teaching and research tool.

The following recommendations are based on what we, the faculty, Trinity College students, and the high school students involved learned from the mentoring and diversity project:

- Lobby for full support of high school principals; it is essential to the success of this program. Students may have to miss some classes. The principal at Bell High School was supportive of the project and allowed students to participate in the project even when teachers objected. At Paint Branch High School, the principal was not fully supportive; therefore, a number of times when students were supposed to participate they did not come.
- Ensure that funding for the program is adequate. At a minimum, funding is needed for transporting both groups of students, for two receptions (one at the beginning of the program and one at the conclusion), and for meals for the high school students while they are at the college.
- Limit the academic content of the course to the literature on mentoring, race, class, and gender.
- Coordinate supervised outreach by the college students; visiting mentees' classes, as the mentees do the college students' classes, and meeting with the mentees' mothers provides excellent learning, sharing, and participatory possibilities. It expands the college students' understanding of issues of race, class, and gender; it further involves the mentees in the process since the classroom visiting is not one-sided, and it encourages greater participation in the program by mothers of the mentees.
- Organize regular discussion group meetings between mentors and mentees to encourage dialogue and mutual understanding of issues. Meetings should be based on assigned readings that are comprehensible to both groups and on daily experiences of the members who participate. Provide a defined starting point for discussion of issues of advocacy, victimization, and transformation, prior to and during the mentoring process. This provides mutual understanding, elimination of fear, and awareness of some of the issues of self-determination and change for both mentors and mentees.
- Expand the grassroots component to include mothers of the mentees. This encourages involvement of mothers in the mentoring process and helps them understand the importance of their support in this process. Efforts at outreach to encourage them to attend are essential.

- Expend more effort to encourage mothers' understanding of the obstacles faced by their daughters, and of how to help their daughters overcome these obstacles and become advocates for themselves as well as their children. After adequate classroom preparation and discussion, the college student mentors can play a central role in this process. This can be an important learning component of the course for both the mentors and the mentees.

It is important to encourage all young women and girls to continue their education. This is especially true for women and girls of color who do not come from the middle or upper class since they are much less likely to have realistic impressions of what the experience is about and what its benefits are. We can help them understand this through such a course as "Mentoring and Diversity." At the same time, the course provides important learning experiences for participating college students. It helps them understand social stratification in very real ways, in terms of the issues of race, class, and gender, and it demonstrates how as students they can play an important role in changing some of those issues.

This report ends with a poem that one of the Bell students wrote for her mentor.

> one day I went to Saint Peter in heaven
> and he told me that the best gift I could ever ask for
> is a good friend.
> He also said, don't come here,
> you are enjoying that gift down on Earth.
> Thanks, Vivienne, for being my gift.

REFERENCES

Andersen, M., and Collins, P. H. *Race, Class, and Gender: An Anthology.* (2nd ed.) Belmont, Calif.: Wadsworth, 1995.

Association of American Colleges. "Passing the Torch: The Rewards of Mentoring." *On Campus with Women,* 1991, *21*(2), 1–2.

Atkinson, P. "Mentoring: Today and Tomorrow." Unpublished paper, presented at the University of Washington, Oct. 13, 1991.

Bell, E. D., and Drakeford, R. "A Case Study of the Black Student Peer Mentor Program at the University of North Carolina at Greensboro and Its Policy Implications." *College Student Journal,* 1992, *26*(3), 381–385.

Bova, B. M. "Mentoring Revisited: The Hispanic Woman's Perspective." *Journal of Adult Education,* 1995, *23*(1), 18–19.

Carden, A. "Mentoring and Adult Career Development: The Evolution of a Theory." *Counseling Psychologist,* 1990, *18*(2), 275–299.

Cook, M. F. "Is the Mentor Relationship Primarily a Male Experience?" *Personnel Administration,* 1979, *24*(11), 82–86.

Dickey, C. A. "The Role of Quality Mentoring in the Recruitment and Retention of Women Students of Color at the University of Minnesota." Unpublished doctoral dissertation, University of Minnesota, 1996.

Dreher, G. F., and Cox, T. H., Jr. "Race, Gender, and Opportunity: A Study of Compensation Attainment and the Establishment of Mentoring Relationships." *Journal of Applied Psychology,* 1996, *81*(3), 297–308.

Goldstein, E. "Effect of Same-Sex and Cross-Sex Role Models on the Subsequent Academic Productivity of Scholars." *American Psychologist,* 1979, *34*(5), 407–410.

Halcomb, R. "Mentoring and Successful Women." *Across the Board,* 1980, *26*(2), 13–18.

Jackson, C. H. "African American Women's Mentoring Experiences." Paper presented at the annual meeting of the American Psychological Association, Toronto, Aug. 1996.

Kalbfleisch, P., and Davies, A. B. "Minorities and Mentoring: Managing the Multicultural Institution." *Communication Education,* 1991, *40*(3), 266–271.

Kim, A. "African American Women in Educational Administration: The Importance of the Mentors and Sponsors." *Journal of Negro Education,* 1995, *64*(4), 409–422.

Merriam, S. "Mentoring and Protégés: A Critical Review of the Literature." *Adult Education Quarterly,* 1983, *33*(3), 161–173.

Missirian, A. K. *The Corporate Connection: Why Executive Women Need Mentors to Reach the Top.* Upper Saddle River, N.J.: Prentice-Hall, 1982.

National Science Foundation/ACM [Association for Computing Machinery]. "NSF Grant to Fund Mentoring Project for Women and Minorities." *Communications of the ACM* (AC Membernet), Jan. 1992, p. S2.

Pearl, A., and others. "Becoming a Computer Scientist: A Report by the ACM Committee on the Status of Women in Computing Science." *Communications of the ACM,* 1990, *33*(11), 47–57.

Phillips-Jones, L. "Establishing a Formalized Mentoring Program." *Training and Development Journal,* 1983, *37*(2), 38–42.

Redmond, S. P. "Mentoring: A Career Training and Development Tool." *American Behavior Scientist,* 1990, *34*(2), 188–200.

Shapiro, E., Haseltine, F., and Rowe, M. "Moving Up: Role Models, Mentors, and the Patron System." *Sloan Management Review,* 1978, *19*(3), 51–58.

Sheehy, G. "The Mentor Connection: The Secret Link in the Successful Woman's Life." *New Yorker,* Apr. 1976, pp. 33–39.

Shrewsbury, C. "What Is Feminist Pedagogy?" *Women's Studies Quarterly,* 1987, *15*(3/4), 6–14.

Tidball, M. E. "Perspectives on Academic Women and Affirmative Action." *Educational Record,* 1973, *54*(2), 130–135.

Tinajero, J. V. "Raising Career Aspirations of Hispanic Girls. Fastback 320." Bloomington, Ind.: Phi Delta Kappa Foundation, 1991.

Wilson, S. A. "The Effect of the Race and Gender on the Formation of the Mentoring Relationships for Black Professional Women." Unpublished doctoral dissertation, Case Western Reserve, 1992.

14

ADVISING YOUNG WOMEN OF COLOR

Susan E. Murphy, Sharon G. Goto, Ellen A. Ensher

CHANGES IN STUDENT DEMOGRAPHICS present challenges and opportunities for today's institutions of higher learning. Opportunities exist in welcoming those with different views and perspectives who bring innovation and creativity. The challenge is to meet the needs of those with diverse cultural values and career goals, as well as allowing individuals to meet their full potential. Women of color in particular may find themselves in a precarious position within higher educational settings, facing challenges related to suspicions of being a product of an "unfair" selection process—all while trying to succeed in an environment that may be culturally incongruous. These women of color face barriers to success twice: as women and as people of color. In a sense, they are in double jeopardy (Pak, Dion, and Dion, 1991) as they must tackle both sets of obstacles.

Increased representation, competition, and heightened sensitivity to ethnicity and race demand greater support for women of color in institutions of higher learning. A critical element of support is found in advising relationships. Cross-cultural relationships in advising require that those in support positions become aware of cultural biases of their own that could interfere with their ability to form effective relationships. These relationships are typically difficult, as both advisor and advisee enter into them with conflicting ideas of what benefits they expect out of the relationship. These difficulties may also stem from cultural differences in the definition of the relationship, the types of communication that occur within the relationship, and the level of trust and perceived effectiveness of the relationship.

In this chapter, we look specifically at the implications of cross-cultural relationships in advising women of color in higher education settings. This chapter outlines the importance of establishing effective relationships, the developmental process, and the manner in which different cultural expectations and values affect the nature of the eventual relationship. The chapter concludes with some practical advice for faculty, staff, and other advisors.

Importance of Advising Women of Color

Cross-cultural advising relationships have become more prevalent as colleges face changing demographics in entering classes. One recent study highlights an 8 percent increase for all minority students in college, from 15 percent in 1976 to 23 percent in 1993 (U.S. Department of Education, 1995). Participation rates in higher education by ethnicity have also changed. In 1995, about 42 percent of all high school graduates enrolled in college, compared to 32 percent in 1972. White student participation is currently close to 44 percent, and African American and Hispanic students are both at about 35 percent. Diversity also exists at the master's and doctoral levels as many of these fields are no longer the exclusive purview of white males (Fox, 1989). For example, in psychology, the number of doctoral degrees awarded to women increased from 24 percent in 1971 to 56.2 percent in 1989 (Brannon, 1996).

Yet the successes for women have been accompanied by mixed success for other minority groups. The increase in women and minorities in many fields suggests the need for more effective cross-cultural advising. Research in cross-cultural advising shows that female and minority students flourish if given appropriate attention, and that they are at a disadvantage if they do not receive advising help. Furthermore, advisors unaware of cultural differences in expectations have been found to exhibit insufficient involvement and inadequate assistance (Friedman, 1987).

Understanding both the development process of the advising relationship and the exact nature of the relationship helps locate facets that are influenced by cross-cultural issues. In the next section, we provide an overview of the developmental stages and highlight different types of advising relationships, varying in intensity and duration. For example, some academic advising, such as advising students about which courses might better fulfill a general education requirement, may occur once a semester. Other forms, such as regular updates on student progress, may occur frequently over the span of a student's college career. Finally, advising in an academic program—usually in the course of academic work such as research—reflects an ongoing relationship that is similar to mentoring.

Relationship-Building Processes and the Influence of Culture

Generally, according to many models of relationship development people seek out relationships in order to satisfy particular needs. One of the original models, social exchange theory (Homans, 1961), views social interactions as similar to economic transactions in which people attempt to "profit" from their interactions with others so that benefits exceed costs. An alternative model views relationships as communal in nature (Clark and Mills, 1993). Some research suggests that women and people from non-European cultures are more communal in their approach to relationships (Triandis, 1995). Miscommunication and misunderstanding may result, or participants may become dissatisfied if the form of the relationship does not meet their expectations. Regardless of the exact nature of the relationship, most begin with an initial phase in which the two participants spend time determining what they might have in common. As it continues, the relationship moves to a phase in which its parameters are explored, communication is increased, and the wish to continue the relationship is made clear. Finally, the relationship moves into a mature stage, where stability and satisfaction are attained (cf. Berscheid and Reis, 1997).

When we think of the effects of cultural influences on relationships, we are likely to conjure up images of people working with others originally from a country other than their own. However, the changing educational demographics of diverse relationships require knowledge of some of the same issues that guide cross-national interactions. Many researchers talk of the move in the United States from a monocultural to a multicultural society. No longer is the melting-pot analogy descriptive of the United States; the model of multiculturalism is becoming more widely accepted (Berry, 1997). Therefore, within these stages of relationship development, we include various social psychological processes that may differ because of cultural influences (see Fiske, Kitayama, Markus, and Nisbett, 1997).

It seems useful to look at culture in terms of one's subjective culture (Triandis and Vassiliou, 1972): the shared values, attitudes, norms, and beliefs that are held by a group (for example, race or national origin). Much previous work has looked at various aspects of subjective culture.

For example, Hofstede (1980) identified four constructs useful in understanding cultural differences: individualism versus collectivism, high versus low uncertainty avoidance, high versus low power distance, and masculinity versus femininity. Other cultural constructs include Confucianism (Hofstede and Bond, 1988), tightness versus looseness (Pelto, 1968), and long-term versus short-term time orientation (Bond, Leung, and Wan, 1982). These cultural values may be particularly relevant for women of color. They may be experienced as dilemmas in reconciling the importance of family versus career, or the extent to which people are expected to look out for themselves versus working toward the best for all.

The constructs are useful both for understanding how cultures might vary and for understanding the likelihood of behavioral tendencies and cognitions of individuals within cultures. That is, although learning another's culture is helpful, culture is not deterministic. Triandis (1995) has argued that all individuals show both high and low power distance and collectivist and individualistic behavior at one time or another. So, rather than saying an individual is collectivist or individualistic, it is more accurate to describe a person as relatively more collectivist (than individualistic), with the realization that the person may act individualistically at any given time.

Acting on cultural stereotypes is limiting because society tends to use many broad categories to describe other cultures. For example, the term *Asian* or *Asian American* comprises Chinese, Japanese, Asian Indian, Vietnamese, Thailand, Hmong, Cambodian, Laotian, and so on. Even though some of these groups have similar values and some overlap in cultural practices, there are many differences among them (Uba, 1994). The same can be said for Latina or Hispanic groups. In addition, the level of the person's acculturation is important to understand but not easy to determine. Some people measure acculturation by the amount of time the individual has lived in the United States, but other research suggests that it is more related to use of native language, ethnicity of friends, and adherence to cultural practices (Suinn, Rickard-Figueroa, Lew, and Vigil, 1987). Therefore, using a person's ethnicity to speculate on her or his cultural values must be merely a starting point for understanding.

Consideration of the individual's circumstances is likely to be more representative of the person's values. Part of cultural advising, then, is to understand the individual's specific context, that is, to have the desire and ability to understand how particular women of color negotiate the expectations of their culture, their specific context, and the educational institution.

Initial Interactions

> Imagine yourself as a new college student at a large state university. As the first in your family to go to college, you are worried about how well you will do. Although you did very well in high school, graduating in the top 5 percent of your senior class, you applied to college at the urging of your guidance counselor. You are unclear exactly why you are at college. In a sense, you saw getting to college as the goal in and of itself. You know it will help you get a good job, but you are really not sure about the type of job you want. You meet with your advisor, and she asks you what you are thinking of for a college major. It seems that you are struggling more than others to adjust to being away from home and to the college environment. Your advisor looks "friendly," but she, like the situation, feels a little intimidating. You are really not sure what to tell her.

During this initial meeting, a number of thoughts go through your mind. The first thing you do is assess what you might have in common with your advisor—in other words, the degree of similarity between the two of you in ideas, values, even taste in clothes. When we meet someone socially, we search for any evidence of similar interests. The purpose of an initial conversation is to answer the questions: Can I get along with this person? Do we have anything in common?

People generally form relationships with those whom they perceive to be similar to themselves in some way (Byrne, 1971). Often differences in gender and ethnicity are salient characteristics that override other similarities or dissimilarities in initial interactions. Research on cross-race mentoring has found that minorities may seek out same-race mentors and are more satisfied with them. For example, African American students who had African American mentors held more positive perceptions and attitudes toward research than those with European American male mentors (Frierson, Hargrove, and Lewis, 1994). In organizational settings, African American protégés tend to have African American mentors, rather than European American mentors (Kalbfleish and Davies, 1991). Minority employees identified as high-potential tend to have a higher proportion of minority contacts in their informal mentoring networks than both their European American counterparts and less mobile minorities do (Ibarra, 1995).

Cultural differences might prevent those within the educational setting from being trusted. Leung (1988) found that collectivists tend to draw a stronger distinction between in-group and out-group members. Therefore, a collectivist student might be particularly wary of an individual perceived as an out-group member (that is, from a different cultural or ethnic group). This strong out-group perception may make the initial phases of advising particularly difficult. The person may not see the potential advisor as a possibility, and therefore may not seek that advisor out, or the initiated relationship might persist and be ineffective without the level of trust needed for advising to occur. On the positive side, this research suggests that once the advisor is perceived as an in-group member by the student, the in-group member is treated with the same level of trust and confidence as any other in-group member.

The initial interaction in an advising relationship, therefore, is very important. Much research suggests that people make first judgments about someone within a very short time and then look for information that confirms their first impressions. During initial interactions in advising relationships, the advisor may be deciding (most likely based on the student's skill set) whether she might be worth taking the time and effort to advise. In these informal or spontaneous advising relationships, initial attraction largely determines the interaction. Informal advising relationships can be very important: research on mentoring in business settings shows that informal mentoring relationships offer protégés more career-related support and result in larger salary increases than formal relationships do (Chao, Walz, and Gardner, 1992). This is not to eliminate the benefits of an assigned advisor. Overall, though, protégés with a mentor do have more positive career outcomes than those without mentors (cf. Dreher and Ash, 1990), indicating that for advising relationships the extra benefits of voluntary relationships, useful as they are, can also be experienced through assigned relationships.

The degree of voluntary initiation of relationships, however, may determine the success of these initial interactions. One student relays a story of an unsuccessful advising experience when she moved to attend a midwestern college from her home in the Los Angeles area. As a freshman whose mother was Asian American and father European American, she was assigned a mentor as part of a minority peer counseling program. Her experience of growing up in the diversity of Southern California never led her to believe that she was a minority in jeopardy of having a difficult time adjusting to college life. She was in fact quite surprised. Although she experienced the normal difficulties associated with growing up with parents who had different cultural values, this was the first time she had to worry about being seen as an unqualified recipient of affirmative-action efforts. Therefore, she felt that the act of forcing her into this special program (had it transpired) would have actually caused more harm than good. Making assumptions based on one's outward appearance or demographic group can be detrimental.

How might cultural differences affect these initial interactions in other ways? To begin with, they may affect whether a woman actively seeks out an advising relationship in the first place. If assigning an advisor has drawbacks, so does relying on the potential advisee to seek out the advisor. In collectivist cultures, the need for an advisor from inside the institution may not be perceived. That is, advisors may be typically expected to come from within the collective (either fellow students or from more familiar settings). The meaning of advising, like mentoring, is different for some cultures. Drawing from experience with Asian-based modes of mentoring, for example, Asian Americans might expect different types of relationships. Goto (forthcoming) argues that in Japanese culture, there is a mentorlike relationship between a teacher (*sensei*) and the student, and between senior *sempai* and junior *kohai* peers. In Chinese and Korean cultures there are similar relations. These are often found outside of the school setting. Students may come to rely on these other types of advising for career-related guidance and may not understand the need to pursue advising relationships within the school context. Therefore, educating students about the benefits of advising relationships that are developed within the institution may be necessary.

Indeed, then, part of the onus for seeking out initial interactions should be borne by the potential advisor. On the one hand, European Americans may not actively pursue advising relationships with students of different backgrounds. They may also be more comfortable in relationships with students whom they perceive to be similar to themselves and less willing to provide critical feedback. On the other hand, female students of color may avoid establishing an advising relationship out of "protective hesitation," to avoid being rejected, or because they hold certain culturally specific beliefs about advising.

Relationship Building

> One of the authors has noticed a pattern of interaction with some ethnic minority students, particularly women, that makes it difficult to develop advising relationships past the initial stages. Often, the informal advising begins after the official business of class assignments ends. That is, many students seek her out to clarify points covered in class or assignments. These students "stick around" for informal chats about issues that are not necessarily directly relevant to the classroom, or are more personal in nature. When young women of color come to

> speak with her they are very grateful for the attention they receive, and immediately leave in an effort "to not take any more of her time." Unfortunately, they miss out on the opportunity for less-formal interactions. It is these types of interactions that most naturally become meaningful advising relationships. Because of their reticence (and thoughtfulness about the other's time), they may miss out on valuable advising.

Once the initial attraction is established, the participants go about the business of relationship building. In relationships that are expected to continue over time, its benefits and potential costs for both parties are assessed. What do I hope to get out of this relationship? What do I have to provide in the way of time and energy? Alternatively, an analysis of the relationship from a communal perspective might focus on the benefits to both parties to determine whether the relationship continues.

Differences based on cultural values have many implications for these early stages of advising relationship. Expectations of the roles within the relationship are uncovered at this point. For example, non-Western-based expectations of advising also tend to be characterized by strong hierarchy or power distance (Hofstede, 1980). Formal language, formal titles, deference, and other indications of reverence are expected between student and teacher, and even between junior and senior peers. This may suit an advisor's particular style and may not impede the building of a relationship—but, more often than not, this hierarchy or high power distance coupled with expectations of more formal behavior is likely to prohibit effective relationships from forming. Cultural differences may affect the amount of time it takes for the advisor and advisee to become comfortable with one another in the relationship as well (Thomas, 1990).

Differences in attributional patterns can also cause misunderstanding in advising relationships. Members of non-Western cultures are more likely to ascribe the behavior of a person to features of the situation, rather than the overwhelming tendency in Western cultures to attribute the causes of others' behavior to the actors themselves (Fletcher and Ward, 1988). When it comes to attributions about one's own behavior, this varies by culture. Differences in attributional styles can make offering advice difficult. Imagine a situation in which a European American advisor attributes a student's poor performance to something about the student's personality (say, low achievement motivation) rather than to something about the situation (such as too many responsibilities at home). The nature of the advice given to the student may not be appropriate if the behavior is mostly a result of a situation and is not about the student's personality. Advisors need to be very careful to give appropriate attention to the situational demands that students may be facing.

In many relationships, the amount of self-disclosure is associated with liking (Collins and Miller, 1994). Furthermore, "disclosing to another communicates that we trust that person to respond appropriately, that we value his or her opinions and responses, that we are interested in knowing them and having them know us" (p. 471). Because of particular cultural values, students may have different ideas with regard to the appropriate amount of self-disclosure, especially if a strong hierarchy exists between advisor and advisee.

In the relationship-forming phase, differences due to expectations of role in the relationship, communication, and attributional patterns may inhibit the ease with which quality advising and mentoring may occur. Understanding cultural differences helps the advisor deal proactively with problems that may arise as relationship building occurs.

Lending Support in the Mature Relationship

In well-established advising relationships, the topics of conversation may change. One of the authors has noticed that a salient issue for many women of color is to balance work and family demands. Take this typical interaction:

> Vicky is near completion of her sophomore year. Her parents have followed a fairly "traditional" life. Vicky's parents both worked, but her mother's responsibilities were primarily to take care of the family. Vicky is starting to explore the professional life and is looking for alternative models. She came to one of us after many conversations about coursework and school and asked, "How did you do it?" She follows with more questions: "How do I choose a profession that's right for me? How do I pursue it successfully? What are the consequences of this profession for my personal life? Have other women achieved this and a successful family life?"

At this point in the mature advising relationship, the objectives of the professional relationship are agreed upon and the participants are enjoying the benefits. During this phase, the participants spend time working toward the goals of what the person hopes to achieve. For example, many of us give specific advice at this point to help in job interviews, job searches, and getting into graduate school. In addition, advice on other career issues, including balancing work and family, may be sought.

A long-term advising relationship takes on many characteristics of a mentoring relationship, and much of the research on mentoring is applicable at this point. Much research has shown that a mentor provides three major functions (Scandura, 1992). The first is support to help the protégé develop in her *career.* This may include helping her choose developmental assignments on the job, working through a difficult problem in the workplace, or giving general career advice for obtaining promotions.

A second function of a mentor is in the area of *role modeling.* Many times a protégé looks to a mentor to show what interpersonal and work behaviors are most useful for getting a job done, either in a particular profession or within a specific organizational culture. Although the role-modeling behavior might be as simple as understanding appropriate dress, it should be respectful of the individual's own choices but still offer guidance in important situations. In one instance, three young women in a class in training and development made an informative presentation to the class. However, their attire was completely inappropriate for the setting; they all wore matching short black cocktail dresses to give their presentation! As a woman and professor, one of the authors felt it was appropriate to give clothing advice to the young women. To impart the feedback, she told them she was giving them friendly woman-to-woman advice, and it was not related to the grading of their projects. She told them that their dresses looked great for an evening out, but not for a presentation. She then suggested clothing that is considered more typical for business attire (and for other formal presentations). Finally, she also self-disclosed about her own missteps in this area. The three young women were receptive and grateful for the feedback.

The last type of support given by a mentor is *psychosocial:* the mentor helps the protégé with other aspects of her career. In this capacity, the mentor acts as a friend and as a counselor. The extent of psychosocial support might be affected by culture. Once the relationship is formed and the mentor or advisor is perceived as an in-group member, if the protégé has a collectivist or communal orientation great loyalty will persist between mentee and mentor. What might happen is that the mentor becomes uncomfortable in being perceived as too much of an in-group member. For example, one of our colleagues recently led a seminar in which an exceptional rapport was developed among the students, and with her. She believed the rapport emerged through much research-based but heartfelt discussion about "cutting edge issues" in ethnic minority psychology. One particular week, they began discussing articles on attitudes toward sexuality. Literally, before she realized what was happening, they started asking her personal questions related to the topic that to this day embarrass her. Given the cultural backgrounds of the students, it seems very unlikely that they had previously had the opportunity to talk about sex to anyone older, including their parents! Once they had developed the rapport with her that she had encouraged, they took it one step further.

Cultural responsiveness appears to be important in the mature advising relationship. Minority students, African Americans students in particular, perceive counselors who are culturally responsive to be more culturally competent than those who are culturally unresponsive (Pomales, Claiborn, and LaFromboise, 1986). Furthermore, counselors "who candidly acknowledge ethnic/cultural differences and the obstacles they produce, instead of projecting an image of 'color blindness' (i.e., cultural unresponsiveness), are perceived as credible sources of help by African American students" (Poston, Crain, and Atkinson, 1991.)

Implications and Recommendations

Throughout this chapter, we have discussed how advising relationships develop and might be affected by cultural influences, using both research findings and stories to highlight the importance of cultural understanding and sensitivity. We would like to conclude with suggestions for developing successful relationships. We have devised this list of recommendations from available research, published counseling guidelines, and our own and colleagues' experiences in advising and mentoring young women and young women of color.

Self-Education

It is important for those involved in cross-cultural advising relationships to gain education about other cultures. The American Psychological Association's *Guidelines for Providing Services to Ethnic, Linguistic, and Culturally Diverse Populations* (1991) suggest that service providers "seek out educational and training experiences to enhance their understanding and thereby address the needs of these populations more appropriately and effectively. These experiences include cultural, social, psychological, political, economic, and historical material specific to the particular ethnic group being served."

Encourage Initiation of the Initial Relationship

As an educator, your availability to students and your willingness to share your own career struggles should serve to attract students to seek you out for advice. We find that openness developed either in the classroom or in office hours gives students a chance to identify with facets of our lives that capture some of the same dilemmas they face. Show genuine interest in your students' academic success and career aspirations. Each of us asks many of our students about their future plans early in college and checks back with the students frequently. We find that by junior and senior year in college many of these students then approach us asking for advice. Our early show of concern is acted upon later as students begin to think of their next career steps.

Build Trust Through Active Listening

When we mention *active listening,* we are not talking about merely using paraphrase or other techniques to ensure that we do the right things associated with making someone feel comfortable. Here, we use the term to refer to active cognitive work to understand a person's values and goals. This initial understanding and respect allows you to help them consider all aspects of a problem and make an appropriate decision. One of us had a student who was struggling to deal with her family's reaction to her leaving for one of the top-rated graduate schools in the country. Her mother told her over and over again how selfish she was for leaving her boyfriend. Active listening revealed that the student felt her mother was being unfair, and that graduate school was very much what she wanted. She realized it would be a struggle without the full support of her mother, but she also realized that her mother was most likely struggling with the anxiety of losing her daughter. By using probing and clarifying questions, the advisor helped the student come to her own conclusions about how best to deal with her mother.

Carefully Explore Values

You can help ensure a successful advising relationship by taking the time to explore the values driving each side of the relationship, a particular student's behaviors and your own; don't let your values interfere with the relationship. This "investigation" can be accomplished by asking the student why she feels a particular way, or by asking what is typical for other people she knows who are facing a specific dilemma. Probing to find out the student's values can help the advisor suspend her or his own values until the situation is understood. It is often the case that we tend to jump ahead and look to our own values when a student approaches us with a problem. For example, a student came to one of us to tell her of her pregnancy. The initial response demonstrated a professional woman's worry rather than joy.

The student quickly said that she and her boyfriend were very happy and glad to be almost through with school. They would get married when they had enough money to have a nice wedding. Her family was happy for her, and most of her other brothers and sisters already had children.

Don't Overrely on Stereotypes

Those of us who have had some exposure to different cultures often tend to rely on the stereotypic bits of information we have about them. Although this may be a useful place to start a cross-cultural relationship, as we have mentioned earlier, each person's situation varies. Another colleague tells a story of a Japanese American woman who approached her after class one day to say that she felt very uncomfortable speaking in class because she was extremely shy. Our colleague, who is Angla, quickly thought to herself that this shyness had something to do with the woman's Japanese background. Instead of assuming this to be the case and moving on from there, she asked the woman to tell her more about her shyness. The student proceeded to tell her that even compared to some friends she had from Japan, she was far quieter. Therefore, letting the student explain the context of her own behavior led to greater understanding for the professor.

Share Insights into Your Own Culture

Many times, students need to understand the perspectives of a potential work culture that may be largely European American. A student came to one of us to talk about a work situation in which her boss asked that she speak only English in the workplace, rather than Spanish. The student was very upset because she felt that the request was insulting. The advisor expressed empathy with the student's situation and then asked her a series of questions to enable her to understand why speaking Spanish might make the supervisor feel uncomfortable. Even though the advisor felt that the supervisor was out of line, she tried to help the student understand why this white male might be threatened. The student then came to her own conclusion that the supervisor was not bigoted but was in fact concerned about workplace etiquette.

Summary

This chapter presents recommendations, based on research and practical experience, to improve the effectiveness of advising relationships with diverse female students. As many of our examples illustrate, higher education may create double binds for students of color, or those who are the first in their family to go to college. Statistics demonstrate that increasing numbers of diverse students are entering higher education, but some find it unwelcoming, as reflected in lower retention rates than for other students. An advisor who acts as a career coach—a role model—and holds positive expectations can be an important source of support for the individual student. Higher education may represent more of a challenge for some students than for others, but with proper advising and support, all of them can flourish.

REFERENCES

American Psychological Association. *Guidelines for Providing Service to Ethnic, Linguistic, and Culturally Diverse Populations.* Washington, D.C.: American Psychological Association, 1991.

Berry, J. W. "Individual and Group Relations in Plural Societies." In C. S. Granrose and S. Oskamp (eds.), *Cross-Cultural Work Groups.* Thousand Oaks, Calif.: Sage, 1997.

Berscheid, E., and Reis, H. T. "Attraction and Close Relationships." In D. Gilbert, S. Fiske, and G. Lindzey (eds.), *The Handbook of Social Psychology.* (4th ed.) New York: McGraw-Hill, 1997.

Bond, M., Leung, K., and Wan, K.-C. "The Social Impact of Self-Effacing Attributions: The Chinese Case." *Journal of Social Psychology,* 1982, *118*(2), 157–166.

Brannon, L. *Gender: Psychological Perspectives.* Boston: Allyn & Bacon, 1996.

Byrne, D. *The Attraction Paradigm.* Orlando: Academic Press, 1971.

Chao, G. T., Walz, P., and Gardner, P. D. "Formal and Informal Mentorships: A Comparison on Mentoring Functions and Contrast with Nonmentored Counterparts." *Personnel Psychology,* 1992, *45*(3), 619–636.

Clark, M. S., and Mills, J. "The Difference Between Communal and Exchange Relationships: What It Is and Is Not." *Personality and Social Psychology Bulletin,* 1993, *19*(3), 684–691.

Collins, N. L., and Miller, L. C. "Self-Disclosure and Liking: A Meta-Analytic Review." *Psychological Bulletin,* 1994, *116*(3), 457–475.

Dreher, G. F., and Ash, R. A. "A Comparative Study of Mentoring Among Men and Women in Managerial, Professional, and Technical Positions." *Journal of Applied Psychology,* 1990, *75*(5), 539–546.

Fiske, A. P., Kitayama, S., Markus, H. R., and Nisbett, R. E. "The Cultural Matrix of Social Psychology." In D. Gilbert, S. Fiske, and G. Lindzey (eds.), *The Handbook of Social Psychology.* (4th ed.) New York: McGraw-Hill, 1997.

Fletcher, G.J.O., and Ward, C. "Attribution Theory and Processes: A Cross-Cultural Perspective." In M. Bond (ed.), *The Cross-Cultural Challenge to Social Psychology.* Thousand Oaks, Calif.: Sage, 1988.

Friedman, N. *Mentors and Supervisors.* New York: Institute of International Education, 1987.

Frierson, H. T., Hargrove, B. K., and Lewis, N. R. "African-American Summer Research Students' Perceptions Related to Research Mentors' Race and Gender." *Journal of College Student Development,* 1994, *35*(6), 475–480.

Fox, M. F. "Women and Higher Education: Sex Differentials in the Status of Students and Scholars." In J. Freeman (ed.), *Women: A Feminist Perspective.* (4th ed.) Mountain View, Calif.: Mayfield, 1989.

Goto, S. G. "Asian Americans and Developmental Relationships." In *Mentoring Dilemmas: Developmental Relationships Within Multicultural Organizations.* Hillsdale, N.J.: Erlbaum, forthcoming.

Hofstede, G. *Culture's Consequences: International Differences in Work-Related Values.* Thousand Oaks, Calif.: Sage, 1980.

Hofstede, G., and Bond, M. H. "The Confucius Connection: From Cultural Roots to Economic Growth." *Organizational Dynamics,* 1988, *16*(4), 5–21.

Homans, G. C. *Social Behavior: Its Elementary Forms.* Orlando: Harcourt Brace, 1961.

Ibarra, H. "Race, Opportunity, and Diversity of Social Circles in Managerial Networks." *Academy of Management Journal,* 1995, *38*(3), 673–703.

Kalbfleish, P. J., and Davies, A. B. "Minorities and Mentoring: Managing the Multicultural Institution." *Communication Education,* 1991, *40*(3), 266–271.

Leung, K. "Some Determinants of Conflict Avoidance." *Journal of Cross-Cultural Psychology,* 1988, *19*(1), 125–136.

Pak, A. W., Dion, K. L., and Dion, K. K. "Social-Psychological Correlates of Experienced Discrimination: Test of the Double Jeopardy Hypothesis." *International Journal of Intercultural Relations,* 1991, *15*(2), 243–254.

Pelto, P. J. "The Difference Between 'Tight' and 'Loose' Societies." *Transaction,* Apr. 1968, pp. 37–40.

Pomales, J., Claiborn, C. D., and LaFromboise, T. D. "Effects of Black Students' Racial Identity on Perceptions of White Counselors Varying in Cultural Sensitivity." *Journal of Counseling Psychology,* 1986, *33*(1), 57–61.

Poston, W. S., Crain, M., and Atkinson, D. R. "Counselor Dissimilarity Confrontation, Client Cultural Mistrust, and Willingness to Self-Disclose." *Journal of Multicultural Counseling and Development,* 1991, *19*(2), 65–73.

Scandura, T. A. "Mentorship and Career Mobility: An Empirical Investigation." *Journal of Organizational Behavior,* 1992, *13*(2), 169–174.

Suinn, R. M., Rickard-Figueroa, K., Lew, S., and Vigil, P. "The Suinn-Lew Asian Self-Identity Acculturation Scale: An Initial Report." *Educational and Psychological Measurement,* 1987, *47*(2), 401–407.

Thomas, D. A. "The Impact of Race on Managers' Experiences of Developmental Relationships (Mentoring and Sponsorship): An Intra-Organizational Study." *Journal of Organizational Behavior,* 1990, *11*(6), 479–492.

Triandis, H. *Individualism and Collectivism.* Boulder, Colo.: Westview Press, 1995.

Triandis, H. C., and Vassiliou, V. "A Comparative Analysis of Subjective Culture." In H. C. Triandis (ed.), *The Analysis of Subjective Culture.* New York: Wiley, 1972.

Uba, L. *Asian Americans: Personality Patterns, Identity, and Mental Health.* New York: Guilford Press, 1994.

U.S. Department of Education. *Digest of Education Statistics.* Washington, D.C.: National Center for Education Statistics, U.S. Department of Education, 1995.

15

LESSONS FROM SELF-DEFENSE TRAINING

Glenda M. Russell, Kari L. Fraser

SEXUAL ASSAULT is one of the most dramatic and fear-producing forms of oppression of girls and women. The actual frequency of sexual assault is superseded by women's fears of being vulnerable to sexual assault (see Gordon and Riger, 1989). The potential of rape limits women's mobility, generates avoidance behaviors, and induces significant anxiety. This chapter focuses on the structures and processes that allow women to move from a position of helplessness and fear to a position of confidence and empowerment in relation to rape.

Women encounter myriad images suggesting that they cannot intervene successfully if they are assaulted (McCaughey, 1997). Furthermore, success in the task violates traditional gender roles (Jackson, 1993; Lamb, 1996; McCaughey, 1997). In short, self-protection against rape represents a paradigmatic case of what women cannot do and thus stands as an ultimate challenge: if a woman can learn to move from a (potential) victim position to an empowered position vis-à-vis rape, she may be able to learn to do so in relation to virtually anything.

We are grateful to the fifty-nine women who became our coresearchers on this project and allowed us to pass on their wisdom and insight to a larger audience. We also wish to thank Deborah Flick, who was involved in the beginnings of this project and contributed much to our understanding of the voices of the women who spoke with us. Finally, we are grateful to Janis Bohan and Frank McGill for their helpful comments on an earlier draft of this chapter.

One approach to rape prevention—and the subject of this chapter—is a full-force self-defense class called Model Mugging (MM). MM training, between twenty-four and thirty hours in duration, systematically teaches women boundary setting and self-defense techniques. The course uses female instructors and male "model muggers" wearing padded suits and helmets. Participants practice techniques in an adrenalized state, using full physical force to fight the muggers to a "knock-out"—the point at which the mugger judges that he would be rendered unconscious were he not protected by pads and a helmet. In addition to the self-defense techniques, MM emphasizes psychological empowerment for participants.

From Fear to Empowerment: Lessons from Self-Defense Training

Given reports of the positive effects of MM in the domains of self-defense and empowerment (Allison and Wrightsman, 1993; Gaddis, 1990; Jackson, 1993; McCaughey, 1997; Ozer and Bandura, 1990; Simonton, 1987), we wondered what the specific elements in the course were that contributed to participants' sense of efficacy. Lacking a significant body of research on MM, we decided an interview study of MM graduates would allow us the greatest latitude in pinpointing those elements. We used a semistructured interview format and placed priority on allowing the respondents to tell their own stories about MM. Our intention was to measure MM outcomes solely through participants' observations. The study did not include a follow-up component.

Fifty-nine female MM graduates, most of them Caucasian, participated in the study. We recruited respondents in two cities. Although we made efforts to invite graduates who represented diversity along many dimensions, we did not attempt to gather a random group of respondents, as we were especially interested in talking with women who were eager to discuss their MM experience. The average age of the respondents at the time of their interviews was thirty-seven (ranging from twenty-two to fifty-seven). Most of the respondents were professionals; approximately half were mental health professionals. We interviewed the women an average of five months after they had graduated (range = two weeks to thirty-two months postgraduation). We interviewed ten of the women individually, forty-six in groups of two to four, and the remaining three women both individually and in a group.

We analyzed the interviews qualitatively, using a modified grounded-theory approach. First, by reading random sections of the interviews, we identified prominent themes in the data and generated a coding schema corresponding to these themes. We then read all of the interviews in their entirety. Consistent with the nonpositivist underpinnings of our approach to qualitative data (Lincoln and Guba, 1985; Sandelowski, 1986), our joint coding was geared toward listening together to the words of the respondents and arriving at a consensus about the issues they presented.

Findings

Readings of the data suggested forty-three major themes.[1] Among them was one we termed "structure and process," a reference to the wide range of characteristics of MM training that contributed to its positive impact on self-defense and empowerment. Our readings of these characteristics suggest that they can be grouped into five major clusters. Here we explain each cluster in detail, using the participants' words as well as our own observations.

Creating a Safe Environment

Creating a safe environment is a necessary condition for productive change to occur in a group context (see for example Yalom, 1995). According to our respondents, MM courses have a variety of properties that promote a sense of safety among participants. For example, the class format is straightforward and predictable. As one participant said in discussing the relative rigidity of the course:

> I don't see it as rigid as much as comfortable that every single thing in the course . . . has a reason for being there, and no matter how irrational it might seem at that moment, the comforting knowledge that, first of all, seven thousand other women have done it; secondly, that so many that [instructor's name] has taught have done it; thirdly, that [instructor's name] has done it. . . .

The instructors' expectations about engagement in the course also contributed to students' sense of safety. Even though the women are expected to engage fully at a physical level, there is no pressure to engage at psychological or interpersonal levels. What limited discussion of psychological issues is invited occurs at a circumscribed depth, and even then participants always have the option of "passing"—choosing to answer a particular question briefly or not at all.

The fact that the primary instructor of the course is a woman helps to create a safe environment as well. Having a woman in charge, especially in matters of self-defense, runs counter to traditional notions of what women do and from whom women can learn (McCaughey, 1997). The female instructor models both the techniques themselves and the fact that the techniques can be performed by a woman. This modeling contradicts what McCaughey (1997) has referred to as the "rape myth": the assumption that men are invincible and women are vulnerable. Having a woman in charge also allows the possibility of seeing women as experts more generally. The participants in our study clearly appreciated having a woman in charge; one graduate called it "essential."

More subtly, the primary instructor provides a focus for students in the class. Especially at the beginning of the course, she is the touchstone to which each student returns. This function was described in a variety of ways. As an example, in referring to the power of her instructor's words, one graduate said they have ". . . stuck in my mind just like a—just like a brick." Another participant described having a flashback during one of the muggings that caused her to stop defending herself. She went on: "The next thing I hear is [instructor's name] calling to me, telling me to fight." At that point, the student resumed defending herself.

Role clarity for male instructors also contributes to a safe environment. Male instructors perform two roles: they offer instruction and they act as muggers in actual assault scenarios. The male instructor acts in the instructor role when he is not wearing his padded helmet. The minute he puts the helmet on, he assumes the role of the mugger and the women treat him accordingly. This convention helps the women know exactly with whom they are dealing at any given time in the course. It may be that this convention generalizes beyond the bounds of the course as well. Many of our respondents suggested that one outcome of MM is enhanced ability to differentiate among men. One woman, a runner, described that her pre-MM response to any man she met while running was to assume that he had violent intentions toward her. She explained that after taking the course her assumptions changed: when she saw a man coming toward her she did not presume to know his intentions, but she trusted herself to deal with them as they were revealed. The graduate added that this change has allowed her to be friendlier toward men in general, a finding similar to Gaddis's in his 1990 study of MM graduates.

Strict boundaries around the male instructor–mugger's behavior also lend a sense of safety. The muggers engage in significant levels of verbal and physical aggression toward the students. However (in contrast to reports by Peri, 1990), none of the women we interviewed suggested that she had ever been touched inappropriately or intimately.

A final factor in keeping the course environment safe is the availability of a code word that all students are taught early in the course. The code word is understood by everyone to be a clear signal that a mugging must be stopped immediately.

All these factors contribute to the women's sense of safety in the course, but their impact seems to extend beyond the course as well. From the experience of MM, our respondents learned the paradox that a safe environment offers them the potential for being aware of their vulnerability and provides a springboard for taking significant risks. The course also seems to promote women's confidence in their ability to deal effectively with men in a variety of settings.

Employing a Highly Structured but Malleable Framework

The MM course has a high degree of structure. We talked with MM graduates who, as a group, had taken classes in several different cities with more than a dozen female instructors, and we repeatedly heard descriptions of the same format and processes. These properties inspire student confidence in the class and give it a momentum of its own. One woman told us, "I actually felt in the end sort of like I'd been spewed out of this machine." Another woman in the discussion quickly added, "—A fighting-woman machine."

The tight structure of the course also counters the confusion and fear of being overwhelmed by the task of self-defense, especially for women who had experienced various forms of victimization. One graduate who had survived child sexual abuse explained it this way: "You know, I think that what's really good about it is . . . it's a very concrete experience. It's very defined; it's bounded; it's clear what's going on; it's clear what the roles are, what the issues are, the potential issues. And there aren't too many things that are very concrete."

Even though MM is highly structured, it is also very flexible in at least two important ways. First, transmission of skills can be tailored to fit the needs of an individual woman. Second, MM presents stimuli that participants can uniquely personalize. One specific method by which this occurs is the conversation scenario, in which muggers enact specific situations that participants describe (McCaughey, 1997; Simonton, 1987). Our respondents reported two major types of conversation scenarios: day-to-day situations that cause a high degree of anxiety (for example, being home alone, walking in isolated places, and venturing into unfamiliar neighborhoods) and scenarios based on actual historical experiences. Rape and incest were especially common. Conversation scenarios allow participants to "figure out what your fears [are] and then put you in situations so you [can] overcome them," as one respondent described it. As such, the scenarios often end years of avoidance. Many women describe these exposure experiences as explicitly life-changing.

Relying on Pedagogically Sound Principles

Much of the process by which learning occurs in MM reflects sound pedagogical principles. For example, graduates frequently commented on the relief they felt at learning a set of self-defense techniques that make use of women's unique physical strengths—such as powerful hips and thighs—rather than upper-body strength. MM also emphasizes fighting from the ground, neutralizing one aspect of many attacks in which assailants throw women to the ground in order to physically and psychologically overpower them. In one woman's terms, "the techniques don't take a lot of strength, are relatively easy to learn, [and] seem to come natural to women. . . ."

Another pedagogical approach of central importance in the course is the constant directive to focus on the power of the woman who is being mugged rather than on the mugger. One graduate described how her ability to focus on the power of the woman changed during the course: "By the fourth and fifth class I made a conscious effort to change the way I was looking at it, just like [instructor's name] said—like concentrate on the power of the woman and all that, and by the end I felt so proud of everybody that it was more like I was just going, 'Yeah!'"

As we analyzed many such comments, an explanation for this phenomenon took shape. When students focus on the mugger's power, they see the woman as a victim and they unwittingly participate in objectifying her. When students focus on the woman, they understand the mugging from her perspective. They see the openings and the moves and understand her as a powerful, self-determining entity. The mugger is, in effect, rendered rather irrelevant. Our data suggest that this focus extends beyond the confines of MM. Participants repeatedly spoke of how MM helped them to maintain their own viewpoints and positions in work and relationship domains.

Another pedagogically sound principle in MM is use of programmed success. Even though the defense techniques are complex, each task to be learned is manageable and is mastered before the next one is attempted. One graduate described how "there was a feeling that you couldn't fail because you . . . were being challenged at a level you could cope with, so you never were going to get thrown something that was beyond you. . . . You could go to kindergarten and not get thrown into fifth grade."

The classes also ensure success by interrupting avoidance behavior. If a woman has trouble with a given task, she is given support to attempt it again immediately, thus countering conditioned avoidance responses (a finding supported by Ozer and Bandura, 1990). As an example, one graduate had survived a rape during which the assailant tied a rope around her neck. Seeing a pillow used in an assault on another student triggered a very strong reaction and she began to cry and hyperventilate. The female instructor gathered the women into a circle to offer support, and then asked this woman to be the next student to be mugged. The woman agreed and was able to "stay grounded" and complete the mugging.

Our respondents also emphasized the importance of learning at a physical level. Their descriptions suggest that repetitively using their bodies in specific ways eventually allows them to bypass many cognitive processes. Many of the women reported that they had limited memory of what they actually did during the muggings; their moves came automatically. One described it as a state of "no mind, no thought." Another noted: "I think . . . MM . . . becomes something your body knows, not something that's cognitive. If I had to be there in the experience, trying to figure out what to do, I'd probably be confused and my processing would take too long to get out of the [assault] situation."

In the same way, learning in MM ultimately occurs in an adrenalized state. The women referred to the "adrenaline rush" of the muggings and to "the emotional intensity that . . . escalates and feeds on itself." A number of respondents made specific connections between their feeling states during the muggings and what they might expect themselves to feel during an actual assault. The fact that they had been able to defend themselves effectively in an adrenalized state in the class promoted their confidence that they would respond appropriately if assaulted in real life.

Students in MM are never passive observers. When one woman is being mugged, the other women are standing in a line close by, yelling support. This support includes a chorus of *No!*s as well as specific instructions about open targets on the mugger and techniques to use. The women who spoke with us described being very focused on the woman on the mat and experiencing her mugging along with her. One respondent observed: "About halfway through the [course], when someone's being mugged, you are all being mugged. And it's not like you just got mugged 30 times; you got mugged 250 times, because you are with thirteen people that went through it all."

The nature of this experience seems to give participants opportunities to learn self-defense skills even when they themselves are not being mugged. In a similar vein, observing the other women's muggings allows students to develop confidence in their judgment about when a boundary violation has occurred—confidence that is a significant challenge for many women (Butler, 1990; Gaddis, 1990; Jackson, 1993; McCaughey, 1997). Graduates spoke of having improved understanding of and willingness to confront boundary violations of all sorts in their lives outside the course.

A final pedagogical principle rests in the observation, echoed by many, that everything in the course has a beginning, a middle, and an end. Many of the endings in particular have a ritual quality. One graduate commented that "there is the sense that there will be some closure and that people are not just left hanging on, unresolved."

Taken together, the pedagogical principles described in this cluster seem to contribute to many of the positive outcomes that the graduates noted. Of particular importance are the notions the women carry with them beyond the confines of the course: they tend to view themselves as stronger, more confident, good learners, physical beings, and capable of giving—as well as receiving—support. Many of the graduates whom we interviewed expressed increased confidence in their own perceptions about boundary violations and more generally. Finally, many of the women reported less polarized views of themselves in relation to men, and enhanced ability to deal with men as individuals rather than as a group.

The Group as the Medium of Change

When asked to describe their fears about the course retrospectively, many women identified concerns about being in an intense group with other women whom they did not know. They wondered how the group would accommodate the differences among participants, especially differences between participants with a history of abuse and those without. Most of the women reported that once the course got under way, however, they experienced the group as warm and supportive. Many of the women expressed surprise at the low level of competition among class members. With respect to differences between women with and without a history of victimization, several volunteered that by the end of the course the boundary between the two groups had blurred considerably. A woman said of her experience with her classmates, "We breathed in union."

One factor implicated in the high degree of cohesiveness among class members was the role of empathy, an important property in therapy groups as well (see for example Yalom, 1995). Graduates told many stories detailing how they developed empathy for other class members. Despite differences among them, women shared a common fear of rape and assault. One participant said, "The common experience as a woman in that class overrides so much." Whereas much of the early bonding in the course appeared to be based on common fears, over time a new bond—that of empowerment—was established and became more central.

The women often were aware of the support they received from those in the line. Members of the class served a metaphorical witness function (Herman, 1992) for one another in their movement from fear (and sometimes victimization) to empowerment, each giving her support to all the other members of her class. The mutuality of these interactions is described in the words of one graduate: "At a basic level, I didn't feel alone. As horrible as [the mugging] was, there was this saving grace of having somebody with me, and my being able to be with somebody." Another graduate said directly, "I did feel very proud of being able to be part of a support group for somebody else."

The group also helped members contain the feelings they experienced during the course. As one participant described this holding function, "The more intense the feeling, the more you had to be with the group to contain it. You needed something bigger than yourself."

Clearly, the group in MM is a powerful force in the change process. Only one woman in the study said she would prefer to learn self-defense in a one-on-one context. She described herself as a very private person who did not like the physical activity, noise, or "enforced bonding" in MM. However, even this graduate acknowledged that she had learned techniques by watching the other women in her class.

Although there is little, if any, explicit political analysis within the course, many of the graduates left MM with at least an implicit sociocultural analysis of what they had previously seen as a unique and personal fear. Many also reported positive changes in their views of and relationships with other women in general. Both of these findings echo those reported by Gaddis (1990) in his study of the effects of MM.

Transcending Gender Roles and Restrictions

Participation in MM entails transgression of a number of gender prescriptions for women. These transgressions are not directly addressed in the course; nonetheless, certain aspects of the course represent behaviors that traditionally have been considered inappropriate for women. For example, there are significant prohibitions against women's engaging in aggression. These prohibitions exist not only among traditionalists but among some feminists as well (McCaughey, 1997). Many of the graduates spoke of their internal resistance to using force to defend themselves. One said that fighting was a "foreign experience" for her.

Further, women have traditionally been discouraged from engaging in dangerous enterprises. A graduate whose childhood experience held an uncommonly high degree of danger put the issue this way:

> I remember when I was growing up, women weren't given a whole lot of dangerous things to face in life. The most dangerous thing I could do . . . was train horses. They were huge; I was small, and I think that's

> one of the reasons I was attracted to it. It was one of the sports when I was growing up that was allowed you, and it could kill you. To break a mustang, you basically went through worse than you went through with MM. But you don't get strong unless you do those things. MM is something designed to make you stronger, emotionally and physically.

A number of respondents indicated that confronting their fears of being aggressive and engaging in a dangerous activity were as difficult as any other aspect of the course.

The flip side of the fear of being aggressive was the fear of becoming universally and unilaterally aggressive. A few women recalled that they had harbored this fear prior to the course. Many more reported that significant others in their lives had voiced this concern. In fact, this fear was not realized for any woman in the study. The techniques learned in MM are almost purely defensive in nature; most do not lend themselves to offensive strategies. Moreover, the graduates often suggested that enhanced perception of boundaries, together with increased confidence in their perceptions, permitted them to have clearer internal distinctions between times when aggression was and was not appropriate (see also Gaddis, 1990). One woman referred to a distinction between her "warrior self" and her "human being" self.

Women's traditional position also involves the expectation that violations against them not only are tolerated but also go unnoticed (Sampson, 1993). In MM, every mugging involves violation. The women do not strike offensively until they decide a transgression has occurred. One woman saw the course as a training ground for learning when violation has occurred:

> I think you get so many chances to experience boundary violations, because not only do you go through each mugging yourself, but you watch everyone else, so that, in that way, you are like this observer that is saying, "OK, don't let him do that," or "Wait" or ["Don't] wait." So you're kind of going through the judgment thing.

A prohibition closely related to that against women's use of aggression is the one against using their own voices. Using one's voice—insofar as it reflects one's presence and self-determination—is a refusal to act the role of "serviceable other," in Sampson's terms (1993). Perhaps the most common pre-MM fear reported by the women in this study was the fear that they would not be able to yell *No!* on behalf of themselves. Several women told us that, at the beginning of the course, when the whole group was instructed to yell, they pantomimed saying *No!*

At the most obvious level, women in the class are saying *No!* to an assailant imposing his will on them. At other levels, the women may say *No!* to other persons or situations as well. One woman suggested that "when I was saying *No!*, it was really *No!* to the whole spectrum of things." A number of women reflected that using their voices for assertive ends was rooted partly in the sense that they no longer spoke in isolation. As one graduate described it, "You can set firmer boundaries . . . if you know that you are speaking for a collection [of women]."

The other side of using one's voice is the experience of hearing voices—or, as one respondent put it, the experience of "not hearing silence." This was stated most poignantly by one survivor of a (pre-MM) rape who told us that being raped had been the loneliest experience of her life; hearing the voices of the instructor and her classmates during her muggings provided relief and healing.

The ultimate goal of MM is that participants develop the willingness and ability to defend themselves physically against an immediate threat. One issue that surfaced repeatedly in the interviews was the connection between having feelings and self-defense. Many women entered the course with the (usually unarticulated) belief that having strong feelings, especially fear, was incompatible with successful self-defense. MM challenged the assumption that fear renders a woman helpless—an assumption rooted in countless media images of women freezing or flailing in response to rape and other forms of violence against them (Meyers, 1997). The course demonstrated that women could fight effectively despite the presence of intense feelings: "I think the process showed you how to use the fear as strength, and I came out of the class basically knowing my fear and using it."

Implications

The findings we describe have broad implications for creating optimal educational environments for girls and women. The MM graduates in our study identified and explained many circumstances that foster women's competence and enhance their confidence as both teachers and learners.

General Principles for Optimizing Educational Environments for Women

First, our findings indicate that women learn well from other women and value opportunities to do so. Our data suggest that women's learning experiences are enhanced if a woman assumes the role of "expert" and controls the learning environment. The woman in charge stands as a same-sex model of what participants can accomplish and precludes some of the alienation that women may experience when being taught by men.

The data also imply that women may benefit from opportunities to identify with other women around their power rather than their vulnerability. Learning environments that reinforce women's strength support women in seeing themselves as competent, capable, and able to protect their interests proactively rather than simply reacting to the behaviors and expectations of others.

Another general lesson taken from the MM graduates concerns the power of positive expectations (Linney and Seidman, 1989). In the face of an extraordinary challenge, courage and confidence were instilled in MM participants by way of an unflagging expectation that all the women would be successful. Coupled with sufficient scaffolding and sound pedagogy, instructors' positive expectations play a critical role as students learn challenging material. The MM graduates point out that such expectations, if clear and consistent, can be internalized by women, increasing their confidence in one another and in themselves.

The MM graduates' feelings of self-efficacy also increased because they were not only successful but successful in new areas. MM challenged some of the participants' beliefs about their own limitations. In doing so, the course often required that women broaden assumptions about their own abilities. The experience of the MM graduates suggests that if a woman moves from thinking *I can't* to believing *I can,* she may bring a newfound level of confidence to subsequent challenges, no matter how different.

Finally, though our data confirm that women learn well from other women, they also illustrate the importance of including men in some learning environments. Specifically, when women are trying to overcome their vulnerability to oppression or intimidation by men, the presence of men in the learning environment allows women to demonstrate their competence specifically in relation to men.

Implications for Specific Learning Environments

The general principles discussed here yield specific implications for enhancing girls' and women's educational experiences in many settings. For example, in the classroom, effective teaching strategies for female students may include using female instructors, providing opportunities for female students to act as "experts" and teach others (including male students), and communicating high expectations for female students' accomplishments.

On many college campuses, emphasis is on treatment after victimization rather than on rape prevention. By contrast, MM is predicated on the belief that prevention is possible and emphasizes the importance of instilling this belief in women. Campus-based sexual assault programs may serve women more effectively by teaching them the skills to forestall an assault and bolstering confidence that they can do so, rather than emphasizing vulnerability. Such programs are also most effective if they involve female instructors; programs should include men as allies, but not as primary experts or protectors.

With respect to MM specifically, tuition for the course varies geographically but is usually several hundred dollars. As such, the course is not readily available to many women. The best way to increase accessibility to MM may be for educational institutions or others to subsidize the course for students.

Regarding campus climates generally, our findings suggest that the visible presence of female faculty and staff may enhance female students' expectations for themselves. Specifically, female students' feelings of self-efficacy may grow when they see other women fulfilling nontraditional roles: teaching in traditionally "male" subjects, coaching male sports, and having parity with men in terms of perceived prestige and expertise. In short, exposure to women in positions of power, and to women working successfully among men, helps counter female students' possible assumptions about sexism in campus administration, fields of academia, and occupations.

Our findings also suggest that campus climates become more hospitable to women as other campuswide prejudices—in addition to sexism—diminish. MM graduates repeatedly commented that to be physically strong and powerful challenged some of their assumptions about what it means to be female. Similarly, women who defy stereotypical gender expectations may be accused of being lesbian (McCaughey, 1997) and exposed to the negative stereotyping that such a label entails. Physical strength is also a component of other negative stereotypes, including, as McCaughey (1997) points out, the stereotype of black women as both strong and mean. In short, women who are perceived as physically powerful are vulnerable to being typecast according to many negative stereotypes beyond the simple accusation that they are unfeminine. Given this interrelationship among prejudices, it follows that campuswide reduction in homophobia and racism, as well as sexism, permits a broader understanding of positive ways to be female.

Our data also imply that college women benefit from having safe spaces where they can come together with other women to offer and receive encouragement and support. Women's groups and women's resource centers play a critical role in encouraging women to realize their individual and collective strengths, while at the same time reinforcing the notion that to seek support is not an indication of personal weakness or incompetence. The MM graduates' descriptions also suggest, however, that female students need opportunities to interact positively and effectively with men so that they can learn to trust in their own abilities to do so.

Regarding counseling centers and the programs they offer, our data indicate that women benefit from experiences that challenge their (sometimes self-imposed) limitations, give them opportunities to take risks (psychologically and physically), and let them be truly courageous. Activities with a physical component are also crucial in supporting women to develop confidence in their physical abilities and to develop trust and acceptance of their bodies. Comments of the MM graduates point to the importance of programs that can be customized to provide adequate challenges based on each woman's unique needs. Programs are also likely to be most effective if they are structured to ensure success and focus on women's competence rather than their vulnerability.

NOTE

1. Descriptions of these themes are available from Glenda Russell, 2315 Broadway, Boulder, CO 80304.

REFERENCES

Allison, J. A., and Wrightsman, L. S. *Rape: The Misunderstood Crime.* Thousand Oaks, Calif.: Sage, 1993.

Butler, J. *Gender Trouble: Feminism and the Subversion of Identity.* New York: Routledge, 1990.

Gaddis, J. W. "Women's Empowerment Through Model Mugging: Breaking the Cycle of Social Violence." Unpublished doctoral dissertation, University of California, Santa Barbara, 1990.

Gordon, M. T., and Riger, S. *The Female Fear.* New York: Free Press, 1989.

Herman, J. L. *Trauma and Recovery.* New York: Basic Books, 1992.

Jackson, S. "Representing Rape: Model Mugging's Discursive and Embodied Performances." *Drama Review,* 1993, *37*(3), 110–141.

Lamb, S. *The Trouble with Blame: Victims, Perpetrators, and Responsibility.* Cambridge, Mass.: Harvard University Press, 1996.

Lincoln, Y., and Guba, E. *Naturalistic Inquiry.* Thousand Oaks, Calif.: Sage, 1985.

Linney, J. A., and Seidman, E. "The Future of Schooling." *American Psychologist,* 1989, *44*(2), 336–340.

McCaughey, M. *Real Knockouts: The Physical Feminism of Women's Self-Defense.* New York: New York University Press, 1997.

Meyers, M. *News Coverage of Violence Against Women.* Thousand Oaks, Calif.: Sage, 1997.

Ozer, E. M., and Bandura, A. "Mechanisms Governing Empowerment Effects: A Self-Efficacy Analysis." *Journal of Personality and Social Psychology,* 1990, *58*(3), 472–486.

Peri, C. "Below the Belt." *Mother Jones,* Sept.–Oct. 1990, pp. 44–67.

Sampson, E. E. *Celebrating the Other: A Dialogic Account of Human Nature.* Boulder, Colo.: Westview Press, 1993.

Sandelowski, M. "The Problem of Rigor in Qualitative Research." *Archives in Nursing,* 1986, *8*(3), 27–37.

Simonton, A. "Facing My Demons." In D. Caignon and G. Groves (eds.), *Her Wits About Her: Self-Defense Success Stories by Women.* New York: HarperCollins, 1987.

Yalom, I. J. *The Theory and Practice of Group Psychotherapy.* (4th ed.) New York: Basic Books, 1995.

PART FIVE

CREATING HEALTHY ENVIRONMENTS

THE PROBLEMS OF EQUITY, justice, and inclusion that plague U.S. society as a whole are reproduced in its educational institutions. Despite the increased presence and visibility of women, the power hierarchies and institutional cultures of educational institutions remain androcentric. How can the structure of higher education be changed? In Part Five, we examine four diverse social problems affecting women as they are expressed in educational settings: access to higher education; alcohol use and abuse; violence against women; and civil rights for lesbian, gay, and bisexual students.

These problems are already painfully obvious to progressive academics. They may seem intractable because they are linked by structural components that reflect intersections of institutionalized classism, racism, sexism, and heterosexism. However, the contributors to this final part of *Coming Into Her Own* do not merely reiterate familiar problems. Instead, each unravels the strands of institutional culture that create tangles of inequity. Most important, each shows specific ways to weave a new, more just community in which diverse students can flourish.

One locus of diversity is age. The increasing numbers of "nontraditional" students in higher education is one of the dramatic shifts of the past three decades. In the mid-1960s there were so few students over the age of twenty-four that no official tallies were kept; by the mid-1980s, they were identified as the fastest-growing group of students in higher education. Moreover, the great majority of these students are women. Current estimates are that 2.5 million reentry women are students in U.S. postsecondary education. In many institutions, the nontraditional student has become the norm.

Because *nontraditional* has usually been defined in terms of age, the diversity of needs within this group was perhaps slow to be recognized. In the final chapter of this volume, Erika Kates reports the results of a national study of support services for a group of reentry women with special needs: low-income single mothers who are receiving AFDC benefits. Kates starts from the premise that the elements of a supportive educational environment for this group can be clearly specified and assessed. Because low-income women must comply with complicated regulations that do not mesh easily with a college's own requirements, they need help negotiating the maze. Second, even with their cash benefits, these women and their families are living below the poverty line. Therefore, they need different kinds and amounts of resources than other college women.

The obstacles seem immense, but the remarkable finding of Kates's Access to Higher Education Project is how well many institutions have managed to provide for the needs of their students who are low-income mothers. Although the programs surveyed in her study were not perfect—many administrators involved with them wished for more resources—their existence expressed real institutional commitment, and they were making a real difference to the students.

A great deal of research shows that low-income mothers want higher education, work very hard to stay in school, and can achieve graduation rates higher than traditional students if given proper support services. The needs of these women, as Kates shows, can be met with institutional commitment and creativity. It is thus particularly ironic that educational benefits for AFDC recipients were slashed in 1996, at the same time that a five-year lifetime limit on cash benefits was imposed. As a result, there are new hurdles for low-income mothers and the institutions that try to support their educational goals. In this case, a blueprint for change may require restoration of some of the successful strategies of the past.

In Chapter Seventeen, Mary Crawford, George Dowdall, and Henry Wechsler focus on traditional-age college students as they explore the implications of a major national study on alcohol use, the Harvard College Alcohol Study. They uncover a gender-linked culture of binge drinking on U.S. campuses that poses significant health risks to millions of students.

Overall binge drinking rates are somewhat lower for women than for men, but bingeing is exacerbated for both sexes in male-dominated or masculinist environments such as fraternities and coed dormitories. Excessive drinking is linked to a wide range of negative consequences for binge drinkers themselves and those who live and work in proximity to them. Clearly, binge drinking is a systemic problem that can best be addressed by changing the culture of drinking and providing positive alternatives to bingeing. The Harvard College Alcohol Study demonstrates that attending a single-sex college dramatically reduces a woman's risk of primary and secondary consequences of binge drinking. This suggests two foci for intervention. First, researchers could study how and why some women self-select the healthier environment of a woman's college. Second, they could examine how the campus cultures of women's colleges function, and use this understanding to derive models of healthier environments. These efforts could inform attempts to change campus drinking cultures at coeducational institutions.

Fraternities have been linked not only to binge drinking but to violence toward women. Yet the majority of interventions to reduce sexual assault on college campuses address only the potential victims, teaching women to restrict their behavior, "just say no," and generally take responsibility for avoiding sexual assault. Deborah Mahlstedt and Carole Corcoran argue in Chapter Eighteen that these approaches obscure the systemic nature of violence against women and do little to reduce its occurrence. They describe the Fraternity Violence Education Program, a unique effort to address dating violence and one that is deeply informed by feminist theory and activism.

In the FVEP, young men develop a safe space where, with the help of peer facilitators, they come to understand the social structural bases of relationship violence. Teaching people to think systemically and acknowledge their complicity in a sexist society is not an easy task; Mahlstedt and Corcoran acknowledge that it takes "time, emotional support, guidance, knowledge, and challenge." The FVEP creates an environment in which college men can examine their own behavior with support from other men and from feminist role models. Even in a supportive environment, change is erratic, marked by "contradictory beliefs, forward movement that unpredictably cycles backwards, unwelcome new awareness, hopelessness when new behaviors seem to fail, as well as the satisfaction associated with successes." Mahlstedt and Corcoran argue that the critical element in program success is the feminist theoretical framework emphasizing the structural, systemic nature of the causes of relationship violence. The success of their approach shows that college men can become allies in creating better educational environments for women.

Unexpected alliances mark a theme running through Chapter Sixteen as well. Janis Bohan and Glenda Russell examine institutionalized heterosexism, the assumption that heterosexuality is the only normal and legitimate sexual orientation. Because of heterosexism, educational settings can be lonely, frightening, and dangerous places for lesbian, gay, bisexual (LGB), and transgendered students. Changing the climate involves interwoven strands of community and individual involvement.

Bohan and Russell conducted an ethnographic study of an institutional crisis: an attempt by high school students in Salt Lake City, Utah—where a Mormon culture that rejects homosexuality is hegemonic—to form a support group for LGB students and their friends. When the school board banned the group, the situation became one in which civil rights were being explicitly denied to a group of students based on religious values institutionalized in their public school. Bohan and Russell's research project explored this volatile situation from within, through structured interactions with groups and individuals involved in the controversy.

The web of interactions revealed in their interviews shows that many people must work together to create safe and healthy environments for LGB students—peers, parents, teachers, and administrators. Given the pervasiveness of homophobia and heterosexism, this may seem a daunting requirement in U.S. culture generally, but it is particularly so in Utah, where religious proscriptions of diverse sexual orientations are extremely influential. However, Bohan and Russell's most striking—and hopeful—finding is that allies may come from the least likely places. In this case, some members of the Latter-day Saints (Mormon) church actively supported the LGB student group, justifying their stance through the church's teachings about love for extended family and friends.

Changing deeply ingrained patterns of classism, racism, sexism, and heterosexism is not easy, nor is changing institutional cultures that support alcohol abuse and dating violence. Yet the projects reported here all show models of healthier institutional environments for women—models that, if implemented, create optimal environments for all students.

16

SUPPORT NETWORKS FOR LESBIAN, GAY, AND BISEXUAL STUDENTS

Janis S. Bohan, Glenda M. Russell

QUESTIONS OF SUBOPTIMAL educational climates for girls and women are complicated by forms of oppression that intersect with sexism. Among these biases are heterosexism (the assumption, institutionalized in the culture, that heterosexuality is the only legitimate sexual orientation) and homophobia (negative feelings and actions toward lesbian, gay, and bisexual individuals). Such prejudices threaten the quality of climate for everyone, especially in the area of gender enactment (see for example Bem, 1993; Hunter, 1993; Pharr, 1988).

The most direct impact of homophobia and heterosexism is on students who identify as lesbian, gay, or bisexual (LGB). For them, the tasks of establishing a sense of identity and forging goals for the future are immensely complicated both by the homophobic/heterosexist attitudes of others and by internalized homophobia—their own adoption of negative judgements about LGB identity and thus about themselves (Malyon, 1981; Margolies, Becker, and Jackson-Brewer, 1987; Martin, 1982; Sophie, 1987).

The sense of isolation, and the potential for harassment and even physical assault, make school an unpleasant and dangerous place for LGB students. Considerable literature attests to these difficulties and their educational costs (for reviews, see Bohan, 1996; Hershberger and D'Augelli, 1995; Savin-Williams, 1995). Adding to these stressors are indications that schools are becoming the battleground for attempts to halt progress toward equal rights for LGB students (Herman, 1997; Pharr, 1996; Rofes, 1997; Woog, 1995).

In recent years, growing sensitivity to these issues has been the basis for efforts to support LGB adolescents (as well as those who are questioning their sexual orientation). Support groups for LGB and questioning young people have emerged across the country, through community-based programs and within schools and universities; such groups have proven extremely helpful to LGB teens (Seattle Public Schools, 1996; Woog, 1995). Here we discuss one such program, focusing on the multiple levels of individual and community involvement that enable such efforts and that constitute educational climate in its broad sense.

The Salt Lake City Project

Our comments are based on a research project inspired by recent events in Salt Lake City, Utah.

Utah is home to the Church of Jesus Christ of Latter-day Saints (LDS), also known as the Mormon church. For the majority of Utahans, the LDS church and what is termed "Mormon culture" deeply influence daily life, including social life, politics, business, the economy, and education as well as religious life. The LDS church condemns homosexuality unequivocally (Comstock, 1996; Schow, Schow, and Raynes, 1991). Because social as well as religious life is rooted in the church, the adolescent who identifies as lesbian, gay, or bisexual faces not only religious but also social exclusion.

Against this background, in October 1995 a group of students at Salt Lake City's East High School petitioned to establish a gay-straight alliance (GSA). Their aim was to provide a social and support network for East High's LGB students and their heterosexual friends. The Salt Lake City School Board and later the state legislature responded by banning all noncurricular clubs rather than allowing GSAs. The club has continued to meet, paying rental and insurance fees for use of school facilities, but the banning ignited a firestorm of publicity.

We undertook a qualitative research project to explore this distinctive situation, where civil rights are expressly denied a group of adolescents, where that refusal is institutionalized within their learning environment, and where it is rooted in a pervasive religious presence. We employed a grounded-theory approach (Strauss and Corbin, 1990) to conduct semistructured interviews with more than sixty individuals during ten multiday trips to Salt Lake. Interviews began with people who participated in the events surrounding East High's GSA; through the use of a snowball approach to participant selection, interviewing expanded to include respondents who were peripherally involved. Many individuals were interviewed several times in an effort to deepen our understanding and keep pace with events as they unfolded. Our analyses of these interviews reveal a complex network of community groups and individuals whose varied participation significantly affected the events that unfolded—and hence the educational climate for LGB students and their allies.

A Multitiered Educational Environment

The influences on and the impact of the GSA were broad indeed, and our work has introduced us to a wide range of perspectives. We have worked hard to be reflexive, to listen carefully, and to construct an understanding of these events that does justice to each of the participants.[1] Our aim in this chapter is to offer a narrative that makes sense of what has occurred in Salt Lake City in a way that honors these multiple perspectives and their relations to one another (Hertz, 1997; Jones, 1997). We discuss several individuals and groups[2] who were involved in these events, often highlighting intersections among them.

LGB STUDENTS. It warrants noting that, in the early stages of the club, members were not expected to disclose their sexual orientation. Club members did identify themselves to us, and we discuss LGB and heterosexual club members separately in order to explore some important differences between the two groups.

From the students' descriptions, their circumstances prior to the club's founding were comparable to those encountered in the psychological literature. Various of the teens reported drug abuse, significant conflict with parents, truancy, dropping out of school, depression, and suicide attempts. Many had been attacked by their peers; such attacks included verbal harassment as well as a few physical assaults in school. Kelli Peterson believed a club would help her and her friends cope with the stresses that LGB teens face. She and a few friends approached the principal, Kay Peterson (no relation), and over time convinced him of the need for the club.

THE IMPACT OF THE CLUB. Consistent with large studies on the value of GSAs for youth (such as Seattle Public Schools, 1996), students at East High tell us that the club has had a very positive impact on their lives. Problems declined; students reported decreases in substance abuse, depression, suicidal impulses and attempts, truancy, and conflict with parents. Their feelings of isolation and vulnerability decreased as the GSA became a vehicle for mutual support. One student described the East High GSA in these terms: "They provide a nice, safe refuge. And, if worse comes to worse, there's places you can go with members of the alliance where you'll be safe."

Typically, according to one of the club's sponsors, teacher Scott Nelson, support revolved around problems of adolescent day-to-day life as well as dealing with homophobic harassment. In addition, the youths clearly helped one another confront and reduce their internalized homophobia. The club also became a source of support for helping members take risks such as disclosing their sexual orientation to their parents, and deal with such intense issues as suicidal impulses.

The members of the GSA also saw themselves as efficacious—a sense often missing among adolescents but apparent throughout our interviews with these teens. As an illustration, here are the words of Erin Wiser: "I can't quit because this is important. . . . So many things I've done really weren't—soccer practice wasn't very important. . . . Yeah, a sense of accomplishment. I stood shoulder to shoulder with thirty, forty, fifty of the most strong-minded, strong-souled students in this valley, and we accomplished something. It's a good feeling."

THE IMPACT OF MEDIA SCRUTINY. Of perhaps greater significance than the club itself was the impact of intense media attention. The school board's cancellation of all noncurricular clubs generated considerable national interest, and GSA youth were pursued by the media (and by others interested in their story, ourselves among them).

The effects of media attention were of two kinds. First, the club itself felt the impact. According to core GSA members, some "media whores," drawn to the opportunity for personal publicity, appeared and disappeared depending upon the degree of media interest, making them unreliable members of the club. The club also became less safe for students who were not comfortable being publicly identified with the GSA. A second impact of media attention was Kelli Peterson's becoming an icon for LGB youth. The intense attention focused on Kelli left her not only famous but without privacy—and often left other club members feeling lost in her shadow.

RESOURCES FOR MANAGING STRESS. The members of the GSA used a variety of resources, internal and external, to weather the aftermath of the club's creation. They began reporting harassment to school authorities—a move that now had an impact because of their principal's commitment to making the school safe for all students. They found strategies for responding to harassment from peers, brainstorming direct and often humorous retorts. Jacob Orosco, for example, told of his response to other males' hostile questions about whether he was really gay: "Why, do you want my phone number?" When he was called a fag, he responded, "So, what's your point?"

Another source of resilience was students' typical refusal to objectify others with hostility. When a state senator made disparaging comments about the presumed sexual nature of what went on at GSA meetings, rather than counterattacking the students invited him to attend a meeting. The students seemed to understand that energy directed toward antagonists would be energy that would not go toward their objectives—"to get together, to have fun, to heal," in the words of one member.

The support these students received from others also helped them be resilient in the face of harassment and media intrusiveness. In interviews, they made it a point to express appreciation for the range of individuals and groups that supported them—including heterosexual students who placed their own popularity at risk.

Heterosexual Members of the GSA

Although much of what has been said applies to heterosexual members of the club as well, some features are unique to club members who identify as allies to their LGB peers.

RATIONALE FOR INCLUSION OF STRAIGHT STUDENTS. Rationales for including heterosexuals in the GSA seem to reflect a mix of altruism, internalized homophobia, and political expediency. Kelli did not want interested heterosexuals to feel left out or others to complain that heterosexual students did not have their own club. Kelli added that having a gay-straight alliance was (desirably) more "mainstream." Another student spoke to the value of excluding no one, urging others who establish such clubs to "never deny yourself the experience of that one kid who would have been left out . . . that one curious, straight kid."

Some GSA members suggested that having heterosexual members in the club demonstrated that the purpose was not to "recruit" people into a "gay lifestyle." One straight member offered, "It's really cool to have straight people in it because I think we're setting an example of, like, that it's OK to be associated with gay people." Other young people suggested that heterosexuals in the broader community could identify more readily with straight than with LGB youths.

MOTIVES FOR MEMBERSHIP. We encountered two major motives for club membership among the heterosexual students. For a few students, membership was a means of enacting sociopolitical beliefs about LGB issues—a stance that Herek (1995 and elsewhere) has termed value-expressive. The other primary reason for joining the GSA reflects what Herek terms social-expressive motives. These students, themselves often socially marginal members of the high school community, joined the GSA because they found in the club a high degree of acceptance. Sprinkled among both of the motivational subgroups were straight students whose willingness to join the GSA had been influenced by prior contact with gay, lesbian, or bisexual relatives or family friends, creating what Herek dubs an experiential-based motivation.

SOURCES OF STRESS FOR HETEROSEXUAL STUDENTS. Straight teens faced some difficulties as a result of their membership in the GSA. Members of their own families sometimes voiced reservations about their being in the GSA. Other students expressed disapproval and even distanced themselves from straight GSA members. Occasionally, heterosexual members were verbally harassed for their association with the club, but most denied any concern about encountering violence. This perception may reflect the influence of Mormon culture, which values civility and eschews confrontation.

Some of the straight teens' negative experiences derived from courtesy stigma (Goffman, 1963), a phenomenon in which those who associate with a devalued group receive treatment similar to that given the target group. Thus, for example, some heterosexual GSA members had been called "dyke" or "fag," and some expressed concern about the effect of courtesy stigma on heterosexual dating opportunities.

A subtle source of stress for heterosexual youth was that they were often rendered invisible by public discourse, wherein the GSA was commonly referred to as "the gay club" in the media and by friends and antagonists alike. Some understood that this sense of invisibility is an experience that LGB people encounter regularly.

MANAGING THE STRESSES. Heterosexual students used stress-management strategies similar to those that LGB members used. Notable among these was humor; the teens laughed at the harassment. Another strategy also paralleled one employed by LGB students: many—especially LDS students—"passed," avoiding telling others that they belonged to the GSA.

Some straight teens also used thoughtful analysis to deal with the stress of belonging to the club. One student spoke of her understanding of the value of tolerance: "I personally think being tolerant of other people is for your own good . . . it makes life much easier for you, 'cause you're not filled up with that rage and that hate because someone's poisoning you with that type of emotion."

Heterosexual students also found support from their LGB peers. In several interviews, when heterosexual members questioned themselves over their own homophobic remarks or over a perceived failure to take a stand, LGB students offered permission to be less than perfect in these regards—sometimes by telling tales of their own homophobic actions.

REWARDS. Membership in the GSA brought rewards as well as stresses to heterosexual teens. Straight members generally were quite enthusiastic about GSA activities and valued the camaraderie and sense of being accepted. Several heterosexual students suggested that the climate of the club had helped them to be more accepting and kinder. One heterosexual student, who is also Mormon, said that she had become more open-minded about religion, less conservative, more outgoing, more assertive, and more fun-loving. Students mentioned an increased sense of efficacy and enhanced self-confidence. They told us that they had learned the value of support when confronted with antagonism from others. Those with political motives felt they were in a position to do some good—in the words of one, to "help the entire society move forward."

The Principal at East High School

Kay Peterson, the principal at East, works to keep in touch with what is happening in his school: "I'll go into the hall and get three kids and say, 'Come have lunch with me on Friday.' I just take three kids; doesn't matter who they are. 'And bring two friends. I'll buy the pizza. . . .' And they all come in my office, we sit on the floor, we make a mess, we eat pizza, the custodians are mad, we clean it up. But I learn a lot."

Even so, he was not aware of the harassment LGB students were experiencing. When students approached Kay to propose the formation of a gay-straight alliance, he expected their proposal would "cause a ripple"; he "didn't realize it'd be a tsunami."

Had the principal voiced strong objections to the idea of a GSA, the matter might have been closed. Instead, he asked the students to gather others and come for lunch to obtain additional information and establish that the idea for the club originated with the students. Early on, Kay "really became impressed that . . . the agenda was driven by the kids who were concerned primarily about the struggles that they were having in schools, and hoping that . . . they could find an official, sanctioned way to support that."

We learned from others who were present at the first meeting that Kay's eyes filled with tears as he listened to the LGB students describe their experiences of harassment at school. He later verified reports of his response: "I don't want to be so noble as to say it's just the milk of human kindness that runs in my veins; it was also guilt that I had been negligent in not seeing that the [harassment] was occurring, or that I had not been vigorous enough, energetic enough in my response to harassment."

This lunch marked a turning point. The GSA students felt heard, teachers who supported the students concluded they had some administrative backing, and Kay determined that his school needed to be made safe for all students, regardless of their sexual orientation. He informed school district officials about the GSA and launched a series of meetings between student government and members of the GSA to ease their discomfort with each other and to help each group see beyond its own stereotypes.

Kay's philosophy on the matter of the GSA is quite straightforward: the issue is not about identity politics. His "biases" have changed, his "perspectives" have changed, and his "sympathies and loves" have changed. But his commitment to ensuring a safe environment for all students at East High remains the motive for his actions. He told us how he represented the matter to his faculty: "This is a recognition that we have kids in our school that are different, and they nonetheless belong to the population that deserves an education, and we're going to serve them."

Interestingly, he takes that position despite his being a member of the LDS church. Several people told us that, rather than focusing on the LDS denunciation of homosexuality, Kay draws on other LDS principles—especially the importance of family. He views East High School as a family of which he is the head and finds it unacceptable to have some members of that family harassing others. Ensuring that everyone is safe is a necessary element of good "stewardship."

Kay has not found support for this position from all quarters. According to some other respondents, he received informal pressure from various community entities as well as opposition from the school board and the legislature. Despite such resistance, and in keeping with his sense of stewardship, he is gratified by teachers' reports that many GSA members' attendance and grades improved after establishment of the club, and he is "flattered" that LGB students now report incidents of harassment, trusting that he will intervene.

Teachers

Teachers at East High School, like most teachers around the country, have little or no training in working with LGB students, and they are continually exposed to negative attitudes toward LGB people. Dealing sensitively with issues of sexual orientation was complicated by the legislature's enactment of SB246, which prohibited school personnel from doing anything that might disrupt the educational climate. Discussion about LGB issues was seen as an example—perhaps the paradigmatic case—of such disruption. Consequently, as one student said, "They really have absolutely no idea how to handle gay students." Students reported not only failures to intervene in harassment against LGB students but also homophobic and heterosexist practices by some teachers.

An assortment of motives underlay various teachers' support for the GSA (cf. Russell and Bohan, forthcoming). Nelson, a heterosexual teacher and early sponsor of the club, recalled that as a high school senior he had failed to intervene when Anglo students taunted African American students. He viewed that as a "missed opportunity where [he] could have made a difference." Georgia Geerling, another heterosexual teacher at East who also volunteered to be an advisor, indicated that her experiences as non-LDS and as the mother of a biracial daughter had sensitized her to the pain of exclusion. In both cases, the GSA provided an opportunity to act on behalf of oppressed youth.

Camille Lee, another East High teacher and herself a lesbian, wanted to be helpful to the GSA but was initially concerned about the impact on her and her job. Camille's initial stance was to work actively behind the scenes. Later she came out as a lesbian, opening the door for her to take a more public stance in relation to the club.

The teachers who were supportive of the GSA enacted their help in a variety of ways. Some accompanied students in their early contacts with the principal. Others helped by supervising GSA meetings, a requirement for all clubs. Some gave advice to students; Barbara Murdock told Kelli about the merits of passive resistance at a point when Kelli was, in her own words, "about to go off and scream at somebody." Some teachers expressed indirect support by setting classroom standards prohibiting harassment of any kind. Members of the GSA were keenly attentive to various teachers' attitudes toward LGB students and attempts to make the school environment safe.

The presence of LGB teachers at East was of particular interest to GSA members. They were quite alert to the actions of teachers who they knew or suspected were LGB. At times, they expressed frustration with teachers who stayed in the closet. In the words of one student: "I mean, I understand; I couldn't not. But it's frustrating knowing that they could've helped me; they could've helped my friends; they could be good examples; they could be out there just showing that there is diversity. They could be visible."

For the students, the lesson of such invisibility was that being in the closet was the appropriate way to live. At the same time, most understood the social and occupational dangers for teachers who disclosed their sexual orientation.

Members of the GSA witnessed the coming out of two public high school teachers in Salt Lake: Clayton Vetter, a debate teacher at a different high school; and Camille Lee at East. The students expressed complicated feelings about teachers' coming out. One described her reaction: "It was almost as if we felt like they were breaking out of their closets to help us. . . . It gave us a sense of almost belonging, because where we were orphans before, now we had someone to look up to."

The students saw these teachers as "role models" with benevolent motives and were grateful for the adults' support. Nevertheless, some students expressed disappointment that the teachers had relied on them to lead the way. Indeed, both Clayton and Camille publicly acknowledged that their decisions to come out were influenced by GSA students. The students sometimes felt a measure of responsibility for the LGB teachers (and at various times for LGB adults in general), and several students acknowledged they sometimes felt pressure from LGB adults who needed the GSA to succeed. The students identified with their teachers' sense that nobody should have such difficult and lonely adolescent periods; in the words of one student, "[The teachers] want to fix it, and [they] want us to help [them] to fix it."

Clearly, attitudes that keep LGB teachers in the closet do a disservice to these teachers and to their students. This was highlighted by the comments of a gay student at a private Salt Lake high school who had several openly LGB teachers. He relied on these teachers as role models, sources of advice and academic help, and people who could help him in his relationship with his parents. Until LGB teachers can come out and receive administrative support for doing so, an optimal environment for LGB students is not attainable.

Parents

The parents of GSA members were implicated in the club's dynamics almost from the beginning. Indeed, had the parents of the founders and central participants blocked their children's efforts to start the club, there might never have been a GSA.

STRESSES. Having adolescents involved in so visible and stigmatized an undertaking was often difficult for their parents. According to the students, most parents shared the fear that the club would make their teens even more vulnerable to harassment. For the parents of the central figures in the GSA—such as Kelli's parents, Dee and Randy Peterson—fears were heightened by constant media presence and speaking engagements, some of which included travel.

Not all parents of GSA members were worried for their children's safety. Mykle Yoshikama's mother, Lynn Scott, believed that violence was an unlikely response in Salt Lake City. However, Lynn watched with concern as her daughter experienced a moderate degree of social ostracism for being a GSA member.

Parents worried about their other children as well, and other family members were indeed affected by the reaction to the GSA. For example, Erin Wiser's mother, Leslie, tells of Erin's younger sister, Bailey, being in seminary (a daily class in LDS doctrine at the high school) when homosexuality was being discussed. Everyone in the class knew that Bailey had a lesbian sister. Bailey was very upset and felt condemned, according to Leslie. She "wanted to crawl away."

SOURCES OF SUPPORT. Parents often identified other parents as their best sources of support. Parents also expressed appreciation for the willingness of some teachers to work on behalf of their teens. Leslie Wiser illustrated this theme when she said: "For these teachers to go out on the line and support our kids and be there for our kids, and for our kids to be able to feel safe after all of this, I mean, they just have been incredible."

AFFIRMING RESPONSES. Despite the stress and concern, many parents felt great pride in the students. Lynn Scott voiced respect for her daughter, Mykle, who was willing to take a firm stand despite ostracism from peers. Even a few LDS parents who condemned homosexuality were said to support their sons' and daughters' willingness to stand for what they believed in. Erin's father, Tim Wiser, referred to Erin as his hero. His pride extended to Erin's peers in the club: "I still feel . . . that our kids are being underestimated. I think the kids are far more intelligent and strong-willed, and they have the fortitude it's going to take to pull this thing off."

Against this background of pride, and despite concerns for the students' safety, many parents helped the teens in a variety of ways, as with moral support and logistical assistance. One parent explained her willingness to be supportive in these terms: "I don't think it's ever wise to hold your kids back. I think that they need to learn. . . . You can't shelter them from being hurt. You can't let them not get on the bike because you know you're going to be kissing that knee. You can't. You have to hold back yourself and say, 'Explore. Get out there and get as much as you can. Enjoy it and experience everything you can grab hold of. Everything.'"

Community

Adults in the community delivered all manner of aid, ranging from financial assistance to moral support. Their strategic support was apparent in the many meetings called on the students' behalf, perhaps nowhere more obviously than in the hundreds of people who rallied at the state capitol to protest the banning of the GSA and other clubs. Moral support was prolific, and the students were very aware of it.

Community supporters spoke of members of the GSA in a variety of terms; representative is the language of Tamara Baggett, an LDS woman and political organizer who viewed the youths as "courageous." For their part, students realized that some LGB adults were living vicariously through them, and that many adults felt that the teens had become their leaders.

Relationships between the students and supportive community members were sometimes laced with tension, much of it deriving from a difference in goals. In particular, when the extreme actions of the school board and the legislature set in motion a crusade for (and another against) LGB youth, the students' initial hope for a support club was overshadowed by public and political agendas. It was sometimes difficult for anyone to remember that these people, who were having such a dramatic impact and were being asked to do and be so much, were not even old enough to vote.

Summary

At this writing, it has been more than two years since the GSA was proposed. The tremendous uproar it raised in its first months subsided and the students returned to meeting, as they had initially envisioned, as a social and support group. The calm was recently disrupted somewhat when two students and the GSA filed suit against the school board, claiming that other clubs continue to benefit from school facilities. This event, however, has not received nearly the attention garnered by the club's founding. Many students seem content—some are even notably relieved—by this diminution of attention. Others, however, are enthusiastic about a return to activism. Throughout the process, the students have continued to benefit from the many tiers of support described above.

Embedded in our descriptions of various levels of community are suggestions about how individuals and groups in each position might foster development and maintenance of healthy learning environments for LGB students. Here we would like to make several more general comments.

First, creating an optimal educational environment benefits from and arguably requires the involvement of many people not usually thought of as participants in educational settings. This may be especially true for young people who are different from the norm in ways deemed significant, and whose distinctive needs traditional educational settings therefore fail to address.[3]

Second, it is inevitable that participation in providing a healthy educational climate brings stresses to all involved. These stresses can be counteracted by active attempts to seek support and nourish resilience, a process we observed in each of the individuals and groups we talked with. We found these two to be commonly intertwined: individual resilience is grounded in collective support.

Third, much of the stress experienced by these students derived from the presence of discrepant goals. The teens wanted a social and support group. Adults in the community often had additional goals for the students. Students were encouraged to participate in ways that were perhaps not always to their benefit, and adults were occasionally disappointed that the students did not move in the direction and at the speed that adults would have preferred. Some of the tension between adults in the community and GSA members was born of a failure on everyone's part to recognize the developmental needs and limitations of these teens.

We have argued that at least some teens benefited from the opportunities afforded by the movement to political activism. On the other hand, some students may have been precluded from participation because of this development. Core members of the GSA were catapulted into situations and challenges that would have strained any adult's coping resources, and they paid a price: encroachments on the process of identity formation, the costs of star status that eventually wanes, and the effective loss of a year's adolescence. If our aim is to help LGB students, we must avoid focusing so intently on their LGB identity that we forget about their individual and developmental needs. We need to be reflective about our own agendas and diligent about not imposing our goals on their lives.

An unanticipated set of findings has alerted us to a fourth important implication of this study. Given the LDS church's stance on homosexuality, one might anticipate universal antipathy to LGB issues among LDS faithful. In contrast to this expectation, we found a small but significant number of LDS individuals who were actively supportive of the GSA—and indeed of LGB rights in general (Bohan and Russell, 1997). The most common rationales underlying such support come, paradoxically, from LDS beliefs, in particular, emphasis on love for and devotion to one's family—including an extended "family" or friends. The very important message of this finding is that assistance might emerge from unexpected sources, and it is crucial that we not miss opportunities for finding support by prematurely excluding certain groups or individuals from consideration.

Finally, although these observations are based on a situation involving high school students in a particular—and distinctive—social context, they can surely be extended to other students and other circumstances. The very extremity of this situation brings into sharp relief issues that underlie the lives of LGB students. Not all live in a setting unique in its religious culture; not all confront such extreme, officially sanctioned prejudice; not all become the topic of national news. But all do face a world that is largely inimical to their identity and that provides few resources for them to cope with that enmity as they negotiate the transition to adulthood. Providing a multitiered support system that nurtures students' resilience holds great promise for making that transition supportive of, rather than detrimental to, their educational experiences.

NOTES

1. We recently conducted a feedback meeting with a large and diverse sample of these individuals, wherein we shared our understandings with them. Participants' responses at this meeting indicated that we have succeeded in this goal.
2. Written permission to record these interviews was obtained from all participants as well as from the parents of participants who were under eighteen years of age at the time of the interview. All participants also agreed to be quoted and to be identified by name in our discussions about this project. Some participants indicated specific areas where they did not wish to be quoted; those limitations have been honored here.
3. This observation has prompted revision of a famous line: *it takes the Village People to raise a child.*

REFERENCES

Bem, S. *The Lenses of Gender: Transforming the Debate on Sexual Inequality.* New Haven: Yale University Press, 1993.

Bohan, J. *Psychology and Sexual Orientation: Coming to Terms.* New York: Routledge, 1996.

Bohan, J., and Russell, G. *Church, State, and Homophobia: Youth Under Siege.* Poster presented at meetings of the American Psychological Association, Chicago, Aug. 1997.

Comstock, G. D. *Unrepentent, Self-Affirming, Practicing: Lesbian/Gay/Bisexual People Within Organized Religion.* New York: Continuum, 1996.

Goffman, E. *Stigma: Notes on the Management of Spoiled Identity.* Upper Saddle River, N.J.: Prentice-Hall, 1963.

Herek, G. M. "Psychological Heterosexism in the United States." In A. R. D'Augelli and C. J. Patterson (eds.), *Lesbian, Gay, and Bisexual Identities over the Lifespan.* New York: Oxford University Press, 1995.

Herman, D. *The Antigay Agenda: Orthodox Vision and the Christian Right.* Chicago: University of Chicago Press, 1997.

Hershberger, S., and D'Augelli, A. "The Impact of Victimization on the Mental Health and Suicidality of Lesbian, Gay, and Bisexual Youths." *Developmental Psychology,* 1995, *31*(1), 65–74.

Hertz, R. (ed.). *Reflexivity and Voice.* Thousand Oaks, Calif.: Sage, 1997.

Hunter, A. "Same Door, Different Closet: A Heterosexual Sissy's Coming Out Party." In S. Wilkinson and C. Kitzinger (eds.), *Heterosexuality: A "Feminism and Psychology" Reader.* London: Sage, 1993.

Jones, S. J. "Reflexivity and Feminist Practice: Ethical Dilemmas in Negotiating Meanings." *Feminism and Psychology,* 1997, *7*(3), 348–353.

Malyon, A. "Psychotherapeutic Implications of Internalized Homophobia in Gay Men." In J. Gonsiorek (ed.), *Homosexuality and Psychotherapy: A Practitioner's Handbook of Affirmative Methods.* Binghamton, N.Y.: Haworth, 1981.

Margolies, L., Becker, M., and Jackson-Brewer, K. "Internalized Homophobia: Identifying and Treating the Oppressor Within." In Boston Lesbian Psychologies Collective (eds.), *Lesbian Psychologies.* Urbana: University of Illinois Press, 1987.

Martin, A. "Learning to Hide: The Socialization of the Gay Adolescent." *Adolescent Psychiatry,* 1982, *10*(1), 52–65.

Pharr, S. *Homophobia as a Weapon of Sexism.* Inverness, Calif.: Chadron, 1988.

Pharr, S. *In the Time of the Right.* Inverness, Calif.: Chadron, 1996.

Rofes, E. "Gay Issues, Schools, and the Right-Wing Backlash." *Rethinking Schools: An Urban Educational Journal,* 1997, *11*(3), 1, 4–6.

Russell, G. M., and Bohan, J. S. "Hearing Voices: The Uses of Research and the Politics of Change." *Psychology of Women Quarterly,* forthcoming.

Savin-Williams, R. "Lesbian, Gay Male, and Bisexual Adolescents." In A. R. D'Augelli and C. J. Patterson (eds.), *Lesbian, Gay, and Bisexual Identities over the Lifespan.* New York: Oxford University Press, 1995.

Schow, R., Schow, N., and Raynes, M. (eds.). *Peculiar People: Mormons and Same-Sex Orientation.* Salt Lake City, Utah: Signature, 1991.

Seattle Public Schools. Safe Schools Anti-Violence Documentation Project's Third Annual Report. Seattle: Seattle Public Schools, 1996. [Available from the Northwestern Coalition on Malicious Harassment, P.O. Box 16776, Seattle, WA 98116, (206) 233-9136.]

Sophie, J. "Internalized Homophobia and Lesbian Identity." *Journal of Homosexuality,* 1987, *14*(1), 53–66.

Strauss, A., and Corbin, J. *Basics of Qualitative Research: Grounded Theory Procedures and Techniques.* Thousand Oaks, Calif.: Sage, 1990.

Woog, D. *School's Out: The Impact of Gay and Lesbian Issues on America's Schools.* Los Angeles: Alyson, 1995.

17

COLLEGE WOMEN AND ALCOHOL USE

Mary Crawford, George Dowdall, Henry Wechsler

ALCOHOL USE AND ABUSE on college campuses is intimately connected to overall campus climate. Consider the following students' accounts of drinking:[1]

> My roommate came home very drunk. I didn't want to deal with it. I had three tests the next day and had planned to study instead of playing "mom." I was really scared though. She was throwing things everywhere and crying. She really stunk and was disgusting. I especially didn't want her to puke in my room. I flunked one test and skipped another, I was so drained. I didn't speak to her at all the next day.
>
> I went to a fraternity party off campus. I had at least 12 shots of liquor and two mixed drinks. That night I went home with this guy I did not know and had sex with him. . . . The guy and his roommates carried me home to my dorm, where two RAs caught me. I went to the hospital for alcohol poisoning and rape. I blacked out. I never pressed charges because he used the condom in my wallet.
>
> A girl I know, who has a very low alcohol tolerance, got so drunk that a friend and I had . . . to carry her for several blocks, trying to keep her from burning us with a cigarette. Since then she has gotten as or nearly as drunk every weekend. It has gotten her into some bad situations and made things very difficult for her roommate and friends who won't confront her forcefully or let me confront her.

In this chapter, we explore the results of a 1993 study of a national representative sample of four-year colleges involving 17,592 students, with a special focus on the 10,132 women in the sample. We first describe drinking patterns among the women and then explore the effects of their binge drinking. Our analyses show that current patterns of alcohol use on campus are linked with numerous negative effects for women, ranging from impaired sleep and study to being the victim of a sexual assault. In particular, we explore the relationships between alcohol use and acquaintance rape.

What factors contribute to a healthier environment for college women? To address this question, we look at institutions and settings where problem drinking is lower. Knowledge of the contexts and effects of drinking among college women points the way to possible interventions for creating safer and healthier learning environments.

The Harvard School of Public Health College Alcohol Study

The Harvard School of Public Health College Alcohol Study (Dowdall, Crawford, and Wechsler, 1998; Wechsler and others, 1994; Wechsler, Dowdall, Davenport, and Castillo, 1995) examined the nature, extent, and associated problems of alcohol use on college campuses with a special focus on heavy episodic or "binge" drinking. This research effort sought answers to three core questions:

1. How extensive is the problem of binge drinking among college students?
2. Who is affected by binge drinking?
3. What can be done about this problem?

The 140 colleges that participated in the HSPH study represent a cross-section of American higher education. Two-thirds are public, one-third private. Approximately two-thirds are located in suburban or urban settings and one-third in small-town or rural settings. Four percent are women-only colleges, and 4 percent are historically black institutions. A twenty-page survey instrument asked students a variety of questions about their drinking behavior and explored problems they experienced as a result of their own and others' drinking. Responses were voluntary and anonymous. Only statistically significant comparisons are discussed in this chapter.

In any study of alcohol use and abuse, the definition of *drinking* is crucial. In this study, a *drink* was defined as a twelve-ounce can or bottle of beer, a four-ounce glass of wine, a twelve-ounce bottle or can of wine cooler, or a shot of liquor taken straight or in a mixed drink. *Binge drinking* was defined as consuming five or more drinks in a row for men, and four or more drinks in a row for women. This definition, which takes into account sex differences in body mass and ethanol metabolism, was based on extensive analyses showing that the gender-specific measure of five drinks for men and four for women accurately indicates an equivalent likelihood of alcohol-related problems (Wechsler, Dowdall, Davenport, and Rimm, 1995).

Some may say, "Four or five drinks? That's not much." This study demonstrates that, in many students, this benchmark is indicative of a heavy-drinking lifestyle. Students who drink in these or greater amounts differ from other students by the frequency and severity of their alcohol-related problems.

Bingeing rates vary dramatically from campus to campus. At its lowest, the binge-drinking rate was 1 percent of the student population. At its highest, the rate was a stunning 70 percent of students. At nearly one-third of the schools, more than half of the responding students were binge drinkers.

Gender Issues in Alcohol Use and Abuse

There is a long history of neglect in studying substance abuse in women (Center on Addiction and Substance Abuse, 1996; Lex, 1990; Vogeltanz and Wilsnack, 1997). Women have been excluded from research samples on the assumption that they are less likely to be substance abusers, or (if they are abusing) that the pattern, contexts, and meaning of their substance use are similar to men's, so that women need not be studied separately. As a result of this cumulative pattern of neglect, substance use in women is much less understood than in men. Alcohol use and abuse are no exception. Today, research samples and clinical studies are more likely to include women, but this does not guarantee that the research is grounded in a gender-sensitive perspective.

Drinking Patterns: Some Group Comparisons

This study found differences and similarities in the drinking patterns of women and men. Most students of both sexes use alcohol. Only one student in six had not done so within the past year; about as many men

(15 percent) as women (16 percent) were in this group of abstainers.[2] Two out of five students drank but were not binge drinkers (35 percent of the men and 45 percent of the women). Binge drinking was reported by 50 percent of the men and 39 percent of the women in the total sample. About one student in five—23 percent of the men and 17 percent of the women—reported frequent binge drinking, defined as three or more episodes within the past two weeks.

Ethnicity was a very important correlate of alcohol use for both sexes. Members of all other ethnic groups were much less likely to binge than white students. For example, among the women in the sample, 44 percent of those who were white, 36 percent of Native American, 17 percent of Asian American, and only 11 percent of African American women reported bingeing.

Fraternity and sorority members were much more likely to be binge drinkers compared to other students. For women, sorority members were nearly twice as likely to binge as unaffiliated women—62 percent versus 35 percent. Among women who lived in sorority houses, an astonishing 80 percent were binge drinkers. This raises the question of whether Greek societies attract binge drinkers, or create them. The data indicate that sororities do not seem to attract binge drinkers in particular, but they may play a role in creating them. One in three women who lived in sororities had binged in high school, only slightly higher than the proportion among other students. But three out of every four women who had not binged in high school became binge drinkers while in residence in sororities.

Group membership tells much about who is at risk for alcohol abuse. First, there is considerable bingeing among women in general. Although women may not match men in the sheer amount of alcohol consumed, they are surprisingly close to men in how often they binge drink. Second, binge drinking is much more a problem for white students than for students of color. Third, involvement in the Greek system is linked to heavier drinking.

Consequences for Women

The women in the sample experienced a number of ill effects from their drinking. Within the school year in which they were responding, they reported:

- Having a hangover (53 percent)
- Doing something they regretted (30 percent)
- Missing a class (23 percent)

- Forgetting where they had been or what they had done (22 percent)
- Arguing with friends or getting behind in their academic work (17 percent)
- Getting hurt or injured (8 percent)
- Damaging property or getting into trouble with the police (3 percent)

Alcohol use is reliably linked to sexual activity among the college women surveyed. After drinking, 16 percent had engaged in unplanned sexual activity, and 9 percent in unprotected sexual activity, within the current school year. Other studies too show a pattern of increased sexual activity and decreased sexual responsibility, leading to increased risk of unintended pregnancies, relationship problems, and sexually transmitted diseases, including HIV/AIDS (Meilman, 1993; Radius, Joffe, and Gall, 1991; Wechsler and Isaac, 1992).

Drinking led to risky driving behavior for the women in the sample. Within the thirty-day period prior to the survey, more than one-fifth (21 percent) had driven a car after drinking alcohol; 5 percent had done so after consuming four or more drinks in a row. Nearly 17 percent had ridden as a passenger with a driver who was impaired (high or drunk). It is worth noting that alcohol abuse contributes to nearly one-half of motor vehicle fatalities, which are the leading cause of death among young Americans (Robert Wood Johnson Foundation, 1993).

In summary, if college women use alcohol, it creates a variety of problems for them. Many of the young women who drank had experienced more than one of these problems, and 12 percent had experienced five or more different alcohol-related problems since the beginning of the school year.

College students are affected not only by their own drinking but by the alcohol-influenced behavior of those around them. This study distinguishes between the *primary consequences* of alcohol use—that is, the drinker experiences some result or consequence of her or his own drinking—and *secondary consequences*—meaning that the well-being or quality of life of an individual is affected by the drinking of others in her or his environment. Within the current school year, 44 percent of the women in the sample took care of a drunken student; 41 percent had their studying or sleep interrupted; 27 percent were insulted or humiliated by a drunken student; 21 percent had a serious argument or quarrel; and 9 percent had their property damaged.

Moreover, alcohol abuse is strongly linked to violence against women. In this study, one woman in four had experienced an unwanted sexual advance associated with others' drinking. More than one in ten had been pushed, hit, or physically assaulted. One in fifty reported being a victim of sexual assault or date rape since the beginning of the school year being surveyed.

Crimes of violence against women are the most underreported category of violent crime (Koss, 1990). The reasons are complex. One factor is that people are very reluctant to use the word *rape* to describe coerced sexual activity between acquaintances (Goodchilds, Zellman, Johnson, and Giarrusso, 1988). To most people, the term signifies the prototypical stranger assault (Warshaw, 1988). When people are asked about specific activities that meet the legal definition of rape (instead of being asked directly, "Have you ever been raped?"), the reported rate of acquaintance rape is typically much higher. For example, in a national survey of more than six thousand students from thirty-two colleges, more than 15 percent of the women had experienced rape, and 12 percent had experienced attempted rape since the age of fourteen. An additional 12 percent had been verbally pressured into sexual intercourse, and another 14 percent had experienced other forms of unwanted sexual contact such as forced kissing or fondling. Of the women who had experienced an act that met the legal definition of rape, only one in four labeled it as that, and only one in ten had told anyone what had happened to them (Koss, Gidycz, and Wisniewski, 1987). Applied to the HSPH College Alcohol Study, the study by Koss, Gidycz, and Wisniewski suggests that even though more than two hundred of the women in the present sample reported having been the victim of sexual assault or rape in connection with their own or others' drinking, the actual number of such incidents may be between four and ten times higher.

Alcohol Use and Acquaintance Rape

More than 80 percent of the rapes that occur on college campuses are committed by a person known to the victim; approximately half are committed on dates (Koss, Gidycz, and Wisniewski, 1987). Acquaintance rape often takes place in the context of alcohol use (Koss and Dinero, 1989; Meilman, 1993). Although the link between alcohol consumption and acquaintance rape is well documented, its meaning and implications are contested (Abbey, 1991; Crawford, 1995).

Understanding the causal relationships between date rape and alcohol use is necessary for designing effective prevention programs (Abbey, 1991). Does drinking cause men to be more aggressive? Does it diminish the ability of women and/or men to communicate clearly with their partners? Does drinking make women less likely to spot a dangerous situation? Do stereotypes about gender and drinking play a part? Any or all of these factors could be involved.

Fortunately, there is a great deal of research evidence that can help sort out the possible causes for the link between alcohol use and violence against college women. The evidence comes from a variety of studies, including surveys of self-reported alcohol use and its consequences (such as the present one), interviews with admitted acquaintance rapists, interviews with survivors of acquaintance rape, and surveys about attitudes and beliefs among male and female college students. Other evidence comes from *discourse analytic techniques,* which involve close study of written or spoken accounts, and *analogue studies,* in which students read scenarios or brief stories about dating situations and assess the behavior of the male and female characters in the stories. These latter two techniques allow examination of people's justifications and attributions of blame for sexual violence. Here we look briefly at the evidence for some of the possible links between drinking and date rape.

One very popular account of the cause of date rape is that it is caused by miscommunication. Communication difficulties between women and men occur, according to this theory, because they have different styles of talk. Even in everyday interactions, they are likely to misunderstand the other's intentions. If alcohol and sexual intent enter the picture, the possibility of miscommunication is heightened, and the resulting communication breakdown ends in rape.

This view is plausible; communication about sexual activity is complicated. People feel vulnerable in sexual situations, and they try to make and refuse requests in ways that avoid overt disagreement. Moreover, sexual scripts that position men as the aggressors and women as reluctant, passive recipients of sexual activity encourage divergent communication patterns in sexual encounters.

Analogue studies have shown that men interpret a greater variety of verbal and nonverbal cues as indicating sexual intent than women do (Abbey, 1991; Abbey and Harnish, 1995). Men perceive women as more interested in sex than women do; they are more likely to interpret a woman's ambiguous cues—complimenting her date, wearing revealing clothes, having a few drinks—as signals of her sexual availability. In general, college men seem to view the world in a more sexualized manner than college women do. Sexual schemas organize and direct men's behavior and filter their interpretation of social milieus. Because it dulls the capacity to analyze complex situations at the same time it increases sexual arousal in men, alcohol use may increase men's misperceptions of women's behavior, leading them to interpret friendliness as an invitation to sex. Alcohol use by women may compromise their ability to send clear refusal cues.

Though much attention has been focused on miscommunication, it is only one of many possible causes of the link between alcohol use and acquaintance sexual assault. Focusing on miscommunication as the sole cause of this form of sexual assault is a mistake. If communication is overemphasized, women are encouraged to accept sole responsibility for rape prevention; they are blamed (and encouraged to blame themselves) if rape prevention strategies fail; and power issues in interpreting relationship violence are obscured (Corcoran and Mahlstedt, 1998; Crawford, 1995; Mahlstedt and Corcoran, in the next chapter of this volume). Other factors are at least as important. Here, we briefly explore the evidence for three other ways in which alcohol and date rape may be linked.

First, women who drink are perceived as more responsible—and men who drink as less responsible—for acquaintance rape. Drinking "justifies" antisocial behavior for men in our society. Many male college students purposely get drunk to experience the disinhibition that comes with drinking (Abbey, 1991). An observer on virtually any college campus readily hears students' tales of their own and others' drunken exploits, such as vomiting in public, throwing furniture out dormitory windows, or driving on the wrong side of the road. These tales are the stuff of ordinary conversation and a common form of boasting. Thus, alcohol use is not just a cause but a reason and justification for otherwise unacceptable behavior. Either consciously or unconsciously, some men may choose to drink in order to make it easier to force sex on a woman—and leave themselves less culpable.

Contrary to the miscommunication model, the majority of acquaintance rapes are planned in advance by the rapist (Abbey, 1991). In interview studies, rapists frequently report using alcohol consumption to justify their behavior; moreover, some criminal statutes hold rapists less responsible for their crimes if they were drunk at the time of the attack, and jurors may be less likely to hold them responsible as well.

College students too share the belief that drinking makes men less responsible for crimes they commit. However, they do not extend the same reasoning to women who become crime victims after drinking. When college students read a story about a woman raped at a party, they held her more responsible if she was described as drunk than if the story mentioned that she was sober. She was also perceived as less moral and likable if drunk. In contrast, the man who raped her was perceived as less responsible if he was described as drunk than if the story mentioned that he was sober (Richardson and Campbell, 1982). Survey data (Warshaw, 1988) and discourse-analytic studies (Crawford, 1995) too show that women who are raped while they are drunk are perceived as more responsible and deserving of blame for the assault. Clearly, "the costs of intoxication are higher for college women than for college men" (Abbey, 1991, p. 168).

Second, alcohol use may affect women's ability to resist sexual assault. Research suggests that rapid resistance is often effective in preventing rape (Bart and O'Brien, 1985; Siegel and others, 1989). A woman who screams, runs, struggles, or otherwise asserts her nonconsent may disrupt the rape episode. However, if the potential victim is drunk, the effects of alcohol on her cognitive and motor functioning may make her less able to assert effective forms of resistance.

Finally, using alcohol may lead others to believe that a woman is sexually available. In one analogue study, students read vignettes about a couple on a date in which the woman had either a few beers or a few soft drinks. Both female and male college students rated the woman who drank alcohol as more likely to want sex, respond positively to a sexual move, and have sexual intercourse (George, Gournic, and McAfee, 1988). In other analogue studies, both women and men who drank on dates were perceived as being more sexual (see for example Abbey and Harnish, 1995). Clearly, there is a stereotype that sharing a few drinks on a date means that the intent of both partners is to engage in sex, and in particular that women who drink alcohol want to have sex.

If using alcohol means that a woman is sexually available, it takes only a few steps of faulty logic to believe that encouraging a woman to get drunk is an acceptable way to make her want to have sex, or if persuasion fails, to make her "fair game" for forced sex. In one study, 40 percent of the young men believed that forcing sex on a date who is drunk is acceptable (Goodchilds and Zellman, 1984). Three-fourths of admitted rapists in one interview study said that they sometimes "got women drunk" to have sex with them; many survivors of acquaintance rape report that their attackers encouraged them to drink for several hours before the attack (Kanin, 1985; Warshaw, 1988).

The Women's College Advantage

Among the more than ten thousand women in the HSPH College Alcohol survey, 5 percent attended women's colleges. Attending a women's college is related to positive outcomes in the area of educational climate, self-esteem, and lifetime achievement (see Sebrechts, Chapter Two of this volume). Research suggests that the social climate at women's colleges differs significantly from that at coeducational colleges. However, until our study (Dowdall, Crawford, and Wechsler, 1998) there was no research on the health-related correlates of attending a women's college in comparison to a coeducational college.

We found that there is more alcohol abuse at coeducational institutions than at women's colleges, though differences do not emerge in all categories of drinking. In the heaviest drinking category (bingeing three or more times in the past two weeks), the difference is striking: only about one in thirteen women at women's colleges binge this frequently, while one in six at coed colleges do so.

Moreover, the two types of college environments are viewed by women differently. For example, 6 percent of women at women's colleges and 29 percent of women at coeducational institutions identified half or more of their fellow students as "heavy or problem drinkers." Fifty-six percent of women at women's colleges agreed or strongly agreed with the statement "Students here admire nondrinkers," compared with only 45 percent of women at coeducational institutions. A smaller proportion of women at women's colleges were involved romantically with another person than at coeducational institutions (31 percent versus 37 percent), and their romantic partners were less likely to have binged on one or more occasions in the past two weeks than the partners of women at coeducational institutions (18 percent versus 27 percent).

There were large differences in the number and kind of alcohol-related problems experienced by women drinkers at each type of school. Waking up with a hangover, doing something later regretted, missing class, forgetting one's whereabouts or actions, arguing with friends, getting behind academically, having unplanned sexual activity, and getting hurt or injured in connection with drinking were all more prevalent at coeducational institutions. Only about 5 percent of women drinkers at women's colleges reported five or more alcohol-related problems since the beginning of the school year, compared to 13 percent at coed colleges. Thus the risk of a constellation of alcohol-related problems is more than twice as high at coeducational than at women's colleges.

Women at coeducational institutions also experienced more negative consequences from other students' drinking, ranging from interruptions of study or sleep to serious quarrels, property damage, and physical assault. The only item with no significant difference between the two types of institution concerned being a victim of sexual assault or date rape in connection with another person's drinking. Moreover, there was a pattern of increased risk of alcohol use and driving for women at coeducational colleges compared with those at women's colleges: coeducational college women were significantly more likely to drive after drinking and more than twice as likely to have ridden with an impaired (high or drunk) driver.

These data demonstrate that with respect to binge drinking and associated risks, women at women's colleges experience a healthier environment than those at coeducational colleges. Students at women's colleges are less likely to binge frequently, have fewer alcohol-related problems, experience fewer negative effects from other students' drinking, and are less likely to combine drinking and driving.

What are the reasons for these differences? There may be several (Dowdall, Crawford, and Wechsler, 1998). Women who dislike alcohol excesses may differentially choose to go to women's colleges. In addition, the interpersonal and social climates at the two kinds of institution may support different choices with respect to alcohol use. The impact of the peer group on college student development, behavior, and attitudes is well established (Astin, 1992). The differences between women in the two settings may also be attributable largely to the presence or absence of men, who are more likely to binge drink. It could also be due to having different female peers in the two environments.

Interestingly, our analyses showed that women's college students spend as much time socializing with friends as do their counterparts at coeducational colleges, and they are equally likely to have five or more close friends. Thus the difference appears related not to the amount of time spent socializing, but to its quality.

Strategies for Intervention

The HSPH College Alcohol Study showed a widespread and destructive pattern of alcohol abuse on U.S. college campuses. However, the pattern is not uniform. Some situations and contexts provide healthier environments for women (and men) than others. In particular, students who remain unaffiliated with fraternities and sororities, those who choose colleges where bingeing is less common, and women who attend women's colleges are at reduced risk of both primary and secondary consequences of alcohol abuse.

Everyone—from the college president on down—is susceptible to denial about the extent of the alcohol-abuse problem and its impact on the life of the campus. To begin to assess the extent of the problem on a campus, consider taking a weekend tour, beginning on Thursday night.

Take a drive around campus with the security guards; observe the clubs on its outskirts. Drop in on the health service. On Friday, see how many classes are offered in comparison to other weekdays, and how many students attend. Observe the fraternity houses and dorms late at night. On any Sunday morning, station yourself outside the residence halls and sorority houses and witness the "walk of shame," a phrase students use to describe women returning from a night of unplanned, and often unprotected, sex. Above all, fight the temptation to think of the alcohol abuse you see as really the problem of "troubled" individuals. When the faces change but the numbers do not, something much more powerful and institutional is happening.

Commitment and leadership at the top are vital to ensure that consistent, long-term prevention and intervention strategies are reflected not just in speeches but in budgets. Over the years, many administrations have opted to keep a low profile on prevention efforts. Denial, a sense of futility, and lack of resources may be at play, but there are other reasons as well. Some administrators fear that taking a visible, systemwide stance might create the appearance that alcohol abuse is unusually severe at their school. Some may be advised by their institution's legal counsel to do as little as possible that might suggest knowledge of an alcohol problem on campus and acceptance of any responsibility for it. But the prevalence of binge drinking on campus is no secret, and it is difficult to see how college administrators can successfully claim not to know it exists.

Colleges and universities offer our most formidable aggregations of specialists in human and organizational behavior, including psychologists, sociologists and anthropologists, linguists and lawyers, teachers and marketing strategists, experts in health and addiction, policy analysts and security specialists, community organizers, family therapists, and system analysts. Yet it is the rare institution that forms a working group of appropriately diverse problem solvers to address the alcohol abuse in its midst. Faculty members can be asked to play a limited but meaningful role in planning and assessment, supporting students and administrators in a campuswide effort. Athletic directors and coaches too can have enormous influence on the drinking culture of a campus.

Resident advisors and academic and retention counselors have been underused. They can enhance prevention and early-intervention efforts, but they need clear roles. Resident advisors cannot be expected to be both monitors and confidants. They need more sustained training and supervision than they typically receive, and better support—including the sure protection of explicit policy. Security officers can also benefit from dedicated training and regular consultation on alcohol-related issues and infractions. It is easy for them to lapse into feeling that by calling abusive drinking to the attention of the authorities they are hurting rather than helping students. Students themselves must carry much of the responsibility for campus change. Student government, peer educators, and campus media can all agree that students are in favor of good times, but not of drunkenness.

At some campuses, new-student orientation is something between a lost opportunity and a weeklong drunk. When they first arrive on campus (usually before other students), many first-year students respond positively to initiatives they would later spurn, particularly if the offerings represent an opportunity to meet their classmates under relatively natural conditions. First-year women need special attention. Many have had little experience with alcohol in high school. They need to understand that because of differences in metabolism women cannot drink equally with men.

Many fraternities and sororities are functional saloons. As noted earlier, fully 86 percent of men and 80 percent of women who live in fraternities and sororities are binge drinkers. The rare president or dean who tells the Greeks to "shape up or ship out," and then keeps his or her word, earns the respect of many. The national organizations must be held accountable for serving underage students in their frat houses and providing an environment where binge drinking is the norm.

State and local officials need to enforce underage drinking laws and strengthen other restrictions to help limit supply. Even more important are the bars and clubs that encourage drunkenness through promoting discount drinks and contests. Colleges have to confront their own power to influence how these clubs operate and are regulated; they are far from helpless or ignorant in these matters. If they want to target heavy drinking, drunkenness, and resultant antisocial behaviors, then campus security and town police should be on the same team, working together. In return, colleges can help local law enforcement agencies through consistent disciplinary policies for students whose drunken behavior violates the law.

A successful and sustainable campuswide effort depends on students themselves generating a code of respectful community behavior. Process is not just important, but crucial. It requires patience, persistence, and humility to enable students to take the lead in making drunkenness an unacceptable excuse for violent and disruptive behavior that violates other students' rights. But a set of policies and exhortations from above simply does not suffice. Students bothered by the secondhand effects of others' binge drinking will gradually feel empowered to speak up without feeling humiliated. It is the students standing at their sides, more than the administrators standing behind them, who most contribute to that feeling.

If colleges really aspire to be civil communities, prevention efforts must empower those students adversely affected by the binge drinking of others.

We once thought drunk drivers were part of life, and smokers had to be tolerated. Today people feel comfortable speaking out against drunk drivers and smokers because we now know the harm they cause others is not an acceptable price to pay for their behavior. The same lessons can help lend a voice to students affected by other students' excessive drinking.

NOTES

1. These quotes are from student responses to open-ended questions in the Harvard School of Public Health Alcohol Study, "Binge Drinking on American College Campuses" (Boston: Harvard School of Public Health College Alcohol Study, August, 1995). Parts of this chapter are adapted from that study.
2. Throughout the text of this chapter, percentages are rounded to the nearest whole number. For precise figures, consult the authors' cited publications.

REFERENCES

Abbey, A. "Acquaintance Rape and Alcohol Consumption on College Campuses: How Are They Linked?" *Journal of American College Health,* 1991, *39*(1), 165–169.

Abbey, A., and Harnish, R. J. "Perception of Sexual Intent: The Role of Gender, Alcohol Consumption, and Rape Supportive Attitudes." *Sex Roles,* 1995, *32*(5/6), 297–313.

Astin, A. W. *What Matters in College? Four Critical Years Revisited.* San Francisco: Jossey-Bass, 1992.

Bart, P. B., and O'Brien, P. H. "Stopping Rape: Successful Survival Strategies." New York: Pergamon Press, 1985.

Center on Addiction and Substance Abuse. *Substance Abuse and the American Woman.* New York: Columbia University, 1996.

Corcoran, C., and Mahlstedt, D. "Preventing Sexual Assault on Campus: A Feminist Perspective." In C. Forden, A. Hunter, and B. Birns (eds.), *A Psychology of Women Reader: Common and Diverse Experiences.* Needham Heights, Mass.: Allyn & Bacon, 1998.

Crawford, M. "Talking Difference: On Gender and Language." London: Sage, 1995.

Dowdall, G., Crawford, M., and Wechsler, H. "Binge Drinking Among American College Women: A Comparison of Single-Sex and Coeducational Institutions." *Psychology of Women Quarterly,* 1998, 22(4), 705–715.

George, W. H., Gournic, S. J., and McAfee, M. P. "Perceptions of Postdrinking Female Sexuality: Effects of Gender, Beverage Choice, and Drink Payment." *Journal of Applied Social Psychology,* 1988, *18*(15), 1295–1317.

Goodchilds, J. D., and Zellman, G. L. "Sexual Signaling and Sexual Aggression in Adolescent Relationships." In N. M. Malamuth and E. Donnerstein (eds.), *Pornography and Sexual Aggression.* Orlando: Academic Press, 1984.

Goodchilds, J. D., Zellman, G. L., Johnson, P. B., and Giarrusso, R. "Adolescents and Their Perceptions of Sexual Interactions." In A. W. Burgess (ed.), *Rape and Sexual Assault, Vol. II.* New York: Garland, 1988.

Kanin, E. J. "Date Rapists." *Archives of Sexual Behavior,* 1985, *14*(3), 219–231.

Koss, M. P. "The Women's Mental Health Research Agenda: Violence Against Women." *American Psychologist,* 1990, *45*(3), 374–380.

Koss, M. P., and Dinero, T. E. "Discriminant Analysis of Risk Factors for Sexual Victimization Among a National Sample of College Women." *Journal of Consulting and Clinical Psychology,* 1989, *57*(2), 242–250.

Koss, M. P., Gidycz, C. A., and Wisniewski, N. "The Scope of Rape: Incidence and Prevalence of Sexual Aggression and Victimization in a National Sample of Higher Education Students." *Journal of Consulting and Clinical Psychology,* 1987, *55*(2), 162–170.

Lex, B. "Prevention of Substance Abuse Problems in Women." In R. R. Watson (ed.), *Drug and Alcohol Abuse Prevention.* Totowa, N.J.: Humana Press, 1990.

Meilman, P. W. "Alcohol-Induced Sexual Behavior on Campus." *Journal of American College Health,* 1993, *42*(1), 27–31.

Radius, S. M., Joffe, A., and Gall, M. A. "Barrier Versus Oral Contraceptive Use: A Study of Female College Students." *Journal of American College Health,* Sept. 1991, pp. 83–85.

Richardson, D., and Campbell, J. L. "The Effect of Alcohol on Attributions of Blame for Rape." *Personality and Social Psychology Bulletin,* 1982, *8*(3), 468–476.

Robert Wood Johnson Foundation. *Substance Abuse: The Nation's Number One Health Problem. Key Indicators for Policy.* Princeton, N.J.: Robert Wood Johnson Foundation, 1993.

Siegel, J. M., and others. "Resistance to Sexual Assault: Who Resists and What Happens." *American Journal of Public Health,* 1989, *79*(2) 27–31.

Vogeltanz, N. D., and Wilsnack, S. C. "Alcohol Problems in Women: Risk Factors, Consequences, and Treatment Strategies." In S. J. Gallant, G. P. Keita, and R. Royak-Schaler (eds.), *Health Care for Women:*

Psychological, Social, and Behavioral Influences. Washington, D.C.: American Psychological Association, 1997.

Warshaw, R. *I Never Called It Rape.* New York: HarperCollins, 1988.

Wechsler, H., Dowdall, G., Davenport, A., and Castillo, S. "Correlates of College Student Binge Drinking." *American Journal of Public Health,* 1995, *85*(7), 921–926.

Wechsler, H., Dowdall, G., Davenport, A., and Rimm, E. "A Gender-Specific Measure of Binge Drinking Among College Students." *American Journal of Public Health,* 1995, *85*(7), 982–985.

Wechsler, H., and Isaac, N. "Binge Drinkers at Massachusetts Colleges: Prevalence, Drinking Style, Time Trends, and Associated Problems." *Journal of the American Medical Association,* 1992, *267*(21), 2929–2931.

Wechsler, H., and others. "Health and Behavioral Consequences of Binge Drinking in College: A National Survey of Students at 140 Colleges." *Journal of the American Medical Association,* 1994, *272*(21), 1672–1677.

18

PREVENTING DATING VIOLENCE

Deborah Mahlstedt, Carole Baroody Corcoran

THE RELATIONSHIP BETWEEN COLLEGE MEN and feminism is usually assumed to be negative. With their tradition of hypermasculine behavior, including violence against women, fraternities might seem the least likely place to locate a feminist-based program to address campus dating violence. However, the experience of those in the Fraternity Violence Education Project (FVEP) at West Chester University (in Pennsylvania) suggests that a feminist approach to prevention education can be effective in giving young men what they need to learn in order to stop destructive behavior. We believe the critical factor in this program's effectiveness is its creation of a safe place for young men to explore ideas about institutional power and control: ideas that are often threatening but that must be understood to stop dating violence.

The program, which began in 1989 as a one-year action-research study, evolved into an established feminist peer education program. The central goal of the FVEP is to convey to men the link between a hierarchical structure of gendered power relations and personal elements of men's everyday experience that lead to violence against women. According to Schwartz and DeKeseredy (1997), the FVEP is the "one exception": a program whose curriculum for fraternity men to prevent sexual violence emphasizes both individual and structural change.

Criteria for Feminist Approaches to Dating-Violence Prevention

Simply involving men in prevention efforts does not make a program feminist, or antisexist; rather, what does so is its assumptions about the causes of violence against women and strategies for change. The FVEP uses a structural feminist, social-change approach to ending male assault (Corcoran and Mahlstedt, 1998). We discuss four basic assumptions of feminist approaches to dating-violence prevention that can be used to develop and assess programs for men.

Centrality of Gendered Power Relations in a Patriarchal System

A feminist social-change approach to prevention is based upon the belief that power relations within a patriarchal system of male dominance stand at the center of the problem. According to this view, dating violence is a consequence of a system of male dominance in which structural inequities, devaluation of women, sexual objectification, and hypermasculinity allow men to maintain control over women through intimidation and use of force (Brownmiller, 1975; Corcoran, 1992; Pharr, 1988; Schwartz and DeKeseredy, 1997). These interlocking elements gain their strength from major social institutions (economic, judicial, educational) that allow them to operate by creating laws making it impossible to hold men accountable for sexual violence. This structural view holds men solely responsible for dating violence. Many campus prevention programs emphasize factors (such as miscommunication) that indirectly make the woman responsible for her abuse ("She did not clearly and firmly say no"). Emphasis on miscommunication in date-rape and battering-prevention programs is dangerous because it leads women to the erroneous belief that assertive speech protects them from date rape and suggests victim-blame (Corcoran, 1992; Crawford, 1995). Although women must develop ways to protect themselves, it does not mean that their "failure" to do so effectively causes their violation.

Men's Responsibility for Taking Action

A feminist approach to dating-violence prevention requires that men take responsibility for ending dating violence through individual and collective action. Preventing dating violence requires that men and women work actively to dismantle male dominance in social institutions and learn to develop egalitarian relationships in their daily lives. Assumption of responsibility may require a man to reflect on his emotional life, interrupt a friend who is degrading women in conversation, or facilitate a discussion with other men on dating violence.

A Safe Place for Self-Reflection and Change

Feminist prevention education acknowledges that social and personal change can be effected if men have structures within which they can examine their own behavior. They need support from other men and feminist role models to do the work necessary for behavioral change and action. Programs based on a feminist approach recognize that the task of examining such issues as institutionalized male dominance, hypermasculinity, and constructions of male sexuality is difficult. It takes time, emotional support, guidance, knowledge, and challenge. Feminists and profeminists understand the profound emotions raised by these issues for men involved in such changes. Authentic, basic caring must accompany the challenge to confront sexism.

An Inclusive Prevention Education for Men

A feminist approach to prevention addresses differences in gender, race, class, and sexuality with regard to the content and process of educating men about dating violence. This approach acknowledges that the dynamics of gendered power relations vary, depending on how one's race, social class, ethnicity, and sexual orientation position one within the larger social structure. These power dynamics intersect with gender in ways that may require new knowledge and awareness to help men understand and change. All intersections of roles—abuser and victim, peer and peer, facilitator and learner—as well as social difference have a bearing on the prevention process.

At first glance, these criteria may seem formidable and not particularly male-friendly. However, if men are viewed as capable of egalitarian relationships and responsive to social injustice, a feminist approach to dating violence effectively educates them to help prevent male violence toward women and supports development of these young men. The context and manner of presentation of feminist ideas is crucial to engaging men in the learning process.

Fraternity Violence Education Project: A Minority Influence Model

The FVEP targets fraternity organizations for change using a minority-influence approach. A central component of the process is in-depth development of leaders drawn from the group targeted for change. Fraternity peer educators influence their individual fraternities as well as the fraternity system at large by serving as carriers of prevention messages, alternative role models for men, and sources for ongoing dialogue. In addition, as active members of their fraternities, peer educators are likely to serve as moderating influences when the possibility of sexually violent incidents arises. As one peer educator (to be identified as number 19) explains, "Women are encouraged to take self-defense classes, to not walk alone at night, to not wear provocative clothing, and to not drink in excess. Men, oftentimes, are not asked to do anything to stop violence against women. The Fraternity Violence Education Project asks that men realize this imbalance of responsibility and take action. It is not always that easy for men to challenge other men's behavior toward women even though they may not like it. We must begin to speak out more and support each other to do so."

Unlike the FVEP, in a typical college workshop for men an educator external to the group tries to reach as many individual men as possible before leaving. Even though one-hour workshops can positively influence attitudes (Fonow, Richardson, and Wemmerus, 1992; Lonsway, 1996), repeated exposure to prevention ideas is needed for in-depth attitudinal change and increased likelihood of behavioral change. In a minority-influence model, by contrast, the peer educator facilitates workshops and remains with the group, thereby continuing to promote reflection and actively challenge the goals and behavior of peers within the system (Moscovici, Mucchi-Faina, and Maas, 1994; Wood and others, 1994). Thus, the presence of peer educators creates an outspoken minority perspective that presses upon the norms of male complicity to maintain silence, devalue women as sex objects, and prove one's masculinity.

Throughout a one-year training program, fraternity men in the FVEP develop the skills necessary to assume a role of peer leadership and take action against dating violence. During the fall semester, the men take a seminar on violence against women for academic credit. Through readings, group discussions, and assignments, seminar participants gain extensive knowledge about sexual violence, have opportunities to reflect on their own behavior, and learn group-facilitation skills. In the spring semester, seminar participants apply their learning by co-leading discussion groups and workshops within the fraternities with experienced peer leaders. Young men who have successfully completed the two semesters then facilitate future seminars. After completing the seminar, peer educators implement programming with fraternities and coordinate campuswide efforts aimed at men.

Creating a Safe, Feminist Space: Content and Process in the Learning Experience

We begin this section with the words of a seminar participant to provide a glimpse of one moment in the course of his evolving process of change:

> The whole time I was worried that some woman was going to get violated . . . later I saw her in our pool room entertaining a circle of guys [surrounding] her. I informed her of the dangers that could happen if she didn't stop. Why does she do this? Why do I care? Before I took this class I would not have cared but now I do. I didn't ask for an attitude adjustment but I don't look or talk to any man the same anymore. I find it hard to have fun at my fraternity events [peer educator number 65].

His words remind us that change is a "messy" process marked by contradictory beliefs, forward movement that unpredictably cycles backwards, unwelcome new awareness, hopelessness when new behaviors seem to fail, as well as the satisfaction associated with successes. We ask that the reader bear this in mind while reading the description of the model that follows.

The content of the seminar and its educational message, designed by the facilitators and one of the authors of this chapter (Mahlstedt), are meant to be clear without oversimplifying the complexity of the causes of dating violence. The process for developing profeminist male leadership through an intensive seminar experience is as important as the content of what participants learn. The goals, processes, and content addressed in the peer training seminar are also the basic elements used to design one-hour workshops facilitated by the peer educators for other college men (Mahlstedt, Falcone, and Rice-Spring, 1993). If a seminar is not a feasible training structure, other in-depth structures such as intensive weekends can work. The content and process components of the FVEP experience apply to these models as well.

Using a rich set of qualitative data, we have identified elements of the men's experience that contribute to their engagement in a structural analysis of violence against women. To avoid a tendency toward hierarchical arrangements, the goal throughout the seminar is to present the material integratively so that the structural and personal components are side-by-side. Similarly, our presentation of the learning experience aims to integrate the content and process aspects of the learning experience. Obviously, involving men becomes the first challenge.

Motivating Men to Get Involved

Four factors motivate college men in dating violence prevention efforts:

1. Compensation
2. Leadership development
3. Personal experience
4. Campuswide visibility

To train men as leaders who will work consistently within their community, the experience must be in-depth, have time available, and not be in competition with coursework. The FVEP is a good example of a field experience, or service-learning, project. Special programs aimed at involving large numbers of men (such as a campuswide event) may use "Greek points" or a monetary award, a portion of which can be donated to a domestic violence shelter.

In addition, professional benefits accrue to young men who have knowledge about gender issues. At least one-third of the sixty seminar "graduates" have received job interviews based on an employer's interest in the project. Certainly, leadership development is important. Peer educators present in high schools, at other colleges, and at conferences. Such opportunities for undergraduate students make participation in the project attractive.

Young men's backgrounds contribute to their motivation. Like women, some young men grow up watching their fathers beat their mothers; in some cases, the men were abused themselves. Some know women who have been victims of violence. Some explain that they "want to make a difference."

What about motivating other men? The same minority-influence strategy can work with other all-male groups on campus, including athletic and intramural sports teams. After several years of pursuit, a seminar for athletes was established at WCU. Larger organized campus events attract and involve the general campus body in an expression of collective action and provide cross-campus visibility. For example, "White Ribbon Day," based on the Canadian men's movement to educate men to stop violence against women (Folliott, Morison, and Kaufman, 1994), is an exclusively male-organized event. Peer educators work with supportive male faculty, professional staff, and students to organize a campus rally and gain commitment from WCU men to not accept or tolerate acts that demean or violate women.

Setting the Tone: The Power of the First Example

Once chosen for the seminar, participants' first exposure to the project should set the tone for what is to come. The seminar begins much like any other course, with an overview of the syllabus and introductions, although the process of clarifying a different "class" structure and authority relations begins immediately. Peer facilitators lead an icebreaker and introductions and then explain the background of the project. I (Mahlstedt) introduce the syllabus and explain the grades, based on the expectations set forth in the syllabus. Early on, we establish my role as a "visiting lecturer/facilitator" to "their" group. I explain that I will attend approximately three of the eight fall-semester classes, for less than one hour each class. Initially, in the spring semester, when seminar participants practice implementing programs, my contact with them increases to provide feedback on their facilitation skills.

While reviewing the syllabus, I introduce the word *feminist* expressly to elicit responses from the men about their associations with feminism. Usually laughter accompanies their replies, which are almost always in a negative category such as "man-hating feminazi." Tongue in cheek, I say "Personally, of course, I would like you to all embrace these ideas and come out profeminist but, unfortunately [smile], people must think for themselves, and so if you do it's by your own choosing." Then, more seriously, "I know these are very difficult things to hear as men. All I ask is that you engage them and enter into a process of looking at your own behavior and the behavior of other men. Your disagreement is encouraged, along with your willingness to accept new things. Only through dialogue can you understand your own position. I appreciate your willingness to participate in this work." Truman, Tokar, and Fischer (1996) found that men's attitudes toward feminism were the most consistent predictor of rape-supportive myths and recommend that rape education address "fears and misconceptions about feminism as construed by men" (p. 561). This process begins in the first class.

After I leave class, the peer facilitators involve the men in an activity about what "being a man" means. They discuss expectations of men and role models, and what they would like to be different. The class ends with a facilitator's close reading of a woman's account of her boyfriend beating her. We aim to establish a tone conveying that the issue itself is always serious, but the process of learning can span a variety of feelings, including frustration, fun, caring, confusion, and excitement.

For those who see feminism as the enemy, our hope is that any associated feelings become attached to me and not the peer facilitators. Initially, the peer facilitators must be perceived as neutral—"one of them." Gradually, as facilitators discuss and reflect on coming to terms with the difficult ideas, participants also observe the caring mentoring relationship I have with the facilitators, which adds a personal dimension to their emerging constructions of feminism. Peer educators explicitly emphasize the process involved in making sense of new ideas in the seminar as well as in the workshops conducted in fraternity meetings. Men must see that they control their own process.

Establishing Clear Goals: Male Responsibility Versus Male Bashing

Since men often expect "male bashing," peer educators initially clarify their goal, which is that men take responsibility to speak out rather than to bash men: "To say that some men do beat and rape women is not male bashing. We feel that this is wrong and want to educate other men to stop this behavior. We ask for your help" (peer educator number 52). Also, men may or will know women who have experienced male violence. More important, women live in a culture of fear and are in the position of viewing all men as potential rapists. Initially, it is usual for seminar and program participants to heatedly deny this "accusation." When explained from a woman's perspective, though, arguing that a woman cannot identify a date rapist or a batterer in advance (Corcoran, 1992), FVEP participants realize that we are not making a personal attack on individual men. Rather, we acknowledge the bind that women face in living with the threat of violence.

With the foundation for the socioemotional climate of the group set in place, the facilitators introduce the theoretical framework.

Packaging a Complex Model: "The Five Points"

In presenting the causal framework of dating violence, we aim to capture the complexity of the problem clearly, concisely, and consistently. Thus, the curriculum for the seminar as well as the one-hour workshops always centers on "the five points":

1. Male institutional and social power
2. Sexual objectification
3. Peer pressure
4. Alcohol
5. Male responsibility

Once the social structure of patriarchy (to be discussed in the next section) is established, the elements within the system are addressed. This occurs through explicit articulation of the relationship between institutional power and a particular element, such as alcohol or sexual objectification. For instance, it is institutional power that allows men to act on their objectification of women through harassment and force ("She deserved what happened [date rape]," "Everyone knows she's a slut," "Boys will be boys"). All resource materials developed by the FVEP—handouts, newsletters, videotaped segments, and a brochure—include these five points (Mahlstedt, 1997).

Feminist approaches to dating violence have not dealt sufficiently with the role of alcohol. In the FVEP, I (Mahlstedt) initially resisted acknowledging alcohol because it is not the root of the problem. Yet it demanded explanation. Koss, Gidycz, and Wisniewski (1987) found that alcohol is associated with the majority of incidents of rape and battering in dating relationships. Responses that "it lowers inhibitions" and "impairs judgment" are inadequate ways to account for a serious, cultural problem. Sanday (1990) first theorized the relationship between alcohol and date rape as a cultural dynamic. Schwartz and DeKeseredy (1997) in their "modified male peer-support model" explain how alcohol consumption facilitates college men's relations with other men, at the expense of women. They note that "some men use alcohol to specifically give them permission to claim that their inhibitions have been lowered." The authors add that they "have rejected any notion that alcohol *causes* the sexual aggression" (p. 152). Their model, however, offers a coherent picture of how power, hypermasculinity, alcohol, and homophobia together operate to create a hostile environment of intense peer pressure that may lead to dating violence. As one participant put it:

> Men believe it is their right to have their way with women, and to criticize them, to degrade them, and to simply use them like toys. I was this way, I admit. I wanted every good looking woman at a party to have sex with me. "Man, I wish I could get her so drunk that she would fuck me!" I probably said to friends. This course questioned my

> actions. At first, I was offended. But after a while, I began to question my own mind. Why exactly was I thinking this way? Why did I feel as though these women were there solely for my pleasure? I could not answer these questions. The FVEP turned on a light in my head. I can honestly say that I will never act towards women in the same way that I have before [peer educator number 48].

The FVEP links alcohol use to the larger social structure through concrete examples. For instance, the peer facilitator explains that if one notices a fraternity brother drunk in a situation in which he compromises himself, someone "grabs him and throws him in a bed with a bucket next to it. But if you see a woman all hammered, all the lights go off [that] she's drunk, she'll be easy." The moral responsibility to take care of someone when he acts compromisingly exists in young men's minds. Why not then take care of a drunk woman, as opposed to taking advantage of her? Because institutional power has allowed men to "get away with it" ("She was drunk so she's just as much at fault"). Thoughts in the person's mind before drinking alcohol influence the behavior that appears with alcohol. Feminist prevention efforts must address alcohol; otherwise, the oversimplified view that it *causes* dating violence remains in people's minds. (See also Crawford, Dowdall, and Wechsler's Chapter Seventeen.)

Thinking Systemically

If the relationship between institutional power and other contributing factors is not explicitly articulated, change becomes focused on individual characteristics (attitudes, alcohol use), leaving the system intact. In a meta-analysis of individual differences and attitudes toward rape, Anderson, Cooper, and Okamura (1997) identified a new factor associated with rape attitudes: political orientation. The authors suggest that "conservative political ideologies that place responsibility on the individual for his or her plight may lead one to believe in women's responsibility for sexual victimization" (p. 312). Such cultural factors influence attribution, that is, how individuals make determinations about the causes of other people's behavior and events by emphasizing certain qualities of the person, or the system (Guimond, Begin, and Palmer, 1989). Furthermore, in their examination of attribution in relation to perceived causes of rape, Cowan and Quinton (1997) found that acceptance of feminist ideas alone may not lead one to think in systemic terms. Cowan and Quinton note that knowledge about a particular ideology alone does not allow us to think systemically; perhaps the ability to do so "requires more than an ideology . . . does it require a general ability or propensity to view causes from a sociopolitical perspective?" (p. 245). These studies support the need to construct ideas about dating violence as a system, as opposed to a collection of contributing factors. The question becomes how to do this.

Use of Participants' Language and Framework as the Point of Departure

As Capraro (1994) observes, starting with the men's current thinking helps them connect with the issue. Men who take the FVEP seminar usually state in the beginning that they were "raised to respect women." This position can make it difficult to grasp a structural analysis of violence against women because they think that if they can teach other men to respect women, then men will not act violently toward women. This "discourse of chivalry" also allows them to view only other men as the problem.

In the seminar, we help men learn the difference between gender relations based on chivalry and those based on equality. Seminar participants first describe gender relations based on past images of chivalry (such as men defending the honor of "good" women or rescuing "ladies" in distress). In discussion, they laugh at these "old" images. When asked about these same images in contemporary gender relations, they reluctantly acknowledge such chivalrous images as opening doors for women and the "slut-virgin" dichotomy. The facilitators explain that chivalry is a system: a broad picture for how men and women are to interact, one that is based on men being stronger than women and having power over other people, including women. The facilitators clarify that to end dating violence, gender relations must be built upon a system of equality, in which all women deserve respect and institutional representation.

Violence as Misuse of Institutional and Social Power

It must be clarified that violence against women is a consequence of misuse of institutional and social power, not of men being inherently violent. Before discussing the dynamics of a male-dominated social structure, we clarify that our social structure is patriarchal. This fact opens up the question of how it may affect others. At this point, men explore experiences in which they felt powerless—including their emotions, how others behaved toward them, and how they dealt with the situation.

Participants then explore the idea that if violence in dating relationships constitutes a misuse of power, it is not inherent to men. Drawing parallels among other forms of oppression—classism, racism, anti-Semitism—helps reinforce a structural analysis of violence that allows seminar participants to explore the structural exploitation of diverse groups of men. For example, devaluation of working-class men and their historical exposure to hazardous conditions in the workplace, or the stereotypes of African American men as oversexualized and raping white women, can be challenged. When explained in these ways, the concepts of male power and control appear to make sense to men, become hard to deny, and reduce defensiveness. We focus on the system, not individual traits, and on complexity, not oversimplification.

Use of Metaphors to Help Men Think Systemically

To shift a peer educator's tendency to make internal attributions about dating violence, metaphors are helpful. The facilitators use Marilyn Frye's metaphor of a birdcage (1983) to explain the subtleties of patriarchy as a system of oppression. First, we suggest that the bars on the cage represent each of the elements of oppression (Pharr, 1988). The bird inside (the oppressed person) sees only one bar when looking out from the cage, yet it knows it is trapped inside the cage. This image helps whenever men focus on one small aspect of oppression and fail to understand why it is important or debilitating to women. For example, when learning about sexual objectification, men's reactions often reflect a single issue or momentary focus ("What's the big deal? It's just one comment"; or "It's the woman's choice to pose for those pictures"). The totality of the system of images as well as all the other elements supporting oppression are lost in the specific incident. When we place one instance of objectification in a context of other elements—the other birdcage bars—it takes on greater significance. Peer facilitators actually draw a birdcage and have participants identify each bar as an element of oppression that contributes to how women experience sexism daily. When they see the elements altogether, a common response is, "I never thought of it that way."

Interaction, Facilitation, and Mentoring: Support and Challenge from a Feminist Perspective

Earle (1996) found that a male-peer model using small groups was the most effective approach to educating young men about dating violence. In the FVEP seminar, the small group becomes a microcosm for how men relate to one another meaningfully on issues they do not often discuss with other men, such as gender role expectations, power, and feelings. The peer facilitators are key role models for the developing peer educators, who subsequently become role models in programs with other men. The facilitators express their own difficulties, what they have accepted, and what they have trouble accepting. To reinforce this approach, seminar participants keep journals, use worksheets to record their reactions to the readings, and document ideas they agreed and disagreed with during each seminar session.

Peer educators develop a strong sense of ownership: this is their project and they are in charge of their process. After three sessions, participant number 64 wrote, "This class is exciting because it is less structured and we're not just talked at. We really do run the class for ourselves. What we put into it will be what we get out of it." Although I (Mahlstedt) visit the seminar, the peer facilitators have control, as when they translate readings and material from outside lecturers into "their own" words.

The men consistently attribute their engagement with a feminist perspective on sexual violence to the safety of being in an all-male group of their peers. In a nonjudgmental atmosphere, they admit to sexist behavior in themselves and other men, which allows them to think about behaving differently. The all-male situation is safe, yet different, because they are discussing issues men usually do not discuss with each other. Thus, it serves as a microcosm in which to experiment with their own behavior in relation to other men—yet another level of learning about gender and masculinity.

Changing the hierarchical power paradigm extends to how men perceive and treat other men. With others, peer educators learn to assume a supportive, egalitarian approach to teaching men about dating violence and to intervening in situations that may be degrading to women. This is not easy. Men often try to change other men in ways that abuse power and reinforce hypermasculinity, through ridicule, threats, and control. For peer educators to break this negative cycle of hypermasculinity, they must practice how to communicate with other men as equals.

Power dynamics linked to race and ethnic differences between men also occur in the seminar and the workshop settings. The qualitative data suggest a tendency for black men to be more willing to acknowledge sexist behavior in themselves and other men. They often demonstrate this willingness through stories of personal experiences. White men appear to appreciate this openness. Also, black men tend to self-disclose more about family experiences of abuse. White men are more likely to self-disclose in their journals, and maybe later in the seminar. The imbalance of self-disclosure and admission of sexist behavior by black men has both positive and potentially negative effects on the power dynamics between black and white men. On the one hand, black men serve as role models of openness and honesty. However, their self-disclosure can also fuel stereotypes of black men's sexism and violence in their families. The white facilitators guard against such negative consequences by encouraging white men to share personal experiences and by frequently reminding participants that statistics on the incidence of rape and battering are the same across all race and social-class groups.

The challenge for young men to examine difficult conceptual and emotional issues must be accompanied by the support necessary to meet this challenge. Some of this support occurs through the peer facilitator-participant relationship. In addition to this level of support, there is the issue of mentoring by an advisor who coordinates the overall effort. Can dating-violence efforts be coordinated solely by men? Can feminist women mentor peer educators and provide them with enough safety to effectively explore issues of power, control, and violence?

Kathleen Carlin (1996) believes that to undo sexist behavior men must be in an all-male environment, which is where the behavior is created to begin with. She recommends, however, that this "men's sphere [be] enclosed and surrounded by women's reality . . ." and that "women listen in" (p. 7) so that male leaders and participants are accountable to the goal of ending men's violent behavior toward women. She explains that it is simply too difficult for most men to constantly acknowledge the seriousness of the problem and risk challenging other men. Carlin, therefore, advocates that feminist women serve as supervisors, mentors, or consultants to men's work with men on violence against women. Also, a strong woman—mother, partner, friend—can have a powerful influence on a man's antisexist development (Christian, 1994). The presence of female authority holds men accountable as well as supporting them to maintain their antisexist perspective.

Mentoring peer educators has been a complex process. I (Mahlstedt) care about them and am uplifted by their work. At the same time, I am torn about the time that mentoring these men takes away from working with women students. I fear being coopted to the extent that their struggles as men mask the seriousness of dating violence and lead me to assume responsibility that is rightfully theirs. Also, entering a room of fifty fraternity men—whether to collect data or observe a program—can be threatening, but it serves to remind me of the power of the all-male group, what young women experience, and the necessity for feminist supervision to reinforce change.

Can a feminist mentor provide these men with enough support? Two of the peer educators completed a minor in women's studies, and fully one-third of them took an additional class with me or another women's studies class, all after their FVEP seminar; this suggests that they not only felt supported but also benefited from their experience. Altogether, three-fourths of the participants continued to maintain contact with me for at least one year following the seminar. One-half of the graduates of the FVEP continued to facilitate programs after receiving credit for the seminar.

Summary

When we began to examine the peer educator's process of change, we asked you to consider the words of the young man (identified as number 65) who wrote about his experience. Obviously, change is never as simple as may inadvertently appear to be the case in writing about it. But when the words of all sixty peer educators are read, it is clear that feminist dating-violence prevention effectively afforded them the safety necessary to confront the issues at the center of the problem: institutionalized male power and control. A seminar participant describes his experience:

> I believe that the underlying cause of violence against women in our society is [. . .] the male-dominated power structure that continues to exist. . . . I had a very hard time understanding this concept at first, and often tried to defend my case against its existence with examples of recent feminist-movement [or] equal-rights successes. However, after reading (and more importantly listening fully to many of the arguments) I began to realize that I was doing exactly what was predicted by some of the readings. It seems silly to me now that I could try to defend my point that in our society men don't hold all the power [peer educator number 32].

Structuring relationships (the all-male peer group with a feminist woman as mentor) and maintaining sensitivity to keep feminist ideas accessible work together to create a safe space for men. The structures for learning (such as using a seminar or intensive weekend) may vary, but it is critical to have a theoretical framework that emphasizes the systemic nature of the causes of dating violence. To ask men to take responsibility by speaking out against dating violence is the goal; silent support is not enough. Young men are capable of creating egalitarian relationships and responding to social injustice. It would be a disservice to them and to women to expect less.

REFERENCES

Anderson, K. B., Cooper, H., and Okamura, L. "Individual Differences and Attitudes Toward Rape: A Meta-Analytical Review." *Personality and Social Psychology Bulletin,* 1997, *23*(3), 295–315.

Brownmiller, S. *Against Our Will: Men, Women, and Rape.* New York: Simon & Schuster, 1975.

Capraro, R. "Disconnected Lives: Men, Masculinity, and Rape Prevention." In A. D. Berkowitz (ed.), *Men and Rape: Theory, Research, and Prevention Programs in Higher Education.* San Francisco: Jossey-Bass, 1994.

Carlin, K. "Working with Batterers: What Is Women's Role?" In K. Carlin (ed.), *Uptake: A Journal for Ending Violence Against Women.* Atlanta: Men Stopping Violence, 1996.

Christian, H. *The Making of Anti-Sexist Men.* New York: Routledge, 1994.

Corcoran, C. "From Victim Control to Social Change: A Feminist Perspective on Campus Rape and Prevention Programs." In J. Chrisler and D. Howard (eds.), *New Directions in Feminist Psychology.* New York: Springer-Verlag, 1992.

Corcoran, C., and Mahlstedt, D. "Preventing Sexual Assault on Campus: A Feminist Perspective." In C. Forden, A. Hunter, and B. Birns (eds.), *A Psychology of Women Reader: Common and Diverse Experiences.* Needham Heights, Mass.: Allyn & Bacon, 1998.

Cowan, G., and Quinton, W. "Cognitive Style and Attitudinal Correlates of the Perceived Causes of Rape Scale." *Psychology of Women Quarterly,* 1997, *21*(2), 227–245.

Crawford, M. *Talking Difference: On Gender and Language.* London: Sage, 1995.

Earle, J. "Acquaintance Rape Workshops: Their Effectiveness in Changing the Attitudes of First-Year College Men." *National Association of Student Personnel Association,* 1996, *34*(1), 2–18.

Folliott, K., Morison, K., and Kaufman, M. *Make a Difference: The White Ribbon Week Student Action Kit.* Toronto: White Ribbon Campaign, 1994.

Fonow, M., Richardson, L., and Wemmerus, V. "Feminist Rape Education: Does It Work?" *Gender & Society,* 1992, *6*(1), 108–121.

Frye, M. *The Politics of Reality.* Trumansburg, N.Y.: Crossing Press, 1983.

Guimond, S., Begin, G., and Palmer, D. "Education and Causal Attributions: The Development of 'Person-Blame' and 'System-Blame' Ideology." *Social Psychology Quarterly,* 1989, *52*(2), 126–140.

Koss, M., Gidycz, C., and Wisniewski, N. "The Scope of Rape: Incidence and Prevalence of Sexual Aggression and Victimization in a Sample of Higher Education Students." *Journal of Consulting and Clinical Psychology,* 1987, *55*(2), 162–170.

Lonsway, K. "Preventing Acquaintance Rape Through Education: What Do We Know?" *Psychology of Women Quarterly,* 1996, *20*(2), 229–265.

Mahlstedt, D. "Getting Started: A Peer Dating Violence Prevention Program for Men." Invited address, Emory University, Atlanta, Feb. 1997.

Mahlstedt, D., Falcone, D., and Rice-Spring, L. "Dating Violence Education: What Do Students Learn?" *Journal of Human Justice*, 1993, *4*(2), 101–117.

Moscovici, S., Mucchi-Faina, A., and Maas, A. *Minority Influences*. Chicago: Nelson-Hall, 1994.

Pharr, S. "Homophobia: A Weapon of Sexism." Inverness, Calif.: Chardon Press, 1988.

Sanday, P. *Fraternity Gang Rape: Sex, Brotherhood, and Privilege on Campus*. New York: New York University Press, 1990.

Schwartz, M., and DeKeseredy, W. *Sexual Assault on the College Campus: The Role of Male Peer Support*. Thousand Oaks, Calif.: Sage, 1997.

Truman, D. M., Tokar, D. M., and Fischer, A. R. "Dimensions of Masculinity: Relations to Date Rape Supportive Attitudes and Sexual Aggression in Dating Situations." *Journal of Counseling and Development*, July/Aug. 1996, pp. 555–562.

Wood, W., and others. "Minority Influence: A Meta-Analytic Review of Social Influence Processes." *Psychological Bulletin*, 1994, *115*(3), 323–345.

19

DEFINING A SUPPORTIVE EDUCATIONAL ENVIRONMENT FOR LOW-INCOME WOMEN

Erika Kates

THIS CHAPTER PRESENTS the findings of a research project whose objective was to document how and to what extent selected colleges provide supportive educational environments for their low-income women students, particularly those who are "welfare" recipients.[1] The description of the supportive resources and strategies is placed within the context of the welfare policies adopted by the thirty-two states in which these colleges are located. A particular focus of the analysis was the extent to which educators—faculty and administrators—became informed about welfare policies and attempted to address any obstacles that arose for students as a result of them.

Elaboration of the research is preceded by brief discussions of two factors that play an important role in low-income women's entering postsecondary education. The first is the significant movement of women over the age of twenty-four into postsecondary education since the late 1960s. Knowing when, why, and how these "older" women entered college during the last three decades—and how institutions responded to them—provides insight into development of the resources that are currently found today on many campuses. The second factor is the role federal and state welfare policies play in enrolling and retaining adult welfare recipients in postsecondary education. The welfare-to-work policies that evolved during the same three decades have critically affected access to education and training.

The research also identifies the barriers to access encountered in 1992–93 and the strategies colleges adopted to mitigate them. The final section outlines how federal and state welfare laws since 1996 have caused a sea change in access. The current incarnation of welfare-to-work policies designed to "change welfare as we know it" raises new questions concerning the efficacy of maintaining supportive college environments.

The Changing Population of Older Women Students

The presence of women over twenty-four on college campuses is a relatively recent phenomenon.[2] In the 1950s there were so few women over thirty that no official tallies existed, but by the early 1980s there were one million women over thirty, and they were identified as the fastest-growing group in higher education.[3] Today, a first impression at some campuses (particularly two-year colleges) is that they are populated largely by older students. In fact the term commonly used to describe them, *nontraditional,* is somewhat of a misnomer since in many colleges they have come to represent the norm.

Several groups or "waves" of older women students have emerged since the 1960s, each propelled by different motives, expectations, needs, and family circumstances. In the 1960s they were primarily affluent, white middle-class women whose earlier education had been interrupted (usually by marriage). As students, they sought primarily intellectual enrichment, rather than careers; as mothers, they usually waited until their children became more independent; and as wives, they were financially supported by their husbands' earnings. Referred to as "returning" students, they were often regarded by educators as "dilettantes."

In the 1970s, with divorce rates increasing dramatically, women turned to education as a form of insurance against divorce and desertion. This second wave, referred to at the time as nontraditional students, was also made up of predominantly white, middle-class women who usually waited until their children were older before entering college. They were also likely to be financially self-supporting.

In the early 1980s, as greater numbers of women entered college following divorce, separation, or desertion, they were more likely than the earlier groups to be entering college for the first time, less affluent, and women of color. They were also likely to have greater urgency in developing financial independence, and to be juggling part-time jobs with their education, enrolling while their children were still young, and experiencing considerable "role strain."[4] They became known as "displaced homemakers" or "women in transition." Many reentry students were highly motivated, often exhibiting higher retention rates than traditional students. Certainly, educators became more aware of these groups as children appeared increasingly on campuses and in classrooms during school vacations.

During the early 1980s, more and more women who were receiving welfare began to attend college. Some had turned to AFDC after losing their jobs in economic recessions, others were responding to a lifelong desire to go to college, and still others were responding to the pressures of welfare policies to become employed. These later groups were often absorbed into programs designed to accommodate earlier ones. They took advantage of already established resources such as women's centers, counseling services, and child care centers. Colleges also began to develop programs and resources designed especially for low-income women.

Welfare Policies and Educational Access

Welfare-to-work programs have also existed for three decades. The sixties and seventies saw the early work experience programs, which focused mainly on women's participation (95 percent of adult recipients are women) in job-search and job-placement activities. The programs were often poorly conceived and implemented;[5] however, they permitted low-income women to participate in postsecondary education—partly because of pressure to become employed and partly because caseworkers had no institutional rationale to deny such access.[6] Thus, during the 1970s and early 1980s, when work incentive programs (WIN) and workfare were introduced, women seldom received encouragement from caseworkers—many of whom had no college education themselves. But neither were they as a group actively prevented from having such access. In fact, they were largely invisible; state welfare agencies were not required to document their activities or record their numbers, and few schools either noticed their presence or cared. Thus, although low-income women may have felt many of their concerns were overlooked or neglected during this period, they also benefited from general lack of scrutiny.[7] During the 1980s, welfare-to-work efforts heated up, and a series of research and demonstration programs were evaluated to assess the effectiveness of specific types of intervention, mostly short-term training and job placement.[8] College attendance was still generally ignored.

In 1988, welfare policy changed dramatically. Congress introduced a comprehensive welfare reform, the Family Support Act (FSA), with a clear focus on moving adult recipients toward employment. Title II of the act, the Job Opportunities and Basic Skills (JOBS) component, *required* a proportion of AFDC recipients in "targeted groups" to engage in twenty hours of work-related activities each week. There was considerable ambiguity concerning how much weight should be given to the human-capital approach (which regarded education and training as both an investment and a buffer zone for families leaving the security of cash benefits) and how much weight should be placed on immediate employment. States were allowed leeway in planning and implementing their JOBS programs. They were required to provide job placement and basic education, but other activities, including postsecondary education, remained optional. *Forty seven states chose to adopt the postsecondary education option,* but (as the research discussed in this chapter shows) their regulations varied widely.

More important, for the first time states were required to monitor the participation rates, hours, and activities of all welfare recipients.[9] Students had to present verification of attendance to their caseworkers in order to receive child care vouchers, and as faculty and educational administrators signed attendance sheets low-income women became ever more visible in educational settings.

The Access to Higher Education Project (1992–93)

The purpose of the education access research project[10] of interest in this chapter was to discover where, how, and to what extent selected colleges provided supportive environments for low-income women, particularly welfare recipients. The research was timed to coincide with the full-implementation phase of the 1988 welfare reform law.

Developing a Conceptual Framework of a Supportive Environment

A conceptual framework of the components of a supportive educational environment was developed (Table 19.1). Nine major components (and numerous subcomponents) were identified, emerging from previous research and years of contact with low-income students, educators, administrators, and advocates. The components included academic policies on recruitment and retention; information dissemination and outreach; academic and psychological counseling; child care resources; financial aid;

Table 19.1. Framework of Supportive Components for Low-Income Students.

Components and Criteria	Measures
General campus environment	The proportion of older students, single parents, and low income students to the total student population.
Administration	Specific programs are established; staff are hired to work with them.
	Recruitment and transfer procedures accommodate the different locations and situations of reentry and low-income students.
Public relations and information	Brochures and catalogs include pictures and text of diverse students.
	Materials list important community and campus resources.
	Newsletters and flyers highlight relevant events and concerns.
Academic	Admissions requirements responsive to circumstances.
	Academic counseling, advising, and tutoring are responsive.
	Faculty have information affecting attendance and performance.
	Academic achievement and persistence are recognized.
Financial	Staff is informed about ways of limiting losses.
	Institution awards tuition waivers and grants.
	Funds are available for emergency loans and grants.
	Fundraising yields special resources.
Student and family support services	Child care resources on site; special arrangements with local centers.
	Family housing is available on campus or nearby.
	Emergency food and clothing supplies are available.
	Family events are organized.

Table 19.1. Framework of Supportive Components for Low-Income Students, Cont'd.

Components and Criteria	Measures
	Health services are responsive to adult and family needs.
	Career counseling is responsive.
Student and peer resources	Student lounge or center with kitchen.
	Student organization, student governance, and newsletters.
	Peer mentoring and advising.
	Traditional students show support and interest.
Institutional research and planning	Institutional records include older students and mention dependents.
	Follow-up studies show success rates.
	Housing and other family friendly resources are planned.
	Special campaigns are planned.
Links and networks	Personnel within an institution discuss concerns and events.
	Communication between institutions expedites transfers.
	Contact with public welfare officials.
	Contact with community-based services, churches, women's groups.

concrete resources such as housing and child care; and peer support (characterized in part by sharing a lore of survival skills). The framework also incorporated linkages within and between colleges, and between colleges and local groups and businesses.

Methodology

The first task was to identify institutions that could be defined as supportive.[11] The second was to develop and test research instruments to request information on all components of the framework. Because of the nature of confidentiality surrounding students' financial status, two questionnaires were developed. One was sent to educators who were most familiar with the population of low-income women, and a second was sent in each case to a financial aid officer with similar expertise. Careful preparation resulted in an overall response rate of 86 percent,[12] with 99 percent of returns usable. After initial analysis of the data, fourteen colleges were selected for site visits in eight states. The visits comprised in-depth conversations with people on campus (chancellors, faculty, financial aid officers, administrators, and students) and off (members of community groups, service providers, and caseworkers).

The second survey was developed to clarify the FSA/JOBS policy for each of the thirty-two states within which the fifty-nine responding educational institutions were located. It was designed to ascertain how the state laws were actually being implemented and to detail the attitudes of JOBS personnel toward access to postsecondary education for welfare recipients. The top echelon of state JOBS administrators were interviewed by telephone.[13]

Research Findings: State JOBS Policies

Because they established the context of educational access for each state, the results of the JOBS surveys are discussed first. The terms under which welfare recipients could engage in postsecondary education varied widely. Among the generous was Massachusetts, which permitted women to receive AFDC benefits for up to thirty-six months for an associate's degree and seventy-two months for a bachelor's degree. Eleven states (34 percent of the sample), among them New York, limited either the amount of time or the level of degree (Table 19.2). States varied in their interpretation of which courses of study offered future potential for employment, and when women should take courses. In some states women were *required* to take summer courses, while in others they were barred from summer school.

JOBS funds seldom paid for tuition because most recipients relied on Pell grants, state scholarships, and loans for educational expenses. The heaviest JOBS expenditures were on child care and transportation costs. The majority of states reported that access to support resources were widely available, but seven states offered limited child care. JOBS funds were used also for (in descending order) books, uniforms, car repairs, equipment, and tools.

Federal policy required states to show that 75 percent of JOBS participants were involved in work-related activities for twenty hours a week. Therefore, a vital component of JOBS policy was how the twenty-hour rule was interpreted. In Massachusetts, taking six to twelve credit hours complied with the twenty-hour rule because recipients could include school-related activities such as laboratory work, academic counseling,

Table 19.2. State JOBS Policies.

	No. of States	Percent of States
Time limits on education and training		
Less than 24 months; or A.A. only	10	32
24–72 months; A.A. or B.A.	11	34
No stated time limits	11	34
Total	32	100
20-hour participation rule		
States with some flexibility of interpretation	19	59
States not showing flexibility	13	41
Total	32	100
Maintaining satisfactory progress		
Difficulties in monitoring progress	8	25
No specific problems	24	75
Total	32	100
Choosing a course of study		
Caseworkers' decisions	20	63
Based on labor market data	10	31
JOBS participants	1	3
n/a	1	3
Total	32	100

library research, and travel. Other states (Tennessee, for example) required the full twenty hours to be met in classroom time. Since a full-time load of five three-credit courses came to fifteen hours, women were required to put in another five hours in volunteer work or a work-study job.[14] In twenty states, participants' courses of study were decided by caseworkers based on prior work records and without aptitude testing or academic counseling. In states with a strict "one course of study" rule, this meant that women could not switch courses or majors if a wrong choice were made. Two-thirds of states reported that caseworkers had no training in postsecondary-education options.

To continue with an education program, participants had to show satisfactory progress. Many administrators assumed that maintaining the same standard required for Pell grants (a 2.0 grade point average) would be adequate. However, this again was subject to interpretation, and in several states caseworkers attempted to collect course grades. One quarter of JOBS officials found such monitoring problematic since college administrators regarded students' grades as confidential information.

Summary

The JOBS survey revealed considerable variation in interpretation of the federal law within and among states. However, when questioned directly about whether they supported the postsecondary option, the majority of JOBS officials stated that both they and their caseworkers did support this option (Table 19.3) because it contributed to:

- Human capital investment: instead of wasting talent, it led to long-term economic advantages for families, businesses, and communities.
- Family well-being: children benefit from their mothers' example and high aspirations.
- Viable economic support: larger families with single heads of household cannot be supported unless they have avenues to higher income.

There was also ambivalence. In states where caseworkers are not required to have a bachelor's degree, they regarded it as problematic if clients appear to have better opportunities than they (the caseworkers) do.[15]

Research Findings: Supportive Educational Environments

The data revealed that no single institution provided all the components outlined in Table 19.1. However, the wide range of resources that were identified testified to strong (and in some instances exceptional) support for low-income reentry women.[16]

GENERAL ENVIRONMENT. The extent to which low-income women can blend into and be accepted in a college environment is an important fac-

Table 19.3. Support Among JOBS Officials and Caseworkers.

	No. of States	Percent of States
Opinions of JOBS officials		
Supportive	14	43
Somewhat supportive	12	38
Not supportive	6	19
Total	32	100
JOBS officials thought caseworkers were:		
Supportive	12	38
Somewhat supportive	17	53
Not supportive	3	9
Total	32	100

tor. Most colleges had sizable numbers of reentry students. More than one-half the colleges had 250 students older than twenty-four, and one-quarter had more than one thousand. Reentry students were 50 percent or more of the entire student population in 83 percent of institutions that responded. In one-half of these colleges, 25–50 percent of reentry students were single parents, and in one-third more than 75 percent were. In a quarter of colleges, the proportion of reentry students receiving AFDC benefits was greater than 50 percent (Table 19.4).[17]

SPECIAL PROGRAMS FOR REENTRY STUDENTS. Many campuses had special programs for reentry students, with program names indicating the specific group focus (Table 19.5). One-third were designed for low-income women (for example, single-parent self-sufficiency programs), one-fifth for single parents (single-parent programs), and almost one-half for general reentry (women's reentry programs). More than 40 percent of programs were begun before or during the 1970s, and nearly half of the remainder dated from the 1980s.

Table 19.4. Reentry Students Receiving AFDC Benefits.

Receiving AFDC	No. of Colleges	Percent of Colleges
Less than 10 percent	8	40
10–24 percent	4	20
25–49 percent	3	15
More than 50 percent	5	25
Total responses	20	100

Table 19.5. Programs for Reentry Students.

	No. of Colleges	Percent of Colleges
Program title focus		
Single parents	5	19
Low-income women	9	33
General reentry	13	48
Total colleges responding	27	100
Program start date		
Before 1970	4	13
During 1970s	10	31
During 1980s	15	47
During 1990s	3	9
Colleges responding	27	100

ADMINISTRATION. A program's longevity and success depend on several factors, one of which is its influence and backing. An indication of influence is the title of the director, and an indicator of its backing is the status of the person to whom the director reports. Just less than 50 percent of programs were run by program coordinators or program directors, 20 percent were run by deans or faculty, and direction of another 20 percent was subsumed under other campus functions such as counseling. Forty percent of program directors (by whatever title) reported to associate or assistant deans, slightly less than one-quarter reported to upper-echelon administrators (presidents, vice presidents, chancellors), and one-fourth reported to directors of campus services (Table 19.6).

ENROLLMENT AND RECRUITMENT. Taking the initial step to enroll in higher education is a daunting experience for many reentry women. They may recall earlier negative educational experiences, be anxious about academic demands, and feel awkward among young people (some of whom may be as old as their own children). Low-income women experience the added stigma of welfare. Effective recruiting requires sensitivity to these concerns and willingness to reach out in different ways. Program administrators usually played a key role in outreach, as did faculty, students, and other college personnel. They all used a wider variety of community resources and agencies than traditional recruiters. Somewhat more than

Table 19.6. Program Administrators.

	No. of Colleges	Percent of Colleges
Program director is called:		
Coordinator, director	21	50
Director, other program	9	21
Dean, vice president	5	12
Counselor	4	10
Faculty	3	7
Total responses	42	100
Program director reports to:		
Associate or assistant dean	17	40
Director of services	11	26
Vice president, vice-chancellor	7	17
Faculty	4	10
President	3	7
Total responses	42	100

50 percent of colleges recruited reentry students through college fairs, transfer compacts, informal coffees, open houses, and mailings. Almost 70 percent used welfare offices, and almost as high a proportion used social service contacts (Table 19.7).

The most effective means of recruiting low-income women included the college's reputation, peer recruiters, word of mouth, orientation workshops, special press releases, and selected mailings. Rockland Community College (New York) and the University of Texas at El Paso used particularly innovative methods. In the former, college counselors worked out an agreement with the local welfare office to allow counselors to talk directly to recipients about college opportunities. In the latter, teachers and counselors working with high school age Spanish-speaking girls included their mothers in their arrangements and outings. As mothers ventured out more and showed interest in developing their own English skills and educational opportunities, bilingual faculty and college counselors directed them to available programs (Table 19.8).

Table 19.7. Special Recruitment Methods.

Special Recruitment Methods	No. of Colleges	Percent of Colleges
Contact with welfare agencies	18	69
Social services	16	62
Women's shelters	5	19
JTPA programs	5	19
Housing	3	12
Churches	2	8
Total responses[a]	30	—

[a]*Multiple responses were permitted.*

Table 19.8. Most Effective Recruitment Methods.

Effective Recruitment Methods	No. of Colleges	Percent of Colleges
Mailings, flyers	12	40
Word of mouth	11	37
Peer recruiters	8	27
Orientation workshops	8	27
College's reputation	3	10
Community-based programs	3	10
Total responses[a]	30	—

[a]*Multiple responses were permitted.*

Several colleges developed special orientation workshops designed to alleviate anxiety and help women feel they "belong." Two private colleges, Champlain and Trinity (both in Vermont), held innovative orientation events: Champlain held a one-week workshop, and Trinity provided a residential orientation. Rockland Community College also held a one-week orientation that included daily sessions using library materials and learning study skills. All three agreed that providing opportunities for women to make connections with their peers during this time was essential. These efforts are reinforced by mentoring and "buddy" initiatives at several colleges.

Clearly, efforts to help women enter college and feel comfortable paid off, for the retention rates were very high. Nearly one-half of responding colleges had retention rates of more than 80 percent. The predominant reasons given for these rates (Table 19.9) reflected considerable emphasis on providing personal interaction with students, and high levels of support services, academic support, special curriculum content, and peer support. Sixty-two percent of program administrators responded that their retention rates were higher than those of traditional students; 20 percent said they were the same as for traditional students.

The presence of leadership was an extremely valuable resource. JOBS policies, state interpretations, and local implementation combined to create confusing situations for low-income women. In only a few instances did caseworkers appear to encourage women in their endeavors. At the University of Tennessee-Martin, caseworkers from a local county agency visited women students regularly to discuss their progress. These contacts were the result of the chancellor's interest; having observed the poverty in rural parts of the state, she felt that education was the key to children's progress

Table 19.9. Reasons for High Retention Rates.

Retention Method	No. of Colleges	Percent of Colleges
Support services	17	52
Personal attention	15	45
Academic support	12	36
Special courses	11	33
Peer interaction	9	27
Screening or follow-up	3	9
Financial assistance	3	9
Total responses[a]	33	—

[a] *Multiple responses were permitted.*

and felt strongly about encouraging low-income mothers. Through her initiative, some units of campus housing were adapted for family use and brought up to code to be subsidized units for low-income families.

Other leaders emerged: a dean of student affairs, exasperated by the onerous reporting requirements of the local welfare office, redid the reporting forms and negotiated less-intrusive attendance checks; a college president who was asked to institute study halls for welfare recipients (to monitor their study hours) refused to do so on the grounds of protecting the confidentiality of their economic status. Others had regular conversations on behalf of groups of students or individual cases that merited intervention.

ACADEMIC CONSIDERATIONS. Welfare caseworkers generally defined which courses women could take on the basis of whether courses were regarded as being directly job related. Since they had no training in either education or career counseling, their decisions often diverged from those of college personnel. Thus, academic courses and expectations raised another set of issues affecting access for low-income women and required administrators to explain to caseworkers the employment potential of specific courses of study.

One-third of colleges assisted all reentry women through their flexible-admissions requirements. Since tracing transcripts of high school courses and grades was difficult or irrelevant for some women (they admitted to not taking school seriously, or to dropping out), many colleges replaced these requirements with essays and other tests. Some colleges experimented with special courses for reentry and low-income women, encouraging them to work in groups and to write about and reflect on their previous experiences. Some, like the College of Community and Public Service at the University of Massachusetts, Boston, replaced the credit-hour system with "competencies," awarding credit for activities such as community organizing and activism. One administrator in a technical college in New Hampshire tested students' potential math ability by asking them to do problem-solving exercises, which she thought were far more illustrative of their potential than standard math tests. As a result, many women at that college went on to enter nontraditional trades and earn relatively high wages.

More than 80 percent of colleges recognized reentry women's academic achievements through a range of informal and formal activities: special scholarships, annual celebrations, a national honor society, a special dean's list, and departmental recognition. Mills College, a private, four-year women's college in California, used a large "brag board" and its newsletter for reentry students to share ongoing information about each other's progress; in Tennessee, Wisconsin, Washington, and Vermont, graduation ceremonies attracted the attention of elected politicians and a governor. In acknowledging the hard work and success of low-income women, these gestures challenged the stereotype many people have of "welfare queens."

FINANCIAL AID. When older women first appeared on college campuses, federal financial aid was only available for full-time students and financial aid forms bore no mention of dependents or child care costs. The surveys revealed that all colleges except one included family living expenses in working out financial aid plans. Some financial aid officers learned to apply specific financial aid funds to specific educational and living expenses to avoid the loss in income many women had experienced.[18] Financial aid officers in two-thirds of the colleges reported no negative impact on students.

However, conflicts between federal and state grants, scholarships, work study income, and loans continued to affect AFDC recipients in one-third of colleges.[19] Almost 30 percent of financial aid officers reported contacting welfare caseworkers over these concerns. The topics they discussed most were food stamps, interpretation of JOBS regulations, and child care.

Low-income women are often thrown by extra expenses that they cannot meet (children's sports activities, school outings, a broken appliance or vehicle). Two-thirds of financial officers reported that their colleges had either grants (26 percent) or loans (69 percent) to help tide families over in such situations. These special resources came from a wide variety of sources: more than 60 percent of college administrators and 42 percent of financial aid officers reported that their colleges applied for outside funds. Most funding requests were submitted to federal and state agencies granting funds for vocational education, displaced homemakers, minority and disadvantaged students, gender equity, and education and training (JOBS). Few private foundations offered funding. Most outside funds came from local fundraising with professional organizations such as the American Association of University Women and local businesses (Table 19.10).

STUDENT SUPPORT SERVICES. Obtaining affordable and reliable child care is a difficult task for many low-income women. Survey responses and site visits revealed a variety of innovative and high-quality child care resources (Table 19.11). Seventy percent of colleges offered child care centers on campus (although 68 percent had waiting lists of ten to three hundred names). Almost 60 percent of centers took children under 2.9 years, but some took children as young as six to twelve weeks. Several centers gave priority to low-income families, setting aside slots for those students; almost 70 percent had sliding fee scales, subsidized slots, or scholarships; and a few were flexible enough to allow students to drop children off for child care on an hourly basis. One community college in Connecticut had a drop-in center that offered free child care in a center boasting a full range of activities. Open between 8:30 A.M. and 3:30 P.M., it was staffed by work-study students, volunteers, and parents. Several campuses had state-of-the art centers, and several offered workshops on parenting and pot luck dinners for families.

Inexpensive or subsidized housing is a crucial resource for low-income mothers (Table 19.12). Forty-one percent of college campuses, mostly the large universities, provided housing. Texas Women's University had converted several buildings into family housing units and applied successfully for funds to build three children's playgrounds and a playroom. A small room off the playroom had two computers donated by the university president, and a window allowed mothers to watch their children while they played. Children also used the computers.

Table 19.10. Sources of Local Funding.

Sources of Local Funding	No. of Colleges	Percent of Colleges
Women's groups	8	44
Clubs and organizations	6	33
Businesses	4	22
Other	3	16
Total responses[a]	18	—

[a] *Multiple responses were permitted.*

Table 19.11. Child Care Arrangements and Child Care Funding.

Child Care Arrangements	No. of Colleges	Percent of Colleges
State-subsidized slots	18	69
Fees on a sliding scale	11	42
Hourly drop-off slots	8	31
Scholarships	7	27
No cost	1	4
Total responses[a]	26	—

[a] *Multiple responses were permitted.*

Table 19.12. Campus Family Housing.

Campus Housing	No. of Colleges	Percent of Colleges
One-bedroom	7	54
Two-bedroom	8	62
Three-bedroom	4	31
Not specified	2	15
Total responses[a]	13	—

[a] *Multiple responses were permitted.*

The surveys and site visits revealed that many colleges helped out with food and clothing. On a number of campuses, administrators had closets in their offices with supplies of children's clothing and clothing suitable for mothers' job interviews. One child care center had a rack of clothing to which people could help themselves. A purchasing agent in a Spokane community college stocked a small room with donated supplies of food, diapers, and other goods; its hours were posted and low-income families could help themselves. One college used its vans to help families with their grocery shopping, and many administrators went out of their way to offer rides to women for caseworker meetings and doctor appointments. In several colleges, traditional students provided resources such as baby-sitting for "mom's night out," and they helped with holiday festivities.

On most campuses, women students were a considerable resource for each other. Peer advising and peer support were considered to be "very effective" in 48 percent and 53 percent of responding colleges, respectively. To encourage such informal contacts, more than half of the colleges had a student center for reentry students that provided quiet places to meet, study, and eat lunch. More than one-third had computers, typewriters, and kitchens, and some had book exchanges, toys, and mailboxes. About 20 percent of colleges had organizations engaged in advocacy on behalf of students.

LINKS AND NETWORKS. Because public assistance, job training, housing, and child care issues are so intertwined, no agency or campus can act in isolation. Therefore, one of the most critical resources were the links and networks established within and between colleges, and between colleges and community-based organizations and businesses.

For example, links between colleges provided an important resource. These connections facilitated transfers—movement between credit and noncredit courses and between one institution and another. Low-income women are far less likely to enter college with a clear plan about how far they wish to go and where they will pursue their studies. They are more likely to begin with a noncredit course or workshop, with a GED or ESL class, and move gradually into degree courses as they gain a sense of mastery in learning. Colleges relied on articulation agreements and transfer compacts, open houses and informal coffees, and strong alumnae and faculty networks (see Table 19.13). Some geographical areas (for example, Spokane) provided seamless links to expedite the movement of women from noncredit, community-based workshops to community colleges and on to take bachelor's degrees in both public and private colleges. Personnel in one program would bring women to look at other schools and help them register for courses. In Wisconsin, where JOBS policies did not permit welfare recipients in a bachelor's program to have child care or transportation benefits, a women's program at the La Crosse campus that offered women a free preparatory course helped them transfer to a local Catholic school that provided financial and other resources to low-income women. In addition, an active network of women's programs and businesses met monthly to raise funds for child care and other needs. These efforts create, and are reinforced by, the links colleges develop with each other.

Well over half of the responding colleges have communications with state agencies, at many different levels. In some communities there is a culture of interagency communication; personnel are well informed of policies and practices outside their immediate domain. College personnel can meet among themselves to resolve questions of attendance, reporting, course choices, and course load. Some who discovered a need for legal advice to deal with evictions, utility cutoffs, domestic violence, and welfare hearings arranged for law students to hold law clinics. One administrator in a very

Table 19.13. Effective Transfer Strategies.

Transfer to Other Colleges	No. of Colleges	Percent of Colleges
Articulation agreements	13	59
Open houses	13	59
Informal coffees	11	50
Transfer compacts	10	45
Faculty and alumnae networks	8	36
Total responses[a]	22	—

[a]*Multiple responses were permitted.*

large university campus in California reported that the group she initially assembled informally to learn more about campus policies and resources began to meet regularly because no similar venue existed to discuss questions and concerns. California is also home to a statewide network of administrators of programs for returning students, and they have become an important voice as policy changes are implemented. In one region, welfare counselors and college personnel formed a group to discuss individual problems (and generic ones) of students involved in JOBS.

There were also numerous college-community links with churches, professional organizations, and businesses. People brought in turkey baskets; provided toys at holidays; held fairs and family events; and raised funds for children's after-school activities, sports equipment, and emergency funds. Several states had effective groups that met families' needs in a wide variety of ways and took great pride in academic achievements and children's progress. Instead of feeling stigmatized, many women felt supported and encouraged.

Summary

In many ways, the commitment to low-income women was surprising in terms of its breadth and the variety of manifestations. Clearly, the kind of persistence such support requires is a resource in itself. On rare occasions, welfare agencies provided concrete assistance, but more often than not agency personnel and JOBS policies provided more obstacles than encouragement. This response arose partially from the ambivalence of the JOBS policies, which—although allowing education and training to "count"—also created parameters that limited choice and created uncertainty. A second serious obstacle was the difference in dominant culture between welfare and education. Welfare imposes restrictions, limits choice, and is sometimes cavalier about the notion of confidentiality. In contrast, educational values espouse confidentiality, choice, and latitude in decision making. To some extent, the obstacles inherent in these culture clashes can be mitigated by savvy and caring personnel who work hard to develop lines of communication and use their political connections and skills of personal leadership. In addition—and not to be underestimated—there was keen interest in the late 1980s in maintaining college enrollments at a time when, demographically, the number of eighteen-year-olds was in steep decline.

There is, however, an important caveat in applying any of the lessons learned from this study. The current situation is very different. Newly available data on the JOBS program reveal that higher education and basic education were the most sought-after activities in fulfilling the twenty-hour work requirement,[20] and newly emerging studies show the efficacy of postsecondary education in reducing welfare dependency and raising income;[21] still, the rules changed dramatically with the passage of the Public Responsibility and Work Opportunity Reconciliation Act (PRWORA) of 1996.

Current Policy: PRWORA and Access to Education and Training

PRWORA imposes huge obstacles to access to substantive education and training; in fact, it virtually eliminates postsecondary education from fulfilling "work requirements." This happens in a number of ways. First, federal law sets an educational limit of twelve months of vocational education as the maximum level that can be attained while receiving benefits.[22] Second, the work requirement now cannot include education and training; instead, it is an add-on to the twenty hours or more of employment or community service that are required. For single parents with limited transportation and child care, this is an almost insurmountable obstacle.

A third factor is the end of the so-called safety net, with the introduction of time limits on cash benefits. Cash benefits have been renamed Transitional Aid to Needy Families (TANF) and are subject to time limits. Federal law limits benefits to families to sixty months within a lifetime; in some states, the limits are twenty-four months in any five years. At the end of the allotted period, a family is cut off benefits regardless of income level. Although the law permits 20 percent of families to be exempt from such restrictions for reasons of disability, illiteracy, homelessness, and domestic violence, a more realistic estimate would be closer to 40 percent.[23]

A fourth factor is that welfare-to-work has become wrapped up in the work-first philosophy, which espouses that "any job is a good job" because it inculcates good work habits and starts adults off on a career path. Instead of perceiving education and training as an investment or buffer zone between welfare and employment, the emphasis is now almost exclusively on employment.

Although forty states applied for and received waivers to the federal policy in order to try out experimental approaches, the majority of states still place severe restrictions on educational access. These limitations also affect a much wider group of recipients than before; not only postsecondary degree programs but those at every point along the education-and-training continuum are affected: English as a second language (ESL) courses, remedial and basic literacy classes, and technical training. As a result, many educational institutions and training centers have experienced dramatic drop-out rates and lower enrollments. New funding sources for work-first programs as well as funding available through PRWORA result in an emphasis on short-term training—often twenty-eight days—or no up-front training at all. Instead, employers are now looked to as providers of training, not only for skills their companies need but also for basic education, GED, and ESL.

Some of these changes may encourage more efficiency and sounder programs, but they also have deleterious effects on proven programs. In Massachusetts, for example, between 1994 and 1997 the fifteen community colleges experienced an average reduction of AFDC recipient enrollments of almost 50 percent. Some states are trying to ameliorate the impact of these trends. Maine uses state funds to pay stipends to low-income women in education, in effect removing them from the welfare system. Some states allow time *before* work requirements begin so that education and training can take place, and still others allow extensions to time limits so educational programs can be completed.

This stemming of opportunities has also produced grassroots and professional-group involvement in advocacy and in the quest for policy change.[24] Questions remain for the colleges discussed in this chapter: How are they responding to these changes? Can the strategies adopted to mitigate welfare policies in the past inform approaches in the future? Can they continue to negotiate, adapt, forge links, and create resources? Or will the culture clash between welfare and education lead to further breakdown in communication, the demise of opportunities for many families living in poverty, and further division between the haves and have-nots?

NOTES

1. Transitional Aid to Needy Families (TANF), formerly known as Aid to Families with Dependent Children (AFDC).
2. In this chapter, the term *college* is used interchangeably with *institutions of higher education* and refers to two-year and four-year, public and private, coeducational and women's institutions.
3. Scott (1980).
4. Swift, Colvin, and Mills (1987).
5. For a comprehensive review of these programs, see Gueron and Pauly (1991).
6. AFDC benefits were available to income-eligible families until children reached majority, and for many years participation in welfare-to-work programs was largely voluntary.

7. For an account of the effects of this invisibility, see Kates (1991).
8. See Gueron and Pauly (1991).
9. U.S. General Accounting Office (1995).
10. The project was funded by the Women's College Coalition, Washington, D.C.; and located at the Project on Women and Social Change, Smith College, Massachusetts.
11. Sites were identified through contacts with participants at conferences, notices in educational newsletters, and specific searches within historically black and tribal colleges.
12. Of the seventy-six colleges that were identified, fifty-nine returned one or both surveys, thirty-two sent additional information (flyers, brochures, institutional studies, and reports), and ten others sent in *only* their own materials.
13. All research was undertaken by the author and two part-time assistants who were AFDC recipients attending college. An advisory group assisted the staff.
14. In two states, JOBS officials had tried, unsuccessfully, to persuade administrators of colleges to institute supervised study halls for AFDC recipients so their participation could be rigorously monitored.
15. One state addressed this situation by providing incentives for caseworkers to obtain more education.
16. This is the term the project decided on for older female students.
17. These numbers were provided by financial aid officers who had access to financial data. College administrators, who also estimated the number of women receiving welfare, *underestimated* the number of AFDC recipients.
18. For many years, women who received Pell grants for their tuition and fees suffered loss of food stamps. A portion of their grant designated to be used for child care or books had been "counted" as income, which resulted in lower benefits. Although this particular conflict was clarified in favor of low-income women in 1986, some financial aid officers remain unaware of these techniques.
19. Although all AFDC recipients qualify for Pell grants, most also take out loans to pay for their educational and living costs.
20. U.S. General Accounting Office (1995).
21. Gittell, Gross, and Holloway (1993). See also Kates (1991).
22. Senator Paul Wellstone's (D-Minn.) amendment to increase this to twenty-four months of postsecondary education was defeated in the summer of 1998.

23. Olsen and Pavetti (1997).
24. The author is cofounder and codirector of the Welfare, Education, Training Access Coalition (WETAC), an organization in Massachusetts that is involved in grassroots organizing, coalition building, legal advocacy, and research.

REFERENCES

Gittell, M., Gross, J., and Holloway, J. *Building Human Capital: The Impact of Postsecondary Education on AFDC Recipients in Five States.* New York: Ford Foundation, 1993.

Gueron, J., and Pauly, E. *From Welfare to Work.* New York: Russell Sage, 1991.

Kates, E. *More Than Survival: Access to Higher Education for Low-Income Women.* Washington, D.C.: Center for Women Policy Studies, 1991.

Olsen, K., and Pavetti, L. *Personal and Family Challenges to the Successful Transition from Welfare to Work.* Paper presented to the Odyssey Forum, Baltimore, Nov. 1997.

Scott, N. *Returning Women Students: A Review of Research and Descriptive Studies.* Washington, D.C.: National Association of Women Deans, Administrators, and Counselors, 1980.

Swift, J., Colvin, C., and Mills, D. "Displaced Homemakers: Adults Returning to College with Different Characteristics and Needs." *Journal of College Student Personnel,* 1987, *28*(4), 343–350.

U.S. General Accounting Office. *Welfare to Work: Participants, Characteristics, and Services Provided in JOBS.* Washington, D.C.: U.S. General Accounting Office, 1995.

INDEX

D

E

F

G

H

I

M

N

O

P

S

T

U

V

W

Y

Z